D1271495

Architecture in Tennessee, 1768–1897

Architecture in Tennessee

1768 – 1897

BY JAMES PATRICK

Contemporary Photography by Michael A. Tomlan

THE UNIVERSITY OF TENNESSEE PRESS : KNOXVILLE

PUBLICATION OF THIS BOOK WAS SUPPORTED BY
GRANTS FROM THE TENNESSEE HISTORICAL
COMMISSION AND THE NATIONAL ENDOWMENT
FOR THE HUMANITIES.

Library of Congress Cataloging in Publication Data

Patrick, James, 1933-
 Architecture in Tennessee,1768– 1897.
 Bibliography: p.
 Includes index.
 1. Architecture—Tennessee. 2. Architecture,
Colonial—Tennessee. 3. Architecture, Modern—19th
century—Tennessee. I. Tomlan, Michael A. II. Title.
NA730.T4P37   720w.9768 80-21089
ISBN 0-87049-223-3

Preface

As early as the spring of 1769, hunters found cabins on the headwaters of the Holston River, and two years later Oconostota, complaining that Virginia's treaty with the Cherokees had been violated, sent word to Lord Botetourt that settlers were living west of the Long Island. Most of these first settlers lived for a few months in hastily constructed cabins, but by 1772 there were already about seventy plantations on the Watauga River, many of them boasting a squared-log house. Before the militia marched across Roan Mountain to defeat the Carolina Tories at King's Mountain in October 1780, Colonel John Carter, merchant, planter, and Worshipful Chairman of the Washington County Court, had built an elegantly paneled dwelling in the fork of the Watauga and the Doe. Colonel Carter's house, a handsome combination of eighteenth-century baroque detail and a traditional plan, is a fragment reminiscent of the elements that had shaped life in the southern colonies since Jamestown—the inexhaustible land, African slavery, a system of trade and banking that reached from the frontier store to the London merchant's counting house, and the arts of the carpenter, mason, and blacksmith. Soon after the Washington County men returned from King's Mountain, John Carter died, bequeathing to his son Landon the possessions that successful planting required: the manor plantation, three slaves, six horses (one blooded), cattle, fifty-two sheep, tools, a wagon, and a cotton wheel.

In the short space of little more than a century, John Carter's civilization of plantations and sailing ships was to be transformed into one of steam and electricity. In 1897 in a Nashville park, Tennesseans built a wood-and-plaster replica of the Greek Parthenon and filled the replica with prize-winning paintings and sculptures to celebrate the hundredth anniversary of Tennessee's admission to the Union. The Centennial Exposition of 1897 was inspired by the World's Columbian Exposition of 1893 in Chicago, and the Beaux-Arts Classicism of the Chicago fair became the accepted architectural style of the Tennessee exposition. Veterans of the battles of Shiloh and Franklin marched along avenues lined with architectural reminiscences of Greece and Rome, even though the exposition also celebrated Tennessee's participation in the emerging world of telephones, electric lights, and transcontinental railroads. There was a history building at the Centennial, but the exposition brought to light an underlying ambivalence toward the past. While there was for the first time a considerable interest in the war and in American history, an orator predicted that Tennessee's future would have in it a little less of Greece and Rome and a little more of the United States of America.

This book is a critical history of the architecture that began when the first squared-log and frame houses were built on the Holston and ended when eclecticism eclipsed traditional imagination and technology displaced the house carpenter. In architecture the years between the building of the Carter house and the Centennial of 1897 compass the eighteenth-century houses of the upper counties and the Cumberland settlements, the delicate Federal of the early nineteenth century, a notable local Greek Revival, Gothic, Italianate, the romantic classicism of southern nationalism, and the long twilight of traditional imagination, during which the modern styles were born. Besides discussing these styles, the important examples, and their architects, I have tried to give the art of Tennessee carpenters and architects a history.

Every student of Tennessee architecture owes considerable debts to those who first undertook the long neglected task of writing our architectural history. *History of Homes and Gardens of Tennessee,* a project of the Garden Study Club of Nashville, was first published in 1936, making available important photographs and documentation which might otherwise have been lost. Nell Savage Mahoney's articles, especially her studies of William Strickland, set high standards for local architectural historians, and more recently Thomas Brumbaugh's *Architecture of Middle Tennessee* (1974) has enriched the bibliography. These authors, as well as the Association for the Preservation of Tennessee Antiquities and the Historic American Buildings Survey, have earned the gratitude of students of local architectural history. And I also thank those who generously allowed me to visit their homes, businesses, and churches, and who shared their knowledge with me. I am grateful as well to the Duke University Library for permission to quote the letters of Adolphus Heiman from the Campbell Family Papers, to the North Carolina State Archives for permission to quote the diary of Juliana Conner from the Alexander Brevard Papers, and to the McClung Historical Collection for permission to quote the Charles Coffin Papers.

Architecture in Tennessee is the result of a happy collaboration. Most of the photographs of extant buildings were made by Michael A. Tomlan between 1972 and 1978, and his suggestions, research, and corrections have substantially improved this book. Photographs made by him are acknowledged in the list of illustrations with his initials; photographs made by others are noted by the photographer's name when it is known. The historical photographs were selected from archives or made available by the owners of private collections and were edited, and in many cases reproduced, by Michael Tomlan. The courtesy of those who permitted the publication of photographs from their collections is acknowledged in the illustration list, and published and manuscript sources, with their depository if the source is rare, are given there. The photographing of extant Tennessee buildings and the reproduction of historical photographs were generously supported by the National Endowment for the Arts and the Tennessee Arts Commission.

Libraries and librarians throughout the state offered indispensable help. I am especially grateful to Jesse Mills, chief librarian of the Tennessee Valley Authority; William MacArthur, librarian of the McClung Collection at the Lawson McGhee Library, Knoxville; Jean Waggener, director of the Manuscript Division of the Tennessee State Library and Archives; and John H. Dobson, the librarian of Special Collections at the University of Tennessee, Knoxville. Mrs. George Fort Milton of Chattanooga, Mrs. T.T. Garrett of Columbia, Ellen Schlink of Lebanon, Ursula Smith Beach of Clarksville, Virginia McDaniel Bowman of Franklin, Ellen D. Hughes of Memphis, Paul Fink of Jonesboro, Walter T. Durham of Gallatin, and William W. Howell of Nashville assisted my research. These historians of Tennessee regions and counties, as well as many scholars known to me only by their books, have made possible a volume that could never have been written if I had been required to master the history of each county, town, and building unassisted. I also acknowledge with gratitude the encouragement given me by the faculty of the University of Tennessee School of Architecture, especially Roy F. Knight, Anne J. Lester, William Shell, and Robert B. Church, III, and by the president of Aquinas College, Sr. Henry Suso Fletcher, O.P. Among the many colleagues who gave me valuable insights, I must mention especially Robert J. Sardello, John E. Fisher, Joseph Peel, and Melvin Bradford. Finally, I must mention my wife, who has borne patiently with this book, whose love for architecture is as great as my own, and with whom I have shared so much that the eyes with which I see are always partly hers. This book is dedicated to Pringle.

A survey covering an entire state and a time span of more than a century is bound to contain some errors. These are my own and persist despite the care of Dianne May and Maudine Prunty, who typed the manuscript. Stephen Cox, who suggested that this book be written, was unfailingly helpful and encouraging, but it was Katherine Holloway, senior editor of the University of Tennessee Press, who helped me finally to bring this complex body of material to publishable form. I know there are footnotes that would make chapters and chapters that could easily make books, but despite limitations of space and shortcomings of my own I hope that this book will provide a helpful introduction to Tennessee architecture of the eighteenth and nineteenth centuries. Writing it has been a labor of love, and has left me with a deepened sense of the importance of our land and architecture. The place where we are born leaves its stamp on us as surely as do the mysterious agencies of family and ancestry. I was born in West Tennessee, reared in Nashville, and have enjoyed the privilege of teaching at Tennessee's University at Knoxville. These are debts books cannot repay.

JAMES PATRICK

Dallas, Texas
January 1980

Contents

Illustrations

Unless otherwise indicated, the following illustrations are photographs. Locations are given when these are not implied elsewhere in the entry, and dates supplied when their omission might foster confusion of the building illustrated with another erected at the same site or in the same city previously or subsequently. These dates, and single dates appearing in the text, give the year of the building's completion. The abbreviations of published sources and depositories used below are taken from the list at the back of this volume.

Architecture in Tennessee, 1768–1897

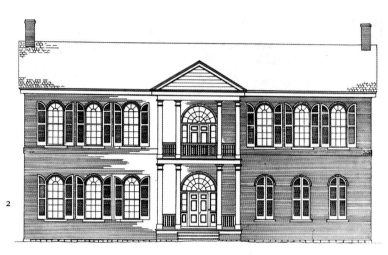

I. EARLY TRAVELERS AND CRITICS

*The first log-hut erected in Nashville was in 1780;
now there is a handsome town, good substantial brick
houses, with public edifices that would embellish any
city in America.*

G. W. FEATHERSTONHAUGH, 1834

Travelers began to praise the look of Tennessee's village and plantation dwellings when their hearth fires were still scattered lights along the muddy trail leading through the wilderness from Abingdon to Natchez. In 1799 Nashville was already a city "with a number of fine buildings," and two years later the Reverend Charles Coffin, newly arrived at Greeneville College, noticed Francis Alexander Ramsey's "large handsome, two-storied stone house" near Knoxville.[1] The following year the French naturalist F.A. Michaux came on James Winchester's Cragfont in the Cumberland settlements and commented that the house was "very elegant for the country."[2] The 1798 edition of Morse's *Gazetteer* called Knoxville, then twice as large as Nashville, "the metropolis of the state of Tennessee," with "regularly laid out" streets, a courthouse, and jail; but before 1820 Nashville, perched above the Cumberland, its brick and frame dwellings scattered around a courthouse that travelers judged handsome, "brick built," and "elegant," had surpassed Knoxville in size and stylish appearance.[3] Though Anne Royall thought Nashville's houses looked "very much like tumbling on your head" from their high bluff as the ferry ap-

proached the town, she recalled that in 1817 Nashville had "a beautiful appearance" from a distance,[4] and in 1827 Juliana Conner wrote, "This is certainly a very well built city—the stores and warehouses are the handsomest I ever saw, generally of brick, handsomely finished and the streets wide and straight."[5] Leroy J. Halsey saw Nashville on an autumn morning in 1830, "its rocks and cedars and house tops partially covered with the first fall of snow, and glittering like a mount of diamonds," and called it "a compact little city . . . confined pretty much to a single hill" but "beautiful even then, set like a gem in the green casket of the surrounding hill-country."[6] A few years later Robert Baird agreed: "It is a remarkably beautiful place. It contains more elegant mansions and pleasant seats in and around it than any other town, of equal size, in the United States."[7]

In 1831 Nashville was a town of 6,000 (1), with handsome churches and public buildings, dwellings like Felix Grundy's at the top of Vine Street (2), and such pleasant country seats as Mayor Robert B. Currey's Meridian Hill and Dr. James Overton's Rock Castle (3). When Baird wrote, the stylish Greek Revival mansion (128) that architect David Morrison had made from President Jackson's plain brick house (127), and the diminutive temple he had built over Rachel's grave in the Hermitage garden (4) were new. In 1829 a

1. The village Robert Baird described was not very different from the view of Nashville published in Matthew Rhea's map in 1834. The cupolas and towers, from left to right, belong to the Christian Church (c. 1826) between Vine (Seventh Avenue, North) and High (Sixth Avenue, North) on Spring Street (Church); Christ Church (1831) at the northeast corner of Spring and High; the Methodist Church (1834) between High and Summer (Fifth Avenue, North) on the south side of Spring; the Presbyterian Church (1836) at the southeast corner of Summer and Spring; and a difficult to identify church, perhaps the Cumberland Presbyterian on Summer near Cumberland Alley. The cupola of the Davidson County Courthouse (1829) in the Public Square is at the right, and the Felix Grundy house is on the horizon near the Christian Church.

2. The Felix Grundy house, Nashville, was an elegant example of the extensive family of two-story, Federal brick houses built in Tennessee between 1800 and 1840.

3. In 1831, Meridian Hill (top center), the residence of Nashville Mayor Robert B. Currey, crowned an eminence south of the city that was afterward remembered as Currey's Hill. Elm Wood (bottom center), Rock Castle (top right), and Meridian Hill represented the continuing influence of eighteenth-century Georgian design.

4. The Doric monopteron in the Hermitage garden is an early example of the self-consciously antiquarian architecture of a regional civilization which saw itself as the heir of Troy, Athens, and Rome.

7

5

6

8

handsome courthouse had been erected on Nashville's Public Square (5), and in 1832 an imposing Greek Revival Presbyterian church was under construction on Spring Street (6). In 1842 the English actor Featherstonhaugh considered Nashville "the center of civilization in the Western country," its Christ Church, "as far as architecture is concerned, one of the most chaste Episcopal churches in the United States" (7).[8]

William Strickland's Capitol, a model of good Greek Revival design borrowed from the Erechtheum and the Choragic Monument of Lysicrates, was begun on Cedar Knob in 1845, and as the limestone temple rose over Nashville, it became the symbol of the region's architectural ambitions (8). An enthusiastic editor wrote that Strickland's Ionic capitals had "in point of beauty of design and excellence of finish" never been excelled in America, calling the workmanship "evidences of the growing taste and skill of our own mechanics,"[9] and to another the building was "an enduring monument . . . of massive grandeur and architectural splendor . . . composed entirely of material found in the State," the doors, sashes, and furniture "made from white oak cut in the forests of Davidson County," the stone "taken from a strata in sight of the building," and the speakers' chairs "wrought in a red variegated marble, found in Hawkins County."[10] In 1863 a visitor to the occupied city called the Capitol "an imposing pile of white marble, more spacious and beautiful than any similar edifice in the Northern States."[11]

5. *The Davidson County Courthouse of 1829 was a late and somewhat provincial member of a post-Revolution family of pilastered and pedimented public buildings, among them the Library Company of Philadelphia (1789–1790) and the Pennsylvania Hospital (1794–1805). When this engraving was made (1831), the Nashville Inn, which occupied the northeast corner of Market (Second Avenue) and the north side of the Public Square from 1783 until 1856, had not yet been given its third story (112).*

6. *The imposing Greek Revival building which Mason Vannoy began in 1832 for Nashville's Presbyterian congregation was the second of three Presbyterian churches to occupy the site on which Strickland's building still stands.*

7. *Christ Church, which Hugh Roland designed about 1829 for Nashville Episcopalians, inaugurated the tradition that Tennessee's Episcopal churches would be Gothic.*

8. *William Strickland's Capitol is one of the most admired buildings in the South. Consistently praised by visitors, it has been the subject of numerous descriptions, woodcuts, and lithographs. Although the city was in Federal hands after February 1862, the Capitol appeared on the twenty-dollar note of the Confederate States throughout the war.*

J. H. Ingraham wrote that the city presented "the most charming aspect . . . of any inland town in the Union. The tall, Egyptian towers of the Presbyterian Church, the Gothic battlements of the Episcopalian, and the pointed turrets of the Baptist, the fortress-like outline of the half finished Capitol, and the dome of the Court house, with the numerous cupolas, galleries, groves, and bridges, together form a coup d'oeil that enchants the eye."[12] After it was occupied in 1862, even the Federals recalled the antebellum town with nostalgia. John Fitch wrote, "Previous to 1861, Nashville was one of the most beautiful, gay and prosperous cities in the Union. . . . The public buildings were of the grandest and most costly character. The State Capitol is said to be the finest structure of its kind in America. . . . Church edifices reared their tall spires on every hand"(9).[13]

9. *Nashville in 1860 was at the height of her antebellum prosperity. On the skyline were the Gothic Revival Hume School (165), completed in 1854; the Episcopal Church (7); the Methodist Church (81); the Christian Church (116); the twin towers of Strickland's Presbyterian Church of 1851; the Capitol (partly obscured by Adolphus Heiman's Masonic Hall of 1860); and the suspension bridge.*

By 1860 Tennessee had two other cities that challenged Nashville's place as the center of commerce and fashion. Memphis, influenced by the styles of St. Louis, Louisville, and New Orleans, was a handsome city, the largest in the state. In 1842 the editor of the *Memphis American Eagle* wrote, "No town in the United States has for the last four years put up so many handsome buildings. . . . Two prodigious hotels, the City and Gayoso, that would beautify any city . . . and no less than four or five Temples of the Living God are . . . being erected" (10).[14] James H. Dakin's Gayoso House (11) was rising south of the center of town, and to come were the Gothic Revival Calvary Episcopal Church

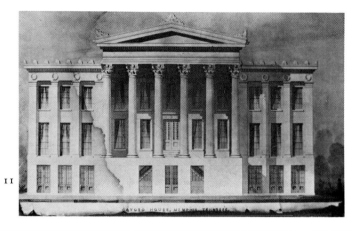

11

10

12

(12), consecrated May 12, 1844; and the "chaste and beautiful" Methodist building (114), completed early in 1845.[15] On November 2, 1846, the *Weekly American Eagle*, noting that "from Exchange Square to beyond Union Street on Front Row, there is now one continued, unbroken line of stores for a full mile," proclaimed Memphis "a young giant of a city, just beginning to raise its proud arms." Soon there were even grander churches, the severely classic Baptist Church (136), completed in 1849; William Crane's Second Presbyterian (13); and the Gothic Revival First Presbyterian begun in 1852. Like Natchez, Memphis had its share of elegant Greek Revival town houses. A visitor noted in the *Daily Enquirer*, April 3, 1849, that numerous beautiful residences, among them Colonel Robertson Topp's (134), presented themselves to the beholder's view on every side.

Knoxville also had fine buildings: the Union Bank (133), built in 1836, the Courthouse (144), completed in 1842, and East Tennessee University (110), built on Barbara Hill between 1826 and 1843; and the city had an especially lovely site, the wooded hilltop between First and Second Creeks on the north bank of the Holston (14). At mid-century the building that visitors to Knoxville admired most was the Asylum for the Deaf and Dumb, a brick block neatly trimmed and fronted with an Ionic porch (15). By 1860 not only the larger towns but Clarksville, Murfreesboro, Columbia, Rogersville, Dandridge, and La Grange had important architectural histories.

Tennessee would remain a rural society throughout the nineteenth century. In 1724 the Reverend Hugh Jones had written that "neither the Interest nor Inclinations of the *Virginians* induce them to cohabit in Towns . . . , every Plantation affording the Owner the Provision of a little Market; wherefore they most commonly build upon . . . their own Plantation."[16] Most Tennes-

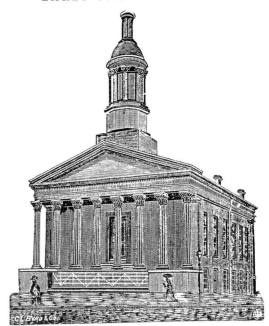

13. Second Presbyterian Church, Memphis, begun in 1846, illustrates the sophisticated use of classical forms that marked the last phase of the local Greek Revival.

seans followed the ancestral pattern of building on their plantations dwellings that ranged in architectural quality from the crude log cabins that cluttered the southern landscape in Frederick Law Olmsted's prewar accounts, to mansions like Isaac Franklin's Fairvue, built overlooking the Cumberland in Sumner County. Fairvue (76) was perhaps the most elegant country house of the 1820s. The farmer William Cantrell called it "the finest embellished and improved place that I have ever seen in the state of Tennessee, or any other state," and Thomas Barry, who was "acquainted with the improvements of the hermitage," judged "those belonging to the Fairvue estate as decidedly superior."[17] Soon both Fairvue and the Hermitage (16), the white-pillared mansion erected after fire destroyed Morrison's building in October 1834, were eclipsed by William Harding's Belle Meade, a mansion a northern visitor thought would "vie with the old manorial estates of the English Barons,"[18] and Belmont (17), the elaborately landscaped villa Adolphus Heiman designed for the Acklens in the late 1850s.

Tennessee was, in Robert Baird's words, "a remarkably beautiful place," and there were reasons why its architecture was more than ordinary. The first settlers and house carpenters brought with them architectural ideals firmly rooted in pre-industrial carpentry and in the lively Georgian building tradition of the seaboard. And the land made Tennessee architecture notable. The valleys of the Tennessee and Cumberland were only the largest of countless rich and pleasant valleys that offered prosperity and invited building. Courthouses and plantation dwellings went up with remarkable speed. Featherstonhaugh remembered that when he had first visited the United States in 1806 "the word Tennessee was mentioned as a kind of Ultima Thule."

10. *Memphis as an illustrator saw it in 1862 was a thriving river town, its public face turned toward the Mississippi, its commercial and domestic life ranged around the four squares (Court, Exchange, Auction, and Market) that the founders had included in their plan in 1818. The Eclipse, one of a succession of steamboats bearing that name, ran between Memphis and New Orleans.*

11. *James H. Dakin's Gayoso House, begun in 1842 on the block bounded by Front, Main, Gayoso, and McCall in Memphis, was a mecca for plantation society.*

12. *Its tall entrance tower centered at the front of the nave, Calvary Episcopal Church, Memphis, begun in 1842 and completed two years later, was a carefully detailed example of the Gothic type which was overwhelmingly popular in Tennessee during the 1830s and 1840s (7, 119, 121, 122, 123).*

15

14

16

In 1834 he saw towns with stylish Greek Revival churches and banks, brick dwellings, and courthouses. Now, he wrote, "No traveler, who comes into the country as I have done, can feel anything but respect for what he sees around him."[19]

Finally, the cultural milieu made good architecture possible in place where there were only imported drama and painting, and where local poets were likely to believe, in Wilkins Tannehill's words, that "it required no great effort of imagination to make a poem . . . that the whole art consists in throwing together a mass of words without rhyme or reason."[20] Because architecture was deceptively utilitarian, religion never considered it frivolous, so that bankers like Drury P. Armstrong of Knoxville and Wesley Wheless of Nashville could be amateurs without losing their character as men of practical affairs. Furthermore, building belonged to the vocabulary of triumphal gestures that southerners—prone always to consider life a tapestry of manners, accomplishments, and conquests—employed when their ability to engage their circumstances successfully seemed unlimited. In this respect Tennessee was a survival from the pre-Renaissance civilization that seemed unaware of the critical, abstract relations poetry or painting could achieve. William Lowndes Yancey is supposed to have answered the charge that southern civilization had produced no great literature with the reply, "Madam, our poetry is in our lives; our fiction will come when truth has ceased to satisfy us; as for our history, we have made about all that has glorified the United States." A Nashville editor wrote in 1846: "The present age is an age of art, not of letters. Energy receives the greatest reward."[21] The rifle and plow played their indispensable part in subduing the land, but Tennessee was civilized with architecture, with whipsaws and adzes, remembered architectural traditions, and the house carpenter's handbooks, chisels, planes, and augers.

14. About 1865 the center of Knoxville was the courthouse, which stood on the north side of Main Street west of Gay Street. The large pilastered building at the left is First Presbyterian Church; the tallest steeple, Second Presbyterian on the north side of Clinch west of Chestnut.

15. The Asylum for the Deaf and Dumb in Knoxville, built by a local carpenter in a city without an important tradition of Grecian design, illustrates the ease with which the style fell within the technical competencies and imaginative commonplaces of the regional civilization.

16. This lithograph of the Hermitage, rendered from an 1856 drawing by Francis W. Strickland, captures the important elements of the southern idyll, the pillared mansion with its formal garden, equestrian gentry, and the benign relations between masters and slaves which the regional apologia presupposed.

17. This painting of Belmont (Belle Monte) idealizes the Acklen suburban plantation as the owner and architect intended it, a romantically landscaped park containing not only the villa but an art gallery, greenhouses, water tower, and summer houses.

By 1860 imagination and toil had converted clay banks and forests into towns and country houses that won the praises of travelers. But it is important to remember that the building of a dwelling, courthouse, or meeting house is merely the beginning of its life. Once built, architecture is lived in, looked at, praised or condemned, neglected or cherished, and finally demolished or preserved. The judgments that determine a building's fate are usually informal, and in that way the critical interpretation of architecture had gone on in Tennessee at least since 1801 when Charles Coffin called Mr. Ramsey's house "handsome." On two occasions before the advent of scholarly architectural history in the mid-twentieth century, the formal critical and historical consideration of architecture was undertaken with some success by local writers. The first of these attempts at systematic criticism took place in Nashville during the 1840s and 1850s, when a circle of intellectuals, booksellers, architects, historians, and clergy, knowledgeable in the theories of Andrew J. Downing and the *New York Ecclesiologist*, made architecture a fashionable topic. Again in the 1890s architecture became important as part of the general recovery of antebellum history that the South began to experience near the close of the century.

By the early 1840s a few Tennesseans became aware of the beauty of their towns and of the part architecture had played in their subduing of the wilderness. Short articles entitled "Our City," published in the *American Eagle* in 1842 and 1843, expressed Memphis' pride in its buildings and its prosperity, while Wilkins Tannehill's "The Town We Live In," a fourteen-part series published in *Port Folio* beginning in 1848, and Thomas Buckley's nine-part "Picture of Nashville," which appeared in the *Daily Evening Reporter* in 1850, reflected a new awareness that Tennessee's towns had an architectural history. Perhaps William Strickland was the catalyst that made architecture fashionable, for when he came to Nashville in April 1845, Strickland brought with him much of the history of national architecture: his apprenticeship under Latrobe; a distinguished Philadelphia practice; and friendship with the great eastern architects, Robert Mills, Isaiah Rogers, and Thomas U. Walter, and knowledge of their work. Strickland, educated in the drafting room instead of the carpenter's shop, was the first of the new professionals, and the obvious excellence of his Capitol made Tennesseans proud and architecture popular. Strickland's modest, rationalist defense of Grecian architecture was published in 1848, and Tannehill himself later wrote two short pieces derived from it.[22] Tannehill also published Strickland's "Sketches of Roman Architecture" in his *Orthopolitan,* and in 1850 Tolbert Fanning announced that Strickland had promised the *Naturalist* an article on architecture.[23]

Strickland's Nashville years, his Capitol, and the regional interest in Grecian architecture were important for the local appreciation of history and good architectural taste, but by 1850 the Greek Revival was already fading in New York and Philadelphia, and a new generation of architects had begun to advocate romantic styles and to defend the theory, derived from the English critics Augustus Welby Pugin and John Ruskin, that truth and goodness, as well as beauty, inhabit architecture, providing an index to social values and advancement and a means of cultural expression. The most successful and important American popularizer of this romantic architectural expressionism was Andrew J. Downing, though he usually failed to do justice to the rich critical and metaphysical underpinnings that gave Ruskin's thought its shape, leaving the American reader of Downing's works with a mélange of practical hints, picturesque designs, and popular naturalism. By 1844 Downing's theories of horticulture and ornamental gardening had inspired Nashvillians—among them merchants John M. Hill, Samuel D. Morgan, William Prichard; publishers Tolbert Fanning, John T.S. Fall, and Anson Nelson; engraver Charles Foster; and bookseller W.A. Eichbaum—to organize a Horticultural Society,[24] and his *Treatise on the Theory and Practice of Landscape Gardening* (1841) and *Cottage Residences*

(1842) were probably available at Berry and Tannehill's and Eichbaum's bookstores. In 1847 admirers of Downing's theories welcomed J.H. Ingraham, an architecture enthusiast, a travel writer, and a teacher who came to Nashville to study for the ministry under the Reverend Charles Tomes, rector of Christ Church.[25] Ingraham tried his hand at design, providing a Gothic plan for the Masonic College of Tennessee, built in Clarksville in 1848.[26] His keen interest in architecture is reflected in his "Letter from Nashville," a description published anonymously soon after his arrival; his article "Rural Taste," which urged planters to secure designs for their houses from Adolphus Heiman; and his letter to the *Naturalist* praising the Horticultural Society's garden.[27] In 1848 William Prichard wrote Downing's periodical, *The Horticulturist and Journal of Rural Art and Rural Taste,* informing the editor that the garden and nursery of the Nashville Horticultural Society were open, that the gardener's cottage was completed with the help of Downing's works (18), and that financial prospects were hopeful.[28] When Tolbert Fanning observed in 1850 that "architectural designs give the most satisfactory evidence of a people's advancement in all that is enobling to man," he was paraphrasing Downing's thesis, published that year in *The Architecture of Country Houses,* that architecture not only addresses the heart, but is "also truthful or significant."[29]

Throughout the fifties articles with titles like "Piety and Beauty" and "Rural Taste" continued to appear in Nashville periodicals.[30]

18. *The gardener's cottage at the Nashville Horticultural Society Garden was built according to principles put forward in A.J. Downing's* Cottage Residences. *Now Morgan Park (Fifth Avenue, North and Van Buren Street), the stream, elevation, and dells which charmed the horticulturists of the 1840s can still be seen.*

The other source of romantic theory accessible to Nashville's antebellum architecture enthusiasts was the American interpretation of A.W. Pugin. Pugin's architectural theory was much like Ruskin's, both emphasizing the relation between art and ethics, or morality and design, but Pugin's theory had a narrower appeal, attracting mostly clergy—especially Episcopalians of high-church views. In England the critical theory set down in Pugin's *Contrasts* (1836) and in *An Apology for the Revival of Christian Architecture in England* (1843) had been made into a science named ecclesiology by the Cambridge Movement—clerics like Benjamin Webb and John Mason Neale who were interested in Gothic architecture and symbolism.[31] The publication of the Cambridge Movement, officially organized as the Cambridge Camden Society in 1839, was the *Ecclesiologist,* and by 1848 an American counterpart had been inaugurated by the New York Ecclesiological Society. Charles Tomes, J.H. Ingraham, and J.L. Gay of the East Tennessee missions were sympathetic to the liturgical and architectural symbolism taught by the *Ecclesiologist,* and through the influence of Tomes and Gay the architects Richard Upjohn and Frank Wills, stalwarts of the high-church party and of the New York Ecclesiological Society, were given commissions in Tennessee during the 1850s.

Amid this growing interest in architecture, the first drawings prepared with the intention of recording local buildings for historical purposes were made. During the 1850s Irish-born W.A. Eichbaum—a bookseller, banker, and enthusiastic supporter of the Tennessee Historical Society—made ink drawings of many of Nashville's important buildings, sometimes sketching them for himself but usually tracing published engravings or the architect's original drawings (19). These, augmented by a few similar sketches prepared by his son, Henry Eichbaum, were acquired by the Historical Society and still provide a valuable graphic source for the study of Nashville's antebellum buildings.[32]

Tannehill, Ingraham, Eichbaum, and Fanning, as well as architects Heiman and Strickland, made the architectural theories of the eastern cities fashionable in their provincial capital at the moment when Tennessee's antebellum culture had come of age; by 1850 many Tennesseans, contemplating the imposing new buildings their cotton, corn, and nascent industrialism made possible, would have agreed with Fanning that their architecture reflected the success of their civilization. But interest faded; the Horticultural Society's garden, its grounds "handsomely arranged, with elevations and dells," and its gardener's cottage "in the rural or English gothic style,"[33] was sold; Tannehill's *Port Folio* and *Orthopolitan* and Fanning's *Naturalist* were discontinued.

19. The Bank of Nashville, constructed in 1853 on the west side of College Street (Third Avenue) south of Union, was a carefully refined romantic Grecian building by James M. Hughes.

Apart from souvenir editions of city newspapers that began to appear as the centennial years rolled around, no history of Tennessee architecture was published in the nineteenth century. This neglect was perhaps part of the forgetfulness that characterized the South after 1865. The effort of southern civilization to establish itself by arms was, at least in retrospect, as indefensible as it was unforgettable; and since the glorious could not easily be disentangled from the reprehensible at such close range, most writers left the important cultural issues alone. There was also a pervasive primitivism, brought on partly by the romantic movement and partly by the regional amnesia, that obscured the real history of the prewar period. This romantic primitivism had been evident even before the war. J.G.M. Ramsey was interested chiefly in the eighteenth century, and in 1853 he was already convinced that the houses of the pioneers had been built without carpenters or masons.[34] In its issue of May 30, 1888, the *Nashville Daily American* described the sale of Adelicia Franklin Acklen Cheatham's furniture and art at Belmont as an auction of "relics at the Old Homestead." Belmont was then twenty-eight years old and had never been a homestead, but by 1888 the antebellum period was already a remote, golden age inhabited by simple and virtuous pioneers.

The second regional contribution to architectural history and ciriticism was made as part of the general reawakening of interest in the southern past that began in the 1880s. It was presaged by the reorganization in 1874 of the Tennessee Historical Society, which had held no meetings since before the war. Then, in 1876, the Centennial of the United States, celebrated with the great Philadelphia Exposition, and four years later the Nashville Centennial reminded Tennesseans that the nation was one hundred years old. In 1889 the death of Jefferson Davis, who had become a symbol of the spirit of the South, gave the region an occasion for recollecting its political history, and three years later R.A. Cunningham began to publish the *Confederate Veteran*, the Nashville periodical which for forty years would keep memory of the cause bright. By 1890 the conviction that the South had a history worth recording was full blown. Although Thomas Nelson Page is best remembered for his romances of southern life, his most important intellectual contribution was probably *The Old South:Essays Social and Political*, which included "The Want of a History of the Old South," wherein Page voiced the regional fear that the past would be forgotten: "There is no true history of the South. In a few years there will be no South to demand a history."[35]

Telfair Hodgson reviewed *The Old South* in the first number of the *Sewanee Review*, observing that "perhaps no conviction has ever been so uniformly held by Southerners, as the one which now exists, that a true history of the Southern people must be written before the materials for that history shall have vanished from the earth."[36] Soon after the United Daughters of the Confederacy was founded in Nashville in September 1894, its members undertook "to collect and preserve materials for the truthful history of the war between the Confederate States and the United States of America."[37] Although the celebration of Tennessee's centennial a year later in 1897 was inspired by commercial interests, much of the meaning the fair had for Tennesseans derived from its character as a great reflection on a century of highly successful existence as a state. Most of the rhetoric praised New South progressivism, but there was a history building at the exposition, and thus the pioneers and the Confederate past were duly celebrated. In the centennial year, the state's first historical periodical, the *American Historical Magazine*, was published in support of the newly established Chair of American History at George Peabody College; the magazine was devoted almost entirely to Tennessee history.

The new concern for history inevitably touched architecture. The first local attempt to preserve historic building took place in 1879, when the Ladies' Hermitage Association began their efforts to acquire Andrew Jackson's plantation house. Although the association was finally successful, the undertaking was complicated by the desire of some Tennessee legislators to make the Hermitage a home for Confederate veterans, another project appropriate to the first generation that remembered the southern past with pride. Like Mount Vernon, whose preservation had been inaugurated by women in South Carolina in 1856, the Hermitage was to be a shrine, not a museum. In the language of its charter, the association was "to beautify, preserve, and

adorn" the Hermitage "throughout all coming ages in a manner befitting the memory of that great man."[38] The architectural significance of the building was weighty but not decisive, for the association conceived the importance of the house in terms of biography and social history, and the preservation of the building was intended to enhance the memory of the man. For the Ladies' Hermitage Association the perfection of historical knowledge was not objectivity but piety.

Nationally, one result of the new sense of history for architecture was the Colonial Revival of the 1880s. That movement was partly the development of the earlier Queen Anne style and partly the domestic phase of the larger Renaissance Revival that took place at about the same time. Although architects trained in New York and Chicago continued to move south during the nineties, it is difficult to discover any direct connection between the literature of the Colonial Revival, the Renaissance Revival, or even the first broad attempts to write a national architectural history and the new awareness of historic architecture in the South. Books like William Rotch Ware's *The Georgian Period, Being photographs and measured drawings of Colonial Work with text*, first published in the year Page's *The Old South* appeared, and Joy Wheeler Dow's *American Renaissance* (1903) undoubtedly had some influence in practice and in schools, but there were reasons why the Colonial past did not fire southern architectural imagination. Except in a few coastal cities like Charleston and New Orleans, and in the Virginia and Maryland tidewater, southerners found no great colonial architecture; and the nineteenth-century buildings that remained were for the most part plantation houses, which by 1900 were remembered as having had little to do with the American past and much with the South's distinctive history. Furthermore, the pieties that illuminated an essay like Thomas Nelson Page's "Rosewell,"[39] a nostalgic description of a great eighteenth-century country house one of Page's ancestors had built in Gloucester County, Virginia, were very different from the technologically and economically determined historiography of the new architects, critics, and historians. Although the theory was not fully worked out until about 1910, J.W. Yost of Columbus, designer of Knoxville's St. John's Episcopal Church (1891), suggested when the American Institute of Architects met in Nashville in 1896 that steel and glass would necessitate an architecture of straight lines.[40] After the Bauhaus popularized the machine aesthetic in the 1920s, technology became the most important source of contemporary architectural theory. Straight lines and standardization were also approved because they seemed to yield maximum economic efficiency. But the economic motive could produce an architecture of opulence as well as one of Spartan simplicity. Harry William Desmond, editor of the newly founded *Architectural Record,* wrote with dispassionate candor in his *Stately Homes in America from Colonial Times to the Present:* "The primary fact about the greater contemporary residence is that it is the house of a very rich man. All the greater residences of the past have been conditioned upon the possession of wealth; but they have primarily expressed something different—an established or impressive social position or some sort of propriety or luxury of life."[41]

Tennesseans, like other American provincials who had little interest in or access to the emerging architectural historiography which proposed technique and economics as the major factors in theory and design, devised a historiography of their own. Those who cared about architecture tended to see a single great tradition of country houses, begun in Virginia at Westover and Carter's Grove, matured at the Hermitage and Belle Meade, and perpetuated after Reconstruction by a new generation of country villas. Although the architects of Tennessee's early-twentieth-century country houses probably understood their work as belonging to the Renaissance Revival, the owners of these mansions read their classic columns in the context of antebellum plantation architecture like Tulip Grove (130) and Rattle and Snap (190).

The regional periodical that gave voice most eloquently to the architectural historiography of the South was *The Taylor-Trotwood Magazine,* published in Nashville from 1904 until 1912 by Robert L. Taylor, a descendant of the Watauga Taylors and governor of Tennessee from 1887 to 1891 and from 1897 to 1899. The magazine offered nostalgic fiction, editorials, and southern literary history. The first article in the first number was an editorial entitled "The Old South," in which Taylor reminded his contemporaries of their obligations to the southern past. Because a strong sense of place was important to the new southern historiography, the magazine frequently included articles dealing with the mansions, gardens, statehouses, and battlefields of the Old South. The Jamestown Tercentennial of 1907 also helped southerners realize the importance of historic places, and it was at Jamestown that Thomas Nelson Page delivered his memorable address extolling Virginia as the mother of European civilization in America.[42]

The first book dealing with Tennessee architecture, May Caldwell's *Historical and Beautiful Country Homes near Nashville, Tennessee,* published about 1911, provided local architectural history that complimented the reawakened sense of the southern past. The author's short preface contained every element of the new regional architectural historiography:

The country around Nashville has always impressed me with its beauty.

For more than a century the people of this section have been home-makers and home-lovers, with an appreciation of the free life of the country inherited from their Anglo-Saxon forefathers.

It has been said that sentiment underlies everything that is lasting and worthwhile. It is the soul of patriotism, the bond of the home, and the foundation of all social and religious customs.

The people of the Old South were full of sentiment and imagination and I have compiled this book with a loving hand, hoping to catch an afterglow of that life which made these homes a region of romance and of dreams.

There was the land itself, the implicit choice of the country house as the most socially significant building type, the identification of southern country life with the traditions of the Anglo-Saxon forefathers, the appeal to sentiment, and the romanticizing of the Old South. For May Caldwell and her contemporaries architectural style was unimportant, while the development of the single significant building type was understood to be self-consistent and continuous from the eighteenth century to the present. In *Historical and Beautiful Country Homes* Renaissance Revival villas—such as Garland Tinsley's Totomoi (1905)—and English country houses—like Claude Waller's Red Gables (1908)—stood alongside early-nineteenth-century Federal examples and grand antebellum plantation houses like Belle Meade in an unbroken and living succession. In 1919, the American Institute of Architects met in Nashville again, and an article entitled "The Architecture of Nashville" was published by the *AIA Journal* in honor of the occasion. After noting the spectacular landscape of the Nashville bluegrass, the author mentioned only the Capitol, other buildings attributed to Strickland, and the "architectural charm" of Nashville's "old time residences."[43] The article was illustrated by eighteen photographs—fourteen of recent and antebellum country houses.

The work that crowned the architectural phase of the regional recovery of the past was *History of Homes and Gardens of Tennessee,* published in 1936, a comprehensive collection of photographs and commentary that spanned the years between John Carter's house at Watauga and modern country residences such as Burlington, built near Nashville in 1932 and described as "Neo-Grec"; Magnolia, near Memphis, inspired by Mount Vernon; and Belcaro, the Knoxville residence of Hugh Lawson McClung, Georgian in style but "rooted in the Italian tradition."[44] The work of the

Garden Study Club of Nashville, *History of Homes and Gardens* was one of several similar books written in the South in the mid-1930s.[45] By then academic architectural history was making its influence felt, for the editor noted that the writers had chosen "to avoid architectural descriptions of the old houses, and to employ the simpler terms used by their builders." Most of the contributors probably did not know much about the technical language the builders had employed, but that was not important, for the book was substantially a *memoria*, an intertwining of memory and imagination to keep in recollection artifacts treasured for their regional and personal associations. *History of Homes and Gardens* was written because, in the words of its preface, the "old order" was passing, the first houses already taken by time, the great plantation houses defaced by "the four bitter years . . . when contending armies struggled for supremacy on Tennessee soil," the "present economic development" an ever present menace.

The architectural amateurs of the 1850s had worked to bring local architecture into the mainstream of national movements and styles. The second regional attempt to deal critically with architectural tradition began with the recovery of history in the 1880s and ended with the perfecting of a historiography to which the great house built on the land was central. Although the style of *History of Homes and Gardens* is uneven and the matter technically (and deliberately) naive, it was written to make good the local love of place. "The Southerner," Ransom wrote in the theme essay of *I'll Take My Stand*, "persists in his regard for a certain terrain, a certain history, a certain way of living."[46] That of course was the point of the local architectural historiography that made Belle Meade a precedent for *fin de siècle* Renaissance Revival villas and Cheekwood (1930) the fulfillment of a tradition to which the Hermitage (16, 189) and Ashwood Hall (191) belonged.

The phase of the regional development of architectural history that began in the 1880s and ended with the publication of *History of Homes and Gardens* had its glaring weaknesses. Most of the writers who took part in it were not well versed in scholarly vocabulary or in the history of building, and the important types of the postwar period—stores, office buildings, factories, city dwellings—were mostly ignored. But May Caldwell and the authors of the Garden Study Club shared a capital virtue: a deep appreciation of the delicate web of imagination that binds man to place by means of houses and gardens. In 1936 Allen Tate, whose poetry presupposes the terrain and seasons of the Upper South, wrote: "I suspect that in the age of social science the term image is not clear; and this, I suppose, is due to the

disappearance, in such an age, of the deep relationship between man and local habitation. An environment is an abstraction, not a place; Natchez is a place, not an environment."[47]

An appreciation of the relationship between man and place had marked local imagination from the beginning. Judge John Haywood observed in his history of Tennessee, published in 1823, that since human action "unconnected with the circumstances of time and place, can at best be imperfectly understood," the writing of history required "attention to the theater of action."[48] That theater was a narrow territory running across the valleys of the Tennessee and Cumberland from the crest of the Unakas to the Mississippi and including in its narrow girth both lush bottomland that made Thomas Dillon write in 1796, "Notwithstanding that I came to this country in expectation of seeing some good land . . . it has exceeded my expectation,"[49] and the "craggy mountains" that reminded Francis Baily of a line from Pope's *An Essay on Criticism*: "Hills peep o'er hills, and Alps on Alps arise."[50] The soil of the river valleys was rich, as was the land that lay atop the limestone of the basin in which Nashville, Franklin, and Clarksville would be built. Trees three feet thick at the butt covered the slopes of the eastern mountains, and there were deer, elk, buffalo, bears, and flocks of Cumberland parakeets.

In 1756 when the colonies of South Carolina and Virginia undertook the building of Fort Loudoun to protect the string of Cherokee villages that lay along the southward flowing Tennessee and its tributaries, the land was sparsely inhabited and partly unexplored. French trappers and soldiers had explored the Tennessee, which they named the Chauvanon for the Shawnees who lived along its banks, and after 1710 the French often visited the salt lick at the bluffs of the Cumberland, and English traders had preceded the fort building expedition of 1756. In 1761 the Colony of Virginia built Fort Robinson at the Long Island, and by 1763, when the peace concluded between France and Great Britain gave the English title to the valleys of the Ohio, Cumberland, and Tennessee, planters and speculators in Virginia, Pennsylvania, and the Carolinas knew that there was a land of unparalleled richness beyond the mountains. Despite danger and distance, settlers began about 1768 to follow the Overhill Cherokee traders who had settled and built in the 1750s, riding or walking down the bridle path that stretched south from the settlements in Botetourt County, Virginia, toward the Holston. About 1772 those who had followed this road beyond the river, and hence beyond the jurisdiction of Botetourt County, Virginia, formed the government that Lord Dunmore called "an inconsiderable yet a separate state," taking the laws of Virginia as their guide. They first leased and later (March 1775) purchased their land from the Cherokees. In 1776 the British disallowed these purchases and demanded that the settlers move back north of the Donelson line of 1771. When Virginia counseled compliance, the Watauga government, which had by then taken the name Washington District, applied to North Carolina, in whose territory their plantations actually lay, for recognition and protection. North Carolina incorporated the settlements south of the Donelson line as Washington District; in 1778 the district was made a county comprising most of the territory that would become Tennessee, and in 1779 the town of Jonesboro was established at the site of the Washington County Courthouse. In the same year James Robertson led a caravan overland to the bluffs where Nashville would be built, and the flatboats that John Donelson guided down the Holston and Tennessee from Fort Patrick Henry and up the Cumberland to the French Lick joined Robertson's party in April 1780. The Watauga and Cumberland settlements, from which Tennessee would be populated and civilized, were now established.

II. TECHNIQUES AND MATERIALS

I have been obliged hitherto to appoint a great many Men at Work, such as Sawyers, others to make Clawboards, others to cut Stone out of the Rocks for Chimneys. The Guard House is finished with a double Chimney. I intend to build a Guard Room for the Officers of the Guard. I send your excellency a draught of the Guard House.

CAPTAIN PAUL DEMERE TO GOVERNOR LYTTLETON,
FORT LOUDOUN, NOVEMBER 24, 1757

During 1757 and 1758 soldiers working under Captain Paul Demere built the barracks, guard house, officer's house, and store houses in Fort Loudoun.[1] The parties originally recruited in Virginia and South Carolina to build the fort had included artisans, some of whom probably remained after the engineer De Brahm, whom Governor Glenn of South Carolina had employed to design and superintend the fortifications, returned to Charlestown in December 1756. The techniques which Demere's carpenters employed were descended from the half-timber construction of the sixteenth century in which the interstices of a braced wooden frame were filled with rubble or brick. In America, where wood was plentiful, the frame was usually covered with clapboard, but beneath this exterior finish was the same masonry-filled frame. The buildings at Fort Loudoun, which required clapboards, although their sills may have been laid directly on the ground and earth or stones substituted for brick, were the well-framed or fair English houses built in the southern colonies since 1607; each member was carefully joined, not nailed, and the tenons of each stud let into the sill and plate. To the French of the Mississippi Valley houses built in this way were *de briquetée entre poteaux* (brick between squared timbers), or *de charpente, remplie de maçonnerie de brique* (of carpentry filled with brick masonry) though other materials, *bousillée* (mud and grass), *pierrottée* (stones and mud), or earth could be substituted for brick.[2] This infilling, called nogging by the English, is found about 1775 at the John Carter house (58), where sun-dried brick was used, and is common thereafter, as in the David Ramsey house (20). The houses in Fort Loudoun were probably built using small stones or earth for nogging instead of brick, but in other respects the houses were typical eighteenth-century structures, the stone chimney foundations of which were discovered when archaeologists excavated the site between 1956 and 1958. These frame buildings probably had steeply pitched roofs covered with wooden shingles. The pack trains which brought powder, tools, and trade goods to the back country forts could also have brought glass and hardware, and any carpenter who made paneled doors or window frames in Charleston could have done so at Fort Loudoun, though some time would have been required for the sawed planks to dry.

In 1779 the town of Jonesboro was established in the territory which the building of Fort Loudoun had tenuously secured, and at its meeting of November 3, 1784, the Washington County Court recommended that "there be a courthouse built in the following manner; to wit: 24 feet square, diamond corners and hewn down after the same is built up, nine feet high between the two floors, and the body of the house four feet high above the upper floor, each floor to be neatly laid with plank. The roof to be of joint shingles neatly hung with pegs; a Justice's bench, a lawyers' and a clerk's table, also a sheriff's box to sit in." The courthouse was to be made of logs squared with a foot adz, joined at the corners with interlocking and diagonally faced notches, and "hewn down after the same is built up" with hand adzes or axes; a new way of building partly adapted from the thick plank buildings of Delaware and partly invented by settlers in western Pennsylvania and the high Piedmont. Apart from the squared-log walls, the construction was familiar to any house carpenter. The floors would be made of plank, probably poplar, sawed with whipsaws at a saw pit or on a scaffold, and neatly laid on hewn or sawed sleepers let into the log walls at the levels of both floors. Rafters set on the topmost log would meet in the center of the house, lathing would be pegged or nailed perpendicular to the rafters at intervals of about ten inches, and wooden shingles fixed to the lathing with treenails driven firm in neatly augered holds. The justice's bench, clerk's table, and "sheriff's box to sit in"—the standard furniture of the eighteenth-century courthouse—would test the carpenter's cabinetmaking skill. Although crudely finished buildings were neither the ideal nor the rule in eighteenth-century Tennessee, during the some twenty-five years separating the building of Fort Loudoun from the founding of Jonesboro, building with squared logs had become popular as an alternative to the nogging-filled, clapboard-covered braced frame. If the house frame were laid up of logs adzed square for a tight fit, the services of the plasterer, brickmaker, and brick layer were not required, while at the same time a strong, well-insulated wall was quickly provided. Trees were plentiful, and chinking—small stones fitted between the logs and plastered with clay—sufficed to seal the house against the weather.

In 1784 a survey of taxable property taken in and near Fincastle, Virginia, about 150 miles northeast of

the Long Island, divided the 59 buildings into 26 denominated "log dwelling houses," 21 "cabins to dwell in," a "double cabin," and 11 "frame dwelling houses."[3] Christopher Taylor's house near Jonesboro, traditionally dated 1777; John Sevier's Plum Grove on the Nolichucky in Washington County (c. 1780);[4] William Cobb's Rocky Mount (c. 1780); and Henry Earnest's house at Chuckey (21) in Greene County were neatly made "log dwelling houses." These were the "very well finished log houses" Coffin saw near Tellico blockhouse on January 24, 1801, and when Michaux visited Greeneville the next year the town had "more than forty houses, built of squared beams, arranged like the trunks of trees of which the log houses are formed."[5] Unlike cabins built of tree trunks, such squared-log or thick-plank houses could be neat and tight and were usually built according to the traditional plans used for stone, frame, and brick dwellings. Frederick Ross noted in his autobiography the considerable difference between "a cabin made of round logs, roof of boards, chimney of sticks, a slab for a door, no window, a puncheon floor," and "a house of hewn logs, a shingled roof, brick chimney, plank floor, and glass windows."[6] But the only difference between a frame house and the "new, two story, hewed log house, chinked and pointed, floors tounged and grooved . . . plain doors and window sash made and put up, a brick chimney with fire place above and below" that Anthony Foster advertised in the *Tennessee Gazette* on January 18, 1804, was the construction of the walls; the walls were built of studs, carefully joined, with the interstices filled with brick or stone.

The origin of squared-log or thick plank construction remains obscure. Log houses were rare in eighteenth-century Virginia, but the technique was common among the Swedes of Delaware Bay, and from Delaware the practice gradually spread into Pennsylvania and the southern colonies. Log houses, constructed *de pièces sur pièces*, their corners formed either by letting the thick planks into a channeled or rabbeted corner post or by shaping the ends of each piece into an interlocking pattern of dovetailed joints, were frequently built in Quebec, and the technique was brought down the Mississippi by the French. Throughout the eighteenth century, dwellings built of round or roughly squared logs, called by the French *maisons en boulins* and by the English cabins or huts, were occasionally erected in the back country, usually for temporary use, but houses built in this way came gradually to be the architecture of the rural poor. Squared-log construction persisted in the countryside, where the technique was sometimes used in building houses but almost invariably in the construction of out buildings and barns, and squared-log houses were occasionally

20. *The David Ramsey house near Viola (Warren County) was built about 1830 using the braced frame construction characteristic of the nineteenth century.*

built in towns. In his manuscript autobiography Nathan Vaught recalled building a log house in the town of Columbia about 1812. Larger structures like Alfred Royal Wynne's inn at Castalian Springs were sometimes built in the 1820s, and in 1831 there were still twenty-one log houses in Nashville.

House carpenters probably came to Tennessee with La Salle in 1682 and Bienville in 1739, and with Major Andrew Lewis and Captain Raymond Demere in 1756. Others followed before the Revolution. John Carter's house at Watauga was probably built before 1775, and twenty years later when Abashai Thomas saw frame houses with brick chimneys in Knoxville, there were brickmakers, bricklayers, and oil makers in the Holston settlements. A house carpenter was practicing his art four years after the *Adventure* reached Nashville, when John Pierce was apprenticed to William Gallapsy,

21. *The Henry Earnest house, built about 1790 at Chuckey in Greene County, is a neat squared-log copy of the traditional stone and frame houses of Pennsylvania and the Shenandoah Valley. The house is banked into the hill, also a Pennsylvania practice.*

and by 1790 a stonemason was at work in Davidson County.[7] Soon after the Washington County Court opened its books in 1779, inventories containing fairly complete sets of tools were recorded. These were frequently the property of planters, for many of the settlers, their sons, or slaves could do some carpentry; but the best work was done by house carpenters and stonemasons who, though they may also have farmed, had some training and more than ordinary skills.

Like other settlers who came to Tennessee before 1800, house carpenters and bricklayers were usually from the nearby back country, the Piedmont, or occasionally from Philadelphia, Baltimore, or Charleston. Artisans in the seaports were often members of the American counterparts of the London guild companies. The Carpenters' Company of the City and County of Philadelphia, modeled on the Worshipful Company of Carpenters of London, was founded about 1727, and by 1770 the Philadelphia company was wealthy enough to build their elegant Carpenters' Hall. By 1788 Charleston's carpenters were participating in important public celebrations, perhaps as the Charleston Carpenters' Society, which existed in 1812.[8] Sometimes artisans working in building trades other than carpentry formed companies, like the Philadelphia Brick Layers' Company, chartered in 1792. Following the practice of the London Company, the Philadelphia Carpenters' Company established a common system of measuring and valuing, settled differences between members, maintained standards of workmanship, and cared for its members' widows and orphans.

Philadelphia, Baltimore, and to a lesser extent Charleston were the port cities where overland trade with the interior South began. Of these Philadelphia, in 1800 the second largest city in the United States, exercised the greatest influence over the back country, though Baltimore always had its share of the Tennessee trade, and after Richmond became a prosperous town most of the goods available in Philadelphia could be purchased there. On January 31, 1767, Governor William Tryon of North Carolina wrote the Earl of Shelburne that John Hawks, the architect of the palace at New Bern, would soon go "to Philadelphia to hire able workmen, as this province affords none capable of such an undertaking."[9] In the early 1790s Rock Castle in Sumner County was built by Daniel Smith's nephews Peter and Smith Hansborough, carpenters who came from Philadelphia to erect their uncle's house, and in 1801 General James Winchester brought house carpenters from Baltimore to finish Cragfont. A year earlier John Steele of Salisbury, North Carolina, a village more remote than Nashville or Knoxville, employed the house carpenter John Langton, who had determined to move from Philadelphia to the North Carolina back country "for the purpose of carrying on his business as a mechanic," and Steele agreed to pay Langton "according to the Philadelphia book of rates."[10]

No copy of the *Rules of Work of the Carpenters' Company of the City and County of Philadelphia* has been found in Tennessee, perhaps because the members were required to surrender their copies when they emigrated, but the practices of the companies of the port cities persisted on the frontier. When the house carpenters of Knoxville, "R. Morrow, Mr. McClure, Mr. McCafry, Mr. Booth, and T. Hope," established among themselves the prices for such items as framing, weatherboarding, making sash, doors, "Modillion or dentle cornice," and stairs in 1801, they were following the practice of the carpenters of Philadelphia, or perhaps of Charleston, where Hope had worked before moving to Knoxville. Five house carpenters in the frontier capital of a newly formed state could hardly publish a handsome book like the *Rules of Work* in which the Philadelphia company had set down their articles of association, prices, patterns, and rules for measuring in 1786, but Thomas Hope did carefully record the Knoxville carpenters' agreement in his *Builder's Golden Rule*. If there was a carpenters' society in Nashville, or if house carpenters there or in Memphis ever met to agree on prices, their rates or articles of agreement have not been found; but the precedent set by the Philadelphia carpenters was still alive in 1819, when the Master Carpenters' and Joiners' Society of Cincinnati published their first list of prices. Nashville did have a Mechanical Society, many of whose members were probably carpenters and bricklayers, and in 1801 the society met at Parker's Tavern on the third Saturday of every month. Two years later the Mechanical Society had a hall of its own, and its members enlivened Nashville's celebration of July 4 with a parade and with toasts: "The mechanical arts, may they meet their due encouragement and their due reward."[11]

The Nashville Mechanical Society was probably not dedicated to the interest of any single trade, but, like the Ancient and Honorable Mechanical Society of Baltimore, founded in 1763, was a social and benevolent association for artisans. The Mechanical Society was succeeded in 1841 by the Mechanics' Institute and Library Association of Tennessee, and three years later the Library Association, with branches in Knoxville, Pulaski, and Lincoln County, as well as Nashville, was incorporated by the legislature. The Mechanics' Union Society of Columbia, chartered in the same year "for the purpose of improving the condition of Mechanics by establishing a circulating Library, and raising funds for educating the children of individual Mechanics," retained something of the character of the eighteenth-century artisans' companies, whose members had also cared for widows and orphans, but, increasingly, the model was the English workingmen's institute, whose purposes were largely educational. The Memphis Mechanics' Institute, organized in June 1854, advertised in the city directory the following year that it provided "Evening school for young men, courses of lectures during the winter season," and a Library Reading Room, as well as "Annual fairs and exhibitions for encouragement of home manufactures."

House carpenters and bricklayers learned their trades through apprenticeship. On November 14, 1796, Thomas Hope advertised in the *Knoxville Gazette* for an apprentice who would learn "the whole art of the house carpenter's and joiner's business," an arrangement like that which bound John Gibson to the house carpenter Thomas Garritt of Williamson County soon after 1800 on the condition that Gibson be taught "the art and mistery of a house joiner" and given $60.00 worth of tools when his term expired.[12] When the apprentice's term was over, he was a journeyman, a workman qualified to work for a master carpenter by the day until his reputation and finances enabled him to join the carpenters' company as a master carpenter.

Colonial carpenters' societies never secured a monopoly—even the Philadelphia company had a competitor, the Friendship Carpenters' Company of Philadelphia, from 1769 until 1785[13]—and the journeyman could always become a master either by undertaking work on his own or by moving to the frontier, where his talent would find a ready market. In America, especially in the South, the organization of the trade

was complicated by the competition well-trained slaves gave journeymen and apprentices. Article XIII of the *Rules of Work* of the Philadelphia company required any member who employed a slave apprentice to pay the company twenty pounds, or a dollar a month for each month a slave journeyman was employed. Throughout the eighteenth century the *Virginia Gazette* contained notices of slaves who were carpenters, brickmakers, and bricklayers, and though slavery was abolished in Pennsylvania in 1780, it flourished in the South until 1865. In 1848 the bricklayers Clark and Bill Jay and the carpenter John Jennings were the most valuable slaves enumerated in the inventory of Isaac Franklin's Sumner County estate.[14]

The skill house carpenters brought to their work was the ability to cut and carve chimneypieces, doors, and moldings and to join wood to wood with mortises, tenons, and pegs in house frames, trusses, and paneling. Every frame house was the work of carpenters who let each stud into the sill and plate, set the corner posts and braces, and attached each piece of weatherboarding to

22. *Cragfont's trusses span the width of the house and are joined to one another with diagonal wind braces.*

23

24

25

26

the studs with pegs. If the house was small, simple rafters would be set at the desired pitch. The longer spans of larger houses often required roofs framed with trusses or principals. Cragfont's trusses (22) are an especially fine example of the joiner's art, a more complex version of the kingpost truss depicted in the Philadelphia *Rules of Work* of 1786. House carpenters also cut and pegged in place the shingles that covered the roof—in 1830 Nathan Vaught decided that selling drygoods would be "Easener and lighter work than putting shingles on the Roof in hot sun." In the tidewater, shingles were usually cedar or cypress, rived or split from a quarter log about three feet long with a froe (a broad, short-handled, dull-bladed axe) and a wooden mallet; but in Tennessee, shingles were rived from oak, poplar, or chestnut.[15] In Virginia, roofs were often tarred or painted, and the practice of painting shingled roofs was still followed in Middle Tennessee in 1811, when the Bedford County commissioners specified that the courthouse roof was "to be painted red or brown as soon as it is covered in."[16]

The skill of house carpenters varied from the mastery displayed at Cragfont and the John Carter house to the plain, substantial work of the typical craftsman, who could produce neat chimneypieces, window frames, and moldings. The carpenters who built the Carter house have not been identified, but the nearly contemporary advertisement that Mardum V. Evengton published in the *Virginia Gazette* on August 16, 1777, catalogs the work a fine carpenter could do:

Wants employment, and is now at liesure, A Master Workman in the various Branches of the Cabinet Business, chinese, gothic, carving and turning; is well acquainted with the theory and practice in any of the grand Branches of the five ancient Orders; viz. Ornamental Architects, gothic, chinese, and modern Taste, &c also Colonades, Porticoes,

Frontispieces, &c to Doors; compound, pick Pediment, and plain Tabernacle Chimney Pieces; chinese, ramp, and twisted Pedestals; geometrical, plain, and common Stair Cases, and sundry other Pieces of Architect too tedious mentioning. . . . I have an elegant Assortment of Tools and Books of Architect.

Evengton wanted prospective employers to know that he could finish doorways (frontispieces) and chimneypieces with plain (tabernacle) or broken (pick) pediments, and build staircases with twisted balusters. A skilled carpenter like Evengton could have produced the paneling and chimneypieces of the Carter house (23) or consoles like those Thomas Hope copied from his handbook and used at Francis Ramsey's house near Swan Pond (24) with ease. The tradition of elegant carving was continued in Tennessee by carpenters like Robert Taylor, who probably made the mantelpieces for Daniel Montgomery's house at Shackle Island about 1835 (25), and the anonymous craftsmen who carved delicate mantelpieces for the Alfred Moore Carter house (1819) in Elizabethton and the Deery Inn at Blountville (c. 1820) and built the doors and fanlight at Clouston Hall (c. 1830) in Franklin (26). The typical Tennessee house carpenter of the early nineteenth century lacked the skill of John Carter's craftsmen, but there were dozens of artisans capable of building plain, solid houses, men like Frederick Pinkley and David Cummins, who agreed in 1799 to build John Overton's Travellers' Rest.[17] Because of carpenters like Thomas Hope and Terrence McAffry of Knoxville, Henry Rieff of Nashville, Robert Taylor of Sumner, and Adam Lowry of Washington County, planters and town dwellers might be expected to build "well-framed" houses with handsome mantelpieces and cornices by 1800.

The art most closely allied to carpentry in the late eighteenth century was cabinetmaking, for joinery, the method of attaching wood to wood with mortises and tenons, was a technique common to carpenters and cabinetmakers. In England, attempts to define the jurisdiction of the carpenters' and joiners' guilds had been unsuccessful, for every carpenter was also a joiner, and since house frames were always put together with joinery, house carpenters were house joiners as well. Because cutting and joining a chimneypiece or staircase required as much skill as making a desk or cupboard, many Tennessee house carpenters were, like Thomas Hope, cabinetmakers when the occasion demanded. Robert Taylor was at work as a house carpenter in Sumner County in 1804, but furniture signed by him also exists.[18] Terrence McAffry, who joined with Hope and other Knoxville house carpenters to establish prices in 1801, advertised as a cabinetmaker from 1810 until his death about 1830, and the

23. *The first story of John Carter's house at Watauga was paneled throughout. The chimneypiece of the south parlor is an especially fine example of mid-eighteenth-century design.*

24. *The consoles Thomas Hope made for the Ramsey house are fine examples of late-eighteenth-century architectural carving. The eave return originally extended the length of the nailer, and the roof may have had a double pitch, the lower (and shallower) beginning four or five feet behind the cornice and forming an overhanging eave.*

25. *The east parlor mantel of the Daniel Montgomery house at Shackle Island (Sumner County) is a good example of late Federal design and execution.*

26. *The doorway at Clouston Hall in Franklin (Williamson County) displays the details characteristic of Federal style: the elliptical architrave, fanlight, colonnettes, and the Chippendale pattern of the sidelight muntins.*

Knoxville house carpenter Nathaniel Hewitt also turned to cabinetmaking.[19] James Purcell of Columbia was a cabinetmaker who took up house carpentry about 1811, and Nathan Vaught, the Virginia-born carpenter who built many of Maury County's antebellum houses and public buildings, was among Purcell's apprentices.

The only woodworking techniques house carpenters left to other trades were sawing and turning. A fine house carpenter left felling trees and sawing them into boards or joists to sawyers, or to sawmills. Turning he left to turners, though if the carpenter was also a cabinetmaker he might have in his shop a lathe for making table legs and bedposts, and it could also be used to turn balusters and newel posts. But carpenters usually did not do their own turning. In the contract signed January 1, 1835, Andrew Jackson specified that his carpenters Joseph Reiff and William C. Hume would pay "all expences of turning." In the 1820 Manufacturers' Census of Tennessee, Moses Cusinberry of Williamson County and Stephen Childrey of Knoxville gave their trade as turner, and turning was still a distinguishable craft in 1847 when George Ireland, turner and carver, kept a shop near Spring and Summer streets in Nashville.[20]

Before 1830 the carpenter's tools were either imported from England or made by a blacksmith, who hammered them out on his forge. Tools were precious possessions, and the wills and inventories of eighteenth-century Washington County list the crosscut saws, whipsaws, augers, gouges, planes, drawing knives, hammers, squares, and chisels their owners considered valuable legacies. When the inventory of Samuel Vernon's estate was recorded in the Davidson County Will Book in 1786, Vernon had "One Cross Cut Saw . . . Three Felling Axes, One Broad Ax, One foot Adze & Some Chisels, Two Hand saws, Two Augers, four Plains in the Stocks, four Plain Bits," enough tools to build a squared-log house but not enough to build a frame dwelling, which would have required a whipsaw. Thomas Hope, some of whose tools had been made in London, was understandably anxious when his mortise chisel, "the largest ever brot to these parts," was stolen in 1797;[21] but by 1800 fairly complete sets of carpenter's tools were common. When the inventory of Robert Patterson's estate was recorded in Davidson County on May 21, 1800, it contained "one Jointer Plaine one hand Jointer Plaine one Jack Plane one Smoothing Plain Stock, one Pair of Compasses (Iron) one Pair Ditto Wood . . . Two Nailing hammers, Two Squares, one Iron, one Wood, one hand saw. . . ." The next year David Hay had "Two Drawing knives, One Hand Saw & Two Augers, One Small [auger], One Broad Ax Two Small [axes], One foot Adze . . . One set

of Tongue and Groove [planes], One Smoothing Plane, Two Moulding Planes, One set of Bench planes, six chisels."[22] Tools were often scarce but seldom unobtainable on the southwestern frontier. When Virginia built the first fort on the Tennessee River, Governor Dinwiddie recommended to Major Andrew Lewis (April 24, 1756) that he enlist "many Tradesmen y't can use the Saw and Ax for the construction of the s'd Fort . . . ," and "purchase w't Horses you may see necessary for carrying Y'r Provis's, Tools &c." The tools eighteenth-century artisans required could be carried on horseback; the materials for the most part lay close at hand.

The wood that made frame construction common in Tennessee before 1800 was taken from the forest with axes and readied for the house carpenter by sawing it into boards and scantling that would be used for flooring, paneling, weatherboarding, and studs. Only large members concealed in the frame, sills, corner posts, and sleepers or joists were usually adzed instead of sawed. When sawmills were inaccessible, logs were cut into boards by sawyers working at saw pits, rectangular pits deep enough for one sawyer to stand in, the log laid across the pit so that a whipsaw could be worked up and down along its length. This was probably the process Sally Smith had in mind in 1793 when she wrote her husband, General Daniel Smith, "There is no sawings done by Captn Smith as yet, nor can I get any others to saw at as reasonable a rate as you gave for what is done, Majr Donelson is the cheapest and he asks 6, 8, & 10 for poplar, walnut, and oak [per] hundred."[23] Forty years later Major Armstrong promised President Jackson that he would set "3 or 4 whip saws" to work so that the Hermitage could be closed against the weather after the fire of October 14, 1834, and as late as 1850 a Nashville writer recommended to farmers that instead of building houses of logs, they have their hands "saw them into boards in a pit, thus making one log go as far as ten put into the house as a whole."[24] Timber was made into planks at saw pits throughout the antebellum period because planters who lived distant from sawmills found the ease and speed of sawing by water power or steam offset by the difficulty of hauling logs to the mill and finished boards back from it.

Before the Revolution began, there were mills in Watauga, Baptist McNabb's on Buffalo Creek, and Matthew Talbot's on Gap Creek. In 1778 the Washington County Court gave James Pearce and Michael Baines permission to establish mills on Little Limestone Creek, and others, like the Dungan mill on Brush Creek, soon followed. Heydon Wells was licensed to build a grist mill on Thomas Creek by the Davidson County Court in 1783, and John Buchanan gave Mill

Creek its name by building his mill there early in the life of the Cumberland settlements. An agreement by which David Rounswell sold Frederick Stump land on White's Creek for a mill with the understanding that the "water works" of Stump's mill would be sited so as not to damage Rounswell's own, was recorded in the Davidson County Will Book on April 17, 1790.

By then at least some of the mills in the territory were equipped with sash saws, vertically mounted blades that moved up and down in a frame, into which a log was fed mechanically.[25] In the eighteenth century, sawmills came close on the heels of settlement. In 1789 a flatboat was built at "Winchester Mills," the "great mills of stone" that the Moravian missionary Frederick C. de Schweinitz came upon near Cragfont in Sumner County in 1799, and these probably included a sawmill at an early date.[26] By 1799 there were four sawmills near Salisbury, North Carolina, and in 1805 Charles Coffin obtained joists, scantling, and weatherboarding from three mills—Wood's, Hickson's, and Fearnsworth's—all located near Greeneville.[27] Nathan Vaught remembered that a sawmill had been built on Lytle's Creek near Columbia in 1809 and that the mill was later fitted with machinery for grinding corn. On March 29, 1811, a boatyard owner on the Caney Fork advertised in the *Tennessee Gazette* that he had "a good saw mill, that can run all summer," and he promised that "Plank or Scantling of any kind that the country affords" could be delivered on any part of the river from the mill to Nashville. In the late eighteenth century sawmills were probably about as accessible as good house carpenters' tools. By 1760 a single factory in Canton, Massachusetts, was producing from 100 to 250 sawmill blades annually, and in 1792, when Nashville merchant John Rice's goods were inventoried, one "saw mill saw" was in stock.[28] Those who wished to build their own mill could hire a millwright like John Harmon, who advertised in the *Carthage Gazette* on August 21, 1811, that he could "erect mills, make repairs &c upon any plan or model" and that "draughts and bills of materials" could be furnished.

As the owner of the mill on the Caney Fork knew, summer or an uncommon dry spell might deprive him of power. On December 19, 1805, Charles Coffin noted in his journal, "On account of the stream failing, Fearnsworth could not saw, till rain might enable him." Steam engines offered an obvious solution, and by December 6, 1831, the *Nashville Republican* could mention "the ruins of the Old Steam Mill" which stood north of town near the Cumberland. By then there was a new steam sawmill in Nashville, probably equipped with the circular blade that had come into use about 1815.

Whether the log was sawed at a pit or on a scaffold with a whipsaw, or by steam or water power at a mill, the planks might be kiln dried, especially if they were to be used for finish carpentry. On June 3, 1805, Charles Coffin "crossed the river at Hickson's Mill, looked at my window plank kiln drying, did what I could to get some of this and some of the weatherboarding soon haled." Once the plank had been dried, the house carpenter could easily make moldings and rails for sash, doors, and shutters with planes, each shaped to produce a tongue, groove, or molding profile.

Settlers who wished to use material more permanent than wood built at first with the stone that lay on or near the surface of the ground throughout much of East and Middle Tennessee. Because these thick-walled stone houses were nearly invulnerable to fire, they have survived in larger numbers than their more numerous frame contemporaries. The techniques used in stone construction were borrowed from Pennsylvania and the Valley of Virginia.[29] The fronts of stone houses were sometimes built of fitted, rough-dressed ashlar, the gable ends and back of lightly worked rubble. Often neat, segmental arches spanned door and window openings and fireplaces; and stone houses often had a water table. A photograph of the Embree house at Telford (Washington County) taken in 1909 illustrates the character of the typical late-eighteenth-century stone house (34). The earliest stone dwelling remaining in Tennessee may be the George Gillespie house at Limestone (54), Jeremiah Dungan's dwelling on Brush Creek at Watauga near Johnson City (56), or the Thomas McClain house in Powell's Valley (Claiborne County), all of which may have been built before 1783. Nashville's first Methodist meetinghouse (c. 1789)[30] and the second Knox County Courthouse (c. 1800) were built of stone. Daniel Smith's Rock Castle near Hendersonville (1796), the Francis A. Ramsey house near Knoxville (1797), the Martin Kitzmiller house (built about 1800) at Boone's Creek (Washington County), and Cragfont (1802) reflect mastery of the craft. Most of the stone houses built in Tennessee during the eighteenth century were not the work of amateur craftsmen but of masons with some knowledge and some skill—men like William Erwin, whom George Augustus Suggs of Davidson County employed in 1790 for nine months for "Two hundred hard dollars" and provisions for a year.[31] A knowledgeable mason like Suggs built the neat one-story cottage (27), a type common in England, which the house carpenter Robert Taylor put up near Shackle Island (Sumner County) in 1822.

Although few houses were built of stone after about 1820, frame and brick houses usually had stone founda-

27. The carefully dressed ashlar, tall profile, and flush chimneys of this one-story stone cottage near Shackle Island recall eighteenth-century precedents still to be seen in Ulster and the English west country. The house was built by the carpenter Robert Taylor.

tions and stone steps. These, however, like stone houses, were often made of stones rough dressed with the mason's hammer. The Union Bank of the State of Tennessee (132), begun in 1834, was perhaps the first dressed-stone building in the state. The most famous building of local stone was the Capitol, built of limestone quarried less than one mile west of Cedar Knob; and certainly Tennessee's most famous stonecutter was Adolphus Heiman, who came to Tennessee about 1837 bearing a letter from Alexander von Humboldt commending the immigrant's skill.[32] In the 1840s Vernon K. Stevenson, an important Nashville commercial and political figure, operated a stone yard not far from the Catholic cathedral.

Michaux remarked in 1802 that masons were "still scarcer than carpenters or joiners" in Tennessee.[33] By *masons* Michaux probably meant both stonemasons, like the artisans who had built James Winchester's stone house, and brickmasons, craftsmen like Mr. Wilkerson of Greene County, who both burned and laid the bricks for Charles Coffin's chimneys and fireplaces in 1806. Although brickmaking and bricklaying were different trades, on the frontier the same artisan sometimes practiced both. Brickmaking required no materials other than clay, a plentiful supply of wood for the kiln, and the brickmaker's mold and plane, but the process of filling the kiln and firing the brick was delicate and time-consuming. Usually, bricks were molded from a mixture of suitable clay and water, allowed to dry in the open air until they could be easily handled, and then stacked in such a way that they would be burned evenly, none vitrified or left unburned. Bricks were burned either in a kiln or a clamp, a temporary kiln built of the bricks that were to be burned. Firing took at least three days, sometimes a week, and then the bricks were

allowed to cool for two weeks. John Sevier noted in his journal on April 26, 1800, that he "put fire into the brickkiln," and on May 2, eight days later, he "finished at night burning brickkiln."[34] This was the process Charles Coffin had in mind when he wrote in his journal on September 17, 1807, "Wilkerson fired his kiln"; and three days later, "Mr. Wilkerson has put no wood today to his brick, thinking them burnt enough."

Bricks made in Tennessee were usually a handsome dark red, and in the eighteenth and early nineteenth centuries often about 9 inches long, 4 inches wide, and 3 inches thick. A District of Columbia ordinance of 1820 specified that brick molds used in Washington should be 9¼ by 4 by 2¼ inches. With the shrinkage caused by firing, this would have yielded a brick about 8½ by 3¾ by 2 inches. This long, narrow face or profile was also preferred in Philadelphia.[35] It was more elegant than the thick Tennessee brick, but also more costly to lay, there being about 50 percent more courses in walls laid with Philadelphia brick 2 inches thick than with a brick 3 inches thick (28, 99).

Antebellum brick houses were great piles of solid masonry with joists led into the brick at floor heights and plaster laid directly on the interior surfaces of the walls (28). Samuel Jackson's town houses in Jonesboro, built about 1820, had end and side walls three bricks thick, about 13 inches, and partitions two bricks thick, about 9 inches; and the Bank of the State of Tennessee built in Rogersville in 1839 (138) had exterior walls three bricks thick at the first story. Walls were some-

28. Even in ruin, The Aspens (c. 1845), Darius Waterhouse's residence at Washington in Rhea County, reveals its solid brickwork.

times laid common bond, with every sixth, seventh, or eighth course of headers so that the longest dimension of the brick extended into the wall, binding it together (46, 101, 109), but the brickwork of the earliest houses, at least their front wall, was usually laid using Flemish bond (35, 41, 42, 44, 88). Brick houses were built in Tennessee before 1800, among them the William Bowen house in Sumner County (35), traditionally dated 1788, and the Buckingham house near Sevierville, built in 1795 (38). Bricks were certainly burned in Knoxville before 1794, when Abashai Thomas saw brick chimneys, and by March 7, 1804, bricks were advertised for sale in the *Tennessee Gazette*. Bricks were sometimes molded in concave and convex shapes for cornices (87, 89).

Besides bricks, masonry construction required mortar, and the best mortar required lime as well as clay. Because lime could be obtained by burning limestone in a kiln, lime was never in short supply in Tennessee; Michaux noted in 1802 that lime was one of the products the Holston country exported downriver to New Orleans.[36] But like brickmaking, the preparation of lime was time-consuming. When Charles Coffin built his house in 1805, he had difficulty procuring enough lime. Coffin noted that lime could not be had for less than eight pence a bushel, nor in less than three weeks' time; and at one point work on the house came to a halt because Mr. Graham, the stonemason, had failed to provide enough lime. One method for producing lime was to layer limestone, free of chert and iron, with wood, burn the pile, and slake the lime with water to float off the few remaining ashes.[37] Coffin's notice of May 10, 1805, that Graham's lime kiln was half done, however, suggests that by then regular kilns may have been used. On another occasion Coffin mentioned that lime had been brought to the building site from the brick kiln.[38]

House carpenters, plasterers, and painters were usually paid "by the measure," a traditional system according to which joists, sleepers, and studs were computed by the square (an area 10 feet by 10 feet in the completed building); plaster by the square yard; moldings and cornices by the linear foot; and items like dormers and porches by the piece. The prices Thomas Hope and Knoxville's other house carpenters established in 1801 were based on this system, and in the contract they signed with Jackson on January 1, 1835, Reiff and Hume computed the cost of rebuilding the Hermitage in the same way. The cost of "Framing 76 sqr Joice at 75 cts per square" was $57.00; "32 square of framing, sheeting and shingling" cost $80.00; and "1 Venetian window," $16.00.[39] On April 24, 1805, Charles Coffin had employed Mr. Drew of Abingdon,

"a good painter" who promised to paint Coffin's new house for "8 shillings a square" and agreed that "windows should be measured as a plain side of the house or room outside and in, only that when I did not finish the inside so as to paint a room, the inside painting of the windows was to be thrown into the outside without any allowance of price."

Stonemasonry was measured by the perch, a volume of 24¾ cubic feet. John Squibb received one shilling and tenpence per perch for masonry erected at Samuel Doak's college in 1802, and three years later Charles Coffin agreed to pay three shillings for every perch of stone laid below grade, sixpence more for that above.[40] In 1820 John Smith charged 62½ cents per perch for stone laid at Samuel Jackson's town houses in Jonesboro,[41] and the perch was still the standard measure for stonework when the Capitol was begun in Nashville in 1845. Brickmasonry was usually valued by the thousand. In 1801 John Sevier paid "three dollars per thousand bricks & 3 Quarters per Arch" to Robert Murray for building his house in Knoxville.[42] In 1860 Adolphus Heiman and John Naff carefully determined that the brickmason Morrell had laid 1,427,585 new bricks at the Masonic Hall in Nashville, so that Morrell could be paid by the thousand.

When payment was not given the house carpenter or mason "by the measure," it was frequently given "by the great," as a single sum due on completion of the work. This arrangement, often used after about 1850, required the carpenter to make an estimate before building was begun rather than waiting to measure the completed work. Provisions for the carpenter or mason and for the apprentices and journeymen employed by them were sometimes furnished by the owner, sometimes by the carpenter, and the party responsible was often specified in the contract.

Iron suitable for lintels, fireplace hardware, nails, and hinges was available in the Valley of Virginia when the first settlers moved to the upper Holston. David Ross's Oxford Ironworks was in operation in Bedford County, Virginia, in 1772,[43] and in 1786 Ross began the correspondence that resulted in the opening of his works near the west end of the Long Island between the North Fork and Reedy Creek sometime before 1791.[44] Nearby deposits were exploited by Colonel Walter King and his partners—the Seviers—from 1795 until 1810 for use at the Beaver Creek Ironworks,[45] located on the south fork a few miles above Long Island. The German stove of local manufacture which Frederick de Schweinitz saw in Sullivan County in 1799 could have been cast at King's works, at the ironworks Nicholas Tate Perkins operated before 1792 near Bull's Gap, or after 1793 at Mossy Creek ironworks in Jefferson County.[46] The Mossy Creek furnace was still in production in 1806, and its products were exported to Virginia as well as downriver.[47] The first ironworks in the Cumberland settlements was begun by James Robertson on Barton's Creek in Dickson County about 1793.

Tennessee ironworks did not produce finished hardware like locks or butt hinges, but bars and castings. Iron was cast either into pigs or useful articles—such as andirons, pots, and skillets—at furnaces where ore was heated white hot with charcoal, making pig iron and an impure vitreous slag. Ironworks were located on streams that provided power to furnish the blast required to raise the temperature of the furnace high enough to melt the ore and to drive the tilt hammer at the forge. Sometimes the wheel drove a turbine or blowing tub that directed a blast through an opening (called a *tuyère*) in the furnace. Sometimes water power operated a bellows that provided a blast, and in the South the *trompe*—an arrangement by which water falling through a pipe entrained air, forcing it through the *tuyère*—was still used about 1840. The pigs, iron not cast directly into hollowware but allowed to run into molds at the bottom of the furnace, were usually reheated and the impurities hammered out by the tilt hammer.[48] The refined iron, or ancones, could then be hammered by blacksmiths to fashion nails, lintels, fireplace cranes and crane eyes, and oven frames.

The American nail-making process was perfected about 1789, and nails were probably being manufactured in the Holston settlements by 1799, when de Schweinitz saw wagoners from Watauga hauling iron and nails across the mountains to the Cumberland settlements. Not long after 1800, one of the Embree brothers was operating a "nail manufactury" in Washington County near the site of Colyar's mines in Bumpass Cove, where Charles Coffin saw the "ingenious waterworks and nail making machinery" on April 22, 1805. Cut nails were advertised in Nashville's *Tennessee Gazette* on June 17, 1801, and on June 23, 1812, David Irwin and Company of Pittsburgh announced the opening of a nail manufactury in the *Nashville Clarion*.

The only materials necessary for building that the land did not afford were locks and hinges, pigment for paint, and glass. In 1750 Martin Bolzius of Georgia explained: "Window glass comes along, already cut, in little boxes from England, and a 4-cornered pane 9 inches wide and 11 inches high costs 6 to 8d. These are set into the grooves of the wood or at the side of the wood by the carpenter or turner who makes the window frame, fastened with a small wooden nail, and secured with putty, which, made of white lead and oil, comes from England."[49] As Bolzius knew, most glass

was imported from England, a practice that continued until about 1800, but during the eighteenth century at least one dozen American glass houses operated intermittently, and a few of these were near towns that traded with the Virginia and North Carolina back country. Caspar Wistar's South Jersey glassworks, begun in Salem County, New Jersey, in 1739, was probably the most successful eighteenth-century American glass house, and in 1769 Wistar was producing "window glass, consisting of the common sizes, viz. 10 by 12, 9 by 11, 8 by 10, 7 by 9." Henry William Stiegel made window glass at his works in Mannheim, Pennsylvania, from 1765 until about 1774, and from 1785 until 1795 Johann Friedrich Amelung made window glass 8 by 10 inches and 7 by 9 inches at his glass house in New Bremen, Maryland. By 1788 there was a glass house at Alexandria, Virginia, and in 1790 another at Baltimore.[50]

The glass Tennesseans began to bring down by pack horse could have been sent from Boston or New York, or even from England, but was probably made in Maryland, at Amelung's New Bremen works, or in Baltimore or Alexandria. A box of glass appears in a Davidson County inventory in 1787.[51] In 1792 William Blount arranged for Sevier to forward the box of glass he had ordered from Richmond for his house in Knoxville, and Daniel Smith received "3 barrels of nails, a bundle of hinges, and 5 boxes of glass," probably for his new house, by wagon.[52] In 1805 Charles Coffin had his glass sent from Baltimore, though by 1801 "excellent window glass" could be bought at Timothy Demonbreun's store in Nashville "by the box or less quantity."[53] White lead for putty to set the glass was available locally by 1805, when Coffin bought his from the Seviers' store.

Since Tennessee ironworks did not make locks or butt hinges, these were also imported. In 1792 the inventory of a Davidson County storekeeper's goods included "forty nine H hinges" and "nineteen door hinges," [54] and large and small H hinges and locks continued to be listed in local inventories until after 1800. Daniel Smith had his "bundle of hinges" sent from the east in 1792, and on December 26, 1805, Coffin received his butt hinges from Boston, though most of them had fallen out of the box and had to be recovered by the wagoner, who mistakenly took them to Newport. In 1792 John Rice had numerous locks for doors and cupboards, and in 1801 the estate of Henry Wiggins included "One Door Lock and brass knob" as well as some H hinges, thumb latches, and iron screws.[55] Because locks were expensive and not always easily available, contracts usually make specific mention of them until about 1850.

Paint was difficult to procure because most pigments

had to be imported and the vehicle, usually linseed oil, was difficult to manufacture and transport and might spoil if left in the barrel too long.[56] Coffin's journal contains several references to his dealings with William Wilson the oilmaker, of Mossy Creek in Jefferson County, who supplied linseed oil for the painting of both Greeneville College and Coffin's house. Pigment was usually ordered from the east, but occasionally bought locally; certainly it was available by 1787, when James Leneer sold "One bag of paint," perhaps whiting, pure ground chalk from which white paint was made, or some other fairly common pigment, to his brother in Davidson County.[57] Coffin had his blue pigment, and probably his green, sent down from Boston, and had whiting sent from Baltimore.[58] The yellow pigment Coffin used to make the paint for the exterior of his house was "yellow paintstone," or "Warm Springs' yellow ocre," rock or earth containing iron oxide that Coffin obtained from Warm Springs in North Carolina.[59] Coffin washed these lumps of iron-laden earth, and his painter pulverized them and mixed them with Wilson's linseed oil. Paint could be made in other ways; Thomas Hope owned "A Reciept for making Paint without Oil or White Lead" by using skimmed milk, slaked lime, and Spanish whiting. But the most common method was mixing pigment with linseed oil. By 1811 Bedford's Medicine and Drug Store in Nashville had linseed oil, also "a very ample supply of every variety of PAINTS & COLORS usual in this country."[60] Paint-making had not changed much by the late 1840s when Isaac Franklin's estate purchased linseed oil, chrome yellow and Venetian red pigment, whiting, and white lead for the Louisiana and Tennessee plantations.[61] Painters were highly skilled craftsmen like the Horns of Nashville, a large family of house, carriage, and sign painters, among whom was the painter of the Union Bank in 1835 and the Hermitage of 1836. Twenty years later examples of graining done by Mr. Horn were entered in the exhibition of the Tennessee Mechanics' Institute.[62]

Most of the materials necessary for building were available locally, and the extant architecture of the eighteenth and nineteenth centuries shows that Tennessee's house carpenters were able to employ these materials skillfully. Although Charles Coffin's house was a type found more often in New England than Virginia, two stories and a basement arranged around central chimneys, the account of its construction that Coffin's journals preserve is a rare and careful history of the materials and techniques carpenters and masons used in Tennessee in 1805.

By April 17, 1805, the laborer Graham was at work quarrying stone for Coffin's cellar walls. On the same

day Coffin called on Mr. Swatral to try to buy lime but found the price too high and the waiting time too long. On the nineteenth Mr. Fearnsworth sent word from his sawmill that Coffin's scantling, the rough finished timbers from which the studs would be cut, was ready. Coffin visited "Friend Embree" at his nail manufactury, probably located near the Embree furnace in Bumpass Cove, and ordered nails for his house on the twenty-second. On the twenty-fourth Benjamin Drew of Abingdon agreed to paint the house for 8 shillings a square, Coffin finding him "nothing but oil & paints." About May 2, Coffin concluded an agreement with the house carpenters Brewer and Rice, and Rice moved into a nearby house with his family.

While the cellar was being dug, lime burned for mortar, shingles, plank, boards, and scantling hauled, Rice and Brewer were carefully cutting each piece of the house frame on the ground, chiseling mortices in sills and plates, and shaping tenons on studs and braces. Coffin noted on June 11 that he had "assisted Rice p. m. in making out stud holes so as not to interfere with the windows." On the third Coffin inspected the kiln-dried planks required for the window frames at Hickson's Mill; weatherboarding began to arrive on the fifth, and on the twelfth and thirteenth sawed joists came from Wood's Mill. By June 25, the excavation for Coffin's cellar was complete, but Mr. Gass, the mason, could not begin the foundation "through Graham's tardiness in burning the lime." On July 2 Coffin wrote, "No lime, no waggoneer, sad delay of workmen on hand." On the same day Coffin "agreed with Wilkerson," the brick mason who would burn Coffin's bricks, lay up the chimneys and plaster the interior of Coffin's dwelling. On the third a wagon appeared with all the lime Graham had produced, a scant two or three bushels. Gass agreed reluctantly to proceed, using mortar made without lime if some allowance could be made in the price for the difficulty of working with clay mortar. The cellar walls on which the sills would rest were completed on July 18.

The frame Brewer and Rice had made would be joined, not nailed, but in 1805 it was customary to pin each rafter to the ceiling joist on which it rested with a large forged nail. Coffin secured "75 spikes 4½ inches long for fastening the Rafters of my house to the Joists" from the blacksmith Clutsinger on July 23. In a week the frame was ready, and Coffin noted on July 31, "Brewer and Rice raised my house frame." It took about three days to get the rafters in place, but the hardest work was the first day. Thirty hands were assembled, and "Brewer entertained them all," though later a disagreement, finally settled amicably and in Coffin's favor, arose as to whether the owner was responsible for providing anything other than the whiskey. In a month the frame was covered with weatherboard. The roof, its oak shingles pinned in place with nails bought from Sevier's ironworks, was finished on September 13, and Coffin noted, "made some variations from Mr. Izard's draught of a door in a copy, which I prepared for my front door." The drawing of the door that Coffin copied had probably been procured from Ralph Izard of Charleston. When "Mr. Izard from Charleston and his Lady" were in Knoxville on July 30, 1806, Coffin called on them, which he would not have done had he not previously made their acquaintance, probably on the journey he made to Charleston in April, May, and June 1803. It was shortly after Coffin welcomed the Izards to Knoxville (September 11, 1806) that he noted in his journal that Thomas Hope had built Mr. Izard's house in Charleston, an arrangement that Hope must have remembered favorably, since he had named a son born December 30, 1803, Ralph Izard Hope. Ralph Izard's brother-in-law was Gabriel Manigault, a likely source for a good design.

During the last two weeks of September 1805, the house carpenters and their apprentices nailed in place the corner boards, water table, and cornice. On the seventeenth "Wilkerson fired his kiln" to make bricks for the chimneys, and on the twentieth the brickmason considered both bricks and lime sufficiently burned. Coffin learned from Colonel William King on October 3 that "Mr. Taggart was engaged to procure my glass according to my request." On November 11 Mr. Wilkerson was hard at work laying off the fireplaces, and Coffin noted, "Susan, Betsy and I went up to the house before breakfast and directed Wilkerson to put the mouth of the oven without the fireplace rather than within it." On the thirteenth Russell sent "the iron bar for the kitchen fireplace and the oven frame." Coffin's intense interest in fireplaces and ovens was probably encouraged by his acquaintance with Benjamin Thompson, Count Rumford's *Essays*. Heating and cooking were among the topics Count Rumford treated most extensively, and as soon as Coffin's books came from Boston in December 1805, he began to read Rumford's works and to follow his advice.

The exterior of Charles Coffin's house was nearly complete when winter came in 1805. On December 17 he agreed to pay Wilkerson the mason "two shillings a square yard for putting on Lathes and either finishing with two coats of plastering and one of whitewashing, or with two smoothed off with particular care so as to fit for painting, and for making Lathes three dollars a thousand in addition." By the twentieth the chimney had reached to the garret joists, and Wilkerson stopped to burn more brick. On the day after Christmas, Coffin

received the box containing building supplies purchased in Boston and was disappointed to find that his package of blue paint had been damaged, and that sixteen pairs of butt hinges were missing. Early in 1806 Mr. Drew came from Abingdon and undertook the painting of the house as he had promised. On August 11, Coffin visited Colonel McClung's house west of Knoxville, "examined the work done on it, found it some of the best in the country, and obtained some knowledge how to direct my workmen in some part of what they have yet to do." The house was State's View, and Colonel McClung's house carpenter was Thomas Hope, whom Coffin was to meet one month later at John Kain's Trafalgar. Coffin paid Rice on October 8, noting, "our conversation and adjustment were with perfect amicableness," and next day settled with Drew the painter. Rice was still at work on Coffin's carefully designed front door on November 5, and Wilkerson continued plastering throughout a second winter.

In about eighteen months in 1805 and 1806 Hughes, Graham, Rice, Brewer, Wilkerson, and Drew had built a frame house with a stone basement, brick chimneys, two stories, and a garret. The wood had come from Fearnsworth's, Wood's, and Hickson's mills. The rock for the foundation had been quarried nearby, and the clay for brick dug and burned just across the Nolichucky. Nails and iron lintels had been forged at Embree's, Sevier's, or Mossy Creek ironworks. Ocher had come from Warm Springs, white lead from Sevier's works, linseed oil from Mossy Creek. Only locks, glass, and a few pigments had been brought from Boston or Baltimore. In 1857 Frederick Augustus Ross described Coffin's house as it must have looked about 1825:

It was nearly square—two stories, a chimney in the middle, giving a little lobby, from which were stairs to the rooms above. The Parlor was to the right, the dining room to the left, the Kitchen . . . back of both rooms—all clustering round that one big chimney very comfortably. The house was painted some tint of yellow, with plain cornice, and modest porch, both white. . . . As you stood in the porch, the orchard was to your right. An open green, on the left, led down to the College . . . . There it stood, like the house, a little piece of Massachusetts, brought all the way to Tennessee. . . . With the boys about it, it was the central object in a noble landscape of rich forests and fields.[63]

The house was a humble fulfillment of the architectural image Charles Coffin had included in the long poem he composed for his Harvard commencement in 1793:

Groves, hills, vales, streams, flocks, pastures,
   fields extend,
Beauties unnumbered in the prospect blend,
And on a cultured hill's most choice retreat,
Peers through its shades the tasteful country seat.

On May 26, 1801, Charles Coffin saw a steam engine at work in Philadelphia, and he noted in his journal: "The machinery is very complicated and the power surprising." By 1831 Nashville still had only a single steam sawmill, but in 1856 about thirty steam engines were at work in the city.[64] *Twyman's Memphis Directory* of 1849 announced that S.B. Curtiss and A.G. Knapp of the Western Foundry and Engine Manufactury could "make to order steam engines complete, embracing Cast, Wrought, and Sheet Iron." During 1850 Henry Ament built "the most extensive and probably the most important workshop and foundry in the west country" in Nashville,[65] and the next year John B. Davis made the first engine to be manufactured locally in Ament's foundry.

Soon Davis's engine was set to work in Warren and Moore's Steam Carpenter Shop, where it powered Woodworth's improved planing and tongue-and-grooving machine, Nye's facer, Daniels' rotary planing machine, and Fay's power morticing-and-tenoning machine.[66] According to the *Memphis Directory* of 1849, G.W. Payne had "in full operation his Machine Turning and Sawing Establishment." In 1854 J.W. Hatcher of Columbia invented a rotary shingle machine "said to be capable of making one thousand to twelve hundred shingles per hour,"[67] and a few years later his townsman Nathan Vaught wrote in his diary: "This year 1858 we went up to Cincinnati and bought a heavy lot of machinery for carpentry purposes. Fitted together, got it in motion early in 1859." The *Plans of Buildings, Moldings, Architraves, Bases, Brackets, Stairs, Newels, Ballusters, Rails, Cornices, Mantles, Window Frames. Sash, Doors. Columns, &c for the Use of Carpenters and Builders,* published by Hinkle, Guild, and Company of Cincinnati in 1862, catalogs the results of steam carpentry, depicting a seemingly infinite variety of building parts, mostly Italianate or Gothic in design. The preface to the catalog admitted that the bad workmanship of competitors had caused "in the minds of many persons, strong objections to all factory work," but insisted that the window frames sold by Hinkle and Guild were made of seasoned lumber and "framed together in the same manner as hand-made work." Furthermore, the low price of manufactured work had induced "farmers and other persons, who formerly lived in log cabins, to build good comfortable houses, and capitalists in our cities have found out that buildings made in this way can be erected and rented so as to pay from ten to twenty percent on the cost." In 1862 Hinkle, Guild, and Company did business in fifteen states from the banks of the Ohio "near the depots of the Ohio and Mississippi, Indianapolis and Cincinnati, and Cincinnati, Hamilton, and Dayton Railroads." Steam was destroying carpentry and regional architec-

tural traditions while it built cities of factories, speculative housing, and capitalists' villas.

Foundries like Ament's in Nashville and the Western Foundry in Memphis made possible the local manufacture of cast-iron building parts. In 1855 the judges of the Tennessee Mechanics' Institute exhibition, Adolphus Heiman, Samuel P. Ament, and James Plunket, praised T.M. Brennan for casting iron door and window caps and columns of the type "now being generally introduced in the Eastern Cities for store fronts . . . taking the place of stone and marble . . . at half the cost." In the judges' opinion Brennan's cast-iron building parts gave evidence of "a decided improvement in the taste of our builders" and displayed the manufacturer's "knowledge of architectural design and embellishment."[68] Columns and caps like those Brennan had entered in the Mechanics' Institute exhibition in 1855 were used extensively on the first-story façades of the four- and five-story business blocks built on Nashville's Public Square during the late 1850s, among them the S.D. Morgan Company building and the Hick's and Ensley Blocks, the last two built by Harvey M. Akeroyd, who in 1859, while Morgan was commissioner, designed the cast-iron balconies and stairs for the library in the State Capitol.[69] In 1859 the architectural firm of J.L. Morgan and M.H. Baldwin advertised in the *Memphis Directory* that they could order from foundries throughout the country "Iron Fronts, Verandahs, Balconies, and Cast Iron Railings of Every Description." The Irving Block, built at the southeast corner of Second and Court about 1860, was an early example of the use of architectural cast iron in that city,[70] and the cast iron front a New York foundry made for William B. Greenlaw's Memphis store and published in their catalog in 1865 was typical of the hundreds brought to Tennessee by coaster, riverboat, and railroad.[71] Cast iron had, as the judges of the Nashville exhibition of 1855 remarked, two admirable qualities: it was "durable and capable of being moulded in any form desired." The material was tough, but it yielded easily to the designer's fancy.

Although the local tradition of fine craftsmanship lingered until joinery was superseded by the nailed balloon frame about 1870, the castings of Brennan's and Ament's foundries and the window frames and newels made by Warren and Moore's pantheon of steam-driven machinery signaled the end of the house carpenter's role in building. Horace Greeley wrote in 1872, "The nail has replaced the mortice and tenon, and economy of material as well as economy of force, is the end we now seek to attain in our building, as in the business of life."[72] After 1850 the new system of rail transportation encouraged the development of national sources of manufacture and supply that could prove profitable only if techniques and building parts were standardized. The house carpenter, the prince of the building trades during the first half of the nineteenth century, would survive either as a skilled laborer in the employ of a contractor or factory owner, or else by disentangling himself from the failing craft tradition, developing his skill in drawing and designing, and advertising as an architect.

In 1846 De Bow's *Commercial Review* reported that Nashville had 4 architects, 247 carpenters, 27 brickmasons, 17 stonemasons, 8 stonecutters, 7 lime-makers, 32 brickmakers, 16 house plasterers, and 23 painters and paper hangers.[73] De Bow's enumeration probably included William Strickland, whose father had been a house carpenter, mason, and master mechanic; Adolphus Heiman, son of a building superintendent in the Prussian royal service, who had come to Nashville a stonecutter; James M. Hughes, a house carpenter turned architect; and G. B. Vannoy, son of the carpenter Mason Vannoy, of the firm Vannoy and Turbeville. Only William Strickland, who had worked in Latrobe's Philadelphia drafting room from 1801 until 1805, had been educated to the profession. The roots of architectural practice lay in the trades. Of Nashville's four architects, only Strickland had not worked with carpenter's or stonecutter's tools in recent memory.

III. CARPENTERS AND ARCHITECTS

Stopped for the night at Mr. John Kain's, where I conversed with Mr. Hope, his house carpenter. . . . He showed an excellent book of architecture.

CHARLES COFFIN

When Charles Coffin called at John Kain's plantation near Knoxville on September 11, 1806, Kain's new house, distinguished by a fine Palladian window and the diapering of its brickwork, was nearing completion (79). Kain had gone to town, so Coffin "conversed with Mr. Hope," and Hope showed him "an excellent book of architecture," probably William Pain's *Builder's Golden Rule,* a handbook containing designs, patterns, and prices published in London in 1782. Although he sometimes relied on Pain's designs and, like most eighteenth-century house carpenters, paid close attention to his employer's desires, Thomas Hope was probably the designer of the Kain house, its architect as well as the builder of its stairs, mantels, and wainscoting.

In the last half of the eighteenth century, the development of architectural style and taste in the South was the work of carpenters who had a good eye for design, who could draw plans, and who usually possessed English handbooks: men like William Buckland of Annapolis, Richard Taliaferro of Williamsburg, John Muncrief and Gabriel Manigault of Charleston, John Hawks of New Bern, and Thomas Hope of Knoxville. Buckland, born in England and indentured about 1754 to Thomson Mason of Maryland, was a carpenter whose talent for carving and design flowered in mansions like Gunston Hall, Whitehall, and the Matthias Hammond House. Richard Taliaferro was a successful planter and the "skillful architect" who undertook the renovation of the Governor's Palace in the 1750s and built several fine houses in Williamsburg and the surrounding countryside.[1] John Muncrief's long career as a house carpenter in Charleston included the building of the Miles Brewton house in the late 1760s.[2] Gabriel Manigault, also a Charlestonian, was a gentleman amateur who built the Joseph Manigault house at 350 Meeting Street (1790–1795); the Branch Bank of the United States (1801), later the City Hall; and the Orphan House, all good examples of post-colonial classicism.

Like Buckland and Hawks, Thomas Hope had been born in England. He was in Charleston by 1788, when he walked with the architects rather than the carpenters in the procession the city held to celebrate the ratification of the Federal Constitution, and the *Charleston Directory* of 1790 located his cabinetmaker's shop at 15 Friend Street. Hope may have built several dwellings in Charleston, but Charles Coffin knew of only one, the

Izard house.[3] About 1796 Thomas Hope came to the newly laid off town of Knoxville, where he opened his carpenter's shop on Barbara Hill and advertised as a house carpenter and joiner.[4] Although he continued to practice cabinetmaking, Hope worked mostly as a house carpenter, building stylish dwellings like Francis A. Ramsey's house near Swan Pond (77), Colonel Charles McClung's State's View (71) on the Kingston Road, Joseph Churchill Strong's town house on Knoxville's Cumberland Street (78), and Frederick Augustus Ross's Rotherwood near Kingsport. Sometimes Hope took his designs from Pain, as he may have done when he built the Strong house. Sometimes he followed plainer, more traditional patterns, as he did at the McClung house. One way or another, Thomas Hope was responsible for some of the best architecture built in the upper counties before 1820.

Hope was but the first of dozens of fine house carpenters (most of whose names and works may never be known) who were more than craftsmen and who brought good style to Tennessee, following the frontier and fullfilling the architectural aspirations of prosperous planters and courthouse commissioners. Samuel Cleague, born in Pennsylvania in 1781, married in Botetourt County, Virginia, in 1800, left Fincastle about 1823 and built his way down the valley to McMinn County, giving East Tennessee a stolid, distinctive family of Federal brick houses (89, 96).[5] Hugh Roland, born in Ohio about 1795, was in Nashville before 1818, when he built the Masonic Hall on Spring Street. Roland, in Louisville in 1830, worked in Memphis in the 1840s.[6] David Morrison, born in Pennsylvania in 1797, came to Nashville before 1828 to build the State Penitentiary (80) and stayed to design many important buildings in Nashville during the 1830s, among them the Hermitage (128), the Methodist Church (81), and the Union Bank of the State of Tennessee (132). In 1833 Morrison provided a design for the new state capitol in Jackson, Mississippi, and about 1840 he was in Memphis.[7] J.C. Trautwine gave up his Philadelphia practice in 1836 to become chief engineer of the Hiwassee Railroad, and while living in Knoxville provided a plan for the Knox County Courthouse of 1842.[8] William H. Clyce was born in Virginia about 1815, but by 1838 he was at work in East Tennessee, where he designed Jonesboro's Presbyterian Church in 1846. William Crane, born in Ohio in 1815, came to Memphis in the early 1840s, designed the Second Presbyterian Church (13), and soon became the city engineer. About 1845 Thomas Blanchard, born in New York in 1815, came to Monroe County, where he built several fine dwellings, among them the Guilford Cannon house (141).[9] The most famous of the immigrant architects was of course William Strickland, who, having failed to secure employment or important commissions in Washington or Philadelphia, came in 1845 to Nashville, where the commissioners of the Capitol offered him a chance to build the new statehouse (8), and wealthy citizens gave him choice residential commissions (149).

Sometimes architects came to Tennessee from Europe, for the state was a land of promise for carpenters and architects as well as planters and speculators. Adolphus Heiman, an ambitious Prussian stonecutter, arrived in 1837 and after 1850 was a popular builder of country houses (17, 167, 171, 173, 174); he was designer of the most important buildings of the University of Nashville (152, 164) and of many churches and schools. Henry Dudley and Frank Wills, English-born partners in a New York firm from 1851 until 1853, designed two of Tennessee's finest antebellum Gothic Revival churches (124, 125). Harvey M. Akeroyd came from England about 1854 and soon gave Nashville its first stylish Italianate designs. The carpenter William Baumann, born in Bavaria in 1807, was in Knoxville by 1855, and though no designs have been attributed to him, his sons Joseph F. and Albert B. were important East Tennessee architects after the war. James M. Hughes, born in Tennessee in 1818 and one of Nashville's most extensively patronized antebellum architects (19, 151, 177), was an exception to the rule that most of the house carpenters and architects who worked in Tennessee during the nineteenth century had immigrated from Virginia, Ohio, Pennsylvania, or Europe.

Although no Tennessee house carpenter is known to have called himself an architect before Hugh Roland came to Nashville about 1818, buildings were usually constructed from a plan. Sometimes owners provided their own designs. Charles Coffin may have drawn the plan he studied on May 30, 1805; certainly he was able to copy and revise "Mr. Izard's draught of a front door" for use of his workmen. But, typically, carpenters and bricklayers furnished plans for their employers as part of their work. On February 2, 1734, the bricklayer Samuel Holmes advertised in the *South-Carolina Gazette* that he could furnish "draughts of houses." In 1769 Ezra Waite of Charleston, who, under the superintendency of John Muncrief, built the porch of the Miles Brewton house and paneled three of its principal rooms, advertised that "after twenty-seven years experience in both theory and practice, in noblemens' and gentlemens' seats," he could "give satisfaction by plans, sections, elevations, and executions at his house in King Street."[10] When the Philadelphia Carpenters' Company built its elegant hall in 1770, the design was

provided by a member, and the first of the company's "Rules for Measuring and Valuing Work" noted that "Drawing Designs, making out Bills of Scantling, collecting Materials, and Sticking up Stuff are to be charged by the carpenter in proportion to the trouble." When Hugh Roland of Nashville advertised in the *Nashville Clarion and Tennessee Gazette* on June 20, 1820, that "Gentlemen in the country can be furnished with Ground Plans and Elevations by sending the size of their intended building," he was following the practice of men like Holmes, Waite, and countless other bricklayers and house carpenters who made part of their living by drawing designs.

Those who considered themselves designers often advertised their abilities. By January 9, 1846, William Crane of Memphis was advertising in the *Weekly Appeal* that he could provide plans, and in 1850 J.H. Ingraham thought Adolphus Heiman would furnish plans for a farmhouse, barn, and stable for about ten dollars.[11] John L. Morgan advertised in the *Memphis Directory* of 1856–57 "plans for houses in detail, together with Specifications, Front Elevations, prospective and otherwise. Particular attention to cottage plans of the latest Northern and Southern style, neatly executed with all the necessary drawings in detail." Two years later P.H. Hammarskold of Memphis advertised in the city directory that he could "furnish designs for . . . Public and Private buildings, with all kinds of Details and Specifications . . . Particular attention paid to Drawings for Country Houses, Churches, etc." Before the war, architectural drawings had become sophisticated and technical, a far cry from the naive sketches produced by the typical late-eighteenth-century carpenter.

Regrettably, none of the plans made by Tennessee house carpenters or furnished by courthouse commissioners during the eighteenth century has been found. With a few exceptions, the elegant drawings John Hawks made for Governor Tryon's palace at New Bern about 1761, some drawings by Buckland, and Joseph Horatio Anderson's designs for the Maryland state capitol in Annapolis, pre-Revolutionary architectural drawings made in the southern colonies were unsophisticated, schematic sketches. No drawing by Hope, none of Hugh Roland's "Ground Plans and Elevations," nor any of David Morrison's drawings has been discovered. Some indication of Morrison's draftsmanship is given by the engravings of the Hermitage of 1831 and the McKendree Methodist Church of 1833 that appeared in the border of Ayres's Map of Nashville, published in Cincinnati in 1831. Although the originals were redrawn by the engraver Samuel G. Munson, David Morrison provided the view of the Hermitage that Munson copied (128).[12] Munson's illustration of the Methodist Church is an architect's elevation (81), not the perspective mapmakers usually preferred, and since the building had not been erected when Munson made his engravings, he probably worked from Morrison's drawing. Two drawings made by William H. Clyce, his design for the Presbyterian Church at Jonesboro (29), made about 1846, and the elevation of The Oaks, the John Roper Branner house (1868) near Jefferson City, survive. Of James M. Hughes's drawings, only the plan of James K. Polk's Nashville residence (30), made in 1848, survives, but his elevation of the Bank of Nashville (1853) was probably copied by W.A. Eichbaum (19). Eichbaum probably copied some of Adolphus Heiman's drawings (155, 165) and engravers may have traced others for use in catalogs (152, 163, 164), but the only drawing known to have been taken directly from Heiman's original is the elevation of the Nashville Masonic Hall that Henry Eichbaum copied at half size and presented to the Tennessee Historical Society on November 17, 1857 (31). None of the "Plans and Elevations of Cottages," "Plans for Church Decorations," designs for private houses, and "City Architecture" that Harvey M. Akeroyd entered in the exhibits of the Tennessee Mechanics' Institute during the 1850s has been discovered. Akeroyd's drawings were the work of a professional, "very elaborately and beautifully finished,"[13] but even in the 1850s much building was still carried out according to simple sketches, like the design for an addition that Nathan Vaught furnished M.D. Cooper gratis by way of a proposal for the job (32). The largest collection of antebellum architectural drawings in Tennessee is the Strickland portfolios. Although Strickland himself did not draw all of them, the best of these plans and elevations illustrate the fine draftsmanship that could be produced in the studios of that period (33). The offices of Strickland and Akeroyd served as schools. Strickland trained many draftsmen who wished to enter the profession, among them his sons Francis W. and James Hartley; and A.C. Bruce, who worked in Knoxville and Atlanta after the war, had been educated in Akeroyd's office during the 1850s.

Once the design had been agreed upon, responsibility passed to the undertaker, who would see the building to completion. The title *undertaker* gradually disappeared from the vocabulary of building after 1820, to be replaced by 1880 with the term *contractor*, but throughout the antebellum period undertaker was the common title for the person responsible, usually under contract and often under bond, for completing the work. The undertaker was often an artisan, usually the carpenter or bricklayer; but sometimes, especially

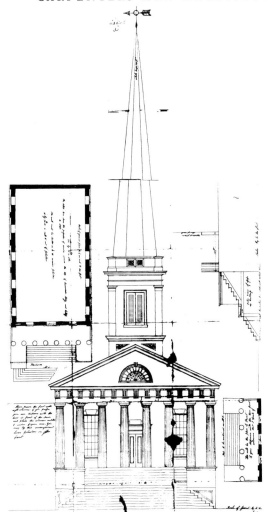

29. *W.H. Clyce's design for the Jonesboro Presbyterian Church (Washington County) shows the carefully executed work of a competent draftsman.*

in public buildings, the undertaker was merely a financially responsible citizen who would guarantee performance, superintend the work, employ and pay the workmen, and if all went well, make a profit for his trouble. Although Charles Robertson is remembered for his military and political careers, the Washington County Court considered him also a responsible undertaker, allowing him "fifty pounds current money for building the court house in the Town of Jonesborough" in 1784.[14] The Embree brothers, Elihu and Elijah, are best known for their ventures in mining and smelting and for Elihu's abolitionist newspaper, but in 1819 they undertook construction of Samuel Jackson's town houses (88) in Jonesboro, employing the bricklayer John Smith under a separate contract and securing carpenters to furnish "door and window frames, and other wooden parts of said house."[15] If the building was costly, and always when it was a public project, the undertaker was required either to produce sureties, financially responsible citizens whose signatures guaranteed his performance, or else to post cash bond. As the Bedford County Courthouse commissioners put

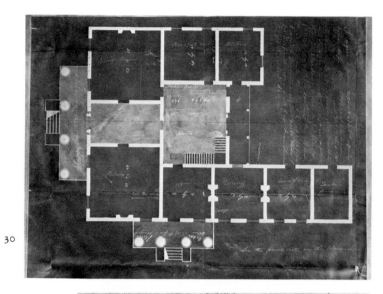

30

31

New front of the old Masonic Hall.
Built, 1818. Wing added in 1847. Newfronted about 1852. Burnt, 185

33

32

the matter, "In order to prevent men who cannot give security bidding . . . no person will be permitted to bid who does not, before the letting, inform the commissioners who his security will be, that they may know whether they ought to permit him to bid."[16] In 1839 the carpenter Herbert M. Ledbetter and the bricklayer William Fields were "held and firmly bound unto the President and Directors of the Bank of Tennessee for the Penal Sum of Eighteen Thousand Dollars" for their completion of the Bank of Tennessee in Rogersville (138), a job for which they were jointly to receive a total of only nine thousand dollars.[17]

Following the practice of Virginia and the Carolinas, the plan of the building was displayed, then the building let to the lowest bidder on an appointed day, often the first day of some regular session of the County Court of Quarter Sessions and Pleas. In 1769 the commissioners of the Williamsburg courthouse, appointed "to agree with an undertaker," advertised, "The plan of the above Court-House may be seen at Mr. Hay's."[18] Five years later the churchwardens of Cameron Parish, having described the additions they wished to make to the rector's house, advised that "those who are inclined to undertake may, by applying to the Reverend Spence Grayson . . . be supplied with a plan."[19] In a moment of whimsy, the commissioners for the first Knox County courthouse set their invitation to bidders, published in the *Gazette* for April 6, 1793, to poetry, promising: "The Plan may be seen in the Ville of Knox, on Monday the first day of court"; but the Charlotte commissioners' prosaic announcement of "the letting of the public buildings in said town to the lowest undertaker on Thursday the 3d of April, 1806," published in the *Tennessee Gazette* on January 25, was typical.

30. *James M. Hughes drew this scheme for remodeling the Felix Grundy house (2) after President Polk purchased the property in 1846. When construction began in 1848, the larger porch was omitted in favor of a distyle in antis scheme, and other changes were made.*

31. *Henry Eichbaum, who shared his father's (W.A.) strong sense of the importance of Nashville's architecture, made this drawing of the Masonic Hall of 1851.*

32. *Nathan Vaught's sketch was the only plan required for the proposed addition to M.D. Cooper's Columbia (Maury County) residence.*

33. *This carefully delineated ink drawing, made in Strickland's Nashville office, may be a study for the Wilson County Courthouse of 1848.*

Planters and town dwellers often superintended the building of their own houses, making agreements with carpenters and bricklayers themselves, as Charles Coffin did in 1805, though sometimes the contract was given to a single workman, who might then act as undertaker and superintendent. This was the choice Robert Armstrong contemplated when he wrote President Jackson in November 1834 that "a Contract will be made, With One person for the Whole repairs or separately with the *Carpenter, Plasterer*, and *Painter*, takeing a Contract from each." Finally, Joseph Reiff and William C. Hume acted as undertakers for the carpentry, with Andrew Jackson, Jr. also signing agreements with the plasterer Higgins, the bricklayer Mr. Austin, and the painters Horn and Wells for rebuilding the Hermitage. In 1839 the directors of the Rogersville branch of the Bank of the State of Tennessee built their new banking house under a contract which made carpenter Fields and bricklayer Ledbetter jointly responsible signatories. Occasionally the house carpenter made contracts with other workmen on behalf of the owner, as the carpenter Adam Lowry did in 1802, when he employed the mason John Squibb "on behalf of Samuel Doak" to build chimneys at Washington College.[20]

Superintending was sometimes done by a master craftsman who was, or wished to become, an architect. George Mason noted on William Buckland's indenture when it expired that Buckland's experience included "the entire Direction of the Carpenter's and Joiner's work of a large House,"[21] and in 1777 Mardum V. Evengton of Chesterfield County, Virginia, advertised: "My chief desire is to act in the Capacity of Superintender, or Supervisor, over any reasonable Number of Hands, either in public or private buildings."[22] By the second quarter of the nineteenth century, supervising was part of the carpenter's and architect's work in Tennessee. The superintendent acted as overseer, employed workmen, guaranteed their accounts, and supervised on the owner's behalf.

Amateurs might also develop reputations for being good superintendents. Drury P. Armstrong acted as superintendent when John Dameron built the Knox County Courthouse (144) in 1842, and served in the same capacity when the new East Tennessee University buildings (110) were built in 1843, noting in his diary on June 6, 1843, "I attended as superintendent on the part of the trustees, and Mr. Crutchfield . . . for the mechanics."

By 1850 superintending frequently justified a fee over and above the profit a workman might make from his labor or an architect from his plans. Strickland was given a fee for his plans for the Capitol, but his salary of

$2,500 per annum was paid because he agreed "to superintend and direct all artisans, mechanics and laborers that may from time to time be employed by and with the consultation and advice of the commissioners and to select and judge of all the materials that may be required for the building in all its branches."[23] In 1860 G.B. Vannoy testified that it had been the custom in Nashville for many years to charge 5 percent on the cost for superintending, and that for the past three or four years carpenters had charged extra for superintending even when they had undertaken the carpentry themselves.[24] Vannoy probably meant that complete architectural services, plans, estimates, specifications, and superintendence should cost 5 percent of the price of construction. This was the practice of New York architects in 1841, when George Wightwick's *Hints to Young Architects, Calculated to Facilitate Their Practical Operations . . . With Additional Notes and Hints to Persons about Building in the Country by Andrew J. Downing* went to press, and in the *Memphis Directory* of 1859 P.H. Hammarskold still advertised terms of "2½ percent for Superintendence." The practice of superintending one's own carpentry gradually disappeared. The conflict of interest was obvious; and in its constitution of 1837 the American Institution of Architects forbade their members receiving "directly or indirectly, any pecuniary consideration or emolument from tradesmen whose works they may be engaged to superintend on behalf of others."

Building was usually carried out under the provisions of a written contract like the agreement of November 1799 between the house carpenters Cummins and Pinkley and John Overton for the construction of Travellers' Rest.[25] Sometimes the contract was supplemented by verbal agreements. On July 31, 1805, Charles Coffin had occasion to remind his house carpenters of obligations "verbally, expressly, and fully agreed upon in the Library, where our written articles were draughted." When the fourth Hermitage was begun in 1834, Jackson's friends assured him that the written contract had been supplemented by detailed verbal descriptions, and the contract of January 1, 1835, noted that "the dementions of the Rooms, The size of the Windows, and a minute description of Worke to be done is not mentioned in this article, but it is understood by the parties, in the presence of the above named Gentlemen."[26]

Contracts were drawn on the assumption that the carpenter or bricklayer would be paid either "by the great" or "by the measure." When a single sum was paid, the carpenter would make his estimate beforehand, agree with the owner for a fixed price, and charge extra only for those changes authorized while the building was under construction. Thus Wesley Wheless agreed to pay James M. Hughes $7,000 for building his Gothic Revival mansion, and during construction authorized changes worth $1,235.[27] But fifteen years earlier the new buildings for East Tennessee University had still been built under an agreement that called for payment by the measure.[28]

Because the measuring of architecture was complicated and easily subject to misunderstanding, measuring and valuing was a service house carpenters and bricklayers were willing to perform whether the work was theirs or not. Samuel Holmes of Charleston advertised in 1734 that he "measures and values all sorts of work."[29] Apart from the articles of association and the plates illustrating the best patterns and techniques, the 1786 *Rules of Work of the Carpenters' Company of the City and County of Philadelphia* were mostly an elaborate, traditional system for measuring and valuing carpentry. When the American Institution of Architects was founded fifty years later, the first members were forbidden to measure or value work "not executed from their own designs."[30] But most architects continued to measure and value work without regard for the institution's new principle. On May 10, 1844, Hugh Roland of Memphis advertised in the *Appeal* not only "Plans, elevations, detailed estimates, &c . . . made out at shortest notice," but "Artificer's work measured and valued; and builders' accounts equitably adjusted on reasonable terms." The intervention of a professional measurer like Roland might have prevented the lengthy altercation between Thomas Crutchfield, builder of the new East Tennessee University dormitories, and Drury P. Armstrong, the trustees' agent and overseer, in 1843.[31] When G.B. Vannoy was asked in 1860 to estimate the value of Wesley Wheless's house, he answered, "I have never measured the work and do not know its cost."[32] Vannoy had in mind the same procedure George Suggs required in 1790, when he stipulated in his agreement with the mason William Erwin: "the Quantity to be Estimated by Judges of Such Work."[33]

Early-nineteenth-century buildings, especially residences, were often the result of close collaboration between the owner and his carpenter, making it difficult to assign responsibility for design. Whether Charles Coffin provided his own design or not, he directed the work closely and helped his carpenters lay out the house frame. Beside his work as superintendent for the trustees of East Tennessee University, Drury P. Armstrong designed his own house, "submitted the plans for creating a columned portico and steeple to the First Presbyterian Church in Knoxville," and "attended to the laying off and properly proportioning the collumns in the portico of the courthouse."[34] In his anxious supervision of the University buildings, which he may actually have designed, Armstrong was following the example of that other public-spirited amateur, Thomas Jefferson, who had provided plans for the University of Virginia in 1819. In 1849 J.H. Ingraham, who knew a good deal less about architecture than Armstrong but who had a dilettante's interest in building and a concern for public education, furnished the design for the new Masonic College in Clarksville (159). Because Ingraham was not a draftsman, G.B. Vannoy drew the plans and elevations.[35] Before James M. Hughes built President Polk's house (151) in Nashville in 1848, there was a lengthy correspondence resulting in many changes, and in 1860 Nicholas Hobson testified that Hughes had been awarded the contract for carpentry at the Wheless house on the condition that he build it to suit the owner.[36] The Hermitage of 1836 and Andrew Jackson Donelson's Tulip Grove are two of the most important and best documented buildings in Tennessee's architectural history, but the houses also illustrate the difficulties which beset attempts to determine the authorship of antebellum domestic architecture. The carpenters Joseph Reiff and William Hume built both houses between 1832 and 1836, and if they furnished the plans for Tulip Grove (130) or suggested the changes that gave the Hermitage its final form (189), they deserve a place with Roland and Morrison as important architects of the 1830s. But the evidence is unclear. No drawings have been discovered; the younger Jacksons, the Donelsons, or some still unidentified architect may have been responsible for these designs.

Part of the difficulty in isolating responsibility for design in the early nineteenth century is the result of the common dependence of carpenters, bricklayers, and owners on the same books for their stylish designs. There were not many architectural books in the South in the seventeenth century—John Carter of Lancaster County, Virginia, had one before 1690, though its title is not known[37]—but after Colin Campbell's *Vitruvius Britannicus* appeared in 1715, dozens of English writers began to produce the treatises upon which colonial house carpenters would rely. William Byrd had ten in his library, all published before 1730, three before 1700.[38] In 1772 Robert Carter's library at Nomini Hall had fourteen architectural books, including William Salmon's *Palladio Londinensis*, and William Buckland owned the same number, among them Batty Langley's *The City and Country Builder's and Workman's Treasury of Designs* (1756), Isaac Ware's *A Complete Body of Architecture* (1756), and Abraham Swan's *Designs in Carpentry* (1759) in 1774.[39] Three years later Mardum

Evengton proudly advertised that he possessed "an elegant assortment . . . of Books of Architect, which I imported from London and Liverpool."[40]

Architectural books remained the single most important common source of design throughout the antebellum period. Thomas Hope brought his copy of Pain's *Builder's Golden Rule*, probably purchased in London before he emigrated to Charleston, to the Tennessee frontier about 1796. When Adolphus Heiman arrived in Nashville about 1837, he brought with him a copy of Giacomo da Vignola's *Regola delli Cinque Ordini d'Architettura* that had probably been in his family for a century.[41] *The Antiquities of Athens*, the famous collection of measured drawings and notes prepared by James Stuart and Nicholas Revett, came to Nashville with William Strickland in 1845,[42] and Strickland and his sons continued to collect architectural books until their library was dispersed in 1859. Andrew J. Downing's works were known in Tennessee in 1848, when William Prichard consulted one of Downing's books to find a design for the gardener's cottage the Horticultural Society wished to build,[43] but Downing's *Cottage Residences* had probably been available several years earlier. James Hartley Strickland owned a copy of George Wightwick's *Hints to Young Architects*, which included an appendix by Downing. Minard Lafever was also represented in Nashville libraries. Henry Eichbaum, an avid amateur, bought Lafever's *Architectural Instructor* (1856), from Berry's Bookstore in Nashville on October 24, 1856, and Lafever's *Modern Builders' Guide* passed from Francis Strickland, who purchased it September 23, 1852, to J.H. Strickland, and finally, on March 21, 1859, to the Tennessee State Library. Books remained important sources of design throughout the nineteenth century. In the 1890s George Barber ran one of the largest mail-order plan businesses in the United States from his Knoxville drafting rooms and published numerous editions of his books and catalogs of designs, as well as the magazine *American Home* (1895–1904).[44]

Given a situation in which any able house carpenter or any competent amateur was an architect, responsibility for the design often shared, and common published sources frequently consulted, the modern distinction between a professional designer and workmen or contractors was moot. Before 1860 the person or persons responsible for determining the design and drawing the plans—whether carpenter, client, or professional designer—was usually called the architect. A bricklayer like Levi Ketchum of Columbia could be named one of two "principle architects" of Columbia's first Episcopal Church building,[45] and in 1847 the official report described Jacob Newman as "principal architect" of the

Tennessee Institution for the Deaf and Dumb in Knoxville (15).[46] Two years later Newman was the bricklayer responsible for erecting the masonry of the Washington County Courthouse according to the plans of Joseph L. Birts.[47] James M. Hughes, listed as a carpenter in Nashville directories during the 1850s, was called the architect of Nashville's Second Presbyterian Church (150) on the silver plate deposited in its cornerstone in 1844.[48] In 1847 Hughes was preferred to William Strickland when President Polk built his house in Nashville (151), and later Hughes provided the plans for the Odd Fellows Hall and for Wesley Wheless' Bank of Nashville (19).[49] Yet Hughes served as carpenter under Strickland at the First Presbyterian Church and the John M. Bass house in 1848,[50] and in 1860 was unsuccessful in his suit to obtain an architect's fee for designing Wesley Wheless' residence. The record of Hughes's suit against Wheless provides an interesting and accurate picture of architectural practice in Nashville in the late 1850s.

About 1853 Wesley Wheless, a wealthy Englishman who had gone into banking with Nicholas Hobson and married Hobson's daughter, decided to build a residence across the Cumberland from Nashville (177). Wheless asked Harvey M. Akeroyd to make a plan but decided not to use Akeroyd's design, paid him a fifty-dollar fee on March 6, 1855, and searched out another architect. On July 16, 1856, Wheless signed a contract with George M. Smith and James M. Hughes for the carpentry. That contract mentions a plan and elevation, and in the trial that followed no witness denied that Hughes had drawn at least the elevation of Wheless' house. Given the unfortunate history of Wheless' business dealings with Hughes, it is remarkable that Smith and Hughes were awarded the contract for the carpentry. Wheless had employed Hughes to build the Bank of Nashville in 1853, and at the trial in 1860 Nicholas Hobson recalled that Hughes had been given the contract for the carpentry only on the condition that he would provide a plan. Hughes had furnished the drawings, but when the bank was completed, he had sued Wheless and Hobson for an architect's fee of $200, and won.

Work on Wheless' house began in the fall of 1856. The foundation was dug, stone was laid, and then the work covered over for the winter. That autumn Wheless solicited a plan from G.B. Vannoy. Vannoy obliged, but when he visited the site several weeks later, Wheless told him that Hughes had the carpentry contract and had furnished the plans. The house was completed in summer, and on July 18, 1857, Smith and Hughes were paid $7,830, the balance due on their account. Then, on October 20, 1858, James M.

Hughes sued in chancery to recover an architect's fee of $800.

When the case came to trial in December 1860, Wheless' lawyer argued that no contract had been made with Hughes for architectural services, that Wheless had provided the ground plan himself, and that Hughes had agreed to build the house to suit the owner. Nicholas Hobson, Wheless' father-in-law and banking partner, testified that Hughes had known of Akeroyd's plans, that he had been anxious to have the job but had told Hobson he disliked working from the plans of others. Hobson remembered that Hughes had warned that Akeroyd would probably make a regular architect's charge, and Hughes had agreed to furnish plans for nothing if the carpentry contract were given to Smith and Hughes. Hughes' lawyer tried to show that Hughes was known to be an architect, that he had actually superintended for Wheless, that professional services were usually remunerated even in the absence of a contract, and that the fee Hughes wished to recover for drawing plans and superintending was customary in Nashville.

Testimony given at the trial showed that during the 1850s Nashville house carpenters often provided plans without additional charge. G.B. Vannoy testified: "It has been customary among carpenters at Nashville for the last three or four years to charge for superintendence where they did the work & for the plan where they furnished the plan"; he added, "And I would have been warranted to charge accordingly had I done the work or superintended, in the absence of any contract." George M. Smith, appearing on Hughes's behalf, testified that carpentry was very different from the architect's work, superintending and drawing plans, and that Hughes had in fact both provided the design and acted as superintendent. On cross examination, Smith testified that he had been in Nashville for fifteen years before he had worked under an architect, and he recalled that when he came to the city in 1829 there had been only one carpenter, Hugh Roland, who called himself an architect.

James M. Hughes lost the case. He was, as Vannoy testified, a "carpenter by trade and architect by profession." Hughes's contract with Wheless, who had not forgotten the bank, contained a formidable clause forbidding Smith and Hughes to charge more than the price agreed for any reason, and besides in 1860, drawing designs could still be considered part of the house carpenter's job.

After 1865 the industrial reorganization of work that divided the traditional building arts into practical and theoretical halves, assigning the practical to carefully supervised laborers who were paid to undertake the job according to a plan, and the theoretical to a new class of professional designers and supervisors, required men like Vannoy and Hughes, house carpenters by trade, architects by profession, to choose either the old art or the new profession. James M. Hughes was listed as a carpenter and builder in the Nashville city directory for 1860, but in 1866 he and his son J.M. Hughes, Jr., both appear as architects. Steam carpentry shops like Warren and Moore's in Nashville drove craftsmen into factories, while the necessity for competent supervision of the increasingly complex techniques of building became obvious. Superintending became a characteristic function of architects, and once superintending was the work of professionals who were at the site only occasionally, architectural drawings and specifications took on a new importance, being as they were the designers' best means for exercising day-to-day control over the work.

The new professional was a man of books and theories. Since Vitruvius, architects had written books containing the theory of their art, and occasionally men like Leon Battista Alberti or Claude-Nicholas Ledoux would present sweeping historical or philosophical theories. But these Renaissance and Enlightenment treatises were not very important in eighteenth-century America. When George Mason recommended William Buckland as "complete Master of the Carpenter's and Joiner's Business both in theory and practice," when Ezra Waite claimed "twenty-seven years experience in both theory and practice," and when Mardum Evengton advertised that he was acquainted with "the Theory and Practice in any of the grand Branches of the five ancient Orders," nothing more than a good understanding of precedents and proportions, and some knowledge of fashionable handbooks was meant by theory.[51] But nineteenth-century architectural theory was of a different order. Andrew J. Downing's advocacy of horticulture and the picturesque, like William Strickland's rationalistic defense of Grecian, were sweeping theories that presupposed aesthetic and psychological principles. As these metaphysical theories became increasingly important among architects and intellectuals, architecture became a profession for the well-read gentleman, not the house carpenter.

Finally, the practical knowledge of statics and materials the architect was bound to gain in his work made him an engineer. Strickland, who usually called himself an engineer as well as an architect, was known for his Delaware Canal and his compendious *Public Works of the United States*, a graphic survey of bridges, harbors, and waterways, as much as for his Greek Revival buildings. J.C. Trautwine, who had studied with Strickland from 1828 to 1831 and had enjoyed a precocious

architectural career in Philadelphia, moved to Knoxville in 1836 to work as Chief Engineer of the Hiwassee Railroad.[52] William Crane of Memphis, who had practiced architecture there since the early 1840s, became the city engineer by 1852;[53] and Adolphus Heiman, probably Nashville's most successful antebellum architect, was employed by M.D. Field as engineer of Nashville's suspension bridge about 1847. David Morrison, who designed many of Nashville's fine buildings of the 1830s, provided the engineering survey that justified the building of the Navy Yard at Memphis in 1842, and in 1849 Morrison was still listed in the city directory as an engineer employed at the Navy Yard. Hugh Roland, in an advertisement published in the *Appeal* on May 10, 1844, called himself an "Architect and Civil Engineer," and promised that he could provide "Drawings, specifications, &c. for machinery, correctly prepared for the Patent office." James B. Cook of Memphis had supervised construction of the Crystal Palace under Joseph Paxton in 1851 and was the designer of submarines and patented jail systems.[54]

Although most architects had probably not read enough Hegel to understand what was happening, the comfortable mid-century liaison between architecture and the new steam and electric technology fell victim after the war to the romantic dissection of reality into a fixed, efficient, historical purpose and a plethora of ever changing forms employed on account of their transitory appropriateness. During the thirty years that separated Appomattox and the centennial, efficiency—most easily understood as profit—became the single justifying value, and beauty an important but secondary and separable good. At no time during the nineteenth century did architects abandon their allegiance to the beautiful, but the foundations shifted. Robert Mills probably spoke for the great architects of the 1840s when he wrote, "The principle assumed and acted upon is that beauty is founded upon order, and that convenience and utility are constituent parts."[55] Mills's first loyalty, and William Strickland's, was to an aesthetic order that unfailingly yielded beauty, convenience and utility being constituent parts. The argument presupposed firm metaphysical underpinnings, an implicit belief in a transcendental aesthetic, and the classical notion of taste, all of which, by 1850, were fading from the experience of clients and architects alike.

On January 9, 1845, William Crane of Memphis offered those who planned to build a more obvious rationale, advertising in the *Appeal* that his services could prevent misunderstandings "involving hundreds of dollars in the differences" which might arise when contractors were "required to estimate and make their calculations from verbal explanations and rude sketches." Crane concluded that "a few dollars paid in the commencement, to an architect who understands his profession, will save hundreds in the end." Doubtless true, but Crane was selling his profession on new grounds. Only five years later Ingraham, urging planters to buy a design from Mr. Heiman the architect, justified his advice that every farmer should build an attractive, comfortable house with the speculation that when the railroad came through, it might offer "Mr. Slack" only $7,000 for his unsightly log house, but "Mr. Goodtaste" $10,000 for his beautiful country villa.[56] The conclusion was: "Good taste costs nothing, Mr. Farmer."

Most architects and their clients probably continued to think about architecture much as they had in the past, but Ingraham's argument, which would become a popular defense of professionalism, illustrates the theoretical result of the industrial reorganization of work. Ingraham's slogan tempted the ignorant and unreflective to confuse art with economics and seemed to justify the abandonment of the traditional aesthetic. The change came slowly. James Marston Fitch observed that at the end of the war the three institutions that would determine the immediate future of architecture, the American Institute of Architects (1857); the first collegiate school of architecture, M.I.T. (1866); and the first architectural periodical, the *American Architect and Building News*, were all concerned chiefly with beauty.[57] Certainly in 1860 the criteria for the successful practice of architecture in Tennessee had not changed much from standards Thomas Hope would have understood. An architect or a good house carpenter still made beautiful designs, and the best praise his work could be given was still the judgment that his buildings were, like Roland's Episcopal church (7), "chaste," or like Adolphus Heiman's Medical Department Building at the University of Nashville (152C), "classical and beautiful."[58] And even in the 1870s and 1880s, when the new apology for the architectural profession was well established, beauty—at a reasonable cost—was what clients valued, even though the theoretical defense of the beautiful was less and less part of the professional rhetoric.

IV. PATTERNS, TYPES, AESTHETICS

*Regularity regards the arrangement of the whole
according to rule—that the doors and windows, as to
size and distance, correspond with one another, and
with the other parts of the building.*

SAMUEL DOAK, c. 1780

Fine house carpenters, craftsmen like Thomas Blanchard or James M. Hughes, who drew and built the best designs, were probably never without handbooks and often traveled; and after 1840 any carpenter who was interested could find copies of the latest works of Andrew J. Downing, Minard Lafever, or Asher Benjamin at a Nashville or Memphis bookseller. But most of Tennessee's early-nineteenth-century buildings were not built by designers of the quality of Blanchard or Hughes or Roland. Nathan Vaught, for example, who was a fine country carpenter from Maury County, in addition to going to Huntsville and other nearby towns on building jobs, took only two long trips in his life, one of those to Virginia to visit an aging aunt. Failing books and travel, a carpenter in Jackson or Rogersville or Newport might simply copy a building he or his client admired, perhaps one the carpenter himself had previously built; or he could ask the owner to describe the house he desired and, relying on his knowledge of house types, begin to build, either with or without a sketch. Whenever he copied older buildings or built from his knowledge of familiar types, the carpenter would also presuppose an aesthetic, one to which he could probably have given only partial expression, nevertheless one having precise content and identifiable antecedents.

For the ordinary carpenter, imitation was often the shortest path to good design, and much of Tennessee's antebellum architecture was simply copied or adapted from Virginia or North Carolina or Pennsylvania precedents. The builder of the Embree house (34) employed the plan William Penn recommended to immigrants in advertisements for his colony: a rectangle divided in half, with one half again divided to make two small chambers,[1] but he probably used it not because he had read Penn's advice to immigrants, but because he had seen a house built according to the traditional plan Penn recommended (50). Similarly, a house like the Greater Dabney house in Goochland County, Virginia, was the model William Bowen used when he built his dwelling on Mansker's Creek in Sumner County about 1788 (35);[2] and the Daniel Montgomery house, a stone, story-and-a-half Federal cottage (36) built at Shackle Island ten miles west of Gallatin, was probably copied from a dwelling like the Mary Harvey Trigg house, Hawthorne Hall, near Fin-

castle, Virginia (37). In Tennessee there are story-and-a-half (or story-and-loft) brick cottages, like the Buckingham house (38) near Sevierville and many similar houses, that imitate buildings like the Wishart house in Princess Anne County, Virginia (39).[3] And there are three-bay Federal town houses, the Eaton house in Franklin (90), the Samuel Polk house in Columbia (91), all copied from dwellings the brickmason may have seen in Abingdon, Staunton, or New Bern. All the house carpenter required in order to build these houses was the training his apprenticeship had earned, a good memory, and perhaps some advice from his employer. Since the eighteenth century was not much interested in novelty and had no experience of the nineteenth-century notion of originality of authorship, these borrowings passed unremarked except for occasional praise. The most elegant of these local borrowings can be traced to seventeenth-century Italy. Country houses like Palladio's Villa Pisani (1553–1555) near Montagnana (40) were ultimately the inspiration for John Muncrief's Miles Brewton house, built in Charleston in 1769, and the nearby Drayton Hall. From the Tidewater the design was brought early in the eighteenth century to Woodlawn (74) and Meridian Hill (3) near Nashville, Fairvue in Sumner County (76), built about 1828, and Hamilton Place in Maury County (41), built in 1832.[4]

These borrowings also perpetuated types, each having rules of its own that carpenters might carry partly in imagination, partly in their hands. Henry Glassie calls these rules unconscious, but not unknown: "They are known, as their proper use proves, and they can be brought into consciousness through question or contemplation."[5] In proof of his thesis Glassie presented an analysis of 182 houses, mostly in Louisa and Goochland

---

34. With its segmental lintels, steep roof, and asymmetrical fenestration, the Thomas Embree house at Telford (Washington County) typified the Shenandoah Valley stone house of the late eighteenth century. ▶

35. The William Bowen house (c. 1788) on Mansker's Creek (Sumner County) is a two-story, hall-and-parlor house.

36. The Daniel Montgomery house at Shackle Island (Sumner County) is a nineteenth-century Federal example of a popular eighteenth-century house type. The elliptical architrave with its decorated keystone illustrates the craftsmanship of the period. The dormers are not original.

37. Hawthorne Hall, built near Fincastle, Virginia, about 1792, illustrates the popular type which the builder of the Daniel Montgomery house (36) followed in Sumner County.

34

35

36

37

38

39

counties in Virginia, suggesting that structuralism can isolate and classify meaningfully the formal element in architectural types, the "universal, the unconscious, the simultaneous, the systematic."[6] It is this formal element on which imagination relies when books and plans are not available.

An analysis of Tennessee architecture built before 1850 would produce results analogous to those Glassie discovered in Virginia. The most obvious example of the influence of the types and transformations Glassie found in Middle Virginia is the extensive family of houses consisting of a central passage joining two symmetrically placed flanking spaces (51). Nearly half (82 out of 182) of the houses Glassie found in his Middle Virginia sample were of this central-passage type,[7] and the same ratio would hold good in any Tennessee region, at least for antebellum architecture. Five examples serve to illustrate the range of stylistic focus, from the plain to the stylistically complete, and the time span (1790–1850) through which this central-passage, two-story type occurs in Tennessee. The steep-roofed, small-windowed brick house John Hoggatt built at Clover Bottom (42), probably about 1800, was a very early Tennessee example of the five-bay Georgian type.[8] The Taylor house, Sabine Hall (43), at Elizabethton,[9] and Windsor (44), the Michael Campbell house near Nashville, both built before 1820, are stylish Federal dwellings. The Anderson house (45) in McMinn County, built about 1835, was the plain work of a country brickmason, and the Hickman house (46) in Dandrige (c. 1840), though its builder did aspire to stylish design, is still a work of vernacular imagination. Yet these are all two-story central-passage houses, and though the builder of the Anderson house lacked the grasp of style that Windsor's mason and carpenters had, he still understood the type, the "universal" and "systematic."

It is also easy to show that variations of and within types similar to the transformations Glassie finds in Virginia occur in Tennessee. There are, for example, central-passage houses having three rather than five openings (65, 77, 102), a pattern found frequently in Scotland and the English west country in the eigh-

40. The garden façade of Villa Pisani (1553–1555) at Montagnana, Italy, is a Palladian original of the popular Ionic over Doric two-story porch.

teenth century.[10] Occasionally this symmetrical window-door-window pattern, designed to express the formal, central-passage house, appears in the older hall-and-parlor plan (two rooms, usually of unequal size, the larger for daytime employments, conversation, and company, the smaller often a bedchamber) in

41. This late Georgian interpretation of the two-story Palladian porch was brought from North Carolina to Maury County by the builder of Lucius Polk's Hamilton Place in 1832. ▶

42. The five-bay façade, cornice, and keystones characteristic of the Federal style are shown in this brick house built at Clover Bottom (Davidson County) by John Hoggatt soon after he acquired the plantation in 1797. The steep roof is one indication of its eighteenth- or early nineteenth-century date.

43. (A) Sabine Hall in Carter County, built before 1820, is a five-bay frame block with Federal details. After 1800 the center bay was sometimes made larger than the flanking bays to give the hall sufficient width. (B) At the back of the house is the kitchen, an independent structure placed close to the main block in the position which the ell would consistently occupy after about 1825.

44. Michael Campbell's Windsor, built on Lebanon Road near Nashville about 1815, was an elegantly finished five-bay Federal brick. The modillioned cornice, plastered lintels, carved keystones, colonnettes, and fanlight give a delicately classic character to the crisp façade. This frontispiece, or door frame, was also used at the John Brown house in Columbia (83), and at Jefferson College near Natchez.

38. The Buckingham house (c. 1795) on Old Knoxville Pike near Sevierville is a one-room wide, story-and-loft house that was built originally according to the hall-and-parlor plan.

39. The Wishart house in Princess Anne County, Virginia, is a seventeenth-century story-and-loft house with a hall-and-parlor plan, perhaps the most important architectural type in the southern colonies during the eighteenth century. The pyramid chimney is structurally independent of the house. The dormer and porch are recent additions.

41

42

43(A)   43(B)

44

45

46

East and Middle Tennessee (63, 64), and the hall-and-parlor plan with its original, asymmetrical façade (52) is also found. The combination of types is never irrational and rarely results in anomalous hybrids, but follows sets and subsets of imaginative rules.

One important question that the persistence of types raises is the relation of apparently vernacular schemes like the hall-and-parlor house, which has little or no place in the history of western styles, to stylish architectural images like the five-bay Georgian house. Is stylish Windsor (44), for example, the perfection of a vernacular building like the Anderson house near Athens (45)? Or is the not-quite-handsome heaviness of the Hickman house in Dandridge (46) the result of the builder's inability to capture the qualities of the stylish type? Glassie answers, I think correctly, that in Middle Virginia the central-passage "I" house is typically an offspring of Georgian neoclassicism, and that wherever its formalizing tendencies are at work, some debt is due that highly self-conscious tradition.[11] Of course there are in Tennessee as well as in Virginia house types that apparently have no stylish precedents: the Penn plan or the hall-and-parlor plan, both of which seem to be transformations of use and necessity by vernacular imagination. If this is the case, it suggests that architectural types have not one but two sources; their roots are either stylish or vernacular, but not both. In this regard it is interesting to notice that there are no vernacular types that have, by some assimilative process, become stylish, though stylish types are always passing into vernacular use, the Georgian central hall house into the "double pen" cabin. But if a type is born as folk architecture—and there is folk architecture as surely as there is folk music—it will, like the hall-and-parlor plan, have no place in the succession of styles. In every whole civilization there will be ballads and Beethoven, limners and Joshua Reynolds, storytellers and Nathaniel Hawthorne; houses like Thomas Embree's and houses like Windsor. Both, the authentic vernacular as well as stylish designs, are distinct from debased popular styles and from the flawed attempts of craftsmen unfamiliar with stylish design to capture it by imitating

detail (47). Both folk and stylish art are integral to civilization, and it is worth noticing that when style fails, the sources of folk art seem also to dry up.

Henry Glassie's structuralist interpretation is only one of several recent attempts to isolate the fundamental imaginative patterns and rhythms that determined design in the eighteenth century. Marcus Whiffen has offered a plausible demonstration that Williamsburg house builders sometimes relied on sophisticated applications of geometry in the planning of their elevations.[12] Thomas Tileston Waterman has suggested that the design of at least a few eighteenth-century Virginia cottages was determined by the builder's use of a modular bay system.[13] The significance of Glassie's work, and of similar shorter studies by Whiffen and Waterman, is the support it offers for the thesis that the sensibilities of a civilization may find their way into buildings without the mediation of self-conscious design processes.

The ordinary house carpenter had models, he knew types, he also had the sensibilities of his time and place, and he knew what was considered beautiful or handsome. Carpenters, though they did not become philosophers, had an aesthetic. Late-eighteenth-century Tennessee is a rare American example of a regional culture that was largely shaped by a common metaphysic, and that metaphysic included a philosophy of beauty that both formed and expressed the sensibilities of schoolmasters, planters, and lawyers, passing from these influential sources into the life of the civilization.

For the Upper South, John Witherspoon, who came from Edinburgh to become president of Princeton in 1768, was the most influential intellectual of the post-Revolutionary generation. He had been educated at Edinburgh, like Glasgow a center of eighteenth-century Scottish intellectual life. Witherspoon had been at Edinburgh when Francis Hutcheson, founder of the common sense school, died in 1746. Witherspoon's contemporary, Thomas Reid, professor first at Aberdeen, then, after 1764, at Glasgow, was probably the most influential of the common sense philosophers, and his thought was perpetuated into the nineteenth century by a succession of disciples that included Duggald Stewart, Thomas Brown, and Witherspoon himself. To do justice to the time and place, Henry Home, Lord Kames, should also be mentioned, for though Kames was not an orthodox Calvinist and on that count experienced repeated difficulties with the intellectuals of the Presbyterian establishment, he largely relied on common sense principles. His *Elements of Criticism* (1762) was the standard treatment of literary aesthetics until the nineteenth century. Although there were differences, Reid, Kames, Stewart, and Brown shared a distinctively Scottish philosophical formulation of the

45. *Probably built about 1830 in McMinn County near Athens, the Anderson house, now destroyed, was an unsophisticated version of the five-bay Federal house type. The plastered lintels indicate the bricklayer's interest in stylish detail. The second-story doorway belongs to local building tradition, the porch to the twentieth century.*

46. *The Hickman house in Dandridge (Jefferson County) has the stolid character of many five-bay bricks built in East Tennessee during the early nineteenth century. The stepped gable was a seventeenth-century feature that survived until 1850 in Tennessee.*

47(A)

47(B)

great neoclassical themes of order, proportion, and reason.

John Witherspoon brought the common sense philosophy from Edinburgh to Princeton, and his pupils of the 1770s and 1780s took it, enriched by the contribution of Reid, Brown, and Stewart, to the southern back country. After William Graham graduated from Princeton in 1775, he moved back across the Blue Ridge to the Valley, then frontier country, and undertook his work as a Presbyterian minister, preaching on Sundays, teaching weekdays. There had been an academy in Rockbridge County since 1749, but Graham was the teacher who made the struggling classical school into the most respected college in the Valley. The academy became Liberty Hall in 1777, and Washington College when George Washington made the school a handsome gift in 1797. Lee's name was added in 1871. But the founder was William Graham, whose biographer wrote, "The extent of the influence exerted by this one man over the literature and religion of Virginia, cannot be calculated."[14] Graham's influence reached to the Holston and Cumberland. Among his Princeton classmates was Samuel Doak, who took his B.A., then studied for about two years under Witherspoon's disciple, John Blair Smith, at Hampden-Sydney before becoming Graham's assistant at Liberty Hall. About 1780 Doak moved to Washington County, and three years later founded Martin Academy, later renamed Washington College, near the new town of Jonesboro. Thomas Brown Craighead, founder of Davidson Academy at Haysboro, a few miles north of Nashville, in 1786, graduated from Princeton in 1775; James Priestly, Craighead's successor and founder of Cumberland College in Nashville; Samuel Carrick, first president of Blount College, Knoxville, in 1794; and Hezekiah Balch, founder of Greeneville College in 1794, came from Princeton or Liberty Hall in 1785; and Isaac Anderson, founder of Southwestern Seminary at Maryville, from Greeneville College. Middle Tennessee's most important antebellum intellectual was Philip Lindsley, a Princeton graduate and disciple of Samuel Stanhope Smith, President Witherspoon's son-in-law and intellectual heir.

Tennessee's eighteenth-century Presbyterian divines, all (with the single exception of Charles Coffin, who came from Harvard) pupils of John Witherspoon or William Graham, constituted an informal intellectual establishment until the southern Awakening broke their hegemony, and throughout the antebellum period they remained pastors and teachers of the planter class and prosperous merchants. In 1798, the year before the revivals began, Jedidiah Morse wrote of Tennessee in the *American Gazetteer,* "The Presbyterians are the prevailing denomination of Christians. . . . In 1788 they had 23 large congregations. . . . There are also some Baptists and Methodists." The Baptists and Methodists would grow, but the important lawyers, planters, and schoolmasters would remain Presbyterians. Andrew Jackson spoke for prosperous second-generation Tennesseans when he wrote on March 25, 1839, "I was brought up a rigid Presbyterian, to which I have always adhered," and from the pulpit and schoolroom desk Jackson's contemporaries and their children would learn a synthesis of Calvinist divinity, Enlightenment classicism, and common sense philosophy which offered a universal constitution, accessible to faith and reason equally, for church and state. The law was as much the creature of Princeton and Liberty Hall as the church. The *Nashville Daily Orthopolitan* of November 21, 1845, reported that twenty-eight men then serving in the legislature had been educated at Washington College.

The tradition of the Presbyterian academy was as comprehensive as it was pervasive. When William Graham compared the philosophy of mind he had derived from Thomas Reid and Lord Kames with the account of human nature the Scriptures taught, "their exact conformity gave him great pleasure, and satisfied him of the truth of his system."[15] The political order, like philosophy, rested upon theological foundations. Witherspoon, Graham, and Doak were pillars of the revolutionary cause, inspired, perhaps, by the Presbyterians' desire to found religious freedom on a scriptural version of natural rights. The Bible, Charles Coffin wrote in 1817, is "the true and only stable foundation of civil liberties, rights, and privileges."[16] "If there be a divine law," Philip Lindsley added in 1827, "none will deny that it is our duty to obey it."[17] In 1861 Frederick A. Ross suggested that the war was fundamentally a conflict between the Puritan, who "recognizes God only as his reason reveals him" and "admits government as he likes," and the Cavalier who honors authority "as authority from God."[18] Deists like Tom Paine dissented from the synthesis whose truth Lindsley, Coffin, and Ross so easily discovered, not because they doubted the existence of reason in nature but because they considered its unvarying order self-evident to an enlightened intellect.

The wisdom of Liberty Hall, Washington, Greene-

47. *(A) The David Kitzmiller house at Gray Station, Washington County, built about 1828, was an energetic attempt to fabricate a stylish two-story brick using a poorly recollected Virginia tradition. (B) The architectural carving which this Federal design required outstripped the carpenter's knowledge and abilities.*

48

ville, Blount, and Davidson was Witherspoon's interpretation of the Scottish common sense philosophy, enriched by appeals to the writings of Reid and Kames, and tempered by Calvinist divinity and the classical authors. The means by which it was taught were lectures—Witherspoon's course on moral philosophy was the first in America to be presented by that method—and the writings of its professors. The most important course of lectures, and the most important treatises, concerned philosophy of mind, or human nature, both inquiries whose purpose it was to discover in intellect the principles of knowledge, morality, and beauty. This psychological method had first been used by David Hume, who had abandoned realism and founded his philosophy on an analysis of the human mind by the time his *Treatise of Human Nature* appeared in 1738. Although the common sense philosophers rejected Hume's skeptical conclusions, they adopted his method and began to write their own philosophies of mind. Francis Hutcheson of Glasgow, usually considered the founder of the common sense tradition, had anticipated Hume by writing *Inquiry into the Original of Our Ideas of Beauty and Virtue* in 1720. Lord Kames's *Elements of Criticism* was published in 1762, and Thomas Reid's *An Inquiry into the Human Mind on Principles of Common Sense* in 1764. Reid had devoted disciples in Duggald Stewart, who collected Reid's works and also published his own *Elements of the Philosophy of the Human Mind* in 1792, and Thomas Brown, whose *Lectures on the Philosophy of the Human Mind* appeared in 1820.

It was as a student of this topic, a pupil of Hutcheson and a contemporary of Thomas Reid, that John Witherspoon lectured on the moral and philosophical questions which largely constituted the Princeton curriculum.[19] When William Graham heard Witherspoon lecture on moral philosophy in the early 1770s, he was challenged by his teacher's observation that many difficult problems remained unsolved. Accordingly, Graham took the philosophical psychology of the Scottish schools as his special study; "The science . . . which engaged his attention more than all others," his biographer wrote, "was the Philosophy of the Mind." Graham based his theories and lectures on his own observations, on Bishop Joseph Butler's published sermons, "Reed's Essays on the Mind," and "some of

the writings of Lord Kames," which Graham preferred to Thomas Reid's philosophy. Graham imitated the curriculum of Princeton, and his students used manuscript copies of Witherspoon's lectures as texts.[20] Samuel W. Doak recalled that his father's writing had been shaped by William Graham's "extempore lectures on the Philosophy of Human Nature," and Dr. Witherspoon's Princeton lectures on "the same and kindred subjects."[21] Samuel Doak recommended that his students read "Watts, Locke, Reed [Thomas Reid], Steward [Duggald Stewart], Brown, &c." Graham's extemporaneous lectures on human nature were never published, but Samuel Doak's *Lectures on Human Nature*, a compilation of notes he had taken in Graham's lecture room, was published posthumously at Jonesboro in 1845. Samuel Doak had delivered these lectures for nearly fifty years, from the opening of Martin Academy in 1783 until his retirement in the late 1820s. As early as December 13, 1802, Charles Coffin noted in his journal that one of his neighbors philosophized "after the manner of Mr. Graham & Mr. Doke."

Although its professors would have denied the relationship, for by then Latin scholasticism was largely forgotten, the common sense philosophy was a back door to the natural law ethics and realist aesthetics of the thirteenth century. Although the analysis began with human nature rather than with first principles, it was the burden of the Scottish tradition that for everything there is a rule, a pattern, a paradigm to which our thoughts, acts, and artifacts must conform if they are to be judged true, good, or beautiful. The moral legacy of the Scottish philosophy is easy to trace, for it passed directly from Francis Hutcheson and Thomas Reid to John Witherspoon, and from Witherspoon to Graham, Doak, and even Charles Coffin, who studied Witherspoon's moral philosophy persistently in 1806. It is more difficult to discover evidence that the aesthetics of Edinburgh ever reached Jonesboro or Nashville. In a single instance, however, both a statement of the aesthetic intrinsic to the tradition and an example influenced by it have survived.

About 1818 Samuel Doak moved from Washington County to a spot near Greeneville, where the venerable schoolmaster built a house and started another school (48). The house, named Tusculum in imitation of President Witherspoon's Tusculum farm near Princeton, was disturbingly asymmetrical and decidedly inferior in style and finish to the nearly contemporary Samuel Jackson town houses in Jonesboro.[22] Yet through its careful adherence to a pattern of modular bays and neat vertical alignment, the house offers a fair illustration of the architectural aesthetic that Samuel Doak had

48. Samuel Doak's Tusculum near Greeneville informed the space it defined with its own reassuring regularity, bringing to the countryside a visual order which was reliable but never overpowering or dramatically formal.

learned from John Witherspoon and William Graham:

To render an object beautiful, in works of art, it is necessary to pay attention to colour, proportion, regularity, and simplicity, and fitness to an end. These are obvious in a well formed house. Colour regards the materials: proportion requires the materials to be of proper size, and to be neatly put together; regularity regards the arrangement of the whole according to rule—that the doors and windows, as to size and distance, correspond with one another, and with the other parts of the building: simplicity respects the omission of all superfluity and fantastical show of ornament: fitness to an end requires that there be nothing wanting, that is necessary to fit it for answering the end for which it was intended.[23]

The architectural aesthetic of Doak's *Lectures on Human Nature* was derived from Glasgow and Edinburgh, where treatments of the topic usually included the well-known list, color, proportion, regularity, simplicity, and fitness, with only occasional variation. Soon after Witherspoon came to New Jersey, probably about 1769, he gave lectures on five subjects, "Eloquence and Composition, Taste and Criticism; Moral Philosophy; Chronology and History; and Divinity," opening his American career with his augmented version of Hutcheson's famous double treatise on beauty and virtue.[24] Of the aesthetic topics, only the lectures on eloquence survive, but in his subsequent work on moral philosophy Witherspoon noted that "the various theories upon the principles of beauty, or what it is that properly constitutes it, are of much importance on the subject of taste and criticism."[25]

Two characteristics of architecture made it the best example of common sense aesthetics. In general, ever since Hutcheson's foundational *Inquiry,* the common sense school had held that the principles of right conduct and of beauty were strictly analogous and equally certain. Just as conscience or moral sense determined right conduct, an innate sense determined the beautiful. John Witherspoon described Francis Hutcheson's "innate sensation" as a faculty that "takes its rise from external objects, but by abstraction, considers something farther than mere sensible qualities."[26] The theme of Hutcheson's aesthetic was the idea that "however we may pursue beautiful objects from self-love, with a view to obtaining the pleasures of beauty, as in architecture, gardening, and many other affairs, yet there must be a sense of beauty, antecedent to prospects even of this advantage." "Had we," he wrote, "no such sense of beauty and harmony; houses, gardens, dress, equippage, might have been recommended to us as convenient, fruitful, warm, easy; but never as beautiful."[27] Form was intellectual, separable from pleasure. "Our external sense" Hutcheson wrote, "may by measuring

teach us all the properties of architecture to the tenth of an inch . . . and yet there is something else necessary, not only to make a man a complete master in architecture, painting, or statuary, but even a tolerable judge in these works."[28] Architectural beauty exemplified an innate order, offering an unexcelled demonstration of the presence of rule in art.

The second obvious resonance of the common sense metaphysic in architecture was the regular and predictable character of the antecedent patterning evident in eighteenth-century design. It was difficult to discover the underlying aesthetic principles in Gainsborough or Haydn but easy to discover them in the works of Robert Adam or Charles Bulfinch. The most easily discernible quality of the metaphysicians' antecedent beauty was "some kind of uniformity or unity of proportion among the parts, and of each among the parts, and of each part to the whole."[29] Hutcheson discovered these fundamental rhythms in Chinese or Persian buildings as well as Grecian or Roman, but noted that "in that kind of architecture which the Europeans call *regular,* the uniformity of parts is very obvious, the several parts are regular figures, and either equal or similar at least in the same range."[30] Lord Kames agreed. "The timid hand of art," Kames wrote, "is guided by rule and compass," so that "in works of art that are original, not imitative, such as architecture, strict regularity and uniformity ought to be studied so far as consistent with utility."[31] For Thomas Reid, regularity was "a sign of intelligence and of mind, as well as of design."[32] At Glasgow, Princeton, and Washington College, the fundamentals of aesthetic theory were regularity, proportion, and simplicity, in Samuel Doak's words, "the arrangement of the whole according to rule."

Although they wrote no treatises, eighteenth-century architects and house carpenters showed in their buildings the same sensibilities as the common sense philosophers. William Adam, like Witherspoon a son of Edinburgh, considered regularity "a most necessary part of architecture," without which "all ornament, however beautiful, becomes confusion,"[33] and travelers often expressed their approval of regularity in design by numerous observations that Tennessee's towns were, like Philadelphia, "regularly" laid off. Eighteenth-century imagination took much delight in the realization of form by means of geometry. This was what pleased Anne Royall when she noticed in 1817 that the cedar trees near Nashville's bluff were "rendered more beautiful by art, being trimmed and cut into cones and pyramids."[34] It was perhaps the same fascination with the realization of geometry in eighteenth-century architectural designs that made William Adam call Sir John Clark's house "a very small box, and genteel, too,"[35] a French traveler call Governor Horatio Sharpe's Whitehall near Annapolis, built in 1765, "a very prety box,"[36] and the commissioners of the Knox County Courthouse of 1793 call their proposed building "a neat little box."[37] The desired architectural image was composed of precise, geometrically determined forms.

The sources available to the country house carpenter who had no books and not much access to stylish models all failed or were drastically restricted by 1860. By then imitation had become unfashionable, for romanticism valued originality and novelty, and if the older house types were still present, it was in spite of studied attempts on the part of the late Greek Revival and Italianate designers to create novel designs. The older sensibilities, formed to favor a highly predictable regularity, also gave way before the romantic metaphysic of change. A succession of English designers—James Malton, John Plaw, and Robert Lugar—began during the 1790s to recommend irregularity in the design of cottages and villas.[38] In 1830 an anonymous American critic wrote, "Beauty is not in favor of the rectangle. . . . We love variety, and nature has largely provided for it."[39] In 1847 the members of the Nashville Horticultural Society consulted the works of A. J. Downing to find a good design for their gardener's cottage, and by the time Haydon and Booth published their beautifully embellished map of Nashville in 1860, most of the city's new buildings were Italianate.

Just as regularity failed to charm the romantic eye, the old metaphysic failed to command the allegiance of the new poets. Eclecticism and subjectivism proved inseparable partners in the destruction of the ordered moral and aesthetic universe Doak and Graham had known. In 1842 the *Southern Quarterly Review* reminded the New England Transcendentalists that "the love of intellectual freedom is not a bond of union, but rather an occasion for separation."[40] Frederick A. Ross argued that those who assumed the sufficiency of reason unaided by authority would pass quickly from an order founded on will to one founded on violence.[41] True to Ross's prediction, the new philosophy sanctioned naturalism in ethics. In aesthetics it taught that man must make for himself a satisfying visual world by arranging nature so as to produce in the beholder the affective pleasures of change and variety. But throughout the years that separated the settlement of the Watauga Valley from Appomattox, most Tennesseans preferred the older intellectual order to picturesque theory. This traditional sensibility formed imagination before architects began to produce designs in the new romantic historical styles, and the regular types and rhythms it inspired lie near the surface of much of

Tennessee's antebellum architecture. House carpenters like Lowry, Pinkley, and Taylor understood it no less than the philosophers Graham and Doak, and though the carpenters could probably not give it words, they could build it.

V. THE EIGHTEENTH CENTURY

The inhabitants of this district emigrated chiefly from Pennsylvania, and that part of Virginia that lies West of the Blue Ridge.

JEDIDIAH MORSE, *American Gazetteer*, 1798

The first European architecture in the territory that would become Tennessee was erected by military engineers and carpenters in the service of French and English colonial authorities who sought to protect their claims in the Mississippi Valley and to placate and control their Indian allies by building forts. In February 1682 the troops and artisans of Robert Cavelier de La Salle built a small fort at the second Chickasaw Bluffs, near the site of Memphis. A map of 1684 called this fortification simply *"fort basti à la prise de la Cicacha,"* the fort built for capturing the Chickasaws, but the place was later given the name Fort Prud'homme for a Frenchman who had lost his way, and nearly his life, at the bluffs, thereby causing La Salle and his party to encamp there while searching for the missing man.[1] Fort Prud'homme was probably a simple campaign fort, a small rectangle of *pieux* (piles, pickets, palisades, or puncheons) set side by side in the ground, perhaps with bastions at the corners, though it would be hasty to conclude that the structure was without architectural interest. Corrupt commissaries, grasping undertakers, and shoddy workmanship plagued the governments of Quebec and Louisiana, but despite these handicaps and the dangers of intermittent Indian warfare the French often built well in the North American wilderness. Three years after erecting the simple fort at the Bluffs, La Salle directed the construction of a house "in the Canadian manner," *de pièces sur pièces*, the corners dovetailed and pegged, at Fort St. Louis near the mouth of Garcitas Creek (Victoria County, Texas), and in 1686 a house designed "in the French manner" and built "of heavy pieces of wood notched into one another, dovetailed up to the height of the roof," stood at the Arkansas Post, near the confluence of the Arkansas and Mississippi Rivers.[2] But there probably were no guard houses or barracks at the first fort on the Bluffs and few opportunities for La Salle's artisans to leave behind examples of the carpentry of Quebec.

In 1739 a new French fortification, named Fort Assumption because it was completed on the Feast of the Assumption of the Blessed Virgin (August 8), was built on the southernmost of the four Chickasaw Bluffs, a few miles south of the site of La Salle's fort of 1682, in order to provide a secure base for the second campaign of Jean Baptiste Le Moyne, Sieur de Bienville, against the Chickasaws. Fort Assumption, the rendezvous for

an expeditionary force of more than 2,000 French soldiers, Swiss mercenaries, Indians, and Negro slaves, was probably designed by Ignace François Broutin, engineer-in-chief of Louisiana from 1730 to 1751, or perhaps by Alexandre de Batz, another engineer and architect in the French service from about 1730 until his death in 1759. Fort Assumption was a large fort of piles, "three bastions bearing on the plain, and two half bastions on the river," and though its plan is not known in detail, this second French fort at the Bluffs was probably similar to the nearly contemporary Fort St. Jean Baptiste at Natchitoches (Louisiana) on the Red River, designed by Broutin in 1733, or the design which Bernard Deverges proposed for the new fort on the Ohio River about 1745.[3] Fort Assumption was destroyed soon after Bienville's return to New Orleans in the spring of 1740, but its abandonment may have had more to do with the doubtful outcome of the campaign than with the predetermination that the fort would be occupied only temporarily; indeed the chronicler of the campaign noted in November 1739 that a fort a fraction of a league west of the Mississippi on the St. Francis River (Lee County, Arkansas), "a slight work with four bastions constructed with rails," would be abandoned because Fort Assumption had been completed at the mouth of the Margot [Wolf River]. If Fort Assumption was typical of its type and era, the carpenters who accompanied the expedition may have built a frame house for Bienville, perhaps, as at Natchitoches, with earth substituted for brick or stone nogging, and perhaps hip-roofed barracks made of *pieux en terre*, rough-hewn posts set in the ground and aligned at the top with a plate, their interstices filled with *bousillée*.[4] Although the fort was occupied for six months, the only surviving description mentions no buildings within the fortification, perhaps because there were none or perhaps because they were considered an unremarkable adjunct to fort building.

The key to the success of French claims to the territory beyond the Allegheny was the Tennessee Valley. Charles Pinckney of Charleston observed in 1754 that the French, "once they had established friendly contact with the Cherokees," would, "according to their well known practice strongly enfort themselves there." Pinkney feared the results: "Our trade and intercourse with all the Indians will be cut off, our out settlements broke up and driven in, our Negro slaves encouraged to rebel against us, and our Planters shut up in the Towns on the Sea Coast, and at length . . . the whole of the two colonies [North and South Carolina] pushed into the sea."[5] The English response to French fort building in the Mississippi Valley came in June 1756, when Governor Dinwiddie of Virginia dispatched sixty artisans and troops commanded by Major Andrew Lewis to assist an expedition promised by South Carolina in erecting a fort on the Tennessee in the territory of the Overhill Cherokees. When Lewis arrived the South Carolina expedition was nowhere to be found, so the Virginians, after delicate negotiations with the Indians, erected a small wooden fort near Chote on the north side of the Little Tennessee River (Monroe County), hoping thereby to forestall the defection of the Cherokees to the French.[6] The Virginia fort was never manned, and in August work was begun on the south bank a few miles up the Little Tennessee on a larger, more permanent fortification. Named for the British commander-in-chief in North America, John Campbell, the fourth Earl Loudoun, the fortification replaced the hastily erected Virginia fort. The work was undertaken by William Gerard De Brahm, a German engineer who had served in the army of Emperor Charles VI in the wars with France and Spain. De Brahm, who had repaired the fortifications of Charleston in 1755 and who later (1764–1770) served as surveyor general for the Southern District of the colonies, was no less a master of the fort building techniques of the Marquis de Vauban, the French engineering genius of the seventeenth century, than his counterparts Broutin and Deverges. Fort Loudoun, though never completed according to De Brahm's complex plan, was to be an impressive fortification, "a Rhombus with two small and two extensive bastions," and with "a hornwork, Cavalier, and Lunettes before the Courtain" overlooking the Tennessee River to the east.[7] Fort Loudoun's curtain and bastions sheltered a guard house, the commander's house, barracks, log storehouses, and a blacksmith's shop.[8] Some of these buildings, probably the guard house and Demere's own quarters, were frame, their sills laid directly on hard packed clay, or else set on stone footings, though the only evidence regarding their construction, apart from Demere's letters, is archaeological, the result of a campaign which by 1958 had discovered the double chimney of the guard house (which Demere called "our state room" and in which he received the Indian chiefs) and the footing of the chimney of the commander's house.[9] The guard house, and probably the other buildings, were designed by Paul Demere and for the most part were built after De Brahm returned to Charleston in December 1757.

Despite the building of Fort Loudoun, the French did as Charles Pinckney had feared, attempting throughout the late 1750s to enfort themselves so as to control the Tennessee Valley. In the autumn of 1756 Captain Raymond Demere, who had commanded Fort Loudoun during the initial stages of its construction,

was convinced that the French would build a fort either at Tellico (Monroe County) or thirty miles further south at Hiwassee Old Town, leaving the English garrison "shut up in a pen and . . . communications entirely cut off."[10] Clearly the French planned such an encircling movement. During 1757 Charles Philippe Aubry, then acting governor of the Illinois territory, and a party of forty soldiers reconnoitered about three hundred miles up the Tennessee or Cherokee River, and on their return built a fort on the north side of the Ohio, which the French called the Vouabache or Ouabache, about eleven miles downstream from the mouth of the Tennessee, a location near the present site of Metropolis in Massac County, Illinois. This fortification, for which Bernard Deverges had provided a plan in 1745, was named Fort Massac, presumably for Massiac, minister of Marine after 1760.[11] At about the same time Fort Assumption (not to be confused with the fort built at the Chickasaw Bluffs by Bienville in 1739) was erected on the Mississippi immediately north of the Ohio and Fort Ascension was built on the Tennessee about fifteen miles above its mouth.[12] These forts could effectively control entrance to the Tennessee, but they were too distant to exercise much influence over the Cherokees of the upper valley. The French intended to build higher up; in their talk with Governor Lyttleton at Fort Prince George (Pickens County, South Carolina) on February 11, 1758, the chiefs of the Cherokees reported the French boast: "They intend to build a fort hard by this and keep it in defiance of us all."[13] By May 1759 a French fort had been built high up the Coosa River, at its confluence with the Coosawatie,[14] a site probably to be located in Gordon County, Georgia, perhaps sixty miles south of Chattanooga. There may have been other French forts actually within the future state. The "remains of an old Shawnee Town which was picketed in as appears by some of them still to be seen," like the furnaces built in the 1760s on the South Fork of the Cumberland and the ancient millstones "set up for grinding" which Donelson found at the French Lick in 1780, were signs of the French presence in the valley of the Cumberland,[15] a presence always just beyond the reach of British arms and intelligence, but one exploited by the Indians. Perhaps it was in part the success of the French fort building campaign which in the summer of 1760 turned the Indians from fickle friends of the British into their emboldened enemies. Fort Loudoun, harassed and starved into submission, was surrendered on August 7, leaving the English without a fort in the lower Mississippi Valley. It was the fall of the following year before English colonial authorities built another fort on a tributary of the Tennessee. Fort Robinson, named for Colonel William Byrd III's partner in the lead mining venture at Chiswell, Virginia, was erected on the north bank of the Holston near the upper end of the Long Island, and "built upon a large plan, with proper bastions . . . walls thick enough to stop the force of small cannon shot," and gates "studded with nails so that the wood was all covered."[16]

Fort Loudoun, and perhaps Fort Assumption and Fort Robinson, sheltered guard houses and barracks built with the techniques and style of the mid-eighteenth century. If the draught of the guard house at Fort Loudoun which Captain Paul Demere promised Governor Lyttleton in his letter of November 24, 1757, was ever sent,[17] it depicted a building not unlike its counterparts at Charleston, just as the carefully drawn designs of Deverges and Broutin, which were regularly forwarded to the governor at New Orleans, and often to Paris, depicted barracks and hospitals influenced by the last stages of the fading continental baroque. And the buildings of military engineers and their carpenters were not the only European architecture built in Tennessee before the peace of 1763. When the Cherokees became restive in 1759, the Overhill traders bemoaned the loss of "Houses, Horses, Leather, and everything they were worth in the world."[18] Between 1710, when a French trader and his youthful assistant Jean du Charleville had opened a store at the site of Nashville for the purpose of trading with the Shawnees,[19] and the late 1760s when John Carter and William Parker operated a store west of the Long Island near the present site of Church Hill (Hawkins County), many Overhill traders had built houses or cabins in the valleys of the Tennessee and Cumberland. But soldiers and traders, though they brought the first European architecture to Tennessee, did not settle the land. The immigration of planters with their wives and children, cattle, tools, and furnishings, and hence the secure beginning of local architectural tradition, is usually dated from 1768 or 1769. The first settlers were not, as they might have been had the immigration begun a decade earlier, French *habitants* who had made their way up the Mississippi and the Tennessee from New Orleans, but English subjects who had pushed across the Alleghenies. The French presence in the valleys of the Cheraqui and the Chauvanon was recollected only in the French Broad, so named because it flowed from Carolina westward into the great valley which the French had so nearly won in the 1760s, and the French Lick, the salt lick near the bluffs on the Chauvanon which French soldiers and trappers had visited long before the English named the river for the Duke of Cumberland in 1750.

The fort building skills which the French and the English had displayed in the valleys of the Mississippi and the Tennessee remained influential in the shaping of a minor architectural tradition until the territory was secured by American settlers and the Indian claims extinguished. No sooner had the wars between the French and British ended than the relentless westward push of the settlers brought them face to face with the Cherokees and Chickasaws. During the 1770s Fort Watauga, also called Fort Caswell and Carter's Fort, was built near Sycamore Shoals; Fort Lee (named for General Charles Lee, commander of the American forces in the South) at Limestone (Washington County); Fort Williams (probably named for Lieutenant Colonel Joseph Williams) on the Nolichucky; and Fort Patrick Henry on the north side of the Holston opposite the Long Island. In 1780 a fort later called Fort Nashborough in honor of General Francis Nash was built at the French Lick on the Cumberland. Fort Blount was built to guard the road to the Cumberland settlements on the north side of the Cumberland opposite Flynn's Creek (Smith County) in 1792, and the blockhouses at Southwest Point and Tellico about 1795. The forts of the Revolutionary period continued the pattern established at Fort Loudoun. Fort Patrick Henry, built in September 1776, was about 100 yards square with three sides built of palisades and a fourth formed by the river's bank, and within it stood a house for the commander and a powder magazine.[20] The French Lick, or Nashborough, fort, built four years later, was a square formed by joining four blockhouses with palisades.[21] The stronghold of Tennessee forts of the late eighteenth century was the blockhouse, a two-story, hip-roofed structure, usually square in plan and often having a second floor cantilevered several feet beyond the walls of the first, which could be used either as a bastion at the corner of a stockaded or palisaded area or built free-standing. Tennessee had no hip-roofed masonry blockhouses like the bastions of Fort de Chartres, the principal Fench fortification on the Mississippi, which had been rebuilt about 1760, nor were there brick blockhouses like the surviving example at Fort Pitt (Pittsburgh), built in 1764, and the traditional accounts of fortified stone or log houses are mostly legendary. For defense the settlers built blockhouses, each the center of a station, like Colonel Daniel Ridley's blockhouse, built in the Cumberland settlements near Mill Creek about 1791, which Featherstonhaugh saw and described in 1834.[22] These were invariably made of logs—Ridley's was more than twenty feet square at the first floor—and perhaps it was the extensive fort building of the 1770s and 1780s which helped make building with squared logs increasingly popular among a population which had seen few such houses in mid-eighteenth-century Virginia or Pennsylvania, the sources of the immigration which populated the Holston and Cumberland settlements during the last quarter of the eighteenth century.

In 1768 the most commonly traveled road to the Holston Valley began in northern Virginia at Harper's Ferry, where the Shenandoah River joins the Potomac, and led southward down the river to the town of Winchester and into the Valley of Virginia, an intricate network of five parallel river bottoms separated by hilly ridges, lying just beyond the Alleghenies. A traveler who followed the Shenandoah to its sources and continued down the Valley would reach Staunton and finally the high ground of what is now Rockbridge and Botetourt counties. This fertile and well-watered region had become a back country crossroads by about 1760. The James rose there to begin its turbulent journey through the Blue Ridge to the newly established village of Richmond and the tidewater plantation lands beyond; and nearby the great road which led southwestward from Philadelphia and Harper's Ferry divided, one branch leading into North Carolina, the other toward the Long Island of the Holston. Settlement had proceeded southward down the Valley of Virginia and westward up the James and Roanoke, and by 1770 the court of Botetourt County was meeting at the site between the headwaters of these two rivers which would later (1772) become the town of Fincastle. From there to the Long Island was less than two hundred miles, not a long journey to an Overhill trader or an adventuresome planter. Settlers could also reach the rich valleys of the Holston's easternmost tributaries by pushing up one of the North Carolina rivers, especially the Yadkin, which rose just across the mountains from Sycamore Shoals, but the road from Virginia was the best and most heavily traveled.

North Carolinians, great speculators like Henderson and Blount as well as countless humbler settlers, would play their parts; and for fourteen years, from 1776 until 1790, North Carolina would govern its trans-Allegheny territory directly, but during the eighteenth century the Tennessee settlements owed greater debts to Virginia and Pennsylvania. The earliest published observation regarding the origin of the immigration is a speech of Governor John Sevier made before the legislature of the State of Franklin in May 1787 and published by the *Georgia State Gazette* on July 28 in which the Governor noted, "A concise narrative of the settling of Franklin would show that the first colony in the country was settled by Virginians about fifteen years ago." Wataugans considered themselves Virginians until the South Fork of the Holston was adopted as the boundary between that colony and North Carolina in 1771; and as the famous

petition addressed on July 5, 1776, to the Provincial Council of North Carolina shows, the settlers had originally relied for title to their lands upon the legality of John Donelson's purchase from the Cherokees made on behalf of the Colony of Virginia in 1771 and had adopted the laws of Virginia as far as their circumstances would admit. Only when their petition to be considered part of Virginia, addressed to the Provincial Council in May 1776, failed to produce either recognition or military assistance did the Wataugans apply to North Carolina, and the settlers north of the South Fork considered themselves citizens of Washington County, Virginia, until 1779. The men who governed the Tennessee settlements (apart from John Carter, whose ancestry remains tantalizingly obscure) were Virginians. Of thirty-seven prominent Franklinites whose biographies Samuel Cole Williams included in his *History of the Lost State of Franklin,* most were born in the Valley of Virginia, only five in North Carolina.

The planters and speculators who made the long journey to the Watauga or the Cumberland settlements faced a lonely existence, usually separated from their neighbors by miles of unbroken forest. In the debates of the Franklin Assembly which the *Georgia State Gazette* published on July 14, 1787, George Elholm noted, "We have neither sumptuous buildings nor towns." The settlements were ten years old before Jonesboro was founded, and in 1795, when the territorial census enumerated 77,262 inhabitants, Tennessee had only nine legally established towns: Jonesboro (1779), Nashville (1784), Greeneville (1784), Clarksville (1785), Rogersville (1789), Knoxville (1791), Blountville (1792), Maryville (1795), and Sevierville (1795), whose total population could hardly have exceeded 2,000. Ninety years before Jonesboro was established, the Lords Commissioners of Trade and Plantations were reminded that the Virginia council had made "several Attempts to bring the People into Towns, which have proved all ineffectual," the colonists being "daily more and more averse to Cohabitation; the major Part of the House of Burgesses consisting of *Virginians* that never saw a town, nor have no Notion of the Conveniency of any Other but a Country Life."[23] The wealth of Tennessee, like that of Virginia and North Carolina, lay on the land, encouraging the tiny, land-loving population to scatter itself across the immense and fertile territory. In 1796 when André Michaux traveled south from Clarksville, then a settlement of fifteen families, to Nashville, he found no dwelling along the bridle path for fifteen miles before he reached White's Creek; and two years later Francis Baily noted that even in long-settled Sumner

County a traveler might not pass more than two or three houses in a day. The most sparsely settled part of the new state was the Cumberland Plateau. In 1796 Baily found not a single dwelling between William Walton's ferry near the confluence of the Cumberland and the Caney Fork and the crossing of the Clinch near Southwest Point (Kingston). The upper counties were more thickly settled, but even there the Moravian missionary De Schweinitz found "but few plantations" on the road from Greeneville to Kentucky in 1799.[24]

Soil and climate had blessed the place, making it not only a bountiful producer of corn, wheat, flax, barley, and tobacco, but also suitable for cotton. Although its importance faded as corn became the regional staple, cotton made agriculture in the new settlements distinctive and profitable. Colonel Carter's estate included a cotton wheel in 1780, the same year in which the famous Indian massacre took place at John Donelson's cotton field in the Cumberland settlements. In 1787 James Winchester sent cotton to New Orleans on flat boats built on the Cumberland in Sumner County, and the cotton factory that John Hague built on Mill Creek near Nashville in 1792 was probably the first in the South.[25] By 1800 Tennesseans were anxious to enter the lucrative trade with England and the coastal cities directly. Sloops and brigs, sometimes built on the lower Cumberland, waited at Smithland to carry Cumberland cotton to Philadelphia and Liverpool.[26] Cotton was still grown in the upper counties during the first decades of the nineteenth century; Charles Coffin of Greeneville noted in his diary his labors in his cotton field.

The typical dwelling of the planter during the late eighteenth century was a squared-log or frame house built according to one of the traditional plans familiar in Virginia or Pennsylvania. Technically, the late eighteenth-century architecture of Tennessee progressed quickly from squared-log construction to frame, and from frame to brick. According to Francis Baily, Nashville's seventy or eighty families lived in dwellings "chiefly of logs and frame" in 1797.[27] One writer recollected that in 1800 there still was not in Nashville "a brick house, a brick chimney, or a *brick-bat*," and that the houses, "with the exception of three or four of stone, were of cedar logs or frame."[28] Michaux observed in 1802 that the town had 7 or 8 brick houses and 120 "built with planks".[29] Fifteen years later Nashville was "principally built of brick,"[30] and when Ayres's Map was published in 1831, Nashville had 263 brick houses, 179 of frame, and 21 log houses. A similar pattern can be traced in Knoxville. James White built his house of squared logs about 1786, but when Abashai Thomas saw Knoxville in 1794 he

wrote, "Here are *frame Houses & Brick Chimnies*."[31] Three years later Knoxville had "100 houses all built of wood."[32] The newest were two-story frame structures, and the town's first brick residence was under construction."[33] In 1802 Michaux wrote that Knoxville was a town of about two hundred dwellings, mostly built of wood,[34] and about 1810 Jonesboro was a town of neat frame dwellings—sometimes squared-log houses covered with weatherboarding—of which only the Chester Inn survives.

The legislation establishing Tennesee's first towns documents the accommodation of seaboard building traditions to the conditions of the frontier and verifies the observations travelers made regarding the materials used before 1800. The act of 1779 which established Jonesboro required that every lot owner should, "within three years after such conveyance, erect, build, and finish on said lot, one brick, stone, or well framed house, twenty feet long and sixteen feet wide, and at least ten feet in the pitch with a brick or stone chimney."[35] The act was descended from English colonial legislation like the seventeenth-century Maryland statutes which required the building of a house twenty feet square in order to secure possession of the lot, and the Virginia act of 1699 which required houses in Williamsburg's back streets to be "20 feet in length and 16 in wideth at the least with a brick chimney thereto."[36] The concern of the North Carolina legislators that chimneys be of brick or stone reflected their conviction that new towns, even in the back country, ought not be endangered by the building of Welch or country chimneys which were made of wood or wattles daubed with clay. Wooden chimneys, which courted conflagration, were prohibited in London about 1400, but they were widely used in the southern colonies, and as late as 1802 the wooden chimneys of Knoxville, were ordered removed.[37] The requirement that houses be "ten feet in the pitch," part of Williamsburg law,[38] had the effect of establishing the minimum allowable perpendicular distance between floor and ridge. The Jonesboro law of 1779 had not mentioned log houses because these were rare in the South before the Revolution. By 1784 North Carolina legislators understood the futility of implying a preference for brick buildings or ignoring the popularity of squared-log construction, so they required of Nashville lot owners only that a "well-framed, square logged, or brick, or stone house" be built, an order which undoubtedly reflected local preferences accurately; and Nashville dwellings were required to be only sixteen feet square, and have eight feet pitch in the clear.[39] In 1794 the Jonesboro law was modified to conform to Nashville's rules.[40]

Very few of the dwellings that made up Tennessee's

eighteenth-century villages have survived; none of the courthouses or meetinghouses. Jonesboro had a squared-log courthouse in 1784. Ten years later Knoxville had its "neat little box" of a courthouse,[41] built of squared logs or frame, and by November 1799 a two-story stone replacement was under construction.[42] The Davidson County Courthouse of 1780 at Nashborough, built "at the public expense of hewed logs," was to be "18 ft square, with a shed or shade of 12 ft on one side of the length of the house, with benches, bar and table fit for the reception of the court."[43] The most important public building in eighteenth-century Nashville—the name was changed in 1784—was the stone meetinghouse the Methodists built on the Public Square about 1790, but it was never floored or glazed and soon fell into disrepair. By about 1807 it had been abandoned.[44]

The most important remnants of Tennessee's eighteenth-century architecture are not in cities, where urban growth and changing fashion routinely caused their demolition, but scattered across the land and concentrated in the upper counties, the territory north and east of Southwest Point, and in Davidson and Sumner. If the few surviving buildings are typical, the eighteenth-century architecture of the Tennessee settlements was derived mostly from the late medieval houses of Scotland and England, transplanted to Virginia and Pennsylvania during the seventeenth and eighteenth centuries, and influenced after 1700 by English neoclassicism. Most of the eighteenth-century architecture that remains was built according to one of three traditional plans: (1) the hall-and-parlor plan common in seventeenth- and eighteenth-century Virginia (49); (2) a variant of this scheme sometimes called the Penn plan (50); and (3) the Georgian central-passage plan (51).

The hall-and-parlor or hall-and-bower house was a well-established type in England and Wales and Virginia in the late seventeenth century.[45] The plan provided one space, usually the larger of the two, for eating, sitting in company, and circulation; and a separate parlor, often used as a bedchamber. In the South during the eighteenth century the plan was frequently repeated on two stories to make a four-room house. Stair arrangements were various. An open stair rising parallel to the front wall was sometimes used. Occasionally cabinet stairs (also called sealed or boxed), often located on the gable wall in the chimney corner, are found; and frequently the two rooms have separate entrances. This scheme occurs in two Tennessee houses that are traditionally dated before 1790: the William Bowen house near Hendersonville (35),[46] a close imitation of the type represented by the Greater

Dabney house in Goochland County, Virginia;[47] and the John Bearden house near Castalian Springs. The most common expression of the plan is an asymmetrical three-bay, window-door-window façade, which is found in squared-log houses like the Christopher Taylor house (1777?),[48] small frame dwellings like the tiny mid-nineteenth-century house in Gainesboro, Jackson County (52), and bricks like the John Neely house in Williamson County (c. 1808).[49] The hall-and-parlor plan occurs with a symmetrical Federal façade at the John Hays house near Antioch in Davidson County (1797),[50] and two years later at John Overton's frame Travellers' Rest near Nashville.[51] This pattern is also found in the late 1820s at the Wylie (63) and Bowman (64) houses in Loudon County.[52]

When the house was large enough, a variant of the hall-and-parlor plan might be built by dividing the parlor (the smaller of the two rooms) into halves with a wall parallel to the façade. The result would be the scheme William Penn recommended to immigrants to Pennsylvania in 1670: "a house thirty foot long and eighteen broad, with a partition neer the middle, and another to divide one end of the house into two small rooms."[53] The Penn plan is still represented in Tennessee by the Thomas Embree house (34) at Telford (Washington County), the Levi Parkins house (53) near Friendsville (Blount County), and the John Carter house (50, 58) in Elizabethton (Carter County). The Penn plan is found as late as 1830 in the frame Hoffman house on Netherland Inn Road near Kingsport. Three of these Penn plan houses belong to the tradition of building in stone that flourished in western Pennsylvania, Maryland, New Jersey, and North Carolina in the last half of the eighteenth century.[54]

The Embree house at Telford, when it was new in the 1790s, followed the Penn plan exactly.[55] About 1770 Thomas Embree left southern Pennsylvania—another source says New Jersey—and emigrated to land on Limestone Creek south of Jonesboro. There his sons Elihu, later famous as the publisher of the *Manumission Intelligencer,* and Elijah, ironmaster and undertaker, were born—probably in the stone house Embree built about 1791.[56] Its two small chambers originally had corner fireplaces typical of this traditional scheme; there are cabinet stairs in the corner by the chimney; the walls are wainscoted, and the reveals of the 18-inch thick stone walls are neatly paneled. The house is banked into the hill, and the basement used for cooking, as it was in most of Tennessee's late-eighteenth-century stone houses. The house has been much altered: porches have been added, the partition between the two small chambers removed from the first story, and the entrance reversed so that the

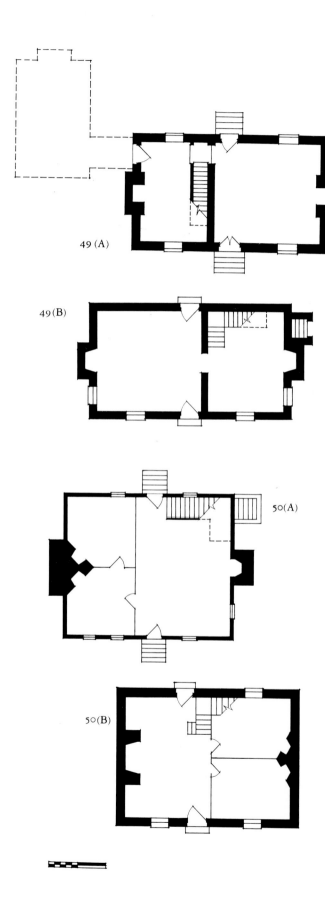

49 (A)

49 (B)

50(A)

50(B)

eighteenth-century front is now the back wall of the house, but a photograph (34) taken in 1909 captures the image Embree, his stonemason, and his carpenter created in the 1790s.

Among the few stone examples, with partitions and corner fireplaces intact is the Parkins house (53) near Friendsville, though, unlike many of the stone houses of Washington and Greene counties, the Parkins house has no basement and is not banked. The George Gillespie house (54) in Limestone approximates the Penn plan but lacks the corner fireplaces.[57] George Gillespie, a Quaker born near Baltimore, had probably built his house at Limestone before 1783. The one-story dependency at the end of the house was perhaps the builder's idea of a satisfactory location (other than the basement) for the kitchen. Locating the kitchen in the ground floor or basement of the house was an urban practice in England, and it is remarkable that this custom was often followed in the Tennessee countryside during the period before 1830: at the Bowman (64) and Wylie (63) houses in Loudon County, at the John Carter house (58) in Elizabethton, and at the Thomas Ripley house (55) in Greene County. The precedents for locating the kitchen in a detached building included in Maryland and Virginia the late medieval custom of attaching a separate kitchen to the house with a covered passageway called a penthouse or curtain; the tradition of Georgian planning, followed in Virginia and the other southern colonies after 1730, according to which the kitchen was often a separate building located as part of a formally conceived scheme for symmetrically placed dependencies; and the Philadelphia custom of building a detached summer kitchen at the rear of town lots.[58] The danger of fire, undesirable heat and odors, and the well-nigh universal practice of giving over the preparation of food to servants or slaves encouraged the building of kitchens, whether in basements or in detached dependencies, which had no immediate access to the hall or dining room of the house. Gillespie, like William Montgomery of Shackle Island (72), put his kitchen in an attached one-story block. The scheme

49. (A) The John Hays house at Antioch (Davidson County) is a late-eighteenth-century hall-and-parlor plan. The kitchen was at the left, connected to the house by a long curtain or covered passage. (B) The George Bowman house, Loudon County, also a hall-and-parlor house, is traditionally dated c. 1828. The basement kitchen was entered from outside the house on the right.

50. (A) The John Carter house (58), Elizabethton, Carter County, was built using the popular Penn plan in which the parlor of the hall-and-parlor house was divided into two chambers. (B) This plan, common in late-eighteenth-century Tennessee, was used by Levi Parkins in Blount County near Maryville about the turn of the century (53).

that finally won widest approval was the service ell, a wing perpendicular to the house, usually joined eccentrically at the rear, which included dining room, kitchen, and smokehouse.

The Jeremiah Dungan house (56) on Brush Creek and the Jacob Range house on Knob Creek (57), both in Washington County, come from the same technical and imaginative tradition that informed the Embree and Gillespie houses, though these houses have only one room on the main floor and are therefore neither hall-and-parlor nor Penn-plan types. At the Dungan house, the kitchen occupies the basement, in which there is a corner oven as well as a single fireplace; the house is banked into the hillside, and access to the first story was provided by a porch. The main floor probably served as a bed chamber, and the second floor has two small rooms opening off a passage located along the rear wall. The most striking features of the Dungan house are the carefully dressed ashlar and the symmetrical arrangement of its window-door-window façade. The formality of the Dungan façade was perhaps less the effect of the formal planning than the result of the circumstance that each floor of the Dungan house had only one room, which meant that there was no lateral partition centered across the width of the house to interfere with the symmetrical placement of the door. The Jacob Range house on Knob Creek, northwest of Johnson City, has one room on its main floor, but its twin chimneys suggest that it may have been built as a hall-and-parlor house. Whether built according to the Penn plan or not, the eighteenth-century stone houses of the upper counties shared certain distinctive details. Chimneys breast into the house, leaving the gables smooth and blank. End walls are pierced only by garret windows. Most of the eighteenth-century stone houses have end chimneys, the usual English and Scottish placement, an exception being the very early Amis house (1780?) near Rogersville, whose builder, following German tradition, planned his dwelling around a single stack of central chimneys.[59] There are often boxed or cabinet stairs, usually located in a corner beside the chimney. The stones are carefully fitted, and the façades of the Gillespie and Dungan houses are dressed ashlar. There is a water table at both these houses, and window and door openings are spanned by shallow segmental arches. The Embree and Dungan houses have wooden blocks about three feet long set horizontally in the

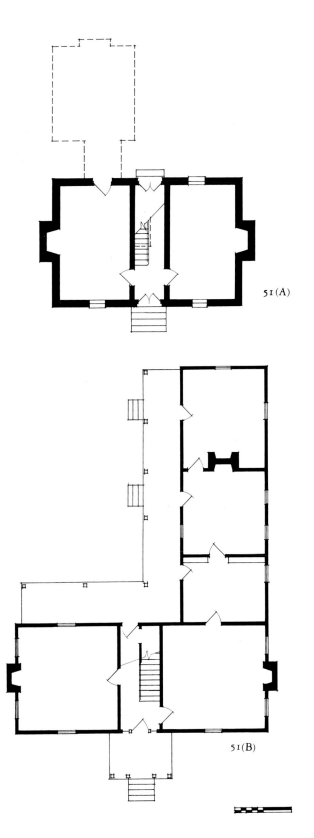

51(A)

51(B)

51. *The formal central-passage plan dominated architectural imagination in Tennessee from 1810 until 1850. (A) The Hughes house (102) in Loudon County (c. 1828) is a small, early version of the central-passage type. (B) The Griffith house, built just before the war a few hundred yards east of the Hughes house, represents the plan with an ell in its developed form.*

52

53

gables just below the line of the plate. As the photograph of the Gillespie house (54) shows, these were used for mounting the returns of the wide eaves typical of late-eighteenth-century Pennsylvania buildings. In Pennsylvania these returned eaves were sometimes joined across the gable to form pent eaves or roofs. Francis A. Ramsey's stone house (77) near Knoxville originally carried these returns at the eave corners.[60]

Although fire and decay have taken most of Tennessee's eighteenth-century frame houses, one fine Penn-plan frame house, probably belonging to the 1770s, has survived. John Carter came to what he thought was the Virginia back country about 1770 or 1771 and opened a store near the site of Church Hill in Hawkins County. Soon after, perhaps in 1772, Carter moved to Watauga, and in 1775, on the occasion of the Transylvania Company's purchases, acquired Carter's Valley from Richard Henderson, who had been given title to it by the famous Path Deed. In the late 1770s John Carter's house was occasionally mentioned as a mustering place and storehouse for powder and lead. Colonel Carter died about 1780, having been for about a decade the political and military leader of the Watauga settlements; chairman of the Watauga government and its successors, the Washington District Court and Washington County Court; and representative to the constitutional convention of North Carolina in 1777. In 1778 Carter was the second richest man in Watauga,[61] and when he died two years later his worth was reputedly the largest ever amassed in transmontane North Carolina. If he was its builder—and it is possible that documentary or other evidence might invalidate the judgment (based mostly on stylistic considerations) that the house is pre-Revolutionary—the house on the Watauga was not the least of John Carter's legacies.

The John Carter house is among the most important witnesses to the persistence of good architectural tradition on the Tennessee frontier (58).[62] The carpentry is excellent; hardwood sills, studs, corner posts and braces are all carefully joined, the wall interstices filled with nogging of sun-dried brick, and the frame neatly covered with weatherboarding. The first story follows the Penn plan exactly: the large hall on the right, two smaller chambers with corner fireplaces on the left. The basement, a full story with a large fireplace, was the kitchen until a wooden ell was built in the nineteenth century, though there was never any interior communication between the basement and the first floor. The Carter house represents the assimilation of the small-scale Penn plan with its tiny cabinet stair to the larger hall-and-parlor Virginia house. Carter took a plan common in Watauga, raised the first-floor ceiling to nine feet, and employed carpenters to create a stylish interior, transforming a three-and-a-half-story Penn-plan house into a dwelling that alludes to buildings like Shirley in Charles City County, Virginia. The single large room of the Penn plan suggests the hall of the early-eighteenth-century Virginia mansion; and like Shirley and Westover the Carter house is set between the road and the river, and has a river front on the Watauga as well as a principal façade facing the road.

From outside the house, the only evidence that Colonel Carter's was no ordinary dwelling was the high first story and the addition of a fourth bay to the familiar window-door-window façade. Inside, the first floor of the house is paneled throughout, the second wainscoted. The style is that of the 1760s. The first story has fluted posts of an Ionic design. The staircase has square, fluted newels and turned balusters. Each of the four fireplaces has a distinctive chimneypiece: a grand meander pattern in the hall; plain paneling in the rear chamber; a circle quartered and reversed in the front chamber (23); a mantel with a pulvinated frieze and an overmantel painting of the hunt, the hounds chasing the stag through stylized countryside, in the second-story chamber. There is also a hanging cabinet of a type usually associated with the architecture of the early eighteenth century in the front, first-story chamber. Watauga was probably governed from this elegant house from the time it was built until 1780,

54. Without its porches, the George Gillespie house at Limestone, Washington County, is much like the Embree house (34), though the ground floor or basement of the Gillespie house was probably never used as a living space. The returned eave indicates the purpose of the wooden nailers in the gables of the Embree, Dungan, and Ramsey houses (24, 34, 56). ▶

55. The façade of the Thomas Ripley house (c. 1810) at Afton, Greene County, is composed in the formal Federal manner, though technically the house resembles the earlier Embree (34) and Dungan (56) houses.

56. The stonework of Jeremiah Dungan's house at Watauga, Washington County, is laid in a neat ashlar, with segmental arches over doors and windows, and a water table.

57. The Jacob Range house is banked into a knoll beside Knob Creek near Johnson City, Washington County.

52. The asymmetrical façade of this small, mid-nineteenth-century dwelling in Gainesboro (Jackson County) suggests the hall-and-parlor plan, in which the dwelling is divided laterally into two equal or nearly equal spaces, the door off center.

53. The Levi Parkins house, Blount County, is a Penn-plan stone house (50B) of the 1790s or early 1800s. Unlike most of the surviving examples in Washington and Greene counties, this stone house has no basement.

54

55

56

57

58 (A)

58 (B)

58 (C)

when Colonel Carter died and the new courthouse at Jonesboro was completed.

The other stylish frame house begun before 1795 was also associated with government. About 1792 Governor William Blount began the dwelling that would serve not only as his residence but as the seat of the government of the Territory of the United States South of the River Ohio. In its present form the Blount house represents a development that may have taken place in several stages between 1792 and 1796 (59).[63] Like the Carter house, Governor Blount's residence was built of frame, its interior wainscoted. In its completed form, the house displays the Georgian preference for symmetrically placed dependencies, the parlor and a bedchamber or office flanking a large central room, and this aspect of its design was widely imitated in the brick plantation houses of the early eighteenth century (3, 41, 74, 129).

The third plan that was important for the development of Tennessee's late-eighteenth-century architecture was the formal, Georgian, central-passage scheme, the "I" plan Glassie found to be common in Middle Virginia. The façade of the Penn-plan stone house had often been asymmetrical, and the dwelling had nestled against a hill. Beginning with the Dungan house (if the traditional date, 1779, is correct) or with Stony Point (c. 1789), façades often display the perfect symmetry of neoclassical design. The site of Stony Point, on a hilltop, silhouetted against the sky, is also new, and though dwellings would continue occasionally to be built banked into a hill, the country houses built after 1795 usually crowned an eminence. The Martin Kitzmiller house (60), built at Boone's Ridge in Washington County probably before 1800, is an interesting hybrid of old and new. On its principal story the house follows the central-passage plan and displays throughout the strictly symmetrical fenestration associated with this formal plan, but the kitchen is banked into the hillside below the road, a practice builders avoided in the nineteenth century.

The new three-bay symmetry can be traced in stone and brick. The Francis A. Ramsey house (77), built near Knoxville about 1798; the James Gillespie house (61), built near Louisville (Blount County) in 1802;[64] and

the William Graham house in Tazewell (Claiborne County), built about 1810—all display the new formal themes and neoclassical details (voussoirs, keystones, and water tables, and at the Ramsey house quoins and stringcourses) in stone, though only the Gillespie and Ramsey houses have the central-hall plan. Three-bay brick houses pick up this new formality as soon as construction in brick becomes common. The John Bearden house at Castalian Springs (c. 1788) already had a formally composed façade, and in the first and second decades of the nineteenth century there are numerous house like the Samuel Lyle house (62) near Jonesboro, and the James Wylie (63) and George Bowman (64) houses in Loudon County.[65] None of these, however, has the neoclassical central passage, and it was well into the nineteeth century before three-bay, central-passage dwellings like the Burford house (65) (c. 1825) at Dixon Springs were common.

Tennessee chimneys tell a story of their own. In early-eighteenth-century Virginia there had been three common chimney arrangements. One, the indoor stack, which located fireplaces back to back on a common interior wall, is seldom to be found in Tennessee, though Charles Coffin's house at Greeneville College, which had chimneys of this type, was probably one of many local examples of this scheme. When chimneys were on an exterior wall (almost always the gable or end wall), they were often pyramid chimneys, structures built outside the house and in principle independent of it, having successive weatherings which moderated the size of the stack, reducing it gracefully from the firebox to the ridge of the dwelling. The chimneys of the Hughes brick house in Loudon County (102) and the John Bearden house in Castalian Springs are local versions of this Virginia and Maryland pyramid type (39). The other arrangement for end-wall fireplaces derived from the medieval custom of building fires against the gable wall and constructing hanging hoods, usually made of lathes or wattles daubed with clay, to carry the smoke through the roof. When perfected by the building of a fire box and chimney on the end wall, this arrangement left a smooth exterior and created flanking interior nooks, one of which was often used for a sealed or boxed stair. The Gillespie and Dungan houses this arrangement, and about 1800 the majority of brick houses built in Tennessee had fireplaces which projected into the house.

It is one of the curious rules of architecture at the turn of the century that as the formal, central-passage house became the most popular type, chimneys began to break through gable walls, and whereas many fashionable dwellings of 1810 had smooth end walls, after 1825 houses routinely display chimneys projecting

58. Probably built before the battle of King's Mountain, the house of John Carter, merchant, soldier, politician, may be the only architectural fragment surviving from the decade when Tennessee was the back country of colonial Virginia and North Carolina. The imposing chimneys, elegant interior finishes, and tall silhouette, the legacies of tidewater architectural tradition, set the house apart from the nearly contemporary stone architecture of Watauga (54, 56, 57). (Three views shown here.)

59

60

outside the gable walls, at first only a half brick, later one brick, two and three. Perhaps this was because the central-passage plan provided a better location for the stair, thereby depriving the chimney nook of its usefulness. Whatever the cause, by 1815 the chimneys of brick plantation houses were usually built so as to project beyond the gables, as they had always done in log and frame houses. "If the building was mine," Maxwell Chambers of North Carolina wrote John Steele in 1799, "I would make two out side Chimneys, it would make your parlors much more roomy, and the house as to outward appearance would look better to my notion."[66]

Another anomalous feature associated with the introduction of the formally planned, central-passage house defies complete explanation. About 1800, just as this house type became common, the practice of building a doorway aligned over the first-story entrance and opening into the second-story passage became more frequent. This second-story doorway does not appear in the houses of the 1780s or 1790s built according to the Penn or hall-and-parlor plans, but it begins to occur in Tennessee, the Virginia back country, and western Pennsylvania (even when no second-story porch or entrance is intended) with the first hint of neoclassicism. This is true at Rock Castle (66), the Francis A. Ramsey house (77), the Wylie house (63), and the Netherland Inn (84). In a house with a tiny cabinet stair such a doorway would have been useful for taking furniture to the second story, but it was precisely when the central-passage plan with its generous stairway appears that these second-story doorways are first found. Perhaps the best rationale was ventilation, although it may also be the case that the second-story door satisfied the late eighteenth-century notion of imaginative completeness, giving the upstairs passage a doorway to match the first-story entrance. Certainly without this opening the transverse upstairs hallway loses much of its imaginative rationale. The resulting space is a narrow dead end, sometimes, as at the William Montgomery house, made into a tiny chamber.

The 1790s saw the building of the first important Tennessee country houses, houses determined by

agrarian wealth, their owners' sense of place and station, and the new formal plan with its central passage and symmetrically placed parlors. After the John Carter house, the first fine plantation house finished in Tennessee was, if the traditional date is correct, Stony Point, the Armstrong house just east of Surgoinsville on the Kingsport road, completed about 1789. Stony Point is a three-bay brick house built on a hilltop site. Its steep roof, modillioned cornice, chimneypieces, and stair date it to the 1780s, and like the Carter house its details recall the pre-Revolutionary architecture of Virginia. Stony Point may have been the first brick, two-story, central-passage design built in Tennessee.[67]

Daniel Smith probably began his house on Indian Creek in Sumner County before William Armstrong started to build Stony Point, but Smith's Rock Castle (66) was not completed until 1796. It is a five-bay, central-hall house, its kitchen in the ell at the rear.[68] The mason who built the stone walls and set the keystones in place was William Stamps, and the carpenter was Daniel Smith's nephew, Smith Hansborough, who gave the first-story rooms handsome, plain paneling and built simple mantlepieces. The scale, the tall ceiling of the first story, the formal façade and central passage, and voussoirs and keystones all bespeak the builder's understanding of style, though the second-story windows are awkwardly proportioned and the interior finishes and details somewhat plain for a house of Rock Castle's grand dimensions.

☆ Cragfont, begun about 1798, represents the conquest of the Cumberland frontier by style. Towering over the surrounding valleys from a hilltop near Bledsoe's Creek, Cragfont's unyieldingly symmetrical mass is bracketed by enormous stone chimneys (67). Even the ell at the rear is centered, making James Winchester's elegant stone house a rare Tennessee example of

59. *Governor William Blount's frame house, built in Knoxville between 1792 and 1796, has had several additions and remodelings. The central block contains a passage and parlor, the east wing a drawing room, and the right a chamber or office.*

60. *The Martin Kitzmiller house at Boone's Ridge, Washington County, is an early central-passage design, though the basement kitchen of the house is banked into the hill, a practice common in the upper country before 1820. The strap hinges, locks, and other hardware are noteworthy.*

61. *The James Gillespie house near Louisville, Blount County, was built in 1802 with a formally composed façade, stringcourse, voussoirs, and keystones (the porch was added later). The stonemason may have taken the Francis A. Ramsey house (77) as his pattern.* ▶

62. *The Samuel Lyle house near Jonesboro, Washington County, probably built before 1820, is the epitome of the handsome three-bay brick—its small windows and steep roof recalling eighteenth-century Maryland and Virginia precedents.*

63. *The James Wylie house near Lenoir City, Loudon County, a three-bay brick with a hall-and-parlor plan and a basement kitchen, displayed the second-story doorway common in late eighteenth- and early-nineteenth-century houses (20, 45, 68, 77, 103).*

64. *The George Bowman house, built about 1828, is a hall-and-parlor house with a basement kitchen.*

61

62

63

64

65

66

the "T" plan of Virginia and Maryland.[69] The interior finishes, noticed by Michaux in 1802, are also exceptional, the stenciled parlor walls and deocrated risers unique in Tennessee. Another house exemplifying the pattern which influenced plantation house design most heavily near the turn of the century is the frame house on Hickory Cove Road near Surgoinsville (Hawkins County) which is traditionally considered the residence of Absolom D. Looney, sheriff of Hawkins County from 1807 to 1812. Probably built during the first or second decades of the nineteenth century, the Looney house (68) is a good example of the nogging filled, weatherboarded, braced frame, and at least some of the vivid interior colors are probably original. The simplified pilasters at the second-story doorway are reminiscent of eighteenth-century Virginia.

Stony Point, Daniel Smith's Rock Castle, and Cragfont are eighteenth-century manors whose builders had not forgotten the faintly baroque neoclassicism of the 1760s, but after 1790 fashionable design took on a more delicate, deliberately classical character.

By 1800 the pattern these first Federal houses would follow was clear. The house would be one room wide, the kitchen hidden in an ell or other dependency, the front—and that was what concerned the eighteenth-century imagination most—strictly symmetrical, its regular rhythm broken only when the center bay was slightly larger than the flanking pairs. The façade merely reflected the plan, invariably symmetrical whether the two principal rooms were square or rectangular. By 1800 lintels were imaginatively important, and in brick houses, when they could not be made from soldier courses, a shape simulating the lintel—and sometimes the keystone as well—was incised in the brick and plastered flush. Woodwork, doorways, mantelpieces, and staircases provided important relief from the severity of Federal plans and façades, though this new woodwork was itself more constrained, less fanciful, more delicate, and more carefully archaeological than the carpentry of the 1790s.

Examples of the new architectural ideal began to appear about 1800. The Alexander Outlaw house, Rural Mount (69), built on the Nolichucky in Jefferson County in 1799, with its formal, five-bay façade and and modillioned cornice, was the epitome of the new

style in stone. The frame house built on Knoxville's Front Street (70) about the same time captures the ideal in wood, and soon there were brick houses like Charles McClung's State's View (71),[70] built west of Knoxville in 1805, and the William Montgomery house (72) that also had formal façades and central halls. Talbot Hamlin thought the large number of these houses still standing in the twentieth century gave Tennessee "a strangely Philadelphia or Pennsylvania look."[71] Indeed, James Parton had noticed it eighty years before: "Tennessee is the Pennsylvania of the South, with a Philadelphia." Nashville, he wrote, "is curiously Philadelphian. The brick pavements, the huge, square, old family mansions of the same material, the unpretending stolidity of the place, the markets, the stores, all have a Philadelphian air."[72]

What gave early-nineteenth-century Tennessee its Pennsylvania air was hundreds of houses and dozens of courthouses built, like the Outlaw and William Montgomery houses, in the new Federal style. Unlike the traditional plans of the eighteenth century, Federal houses were routinely stylish and could be executed successfully only by carpenters with skill and some design ability. The best called themselves architects, and the first to do so in Tennessee may have been Hugh Roland, who advertised in the *Nashville Clarion and Tennessee Gazette* on January 20, 1820, his willingness to provide plans, elevations, and estimates.

Roland and his contemporaries represented the tradition of Wren and the Adams, mediated through the English handbooks, a few eighteenth-century American masters like Robert Smith and William Buckland, and the traditions of provincial practice which the carpenters' companies institutionalized. But Tennessee's architectural heritage might well have been otherwise—Memphis as reminiscent of New Orleans as Nashville was of Philadelphia. At the conclusion of the French and Indian War in 1763, France gained the assent of its Spanish ally to the Treaty of Paris (and simultaneously consolidated its American territories) by ceding Louisiana to Spain, thereby making Spain master of the lower Mississippi, an arrangement which lasted until European political events caused the retrocession of Louisiana to its French founders in 1800. During the 1790s a vacillating Congress, seemingly incapable of appreciating the importance or the interests of the English speaking settlers in the Mississippi Valley, made Tennesseans dream of a southwestern nation, carved from the territories of Spain and the United States and controlling the river and the rich valley. In 1789 the Cumberland settlers named their district Mero in honor of Esteban Miró, the Spanish governor at New Orleans, who controlled the trade of

65. *About 1826 the builder of the David Burford house near Dixon Springs, Smith County, used the somewhat old-fashioned three-bay façade with the common central-passage Federal plan.*

66. *Rock Castle, Sumner County, completed about 1796, is a handsome plantation house of the rich, plain post-colonial style which preceded nineteenth-century Federal.*

67

68

the Mississippi. John Sevier's policies during the collapse of the Franklin government of 1787 are usually thought to have been directed toward reapprochement with Spain, and a decade later William Blount was expelled from Congress because of his intrigues with the Spanish. The most important symbol of Spanish influence in Tennessee territory was Fort San Fernando de las Barrancas (Fort St. Ferdinand of the Bluffs), which was erected in the summer of 1795 on the southernmost of the four groups of Chickasaw Bluffs that interrupt the low-lying east bank of the Mississippi between the northern boundary of Lauderdale County and Memphis. Intended to provide a base from which Spanish troops and His Majesty's Light Squadron of Galleys could control the upper Mississippi, Fort San Fernando was designed and built by the engineer Juan María Narcis Perchet, who during the construction of the fort was directed, and occasionally harassed, by an elaborate bureaucracy which included not only the commanders of Fort San Fernando, Elías Beauregard, Vicínte Folch y Juan, and Josef Deville Degoutin Bellechasse; but Manuel Gayoso de Lemos, governor at Natchez, and the governor-general at New Orleans, Baron de Carondelet.[73]

The fort itself, erected just south of the Margot (Wolf) River on the northernmost promontory of the fourth Chickasaw Bluffs, was a square with four bastions. Between the fort and the Mississippi were the beginnings of a town; on Victor Collot's map of 1797, based on observations and sketches made the preceding summer, the twelve buildings which had sprung up outside the walls are clearly visible. Just south of the

67. James Winchester's Cragfont (c. 1802), a Maryland manor house transplanted to the Cumberland country, commands Sumner County's rolling terrain from a hilltop overlooking Bledsoe's Creek.

68. The Looney house near Surgoinsville, Hawkins County, though probably built in the 1820s, belongs imaginatively to the late eighteenth century.

69. Rural Mount, the Alexander Outlaw house, built near the Nolichucky about 1799, is an early and highly developed example of Federal design, resembling in its refinement and proportions the nearly contemporary William Montgomery house in Sumner County (72).

fort was the garden intended to supply the garrison, and next south, a hospital. Collot's map depicts a large habitation, perhaps the commander's house, on the southernmost point of the bluffs, which was also the intended site of a second four-bastion fort, located so as to secure the southern approach to the bluffs. In his written account Victor Collot noted that the settlement included "a handsome house for the governor, an ill-constructed barrack for the troops, and a powder magazine covered with tiles."[74] The handsome residence for the commander, probably built at the behest of Vicente Folch between July 1795 and June 1796, may have resembled the house of Don Manuel Gayoso de Lemos at Natchez,[75] which was raised on a brick basement and surrounded by a gallery, though Collot's account implies that the commander's house was in the fort. Certainly Folch's persistent requests for lime and carpenters suggest that Perchet, who had brought his architecture books to the site, was building a house typical of the best Louisiana architecture of the period.[76] If the commander's house resembled Gayoso's Concord at Natchez, Perchet probably built it of brick (the basement) and of *briquetée entre poteaux,* brick placed between the members of a wooden frame, and usually covered with stucco. The ill-constructed barrack was probably made of squared or rough-dressed timbers set upright in the ground, or constructed of squared logs.

Fort San Fernando was held only until March 1797, when the treaty of San Lorenzo el Real, which confirmed American claims to the east bank of the Mississippi, took effect. The fort was dismantled, lumber and old iron shipped away, and its ruins went unnoticed twenty years later when Memphis was laid off. This

70

71

fragment of late-eighteenth-century Spanish colonial architecture was largely without influence, leaving local architectural tradition firmly in the hands of men like Thomas Hope and Hugh Roland, who represented the English traditions of Charleston and Philadelphia.

72. *Robert Taylor built this five-bay brick house for William Montgomery near Shackle Island, Sumner County, in 1804, under a contract stipulating that the house was "to be divided into two rooms and a passage." By 1815 this formal, central-passage house was overwhelmingly popular among Tennessee planters.*

70. *The new interest in elegant regularity is evident in this five-bay frame (probably not John Chisholm's tavern) that stood on Front Street behind Governor Blount's house in Knoxville. The plain, gently tapered or battered chimney was typical of the late eighteenth century.*

71. *Although State's View was damaged by fire in 1823, its plain, precise character probably remains unchanged from 1809, when Thomas Hope built the house for Charles McClung at Ebenezer near the road from Knoxville to Kingston. The frame addition is recent.*

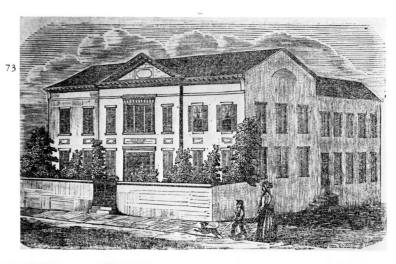

73

74

7

76

VI. THE FEDERAL STYLE

An inverted portico is supported by two massive stone columns of the doric order . . . and though not strictly referable as a whole to any one particular order of Architecture, yet it combines convenience and a freedom from tawdry appendage, with great architectural beauty.

"THE METHODIST CHURCH,"
Nashville Republican and State Gazette
OCTOBER 15, 1833

The architect Hugh Roland was in Nashville by the spring of 1818, for on June 24 of that year the cornerstone of the Masonic Hall was laid,[1] and one year later, in June 1819, the Masons were able to entertain President Monroe in a stylish Federal house with panels, colonnettes, three-part window, modillioned cornice, and pedimented gable (73). Although an elliptical fanlight would have made the Masonic Hall even more stylish, Roland's building was a fair example of the delicate classicism that Samuel McIntire and other eastern house carpenters and woodcarvers developed from Renaissance architectural treatises and the rich tradition of English handbooks. Consisting mostly of a system of small-scale copies of classical details and the extensive use of elliptical architraves and blind arcades, the new style was ready-made for woodcarvers

73. *Nashville's Masonic Hall, 1819, the first known work of Hugh Roland in Tennessee, was a stylish Federal house with public rooms on the first floor and space for the use of the masonic organizations on the second. Built on the north side of Spring (Church) and east of Summer (Fifth Avenue), Roland's building was remodeled in 1850 by Adolphus Heiman (31).*

74. *John Nichols' Woodlawn, the center of a plantation that stretched from the Harding lands to the present site of Montgomery Bell Academy, was a Georgian house with hipped roof, symmetrically placed dependencies, and railing and two-story porch. The precedents were the late baroque plantation houses of Virginia and the Carolinas, though here the ellipses and fanlight give a Federal character.*

75. *The De Vault house, built in the village of Leesburg, Washington County, about 1824, was a two-room-deep house with a vernacular Federal interpretation of the two-story Palladian porch. The house was a stage point, where horses were changed and guests might lodge for the night.*

76. *Like Hamilton Place (41), Fairvue in Sumner County has a classic porch derived from Palladian precedents. When Fairvue was built (c. 1828), this elegant house set new standards for plantation dwellings.*

and carpenters who were usually ignorant of architectural theories but thoroughly competent with planes, gouges, and chisels. Buildings had been erected in the Federal style two decades before Roland came to Nashville. In 1796 John Hays had given his hall-and-parlor house at Antioch (Davidson County) a Federal façade,[2] and three years later Governor John Sevier agreed to pay his brickmason extra for each arch, a sure sign that Sevier's Knoxville dwelling was Federal.[3] In 1804 James Park's fine Federal house, still standing at the southeast corner of Cumberland and Walnut in Knoxville, was completed.[4]

From the beginning Tennessee Federal style was complicated by the persistence of eighteenth-century details and images. One obvious example of this stylistic complexity was the use of the two-story porch (usually two superimposed one-story porches) of vaguely Palladian provenance, which was among the most popular features of Tennessee plantation houses from 1815 to 1840. This porch occurs during the first decade of the nineteenth century at the Elkanah Dulaney house in Blountville (98) and at Woodlawn near Nashville (74), and about 1818 at the Felix Grundy house (2). Both the Green house in Jonesboro and the De Vault house in nearby Leesburg (75) perpetuated this feature in the upper counties during the 1820s, each having a porch supported by four turned columns and surmounted by a pediment with a deep, complex cornice built up of intricately sawed and drilled shapes.[5] At each story the columns carry elliptical arches, and the mutules are of the type popularized by early-nineteenth-century handbooks, in which the guttae, instead of being short, cone-shaped projections from the face of the mutules, are holes drilled in them. These Washington County examples are hydrid, the result partly of a remembered eighteenth-century device, the triple arch; partly of a local tradition of carpentry; and partly of a Palladian tradition of two-story, country-house porches. This stylish image can be traced from Woodlawn near Nashville[6] to Isaac Franklin's Fairvue (76), built in Sumner County in 1828,[7] and Lucius Polk's Hamilton Place (41), built in Maury County about 1832.[8] These houses imitate the type represented by the Miles Brewton house in Charleston and Palladio's Villa Pisani. Woodlawn's symmetrical dependencies attest its Palladian inspiration, though the great elliptical windows of the second story are Federal. Fairvue's porch is Palladian, but other details, the elliptical architraves and the dormers on the river front belong to Federal style. The Polk house copies the orders of the garden façade of the Villa Pisani exactly—Tuscan on the first story, Ionic on the second—and displays Pal-

77

78

ladio's triglyphs in the frieze. The plan of the Polk house is also Palladian, arranged around a central hall with two staircases placed symmetrically. The engraving of Currey's Hill near Nashville made about 1831 (3) illustrates the popularity of the Palladian porch at a time when houses with Federal details were also being built. At its best, at Fairvue and Hamilton Place, the form consisting of two superimposed orders, the uppermost carrying a pediment, is an elegant imitation of eighteenth-century architecture, but at the nearly contemporary De Vault house (c. 1826) the Palladian theme is confused with the triple arch, Federal in spirit, and the order is a naive carpenter's Tuscan. The David Kitzmiller house (47) at Gray Station (Washington County) exemplifies the confusions that may occur as stylish architectural themes and details pass into popular use. The carpenter knew that he wanted a two-story porch, and he had seen the fashionable details he associated with the house he had in mind, but he lacked the knowledge, imagination, and skill necessary to build a Fairvue. All these houses—Woodlawn, the Felix Grundy house, the De Vault and Green houses, Fairvue, the David Kitzmiller house, and Hamilton place—have some Federal details. Some are stylish, others less so. Despite their pervasively Federal character, the dominant image conveyed by the two-story porch affixed to the center of a three-or five-bay brick block is Palladian. The Palladian porch in its varied adaptations is a parable of Tennessee's Federal architecture, which is sometimes stylish, frequently not; often complicated, even dominated, by remote precedents and eighteenth-century themes; and frequently built by carpenters who lacked mastery of its details. This is not to say that Tennessee had no distinguished Federal architecture. The William Park house in Knoxville; Clouston Hall in Franklin (26); the Daniel Montgomery house at Shackle Island (36); the Samuel Polk house in Columbia (91); and Rokeby, the John Childress house near Nashville[9] would bear comparison with good Philadelphia and New York examples. But much that remains is not so stylish, not even decisively Federal, because this architecture when it was built encompassed a wide range of stylistic focus and technical competency, as well as themes belonging to more than one phase of post-Renaissance classicism.

A brief look at the work of three important carpenters or architects who built in Tennessee before 1840—Thomas Hope (c. 1757–1820), David Morrison (1797–1860?), and Nathan Vaught (1799–1880)—illustrates the complex character of Tennessee Federal. The first house Thomas Hope designed and built in Tennessee was probably Francis Alexander Ramsey's dwelling near Knoxville, begun about 1797.[10] The house was a three-bay stone house of the type Ramsey probably remembered from Limestone, where he had spent his youth, and where the Gillespie house had stood since the 1780s; but Hope's use of stylish details and of the formal Georgian plan made it something more than a Watauga stone house (77). The Ramsey house had quoins and a stringcourse, picked out in a distinctive blue limestone, and the flat-arched openings have carefully worked voussoirs with elongated keystones. The graceful consoles at the eaves are fine examples of the house carpenter's talent for woodcarving. The kitchen was located not in the basement but in a flanking block. There is not much that is Federal about the Ramsey house, and it is probably best remembered as an elegant fragment of the late Georgian neoclassicism popular in coastal towns in the early 1790s, limited and transformed, of course, by local resources and influenced to some degree by the older tradition of stone buildings.

Two of Hope's other projects are conservative combinations of Georgian and Federal elements. In 1814 Hope completed for Joseph Churchill Strong a two-room deep brick house (78), one of the few in Tennessee to have the full, Georgian four-room plan, at the southwest corner of State and Cumberland in Knoxville.[11] With its hipped roof, projecting center bay, pedimented gable, and deep cornice, the house was reminiscent of an earlier generation of tidewater Georgian houses like the Hammond house in Annapolis (1773–1774), or even Mount Pleasant (1761) and Laurel Hill (1762) in Philadelphia,[12] but this elegant type was never popular in Tennessee, the only surviving example being the John Williams house (c. 1815) near Knoxville, where the carpenter made a half-hearted attempt to use the pedimented center bay as the dominant feature of a handsome five-bay brick.

The same conservative ideas were probably at work in Hope's design for Rotherwood, Frederick A. Ross's plantation house near Kingsport. Hope was working at Rotherwood at the time of his death in 1820, though his letter to his wife shows that when he fell ill, the carving—presumably window frames, chimneypieces, and cornices—had not been completed.[13] Still, the design may have been Hope's, though Ross, whose father was the wealthy David Ross of Augusta County, Vir-

77. The Ramsey house, built by Thomas Hope about 1797 near Knoxville, has the formality of the new Federal style but actually is rooted in Georgian precedents, the sources of the quoins, keystones, stringcourse, and consoles.

78. The house Thomas Hope built for Joseph C. Strong about 1814 in Knoxville displayed the carpenter's command of fashionable English and seaboard precedents.

79(A)

79(B)

80

ginia, would probably have had ideas of his own. Frederick Ross described Rotherwood as "a brick building, two stories, hipped roof, a cupola, with railing, having ordinary porches front and rear."[14] The hipped roof, cupola, and railing locate Rotherwood at the end of the Virginia tradition of mansion building that had begun with the Governor's Palace at Williamsburg, though Rotherwood would have been much smaller.[15] Its plan was square, a dining room occupying one side of the house, the parlor and library across the hall, and, like the Knox County Courthouse of 1800, Rotherwood was stuccoed white.

Thomas Hope did design some houses near Knoxville which seem to fit comfortably within the typical five-bay Federal pattern that was commonly used for plantation dwellings after 1800. Charles McClung's State's View (71),[16] which Hope built near Kingston Pike west of Knoxville about 1805, and Trafalgar, the Kain plantation house (1806–1807) constructed northeast of Knoxville on a site later occupied by the John Sevier Yards of the Southern Railroad (79),[17] were built according to this pattern as was the Armstrong house, another plain Federal brick dwelling with a symmetrical façade and central-passage plan which might reasonably be attributed to Hope.[18] Before Thomas Hope came to Knoxville he had worked in Charleston, leaving for the frontier just as the Federal style became popular in the southern port cities. Although he could carve delicate Federal mantels, the evidence suggests that the architecture Hope considered stylish was not the American Federal of the early nineteenth century but a neoclassicism enriched by remembered Georgian details. The Palladian window with consoles at its mullions that Hope employed at Trafalgar was a combination of elements popular in England throughout the last half of the eighteenth century.[19]

Thomas Hope was an Englishman who probably never saw Philadelphia, New York, or Boston, but David Morrison was born in Pennslvania about 1797

and knew something of the eastern cities. He was probably in Tennessee by 1828, for Fairvue in Sumner County was built by "Mr. Morrison" and "Mr. Wilson" that year.[20] Certainly the times were right for an ambitious house carpenter in Middle Tennessee. In 1825 William Carroll had been elected governor on a platform that promised the construction of a penitentiary and an asylum, and in 1829 David Morrison was chosen architect of the prison.[21] Morrison went north early in 1830 to study newly designed prisons, and determined to follow the plan used in Wethersfield, Connecticut. The penitentiary was begun near the present intersection of Charlotte and Sixteenth streets on April 1, 1830, and dedicated the following New Year's Day.[22] The building was a long block with neoclassical details, crowned by a monopteron, the circular temple form that Morrison considered the epitome of stylish design (80). Eastin Morris, who was a member of the penitentiary building commission, noted with pride in his *Gazetteer* in 1834 that Morrison was "an experienced architect" and that the building had cost less than $50,000. The penitentiary also impressed Featherstonhaugh when he visited Nashville in 1834; thirty years later a northern visitor noted that it looked "substantial enough to last for a dozen centuries."[23]

81. *Nashville's Methodist Church of 1833 designed by David Morrison was the first to occupy the site of the present McKendree.*

79. *(A) The zigzag diapering of Trafalgar's brickwork was an English detail found frequently in tidewater Maryland and Virginia. (B) Hope used consoles similar to those found at the Ramsey house on the mullions of the Palladian window (24, 77).*

80. *David Morrison's penitentiary, built near Nashville in 1830 in a highly conservative neoclassical style (stringcourse, quoins, rusticated voussoirs), was erected in conformity with the new idea that prisoners could be reformed through labor and incarceration. The building replaced the stocks that had stood in the courthouse square and, with the branding iron, had served as punishment for all but capital crimes.*

Another nearly contemporary public building that can be attributed to Morrison with certainty was the Methodist Church, built on Nashville's Spring Street in 1833. By October 15 of that year, the building was sufficiently complete to allow the *Nashville Republican* to carry a flattering description noting that "the plan, though with some, perhaps unimportant, alteration, was originally designed by Mr. D. Morrison." The alterations had not been unimportant, for the building had been constructed with a short central tower and steeple instead of the monopteron Morrison's design had included (81), but the Palladian window with its blind arcade and the fluted Doric columns *in antis* were constructed as designed. Although Morrison and Minard Lafever were both born in 1797, Morrison's Nashville work shows little influence of the free Grecian style Lafever presented in his first book of designs, *The Young Builder's Instructor* (1829); Morrison instead displays a dependence on stylistic themes as old as William Kent's Horse Guards (1749).[24]

and the remainder of brick, and the two fronts are ornamented with four white pilasters each. The dome contains a good town clock, and is supported by eight columns of Ionic order."[26] The monopteron, basement, and quoins suggest that Morrison may have been the architect, and if so, the panels and pilasters make it the most obviously Federal of his Nashville designs.

Stylistically, Morrison's work of the period 1828–1831, Fairvue (if he was the architect), the penitentiary, and the Methodist Church, all display the complexity that characterizes much of Tennessee's Federal architecture. There are elements of eighteenth-century design (quoins, rustication, railings, Palladian windows, blind arcades) and the monopteron borrowed from the Greek Revival, but there is not much of the distinctively Federal interest in the contrast between simplicity and delicacy, and there is only one elliptical architrave (Fairvue). Educated in the diffuse tradition of post-colonial classicism, Morrison apparently avoided innovations until he took up the Greek Revival style about 1831.

Morrison's work was popular in Nashville, and the architect consistently received the encouragement of Nashville's Democratic establishment. After he completed the penitentiary, Morrison renovated President Jackson's Hermitage.[27] The next year (1833) Carroll recommended him to Mississippi authorities as a good architect for their new statehouse in Jackson; and in 1834 he designed the Nashville banking house of the Union Bank of Tennessee. In 1842 Colonel Morrison surveyed the Wolf River to demonstrate the feasibility of using the stream to furnish power for the Navy Yard at Memphis, and in 1845 Morrison, then employed at the Navy Yard, was in correspondence with President Polk on matters of patronage.[28] Morrison was listed in *Twyman's Memphis Directory* (1849) as an engineer.

82. *The Lunatic Hospital (later City Hospital) in Nashville, built near Middle Franklin Turnpike (Twelfth Avenue, South) a few blocks south of Broad in 1833–1835, had Morrison's popular monopteron, though no documentary evidence associating the architect with the hospital has been found.*

Between the building of the Penitentiary in 1830 and the construction of the Methodist Church in 1833, two other buildings bearing the marks typical of Morrison's designs were completed in Nashville. The Lunatic Hospital (82), also part of Carroll's platform, was built during 1831, and if Morrison was not the architect, its designer nevertheless employed the fashionable monopteron.[25] A new Davidson County Courthouse was also built in 1829 (5). Eastin Morris called it "a spacious and commodious edifice," noting, "the foundation, and part of the lower story is of fine hewn stone,

83. *The John Brown house, Annoatuck, built by Nathan Vaught near Columbia in 1818, is a simple, handsome Federal house typical of Vaught's work in Maury County. The porch is a later addition.*

84. *The Netherland Inn, built about 1812 at Boatyard [Kingsport] in Sullivan County, stands near the Holston River at the south end of the Long Island. This photograph, taken when the building was under restoration, shows it without the porches, probably much as it was when newly built.*

85. *The Alfred Moore Carter house, built in 1819 in Elizabethton, Carter County, is a handsome example of complex, overdelicate, late Federal style. The mantelpieces are especially noteworthy.*

83

84

85

86

87

Unlike David Morrison, who traveled more than once from the South to Pennsylvania or Connecticut and who called himself an architect and had some grasp of Greek Revival theory, Nathan Vaught was a first-rate country carpenter who built in the unself-conscious Federal style of the early nineteenth century. Vaught, left an orphan in 1807, was articled to James Purcell, a Maury County cabinetmaker. In 1811 Purcell took up house building, and Vaught of course learned both trades from his master. "Youth and Old Age," the manuscript diary written by Vaught in 1861, is the biography of a conscientious workman whose vocabulary was free of stylistic terms and theory and who, given the sound traditions of building which he had developed early in his career, practiced his trade successfully, unaware that architectural fashion had gone through several revolutions during his lifetime. The first house carpenter's job Vaught undertook was a log house on the Columbia Square in 1812, and the first house he built on his own was a residence for John Brown, called Annoatuck (83), which still stands in Columbia, though a portico has been added and a few other details altered. When it was new in 1818, the John Brown house was a plain, five-bay brick house with plastered lintels and handsome front door of the kind Vaught described as "circle headed." Two years later Vaught went to school for several months to learn to read, write, and figure, paying for his education by doing carpenter's work for the schoolmaster.

One of the finest houses Vaught built was Clifton Place, General Gideon Pillow's plantation house in Maury County.[29] In 1838 Vaught undertook the carpentry on Pillow's house, though it is clear from Vaught's diary that his employer determined the design and employed a carpenter and brickmason to work under his superintendency. Vaught's unreflective loy-

alty to traditional practices is typical of the place and period, and that explains in part the existence in Maury County of numerous plain, pleasing brick houses that reflect a better understanding of technique than of style. One of the few self-consciously stylish buildings Vaught undertook was the Columbia branch of the Bank of the State of Tennessee (1839–1840), a Greek Revival banking house which still stands near the square in Columbia.

Although the architecture of Thomas Hope, David Morrison, and Nathan Vaught was often handsome, occasionally stylish, their designs were not formed by a clear, consistent tradition of Federal design. Hope and Morrison were both influenced by eighteenth-century architecture, and Vaught was a country carpenter who learned as he worked and in his diary never offered a comment on style. Yet there were fine Federal houses in Tennessee, though in most cases the name of the carpenter has been lost. Several remain in the upper counties. Mary Patton Taylor, widow of General Nathaniel Taylor, built a frame house—Sabine Hall— near Elizabethton about 1818 (43). The A-A-B-A-A rhythm of its façade recalls the Netherland Inn (84), and the neat Federal pediment, fanlight, and pilasters at the entrance support the family tradition that Philadelphia carpenters built the house.[30] The most stylish Federal house in East Tennessee is the Alfred Moore Carter house (85), built in Elizabethton about 1819 by Colonel John Carter's grandson.[31] The local memory that the carpenter or architect was from New Jersey is not improbable. The carpentry is technically superb, though marked by the disturbing complexity that beset Federal detail in its decline; the profiles are too deep, the projecting elements too flat and thin, the design unnecessarily intricate. The façade of the frame dwelling is finished with boards butt joined and nailed or pegged flush against the studs, not lapped like weatherboarding, to provide the smooth surface neoclassical taste preferred. Although most of the two-story porch is a replacement, the familiar Palladian precedent was followed. The Deery Inn in Blountville also deserves mention among the stylish Federal houses of the upper counties. Begun about 1813, the frame house has a Federal doorway with distinctive Chippendale muntins, and window frames with baroque keystones (86).

Given the early date of their settlement, it is remarkable and unfortunate that relatively few examples of stylish Federal architecture have survived in Washington and Greene counties. The Snapp house (87), overlooking Limestone Creek from a hill a few miles south of the village of Limestone, is an impressive Federal

86. The Deery Inn, Blountville (Sullivan County), is a block of frame row houses with carefully detailed doors and windows. The building is the result of successive additions and remodelings of an eighteenth-century stone house (still serving as the kitchen), a log house (right-hand corner), and a store (left-hand corner), all joined together early in the nineteenth century to create an elegant complex, including not only the store and dwelling but an inn. The parlor chimneypiece is among the finest examples of Federal craftsmanship in Tennessee. The bracket over the entrance is not original.

87. When the Snapp house on Limestone Creek, Washington County, had its original porch, it was a much more handsome building, but even now it retains the dignity of the Federal plantation house.

central-passage house with superb mantlepieces. The Valentine Sevier house, a neat central-passage Federal town house built in 1821, still stands on Greeneville's Main Street, and the Felix Earnest house, east of town on the Nolichucky, is a beautifully detailed plantation dwelling, but the most magnificent Federal house ever built in Greene County, the John Dickson mansion, built five bays wide and two stories tall on Main Street in Greeneville about 1818, has been razed.[32] The tiny B.G. Young house near the intersection of Boone's Creek Road and highway 137 is an example of a small scale type that was probably numerous a century ago. Many of Jonesboro's early brick buildings are rather plain and heavy. One of the best Federal designs in Jonesboro is Sisters' Row (88), the block of three town houses that Elijah and Elihu Embree built for Samuel Jackson on Main Street between 1819 and 1822.[33] The mason was John Smith, but the name of the carpenter who made the carefully detailed doorframes and mantles and framed the graceful elliptical openings between the parlors has been lost. The moldings, as was often the practice in Washington County, are not shaped with planes, but made up from layers of wood, cut and drilled into appropriate shapes in the fashion usually associated with the Pennsylvania and Valley Germans. The cornice of the central house, which may be origi-

88. *Sisters' Row, three town houses built by Samuel Jackson in Washington County on Jonesboro's main street in 1819–1822, is a neat block of Federal row houses, typical of the dwellings that lined the streets of Tennessee's early-nineteenth-century towns.*

89. *Samuel Cleague, undertaker and planter, built his house in McMinn County a few miles north of Athens about 1828. The heavy, plastered lintels and step gables are typical of Cleague's work.*

90. *The Eaton house, built in Franklin (Williamson County) about 1813, exemplifies a popular antebellum town house plan: three bays built two stories tall, the elegantly finished doorway leading into the passage and stairs.*

91. *Samuel Polk's residence in Columbia (Maury County), built about 1817, is a handsome three-bay Federal town house. The molded keystones were also used at the Saunders-Marshall house, on Third Avenue in Franklin, about 1803.*

92. *The three-bay, two-story house remained the epitome of urban architectural fashion until 1860. In the 1850s, the camera recorded this image of the good life as a Nashville burgher lived it in his College Street (Third Avenue) establishment: house, family, servant, hack, and parrot. A nearly identical house still stands at 908 Second Avenue, South.*

89

90

91

92

93. *Thomas Hardin Perkins' Meeting of the Waters in William-son County is a grand Federal plantation house built about 1810.*

nal, is an exception to this practice. Throughout, the builders produced a credible version of a stylish Federal town house.

The scheme of two apartments in Samuel Jackson's row of three town houses, the narrow two-story house with a passage and staircase along one side, popular in New York and Philadelphia by 1800, was used often in Tennessee after about 1810, its characteristic feature being the door-window-window façade the arrangement generates. About 1828 Samuel Cleague used this scheme near Athens, where he built a tall, three-bay Federal house in the countryside (89).[34] Two earlier Federal town houses, the Eaton house, built in Franklin about 1813 (90), and the Samuel Polk house (91) in Columbia,[35] also follow this scheme. Both have the characteristic elliptical fanlight, and the keystones of the Polk house are especially noteworthy. Although the details changed, this house type remained popular in towns throughout the antebellum period (92).

Five-bay Federal brick houses, patterned after the type represented by the William Montgomery house in Sumner County (72), continued to be built until 1850. Among the notable examples of this development are Two Rivers, built perhaps as early as 1810 on Del Rio

Pike in Williamson County;[36] the Greening or Swafford House in Pikeville (1820?), the Robert Wilson house in Maury County;[37] the John Childress house, Rokeby, near Nashville, (c. 1820);[38] Meeting of the Waters (93), also in Williamson County;[39] the John Fain house (94) built near Dandridge in 1843; and the

94. *Despite its dormers and porch, the Fain house built in 1843 near Dandridge, Jefferson County, is the same conservative, symmetrically planned, five-bay Federal brick which had become common before 1810.*

95. *John Fonville built the Mentlo house in Sumner County near Gallatin in the early 1830s.*

96. *The handsome Elijah Cate house near Athens in McMinn County was the work of Samuel Cleague, who lived nearby. Its somewhat naïve detailing makes it typical of a period and place in which the sources of Federal style were too remote to perfect style.*

97. *The David Campbell house, Knox County, is a plain, early example of the familiar pattern, its plan nearly identical to the later, more stylish Mentlo house (95) and Meeting of the Waters (93). These five-bay brick houses represent a vast and largely undervalued family.*

94

95

96

97

99

98

100

101

Newton Jordan house (1845) near Triune in Williamson County.[40] The three nearly identical, plain, well-proportioned houses—the David Chenault house (c. 1830), the James B. Jameson house (1832), and the Daniel Wade Mentlo house (1835)—John Fonville built near Gallatin, giving each a distinctive porch, are especially fine Middle Tennessee examples of the five-bay Federal type (95).[41] In the early 1830s Samuel Cleague, probably assisted by his son-in-law Thomas Crutchfield, built at least two five-bay Federal bricks of distinctive beauty: Brazelton Place at New Market and the Cate house (96) near Athens.[42] All these stylish or nearly stylish houses stood among dozens of plainer five-bay bricks like the Anderson house (45), also built near Athens, and the David Campbell house on Kingston Pike (97).

There were always variations of the five-bay scheme: the Elkanah Dulaney house in Blountville (98), a three-bay Federal block with a Palladian porch, built about 1802; the diminutive Andrew Johnson house in Greeneville (99), a tiny hall-and-parlor house with a formal, three-bay façade; the Blythe house in Gallatin (100), where the two windows customarily used in each of the parlors are replaced by a single Palladian window; Woodlawn, (1807) near Nashville, which has large horizontal ellipses as second-story fenestration (74);[43] the three-bay Vance building, probably built originally as a store or bank, opposite the courthouse in Dandrige (101), and the John McRae house on Court Square in Charlotte, built with four doorways, perhaps to enable the householder conveniently to operate his

store. Three-bay houses could have handsome details, as the Ramsey (77) and Hughes (102) houses do; and sometimes the bay system that Federal design implied was used to create regular but asymmetrical facades, a practice illustrated by the Samuel Doak house (48), the Deery Inn in Blountville (86) and the John Craighead house (103).[44] Stone was seldom used after 1810; most formal, central-passage, five-bay houses were built of brick or frame. With a few exceptions, like Sabine Hall and the Alfred Moore Carter house, the frame dwellings of the early nineteenth century have disappeared. One of the few remaining stylishly detailed Federal houses in West Tennessee is frame: the Holcombe house, Westover of Woodstock, built in La Grange about 1830 (104).

At least three Federal cottages of a story-and-a-half remain in Tennessee. Clouston Hall (26) and the Fountain Branch Carter house were built in Franklin, probably during the early 1830s, by house carpenters who had mastered the Federal system of detail.[45] The Daniel Montgomery house at Shackle Island (36), also a beautifully detailed Federal dwelling, is attributed to Robert Taylor,[46] the house carpenter who built the nearby William Montgomery house in 1804 and who lived not far from the Montgomery plantations.[47] Another example of this story-and-a-half Federal type stands in ruins. The John Kitzmiller house (105) on Maupin Hollow Road in Washington County, probably built in the 1820s, was a stone cottage of this type with a doorway and porch identical to the porch and door of the De Vault house (75).

98. The Elkanah Dulaney house in Blountville (Sullivan County), built near the turn of the century, had the two-story porch and central-passage plan characteristic of the most popular early-nineteenth-century designs.

99. In Greene County, Andrew Johnson's second Greeneville house was a neat hall-and-parlor Federal dwelling, its plan nearly identical to the John Hays house (49A) in Antioch (Davidson County). The thick bricks, used frequently in Greeneville during the 1830s and 1840s, were the work of brick layers and brickmakers willing to trade elegance for economy and ease.

100. The designer of the Blythe house in Gallatin (Sumner County) used twin Palladian windows, the architectural feature most obviously associated with the Federal style.

101. The Vance Building, an adaptation of the three-bay, central-passage plan to commercial uses, was built opposite the courthouse in Dandridge, Jefferson County, probably in the 1820s. The plastered lintels, circular architraves, and cornice are characteristically Federal.

102. The Moses Hughes house, built about 1828 in Loudon County, has the central-passage plan (51A) and plastered lintels that characterized stylish architecture in the late 1820s. The bulk and double weathering of the chimney is the legacy of the Virginia pyramid chimney. Compare the Thomas house, Madisonville. ▶

103. The John Craighead house (1818), Knoxville, was a plain, neat brick with regular fenestration, plastered lintels, cornice, and a basement kitchen. When this photograph was taken, its original six-over-six windows had been replaced with late-nineteenth-century sash, the second-story doorway boarded up.

104. With its Federal doorway and mantelpieces, Westover of Woodstock, the Beverley Lafayette Holcombe house at La Grange (Fayette County), belongs to the first generation of stylish buildings erected in West Tennessee.

105. Built about 1825, the John Kitzmiller house was a central-passage, story-and-a-half stone cottage, its porch detailed in the manner of Washington County.

102

103

104

105

107

106

108

109

Between 1800 and 1840 Tennesseans built mostly dwellings, but every county had its courthouse. The predominant pattern was the hip-roofed, nearly square, two-story block, usually with cupola, a type occurring frequently in early-eighteenth-century meeting house and school designs, and frequently used for public buildings in the southern colonies during the eighteenth century.[48] As the Court minutes for 1816 which ordered "the cupola and roof . . . removed . . . the gable ends raised and a new roof without cupola put thereon" show, Knox County's stuccoed stone courthouse of 1800 had been of this type. The Williamson County Courthouse of 1809 was a two-story block, forty feet on a side, "Built of good well burnt brick . . . on a good Stone foundation . . . four windows on each side and end, and arched over the top"; its roof "drawn from each square to the centre so as to form a Cupola on top";[49] and in 1811 the commissioners of the Bedford County Courthouse instructed bidders that the building contemplated for Shelbyville was to be 42 feet by 38 feet, two stories, built of brick, "the roof to be hipped and on top to have a cupola."[50] Two-story brick courthouses with hipped roofs were built at McMinnville (1811), Jackson (1824), Nashville (1829), and Gallatin (1837). An important precedent for this type in Middle Tennessee may have been the "handsome brick built" Nashville courthouse of 1800–1801, two stories tall and 40 feet on a side,[51] a building Bishop Francis Asbury considered "elegant" when he saw it in 1808.[52]

The second Knox County Courthouse was demolished in 1840, and the Davidson County Courthouse of 1801 about 1828, but the Dickson County Courthouse, built in Charlotte by Phillip Murray in 1833, is a hip-roofed Federal block of this type.[53] Five years later John Dameron built, and probably designed, the temple-form courthouse at Rogersville (106), the only remaining building of its type in Tennessee.[54] The scheme Dameron used had probably come down the valley from Botetourt, where Thomas Jefferson had furnished a plan for the courthouse in 1818.[55] A similar Jeffersonian temple form had been used when the Greene County Courthouse (107) was built about 1824 by Thomas Crutchfield, who, with his father-in-law Samuel Cleague, had moved to Tennessee from Botetourt County about 1823,[56] so Jefferson's plan may have been the model for both the Greene and Hawkins county courthouses.

It is an interesting index to the character of Tennessee society that, after courthouses, the most imposing institutional projects undertaken in the early nineteenth century were college buildings. Between 1796 and 1806 the trustees of Greeneville College erected a two-story building, 32 feet by 26 feet, which was stylish enough to boast a belfry. Both Greeneville College and the larger brick building Samuel W. Doak built at Tusculum Academy about 1841 show the influence of the college structure Doak and Balch would have known best, Princeton's Nassau Hall (108), and like the Princeton building both the Greeneville and Tusculum buildings (109) were Federal blocks with slender belfries.[57]

East Tennessee College, chartered as Blount College by the legislature in 1794, occupied a two-story frame house at the corner of Clinch and Gay streets in Knoxville in 1796. In 1810 the trustees, attempting to raise money for new college buildings, conducted a lottery and solicited Thomas Jefferson's support. Although Jefferson refused on principle to purchase a ticket, he did reply on May 6 offering his architectural opinion that "the common plan followed in this country . . . of making one large expensive building" was "unfortunately erroneous" and suggesting that it was "infinitely better to erect a small and separate lodge for each separate professorship." He later proposed this plan for the University of Virginia. The trustees of East Tennessee College did remember Jefferson's advice that universities should be decentralized. In 1826 they secured, in Pryor Lea's words, "a considerable eminence in view of the town and near to it, between the River and the Main Stage Road, to which the attention will be attracted from each of those common highways, and from which the prospect is delightful."[58] By October 1828 the main college building, called by its detractor Dr. John C. Gunn "that great rotunda—that monument of folly, the college," was completed on Barbara Hill, and later one-

106. *The form and porch of the Hawkins County Courthouse of 1839 at Rogersville imitate a Greek temple, though the bell-shaped cupola, often used atop public buildings in East Tennessee until 1860, was a Federal survival. The porch and cupola depicted were altered about 1929.*

107. *The Greene County Courthouse of 1825 was built according to a scheme borrowed from Jeffersonian classicism.*

108. *Robert Smith built Nassau Hall at Princeton in 1758, and his design became the model for many other schools, including Tusculum.*

109. *Tusculum Academy, built near Greeneville in 1841, with lecture halls, library, and chapel under one roof, illustrated the scheme Jefferson had sought to supplant with his decentralized design for the University of Virginia.*

110

111

story dormitories were built around it. The original building cost, in Gunn's words, "$2,726 of the people's money, including its glittering spire," a feature which Henry Ruffner, who saw the building in the summer of 1838, thought made the college resemble a church.[59] Between 1839 and 1843 the original dormitories were replaced by Thomas Crutchfield, who, under the watchful eye of Drury P. Armstrong, completed the three-story brick dormitories and professors' house.[60] If the scheme stood in 1843 as it looked when the oldest extant photograph was made, perhaps about 1875, the East Tennessee University buildings were, after the structures on Nashville's Public Square, the

110. This photograph of East Tennessee University, Knoxville, probably taken about 1875, shows the center building of 1828 and the flanking dormitories of 1842–1843. The small building at the right is the east professors' house, also built about 1843. The trustees, in the Knoxville Register *for October 22, 1828, proclaimed the main building unsurpassed "in point of elegance and adaptation to the objects in view."*

111. Cumberland Hall, the main building of the University of Nashville, was built between 1805 and 1825 near the present intersection of Third Avenue, South and Lindsley. The building contained meeting rooms for the Agatherian and Erosophian societies as well as lecture rooms, dormitories, and a chapel.

112. The Nashville Inn stood on the north side of the Public Square near the end of the beautifully arched stone bridge built across the Cumberland in 1823. The wings with their elliptical windows probably belong to the first decade of the nineteenth century; the third story of the main block was added after 1831.

most imposing group of Federal buildings in the state (110). In contrast, the University of Nashville was housed until about 1850 in Cumberland Hall (111), an unprepossessing brick block begun in 1805, to which periodic additions and renovations were made.[61] The other important antebellum Tennessee university, Cumberland in Lebanon, was begun in 1842 and was completed in a romantic Grecian style about 1859 (153).

By 1830 the hamlets of the late eighteenth century were becoming handsome towns, built mostly in the Federal style. Nashville, a busy riverport of more than 6,000, was the loveliest of all and at its center stood the state's finest cluster of Federal designs: the Davidson County Courthouse (5); the City Hotel on the east side, the Nashville Inn (112) on the north; the Nashville Branch of the Bank of the United States (113) at the northwest corner; the city market on the west; and stores like Thomas Kirkman's on the south.[62] Eastin Morris described the bank, built in 1827, as "a handsome brick building with plain columns,"[63] and an engraving made two years earlier for Ayres's map depicts a temple-form building—a fanlight in the pediment and windows and door in blind arcades—all characteristically Federal. The Nashville Inn (5, 112), throughout its successive remodelings, also remained an essentially Federal building with columned porches and elliptical attic windows, "rooms handsomely furnished . . . and everything *comme il faut*";[64] and the Federal fanlights and door enframements of the City Hotel are shown in an engraving of 1831(5). In 1859 Parton described the hotel as "a huge tavern, with vast piazzas, and interior galleries running round three sides of a quadrangle, story above story, and quaint little rooms with large fireplaces and high mantles opening out upon them; with long dark passages, and stairs at unexpected places; and carved wainscoting. . . ."[65] Along the west side of the Public Square was the market house, completed in January 1829, which contemporaries believed was surpassed only by Boston's Faneuil Hall. The market house was 270 feet long and 62 feet wide, its Federal character established by "two elegant elliptical arches, each seventeen feet in the clear, supported by a row of pillars, each two feet thick, extending the entire length of the building."[66]

Tennessee had an interesting, often distinguished, Federal architecture. But one architectural form common in the villages of the coastal South was rare in

114. *The First Methodist Church of Memphis was built between 1842 and 1845 at the northeast corner of Second Street and Poplar Avenue. The site of this conservatively designed Federal church building is now occupied by a Gothic successor begun in 1889.*

Tennessee's Federal towns, for before 1830 there were few stylish church buildings in Nashville, Knoxville, or other county seats. Memphis' Presbyterian Church, built in 1834 at Third and Poplar, was a plain building. In 1842 an editor noted the "stumpy architectural proportions of the steeple," adding, "but as it is the handsomest in the city, we'll let it pass."[67] The Methodist Church, "that chaste and beautiful building," begun in 1843 and dedicated in February 1845, was the first stylish Federal design in Memphis (114).[68] Knoxville had no steeple until Drury P. Armstrong drew designs for a steeple and portico for the Presbyterian Church in 1832 and raised the funds to add these embellishments.[69]

113. *The Nashville Branch of the Bank of the United States, built in 1827, stood at the northeast corner of College Street (Third) and the Public Square. The details are characteristically Federal, the temple form and two-story order borrowed from the early nineteenth-century classicism of Latrobe and Jefferson.*

VII. CHURCH BUILDING

They appear also to be less religious, although they are very strict in their observance of Sunday. There are few churches in Tennessee.

F. A. MICHAUX, 1802

Until the great depopulation of the 1940s, the forms that dominated the southern countryside were invariably ecclesiastical, distant cousins of James Gibbs's St. Martin-in-the-Fields or St. Michael's in Charleston. With the passing of the village and the crossroads hamlet, the countless tiny, white buildings have been less well tended, and many of the Shilohs, Antiochs, and Bethels of southern memory have decayed, awaiting their resurrection in the suburbs and slums to which the worshipers of the rural South have migrated. Now Tennessee's towns and cities are full of church buildings. Although their spires cannot compete with office towers and high-rise apartments, there are 500 in Nashville and Memphis and nearly as many in Knoxville and Chattanooga. But when Michaux visited Tennessee in 1802 he noted the absence of church buildings,[1] and De Schweinitz wrote of Knoxville in 1799: "There is not a single house here for religious services."[2] Meeting houses were built in the countryside soon after the first settlers arrived, buildings like the house that gave its name to Meetinghouse Road near Sapling Grove before 1774,[3] or the Sinking Creek or Buffalo Ridge churches in Washington County, but few churches were built in towns before 1820. These first buildings were often uncomfortable and uninviting. The Buffalo Ridge Church, built in 1793, was typical. It was a log building, chinked with small stones and mortar, the floor made of puncheons (logs laid directly on the ground and planed level on one side), with one small window, unglazed and located high in the gable wall so as to admit light without inviting Indian attack.[4] Seats were made of split logs. The Buffalo Ridge Church was not replaced until 1848, when a second building was begun by Martin V. Kitzmiller,[5] but by then the Kitzmiller family had already built three large, well-finished houses in Washington County—at Gray Station, on Boone's Ridge, and on Maupin Hollow Road (47, 60, 105). F. A. Ramsey built his house at Swan Pond about 1797, but Lebanon Presbyterian Church, near the confluence of the Holston and French Broad, was made of squared logs.[6] George Bowman of Loudon County was typical: about 1828 he built a brick dwelling for himself and constructed a log building for Sunday worship.[7] Although Samuel Doak's lectures included the topic "On Beauty" and his Tusculum near Greeneville was a regular and neatly built brick house, he preached in borrowed dwellings, log meeting-houses, buildings like Lick Creek Meetinghouse, Erwin's Meetinghouse, Patterson's, Brotherton's, Harmony Meetinghouse, Washington Meetinghouse, Hebron, Bethel, and Strothers (115).[8] But during the eighteenth century there was no building in Tennessee for public worship that approximated in architectural quality the beauty of the finest dwellings. Indeed, few stone or brick churches were built before 1820, only a handful in towns.

Before 1790 a stone meetinghouse was begun by the Methodists in Nashville's Public Square, and in 1796 the legislature secured to the Methodist Society the right to use the building but not "to debar or deny any other denomination of Christians the liberty of preaching therein."[9] This stone house was one of two meetinghouses in Nashville that Morse's *American Gazetteer* listed in 1798, the other being perhaps the Baptist Church on Mill Creek four miles from the town.[10] By 1807 the stone building was dilapidated, a newcomer remarking that Nashville did not afford "a house for the public worship of God."[11] The next year Nashville Methodists built a "new, neat brick house 34 feet square, with galleries," near Eighth and Broadway; but despite Bishop Asbury's conviction that the new meetinghouse stood "exactly where our house of worship should by right have stood,"[12] the church was too far from town, and in 1817 another building was erected on Spring Street.[13] In 1808 Williamson

115. In the early nineteenth century, small churches like Strothers Meetinghouse (removed from its original site to the Scarritt College campus in Nashville when this photograph was made) were often windowless and built of squared logs or thick planks.

116

117

118

County Methodists had a brick meetinghouse in Franklin, and a frame one five miles in the country.[14]

It took Francis Alexander Ramsey and his neighbors near Lebanon-in-the-Forks fifteen years to replace the windowless, squared-log building with stone. In Knoxville, Nashville, and Maury County, brick churches were begun about 1812, but the first meetinghouses completed in towns were the buildings Presbyterians occupied in Nashville and Knoxville in 1816.[15] Baptists probably had no church building in any Tennessee town until 1821, when their tall brick meetinghouse (116) was begun on Spring between Vine (Sixth) and High (Seventh).[16] None of these first brick buildings remains, though the type is still represented by such plain, two-story meetinghouses as Zion Presbyterian Church, Maury County (1849), a handsome building which perpetuated the local preference for the late medieval stepped gable as well as the eighteenth-century custom of building galleries along each side to provide maximum capacity (117), and Bolivar's Presbyterian church building (118), built in 1853, in which the second story has always been the property of the Masonic lodge, an institution usually considered the moral auxiliary of the church in antebellum southern society.

Church building was relatively unimportant in Tennessee before 1830. In 1799 Knoxville had a hundred houses, a dozen stores, some cabinetmakers and tanneries, a newspaper, and a limestone courthouse, but there was no church building. Until the Hebron Presbyterians moved to town in 1816, there was no church in the town of Jonesboro;[17] it was 1834, fifteen years

after the town was laid off, before Methodists built the first church in Memphis. "One bleak Sabbath in March, 1832," Francis Owen wrote, "I reminded them that there was not a house in this town dedicated to the worship of Almighty God, no temple lifting its steeple Heavenward."[18] But the Methodist church of 1834 had little of a distinctively ecclesiastical character. About 1839 J. H. Ingraham wrote at Memphis, "From Vicksburg to this place, I have seen nothing that looks like a place of worship. There may be meetings held, indeed, in private houses; but nowhere is the spire visible."[19] Two years earlier George Rogers had remarked that a meetinghouse near Jackson was "a mere pile of round logs, with openings between nearly as wide as the logs themselves, such are all the meetinghouses in that country."[20]

The plainness of Tennessee's first meetinghouses and the tardy appearance of town churches are in part to be explained by factors intrinsic to frontier life and religion. Among the Methodists, distrust of wealth made churches plain. The Christmas Conference of 1784 had decreed: "Let all our Chapels be built plain and decent; but not more expensively than is absolutely unavoidable. Otherwise the Necessity of raising money will make Rich Men Necessary to us. . . . But if so we must be dependent on them, yea, and governed by them." And the absence of churches from the first towns and villages is not so strange as it at first appears. In 1800 the population lived mostly in the countryside and often could reach an outlying meetinghouse more easily than a village church. Charles Coffin's journals suggest that in 1806 there were about a dozen meetinghouses in the countryside of Greene and Washington counties. In towns, courthouses were available for public worship. Although Hezekiah Balch had a meetinghouse in Greeneville by about 1796, both he and Charles Coffin preached routinely in the Greene, Washington, and Hawkins county courthouses, and it was December 1824 before Coffin could write Leonard Woods, "It begins to be an object to build decent churches." "They have not a church," Juliana Conner wrote in Jackson in 1827, "but assemble in the Court House, which is a neat handsome brick building."[21]

The apparent lack of zeal for church building during the eighteenth century is also partly to be explained by the laxity of religious practice before the revival of 1800. Tennesseans of the Jeffersonian era were not church-going southerners of the late nineteenth century. George Roulstone inaugurated the *Knoxville Gazette* in 1791 by publishing Paine's *Age of Reason* in installments, and fifteen years later Charles Coffin was still much troubled by encounters with deists and unbe-

116. *The Nashville Baptist Church, built on the south side of Spring Street between High (Sixth) and Vine (Seventh) between 1821 and 1826 belongs to a little studied family of early nineteenth-century southern churches that includes such surviving examples as Latrobe's Episcopal Church (St. Paul's) in Alexandria, Virginia (to which the Nashville building has an especially close affinity), and the Presbyterian Church in Rodney, Mississippi. In 1827 the Nashville congregation joined Alexander Campbell's movement, making the building the Christian Church.*

117. *Zion Presbyterian Church in Maury County is an essay in architectural conservatism. The distyle porch had been popular almost twenty years earlier (81, 137), and the crow step gable persisted from the late medieval style in Virginia. Zion is one of the few remaining nineteenth-century buildings having the long galleries typical of the eighteenth-century urban meetinghouse.*

118. *The First Presbyterian Church, built about 1853 in Bolivar (Hardeman County), illustrates the adaptation of the tall eighteenth-century church form to local use. The first story was for public worship; the second housed the town's Masonic Hall.*

lievers in Greene County. When the revival came to the frontier in 1800, it brought its own temporary solution to the requirement for buildings. As James Gallaher wrote in the *Western Sketch-Book* in 1850, camp meetings had been possible because most of those attending had recently walked or ridden from Virginia or North Carolina and during the journey had learned to camp around their wagon and cook their food in the open countryside. There were also economic reasons why many ministers preferred not to live in town. Baptists most often built churches in the country and Presbyterians in town because Baptist preachers, who seldom took pay for their ministry, were usually farmers, while Presbyterian ministers usually kept schools.[22]

Yet when every apology has been made, there remains the anomaly that during the first forty years Tennesseans cared more for the symbols of agrarian success than for the houses in which religious exercises were conducted. We are left with Bishop Asbury's comment that the stone building built on Nashville's Public Square in 1796, "if floored, ceiled, and glazed, would be a grand house"[23] and with the attendant puzzle of a culture in which very strict observers of Sunday built few churches. By 1644 the Virginia colonists had begun a brick church at Jamestown; when Tennessee was settled, missionary priests had already built their chains of baroque chapels across Spain's North American possessions. But before 1820 little that deserved the name architecture had been built to house public worship in Tennessee. In 1850 a Nashville architectural critic could think of no more telling way to describe an ugly barn than by calling it "a great, awkward, log meeting-house-looking affair."[24] The editor of the *Banner of Peace and Cumberland Presbyterian Advocate* wrote on November 7, 1844: "There is neither slander nor unjust complaint in saying that there is great neglect of those sacred places. Some neglect to rear a place for the worship of almighty God; more neglect the comfort and convenience of those places they build."

Unlike their European ancestors, Tennesseans considered the building of beautiful churches unnecessary or undesirable. The great medieval thinkers had taught that because grace perfected nature, the natural world could be transformed by a supernatural order whose final, uncreated glory the created realms of art and sacramental signs anticipated. One result of this theology was a superb tradition of architecture and iconography which stretched from Hagia Sophia and the Palestinian basilicas to Reims and St. Peter's. Rationalists like Paine and Jefferson, considering the truths of religion to be natural or rational truths, usually held the beauties of art and nature to be purely

natural beauties, and sometimes the rationalists argued that when human intellect had been sufficiently enlightened by benign scientific knowledge, when causes were clearly understood and superstition abolished, natural insight would render meaningless the notion of a supernatural order as understood by European Christendom. Still, the rationalists considered art important, and from their ranks came the romantics who mistook aesthetic for religious experience. The great succession of dualists, the Gnostics, Bogomils, and Albigenses, had troubled European history by teaching that God had abolished nature, rendering its existence unnecessary, or nearly so.

Among these sectaries, art and architecture could never flourish, and each of these opinions was broadly represented in early-nineteenth-century Tennessee history. But the local solution, while perhaps owing a special debt to the venerable tradition of radical dualism, was of an order all its own. While professing the reality of nature, certainly of planting, begetting, speculating, and profit-taking, the typical Tennessean would also have been quick to profess the irrelevance of nature to creation's final purpose, universally conceived after 1820 to be the salvation of the soul. God did not inhabit and transform the created order but dwelt in an inaccessible heaven about which this world revealed little or nothing. The created order was by nature irredeemable. In a world devoid of the Presence, art could discover no anticipation of glory. The mysteries Christendom had traditionally celebrated could have no virtue of themselves but were occasions for obedience and recollection because God could not, on systematic grounds, inhabit matter. This folk Gnosticism inhibited painting and might have prevented the building of fine churches indefinitely had not alternative theories gained ground after 1830. The problem was clearly and unavoidably theological, and that in an age when theology books were generously represented in inventories and when theological matters were discussed more than any other topics except farming and politics.

John D. Blair, the distinguished Virginia Presbyterian, stated the ground of the theory about 1825. The sacramental bread and wine were "intended only to bring the death and sufferings of the Lord Jesus more strongly to rememberance.... As we derive our ideas in general from outward objects, so those external signs are designated ... to affect the heart."[25] In his haste to avoid an older theology, Blair had adopted the Lockean philosophy of impressions and ideas and had made the sacraments mere instruments for arousing appropriate sentiments. Once the older conviction that the sacraments somehow conveyed the Presence had been reduced to psychology, the relation between symbol and effect could be stated inversely. By 1870 the eminent Presbyterian theologian Richard D. Beard was convinced that baptism, "though useful, and to be observed," was, "properly received, an expression of what is in the heart and nothing more." Whether the Christian sacraments were reminders of sentiments that should be in the heart or expressions of feelings already there, local theologians agreed that nature was never made glorious by an indwelling presence in this world's history. Beard reasoned: "Baptism is evidently a symbol. There is nothing spiritual in it, considered in itself. There is nothing spiritual in the Lord's supper, considered in itself. As a symbol, however, it is exceedingly expressive. . . . That which is external is to be regarded as an expression of that which is internal. In no other sense is what is external to be regarded as constituting a part of our religion."[26] There was no real relation between the spiritual and the symbolic, hence none between supernatural reality and art or architecture. The sacraments suggested, but did not mediate, reality. Timothy Dwight, an influential theologian who became president of Yale in 1795, concluded that "the scriptures expressly declare that Baptism is not the great instrument of regeneration,"[27] and the Reverend Thomas Hawkeis, once chaplain to the countess of Huntingdon, argued that holiness and charity were not "giving alms to the fraternity of mendicants, building churches, endowing monasteries . . . but pure affections."[28] The contrast between the plain, unadorned, pure, simple, inward, spiritual, and true on the one hand and the external pageantry, pomp, formality, display, and falsity on the other were clearly established. The regional deity did not impinge upon man's historical being in ways involving the material world. He was not especially pleased with alms, sacraments, or architecture.

The position had one important corollary and an important consequence. The corollary was the proposition that the printed word was the primary, indeed the only, means of revelation. Printing had engendered a revolution by abstracting truth, now understood as printed texts, from history. As the men who chose the word knew, a meetinghouse is not a church. In one, God speaks in homilies and texts for the worshipers' edification; the other shelters a presence. No holy places could be built in Tennessee, for place could not be holy if true religion was invariably conceptual, psychological, spiritual, and inward. Architecture, like nature, is objective and historical. And so log and plain frame meetinghouses grew apace alongside Cragfont and Stony Point. Our fathers' God did not need a place of presence, priests to mediate his graces, or nature to

direct the believer to its sacramental perfection. He dwelt not in houses, water, wine, or art, but in the printed word and pure affections. He was everywhere or nowhere. The Romantics who were coeval with the founding of the interior South were convinced that God was everywhere, that He was Nature or History. The southern believer would probably have preferred the view that God was, with respect to nature, nowhere, but alive in the hearts of believers. In 1852 Emerson had refused to celebrate the Lord's Supper unless the bread and wine were removed, presumably because these materials inhibited true spirituality. Emerson's southern contemporary might have agreed on the point of metaphysics but would have gone on to insist that, granting the essential irrelevance of nature and art to the realm of final glory, men ought to obey the scriptural text which commands the act. Neither the transcendentalists nor early-nineteenth-century Tennesseans were much concerned with church building.

The pure religion of early Tennessee civilization was not destined to hold the field unchallenged. In the 1820s those Anglicans the pioneers had left behind were themselves crossing the mountains, and with them came a new awareness of the affirmation that Christendom had traditionally made to time and place by means of architecture.

The Nashville congregation was founded by missionaries from the East. The Reverend Mr. Howell, "quite a young man recently from New York, agreeable and pleasant in his manners," was there in September 1827, when Juliana Conner wrote: "They are about erecting an episcopal church, as they have a clergyman and a very respectable congreagation, which assembles in the Masonic Hall." The Reverend Mr. John Davis, a deacon sent south by the missionary society, was in Nashville when James Hervey Otey, newly ordained to the priesthood, returned in the summer of 1827 to Williamson County, where he became rector of St. Paul's, Franklin, a parish officially organized on August 25 of that year. The Nashville congregation had not erected its building in July 1829, when Bishop Ravenscroft of North Carolina found the members of the Nashville Church still under the leadership of Mr. Davis, "all zealous for putting the congregation once more on a regular footing and exerting themselves to build a church and obtain a resident minister." Daniel Stephens had taken charge of the congregation newly formed in Columbia shortly before the convention which founded the diocese was held on July 1, 1829, and soon Otey and Stephens were joined by the Reverend George Weller, who accepted a call to Nashville the following December.

119

James Hervey Otey, a man of commanding stature and presence, deep piety, unflinching principles, and utter dedication to the church whose theology and liturgy he had discovered through reading the *Book of Common Prayer,* was the pivotal figure in establishing the Episcopal Church in Tennessee. It was the Nashville congregation, however, under the leadership of George Weller, whose members built the first Gothic Revival church in the diocese. On July 5, 1830, the cornerstone of Christ Church was laid on the site in the northeast corner of Spring and High Streets before a crowd which included members of the Franklin and Columbia congregations. The stuccoed stone building, designed by Hugh Roland in a castellated style with a central tower containing a narthex (7), was consecrated by Bishop Meade of Virginia on July 4, 1831.[29] A few

119. Completed about 1834, St. Paul's, Franklin (Williamson County), may have been inspired by Hugh Roland's Christ Church. St. Paul's and the nearby Masonic Hall display the distinctive local interpretation of Gothic detail.

120. Immanuel Church, built in La Grange (Fayette County) in 1843, is a good carpenter's naive idea of ecclesiastical Gothic, with Ionic pilasters borrowed from the Greek Revival.

days earlier, on June 28, Bishop Meade had laid the cornerstone for Otey's own parish church, St. Paul's, Franklin (119), a building Bishop Otey described to the convention five years later as "commodious and beautiful, built after the Gothic style."[30] The cornerstone of St. Peter's Church, Columbia, was laid on July 2, 1831.[31] Gothic Revival church buildings may have been built before the Episcopalians began their grand succession of steep-roofed buildings with entrance towers and pointed windows. Holy Rosary Cathedral, a brick building 30 by 75 feet that stood on the west side of High Street (Sixth Avenue, North) just south of Line (Jo Johnson), was completed but "not yet opened for services" when Juliana Conner visited Nashville in 1827.[32] Neither this first Catholic church building in Tennessee nor any other church buidling erected before Christ Church is known to have been in the Gothic style.

122

121

Once Episcopal churches were built at Nashville, Franklin, and Columbia, the Gothic style spread rapidly to West Tennessee. Soon there were towered and castellated wooden or brick buildings in the county seats and larger towns and in the open fields near centers of plantation population: Immanuel, La Grange, completed in 1843 (120); Calvary, Memphis (12), begun in 1842 and consecrated two years later; St. Luke's, Jackson, completed in 1844; and Zion Church, Brownsville (121), later renamed Christ Church, built in 1846. The West Tennessee tradition of Gothic Episcopal churches was perpetuated in the 1850s by St. Mary's, Memphis (1858), St. Matthew's, Covington (1858); Ravenscroft Chapel, built in 1858 on Ravenscroft Plantation east of Randolph; and St. Thomas, Somerville, (1858–1859). The Gothic Revival came more slowly to East Tennessee. St. John's, Knoxville, begun July 22, 1845, [33] was probably the first Gothic building erected east of the Tennessee River. The next was the building George Spencer designed and built for the congregation of St. James, Greeneville (122) in 1848–1849.[34]

St. John's, the plantation chapel at George Polk's Ashwood Hall in Maury County (123), symbolized the successful transplanting of the style; when it was completed in 1842, it inspired poetry and praise from J.H. Ingraham and David C. Page, rector of Calvary Church, Memphis.[35] Episcopalians, more than any other group, brought the notions of fine church building and of historical style to Tennessee. They remembered Virginia, and England, and a history that was more than print. Episcopalians practiced a sacramental piety that made it fitting that God should be worshipped in a suitable house, and they could usually afford to build. Yet the peculiar disjunction between grace and nature that marked the regional religion had been institutionalized long before Virginia piety had taken root, and this disjunction did not die easily. Thus even James Hervey Otey, who had presided over the Gothic explosion in Tennessee, was unwilling to consecrate the chapel J.W. Niles had built on his farm near the banks of the Tennessee a few miles from Madisonville because of the crosses on its gates and gables. The story

is a parable of the conflict between the antisacramentalism of the frontier, the principles of a great American architect, and the sensibilities of a great churchman.

The Gothic Revival had first appeared as one of several manifestations of the longings of English romanticism for the antique, but during the 1830s the revival of Gothic architecture had become inextricably tangled with the cause of theological reform which the Oxford Movement was encouraging in the English establishment. The noise of the battle which followed upon the reassertion of traditional principles by John Henry Newman, E.B. Pusey, and their supporters reverberated in Tennessee. The famous polemical tracts Newman and his friends had written were soon on sale at Berry and Tannehill, Booksellers, in Nashville,[36] and by 1846 Isaac Anderson and Frederick A. Ross had undertaken a new series of the *Calvinistic Magazine* in order to bolster Presbyterianism and to still "the voice of Puseyism."[37] The *Banner of Peace and Cumberland Presbyterian Advocate* and Nashville's *Christian Review* warned of the dangers of the Romeward movement within the Protestant Episcopal church. The architectural symbols of the movement were the Gothic Revival churches of the 1840s and 1850s. Unlike earlier Gothic buildings, these churches were often the conscious results of the ecclesiological theory of the Englishmen Benjamin Webb and John Mason Neale and of the architectural theory of A.W. Pugin. According to these thinkers, the architecture and liturgy of the Middle Ages would, if successfully re-created, evoke by its symbolism the piety and ethics of the thirteenth century. This theory was propagated in England by the writings of Pugin—especially *Contrasts* (1836) and *The True Principles of Christian or Pointed Architecture* (1841)—and by the *Ecclesiologist,* and in the United States by the New York Ecclesiological Society and its journal, the *New York Ecclesiologist,* which was published from 1848 until 1853. The New York society included among its members Episcopal clergy and several professors and students of the General Theological Seminary, as well as architects who espoused Gothic Revival architecture and ecclesiological theory. Among the students who belonged was John Henry Hopkins, Jr., whose father, the Episcopal bishop of Vermont from 1832 to 1868, had written in 1836 the first American treatise on Gothic, *Essay on Gothic Architecture, with Various Plans and Drawings for Churches, Designed Chiefly for the Use of Clergy.* Richard Upjohn was made an honorary member in 1849,[38] and Frank Wills, who had practiced in Exeter, England, where he had belonged to the diocesan architectural society, was the New York society's first official architect. In 1850 Wills wrote the most comprehensive American ecclesiologi-

121. The large, gracefully shaped windows of Christ Episcopal Church in Brownsville, Haywood County, make it a lively, sunlit representative of a church type that tended to be romantically gloomy.

122. St. James, Greeneville, designed by George M. Spencer, is an interesting combination of Greek Revival and Italianate forms to which pointed windows and Gothic details are applied.

123. The Polks built their Maury County plantation church in Gothic style in 1842. Situated on a gently elevated site near the common boundaries of the Polk plantations, St. John's is Tennessee's clearest image of plantation Episcopalianism.

cal treatise, *Ancient Ecclesiastical Architecutre and Its Principles, Applied to the Wants of the Church of the Present Day,* a work in which he argued that in church buildings the soul "animates the frame and speaks in every stone," the edifices themselves teaching Christian doctrine.[39]

Through a series of commissions, many gained through his association with the ecclesiological society, Frank Wills brought ecclesiologically correct Gothic to the South. In 1851 Wills, who had come from Frederickton, New Brunswick, to New York before April 1848, formed a partnership with another English architect, Henry Dudley, also from Exeter; and though the partnership lasted only three years, the association endured.[40] Dudley later completed the Church of the Nativity in Huntsville, Alabama, which stood half-finished when Wills died about 1857,[41] and undertook the building of the Church of the Advent in Nashville, a commission which would almost certainly have been Wills's. Frank Wills's first building in the South was probably the lovely Chapel of the Cross in Madison County, Mississippi; his last the Church of the Nativity.[42]

Clerical interest in ecclesiology was probably stimulated in Tennessee by the Reverend Charles Tomes. Tomes served as rector of St. John's, Knoxville, from 1844 until 1846, during which time he erected what may have been East Tennessee's first Gothic Revival church and established the Episcopal congregation at Greeneville. From 1846 until 1848, Tomes was at Sing Sing, New York, and in Christ Church, St. Louis. From that time until a few months before his untimely death in 1857 Tomes was the rector of Christ Church, Nashville, resigning that important charge only in April 1857, when he accepted the call to the newly founded Church of the Advent. Tomes became Bishop Otey's son-in-law in 1846 by his marriage to Otey's daughter Henrietta. He was also the rector under whom both J.H. Ingraham and his less well-known brother J.P.T. Ingraham served, the former as a theological pupil from 1848 until 1852 and the latter as curate of St. Paul's

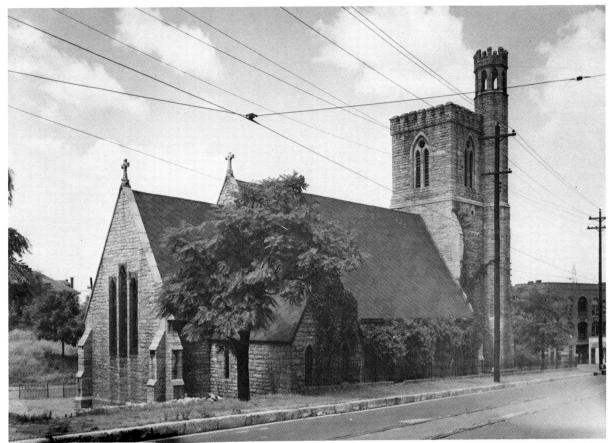

124(A)

mission church from 1848 until 1850. The Reverend
Charles Tomes probably asked Wills and Dudley to
provide plans for the Church of the Holy Trinity (124)
late in 1851, for at its meeting of January 5, 1852,
Tomes became a member of the New York Ecclesiological Society, and the cornerstone of the new church
was laid on May 29. Like Wills and Dudley, Tomes had
immigrated from England. Something of a Puseyite, he
had inaugurated daily services and refused to preach
the traditional Protestant eulogies at funerals. At the
laying of the cornerstone of Holy Trinity, Charles
Tomes defended ecclesiological theory. Christian
temples should "address themselves to our religious
sensibilities." Tomes deplored "the neglect to make
them thus expressive which makes our Church buildings so uninteresting, so unsatisfying." Church buildings should "answer to some of the wants of religion
that stir within us" and "speak to the heart."[43]

Tomes's commitment to ecclesiology and to a moderate Puseyism continued. In the spring of 1857 he
sought to abolish the system of pew rents in Christ
Church, but he lost the battle and resigned to found the
Church of the Advent, where every pew would be free.

124 (B)

124. (A) The church as built was given a gabled vestry room, and
castellations replaced the pinnacle on the tower. (B) In 1852 Frank
Wills of New York designed the Church of the Holy Trinity in
Nashville according to the principles of symbolism and ecclesiology.

125 (A)

125 (B)

His intransigence on this point was probably born of his adherence to the views put forward in J.M. Neale's *History of Pues* (1843), which considered pews a seventeenth-century invention, a source of snobbery, and a hinderance to the evangelization of the poor. Tomes fell ill a week before the first services were to be held in the new parish and died on July 10, 1857. On the following New Year's Day, Charles Todd Quintard became rector of the Church of the Advent. Whether Tomes had initiated inquiries before his death or whether the matter had waited Quintard's election, Henry Dudley was named architect of the new building. Work was begun in 1859, but the war intervened, and the Church of the Advent, widely considered the handsomest Gothic Revival building in Tennessee (125), was not completed until 1870.[44]

Buildings like the Church of the Holy Trinity, the Chapel of the Cross, the Church of the Advent, and Richard Upjohn's southern churches provided an appropriate setting and occasion for the revival of medieval liturgical customs and long forgotten doctrines. In England the Oxford Movement and ecclesiology had come of age, and there was growing concern among traditional Anglicans that "The 'Restoration of Churches' is the Restoration of Popery," the title given a famous sermon of 1844. In America the labors of the ecclesiologists were greeted by sentiments expressed in such tracts as *Puseyite Developments or Notices of the New-York Ecclesiologist, Written by a Layman,* in which the Romeward tendencies of the society were cataloged.

Against the background of continuing controversy concerning the revival of medieval theology and the increasing popularity of ecclesiological Gothic, Bishop Otey was asked to consecrate the church that the children and son-in-law of John McGhee—Charles McClung McGhee and Margarett McGhee Humes Niles and her husband J.W.J. Niles—had built at Riverside. The building, erected to fulfill the intention of John McGhee, was begun on a hilltop near the site of the Tellico blockhouse about 1851, but the work was abandoned soon after the foundations were laid. In 1853 the Niles family returned to their Monroe County farm, intending to make it their permanent home, and over a period of two years the building was

completed. The plans for the church and its furniture had been drawn by Richard Upjohn, who had given the Reverend J.L. Gay, minister in charge of the East Tennessee Missions, a handsome brick building with buttresses, a steep roof, pointed windows, and a Galilee porch (126). One of the finest architects of the American Gothic Revival, Upjohn was a staunch advocate of that Puseyism which valued sacramental piety and of the ecclesiological theory which understood architecture to be an expression of theology. Upjohn was also a close friend of the high-church bishop of New York, Benjamin Onderdonk, and Upjohn had once declined the opportunity to design a church on the grounds that the action would violate his religious principles.[45] Otey almost certainly knew the architect's name and his convictions. It had been Otey's painful duty to prosecute charges of immorality against Bishop Onderdonk in 1845, and the religious press of Tennessee had never allowed the Episcopal bishop to forget that sin had been found among the defenders of Puseyism, with whom, by 1850, all Episcopalians were inextricably linked. In 1845 the editor of Nashville's *Christian Review* wrote: "I humbly ask my Episcopal friends, if the immoral conduct of their bishops does not effectively nullify the authority of their divine acts in the church? . . . Will the Bishop of Tennessee . . . so far condescend to stoop from his divine authority, as to give a poor humble subject of his diocess of Tennessee information on this subject."[46] A decade of such undeserved provocations had probably not made James Hervey Otey feel more kindly toward Puseyism or symbolism (the name frequently given the theoretical aspect of ecclesiology), movements which usually appeared together and which Otey knew to savor of doctrinal revolution. On a fine August morning in 1857 Bishop Otey beheld Upjohn's church at Riverside and refused to consecrate it because of crosses on its roof; the baptismal font planted squarely in the aisle in imitation of antique practice; the altar with five crosses, candlesticks, and flower vases; the sentence "Reverence my Sanctuary—I am the Lord," painted on the chancel arch "in beautiful German text"; and the verse "Whoso eateth my Flesh and drinketh my blood hath eternal life" written both over the altar and encircling the windows at the rear.[47] When Bishop Otey arrived at Riverside in August, Charles Tomes's death was but one month past, and it is hardly possible that Upjohn's church could have failed to remind him of his promising young son-in-law, who had crowned a life of exemplary service by entering into controversy with the powerful congregation of Christ Church and by losing on an issue which sober minds could hardly consider important but which was dear to the hearts of ecclesiologists and Puseyites.

125.˘ (A) *The design Henry Dudley provided in 1859 for the Church of the Advent made it the largest and finest Gothic building proposed for antebellum Nashville. (B) The church, which stood on the east side of Vine (Seventh Avenue) south of Church, was not completed until 1870, by which time the original design had been modified.*

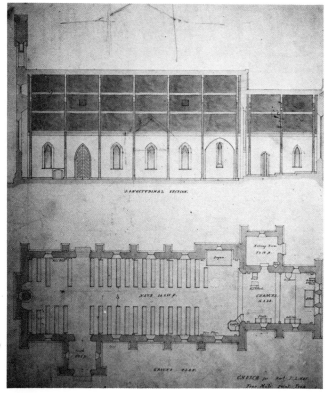

126(A)

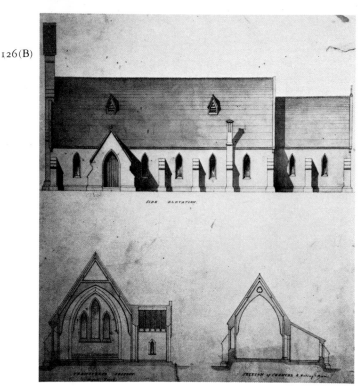

126(B)

Ironically the rector of St. Andrew's Church at Riverside was Charles Tomes's former pupil, J.H. Ingraham, who had returned to Tennessee from Natchez to take charge of the new parish and to found a girls' school to be called Riverside Academy. Ingraham, aware that Bishop Otey might be displeased by the building and its appointments, had tried unsuccessfully to warn the bishop, but Bishop Otey had not found time to inspect the premises before the service of consecration. Surprised by what he saw on entering the church, Otey quietly ordered the candles taken to the vestry room, and later in the day he and the Reverend J. L. Gay discovered that the superaltar could be removed.[48] Although the church was finally consecrated, a proper deed was never secured, and Ingraham soon resigned.[49] Finally St. Andrew's was abandoned. Soon the building decayed, leaving only fragments of its marble water table and churchyard cemetery to mark the site.

The difficulty at Riverside occasioned a controversy that continued in the church press through the winter of 1857 and spring of 1858. The bishop claimed the right to judge the appropriateness of the appointments of churches. The *Episcopal Recorder* sympathized with his principles but considered his actions intemperate and perhaps unlawful. The *Churchman* thought Otey's action a blow aimed at high-church doctrine and ecclesiology. Bishop Otey himself understood with unerring judgment the importance and significance of the issue. He approved of "spiritual suggestion,"[50] but symbolism, the name members of the New York Ecclesiological Society had chosen for their theory that externals convey spiritual realities, he found too dangerous.

In 1858 Bishop Otey gave this account of the happenings at Riverside to the Diocesan Convention:

> When I approached the church and beheld on every gate of the yard a cross, three crosses on the roof and in the gable or belfry and on entering the church saw under the chancel window an altar that might properly be called high, occupying a large space with three steps rising to its base, with five crosses painted on its front, a moveable cross on the window above; and besides all this two large candlesticks of turned wood, placed there, not to give light to the house, but avowedly to enlighten the inner man, the mind, the soul, by ther mysterious power of symbolism, I felt that the time had come for me to interpose . . . .

126. *(A) Church for Four Mile Point, Monroe County. (B) Richard Upjohn's design for St. Andrew's exemplified the romantic liturgical and architectural medievalism of the Cambridge Movement and its American counterpart, the New York Ecclesiological Society.*

By arousing "the mysterious power of symbolism," Upjohn had violated the disjunction between spirit and matter which constrained even Bishop Otey. It was the "system known as symbolism," the "introduction of symbolism by means of material forms or figures" to which the Bishop objected. In 1846 Frederick A. Ross had written, "The sober Christian, denies that *sensible* acquaintance with his Maker or with disembodied spirits, has been allowed in the flesh, since the days of miracles which established the Scriptures."[51] Although on reflection Ross might have qualified his remark, he clearly found it reasonable to conceive of the Maker as chief of disembodied spirits, master of a Cartesian heaven in which glory did not mean the transformation but the abandonment of the flesh. Ross and Otey were grasped by the conviction that God had inhabited matter only once, that he did not do so now in what the older religion had called sacraments, and that, given these presuppositions, painting and architecture ought not tempt the heart to the contrary by some "mysterious power of symbolism" that might lead to reverence or adoration.

Reservations such as Frederick A. Ross and Bishop Otey held would not long influence church building in Tennessee. Indeed, history, and beauty, had been reintroduced to local church building by the succession of Gothic Revival churches that Otey himself had encouraged since 1830. The Baptists completed a handsome Gothic Revival building in Nashville in 1841. A Greek Revival church building was completed by Nashville Presbyterians in 1836, and in 1846 the Second Presbyterian Church added another. In Knoxville the Gothic St. John's (1846) was followed by a fine Grecian Presbyterian church in 1852 and by a Gothic Revival Catholic church the same year, and Episcopalians continued to build romantic Gothic buildings like the wooden Church of St. Mary (1858) on Poplar Street in Memphis and Grace Church, Spring Hill, a very advanced board and batten building of the late 1850s. Yet half a century had passed before church building was considered important. Michaux's observation that Tennesseans "appear also to be less religious, although they are very strict in their observance of Sunday," led him to notice, "There are few churches in Tennessee." In the royal domain of Satory near Versailles, where Michaux's family were traditionally the groundskeepers, religion was a texture of time-honored observances taking place in a rich setting of medieval and Renaissance buildings, and Sunday was a time of feasting. Tennesseans puzzled Michaux because they kept somber Sundays but built few churches. They did so because the soul was one thing, the body another.

VIII. THE GREEK REVIVAL

All the civilized world acknowledges the existence of permanent principles established by the wisdom, strength, *and* beauty *of the proportions and symmetry of the Grecian Temples.*

WILLIAM STRICKLAND,
"The Three Orders," 1848

On December 6, 1831, David Morrison, the architect employed by President Jackson to remodel the Hermitage, described the completed work in a letter to his client:

The Hermitage as improved presents a front of 104 feet, the wings project 9 feet in front of the center building and are connected by a colonnade of the same breadth. The colonnade consists of 10 lofty columns of the Doric order, the entablature is carried through the whole line of the front, and has wreaths of laurel leaves in the frieze, on the cornice is a blocking corse that supports an appropriate balustrade. The upper story consists of a Portico surmounted by a pediment which breaks the monotony of the composition in a very satisfactory manner.[1]

The architecture of columns, entablatures, and cornices required for its successful execution a designer knowledgeable in antique precedents and familiar with academic architectural vocabulary. In 1814 George Tucker described this new professionalism in his essay on architecture: "Ever since the rules and proportions of Greek architecture have been digested into a system, it has been held a valuable accomplishment to relish and understand them. The art which it has cost much labor to acquire, and which distinguishes its possessor from the common mass of mankind, he will seek to display by a rigid observance of its precepts."[2] David Morrison's knowledge of theory and command of technical vocabulary identify him as an architect like Latrobe or Strickland, a designer and superintendent, not an artisan or mechanic. The designing house carpenter would disappear only when steam and nails made his art redundant, but the Greek Revival offered architects an appropriate occasion to display the imagination and theoretical knowledge carpenters often lacked.

The American Greek Revival had roots in English neoclassicism, and Palladio, Inigo Jones, Sir Christopher Wren, and James Gibbs were the fathers of a rich tradition of classical taste that passed through several stages before the Federal style of the 1790s was developed. In March, 1787, Thomas Jefferson, then minister to France, stood in Nîmes "gazing whole hours at the Maison quarée, like a lover gazing at his mistress," and the antiquarian phase of the Revival was inspired by the admiration Jefferson and his contemporaries felt for classical, especially Roman, models. In both England and America the Greek Revival also owed much to a heightened appreciation of the classical past that late-eighteenth-century romanticism encouraged. Stuart and Revett published their *Antiquities of Athens* in 1762, and the Elgin marbles and Byron's poetry played their parts in capturing English imagination. Jefferson's Virginia Capitol (1789), built in imitation of the Maison Carrée, was followed by Benjamin Henry Latrobe's Bank of Pennsylvania (1798), the Baltimore Cathedral (1807), and the works of Robert Mills (1781–1855), William Strickland (1788–1854), and John Haviland (1792–1852). Although Latrobe and Strickland imitated antique models in their Grecian designs, slavishly as Latrobe put it,[3] they were not purists. Latrobe had prepared a Gothic as well as a classic design for the cathedral, just as Adolphus Heiman would prepare both Grecian and castellated designs for the Tennessee Hospital for the Insane fifty years later.[4] Strickland defended the Grecian style, though he had begun his career with the Gothic Masonic Hall in Philadelphia and built his last church, First Presbyterian in Nashville, in Egyptian Revival style. But Greek Revival, or Grecian as antebellum architects usually called it, was favored for public buildings in the interior South after about 1830 to the near exclusion of Gothic and the other styles.

The local success of the Greek Revival was the result in part of the regional acceptance of political and educational theories which seemed to the typical southerner to perpetuate the classical ideal. Many apologists for southern civilization saw the South as a society of traditions and unchanging principles, and an architecture that rested on precedent seemed to echo that unvarying order. Strickland is supposed to have told his pupils that one need go no further than *The Antiquities of Athens* to discover a good design.[5] True to his theory, he had modeled the Second Bank of the United States at Philadelphia after the Parthenon and the Tennessee Capitol after the Erectheum and the Choragic Monument of Lysicrates. The writer of an article entitled "On the Intellectual and Moral Relations of the Fine Arts" that appeared in the *Southern Literary Journal* in 1837 spoke of "the progress of the fine arts to that perfection, which they attained long ago in the days of ancient Greece" and called the Greeks "those standards of mankind."[6] George Tucker, noting Jefferson's reliance on the Maison Carrée, remarked that the authority of the ancients was final and concluded that "a candid view of the principles upon which Greek architecture is founded, leads us to doubt whether its empire over human taste is not too firmly fixed to be shaken or controlled."[7] The study of the classics was encouraged

on similar grounds. The first volume of the *Southern Literary Messenger* contained an article entitled "Study of Latin and Greek Classics," in which the author concluded: "Let all remember this, and seek not only rule of guidance, but successful illustration among the pages of the past."[8] The second volume of the same journal included an essay entitled "The Classics," which reiterated the theory and assured students that "the exercises which we recommend are those in which were trained all the best models in science and general literature, whom they most revere and admire."[9] In the same year the journal published a "Classical Bibliography," recommending a list of books to be purchased by those who wished to own a fine classical library.[10] In an essay defending the study of Latin and Greek, George Tucker noted with regret that "the speculative spirit of the age requires a reason for everything."[11] For Tucker, the prototypical academician of the Jacksonian Age, the best authority was tradition.

In politics, Greek Revival theory suited the desire of southerners to see themselves as heirs and imitators of the Greek *polis*. Americans were generally sympathetic toward the Greek struggle for independence,

127. The second Hermitage, Davidson County, was a plain Federal house, two rooms deep and two stories tall.

but, ironically, regard for the peculiar domestic institution that had played so great a part in the societies of Athens and Sparta also encouraged southern interest in classical civilization. In April 1850 the *Southern Literary Messenger* devoted twenty-two pages to "Observations on a Passage in the Politics of Aristotle Relative to Slavery," and even earlier De Bow's *Commerical Review*, published in New Orleans, had argued that slavery, relative isolation, and the attendant necessity for native industry and commerce had been foundations of the greatness of Greek art.[12] The enemy was change. A reviewer, writing for Charleston's *Southern Quarterly Review*, observed of the contributors to Emerson's *Dial*: "The transcendentalists are enemies of antiquity, and equally hostile to existing institutions, and prevailing systems of morals, in philosophy and religion. They are the champions of change and reform in all things."[13] During the forties and fifties southern politicians emphasized the close relation between their own institutions and classical civilization. There remained, of

course, the expansionist, progressive, pioneering face of the South, the South whose sons were ready to sell out and move to Texas. Yet prophets of change never met more than half-acceptance south of the Ohio, a desire for the fruits of transcendental theory without its disabilities—for gins, steamboats, and railroads without abolitionism, deism, or constitutional revolution. General Jackson's determination to have the Homeric tale of Telemachus and Ulysses on the walls of the Hermitage hall brought into local history the tradition which Washington had claimed by ordering for his chimneypiece at Mount Vernon "A Groupe of Aeneas carrying his father out of Troy."[14] The patrimony of Troy flourished on the banks of the Potomac and the Cumberland.

Tennesseans—not only the Donelsons, McClungs, and Polks, but the sons of middle-class farmers—were educated to value classical ideals and classical civilization. The wisdom Samuel Doak taught at Washington College and Charles Coffin at Greeneville was the classical wisdom of Homer and Cicero, informed by the Bible, Locke, and the Scottish philosophers; and when Mr. Carrick opened his academy in Knoxville in 1792 he advertised his ability to impart "a Competent Introduction to the Latin and Greek Languages."[15] Homer, Xenophon, Cicero, and Euclid were in the library of Nashville's Davidson Academy before 1786, and for eighty years the classical tradition flourished in its successor schools, Cumberland College and the Univer-

128. Architect David Morrison made the drawing from which this engraving was taken in December 1831, just as the work of transforming the Federal Hermitage into a Greek Revival plantation house was completed.

sity of Nashville. In 1838 entering freshmen at East Tennessee College were examined in Virgil, Cicero's orations, and the Greek reader, as well as arithmetic, English grammar, and geography. According to the announcements for 1846, freshmen at Lebanon's Cumberland University would study Sallust, Cicero, and Xenophon. Sophomores went on to Cicero and the *Graeca Majora,* and juniors added Sophocles or Euripides. Cave Johnson, Jackson's confidant and later postmaster general, was expelled from Cumberland College in Nashville because his Latin pronounciation was faulty,[16] and while David Morrison labored to remodel the Hermitage into a noble Doric pattern, young John Donelson Coffee, another of the general's connections, was struggling to learn his Latin and Greek under the stern Professor Cross, and failing at the latter so badly that General Coffee and the boy's uncle John C. McLemore felt constrained to plead his case with President Philip Lindsley.[17] Ten years later young Jethro Gatlin, some of whose letters have also survived, was still struggling to satisfy Mr. Cross; and Cicero, Sophocles, and Aristotle's *Ethics* were very much part of the curriculum at the University of Nashville.[18] When the English traveler J. S. Buckingham passed through Greeneville and Blountville in 1841, he was struck by the irony of Tennesseans proclaiming themselves the particular heirs of Greek civilization:

Though the farmers of Tennessee may have their country studded with such classical names as Athens, Sparta, Troy, Carthage, Memphis, and Palmyra . . . it will take some time before their prose compositions will equal those of Demosthenes, or their poetry rival that of Homer; there being only one feature in which they resemble the Athenians—though it must be admitted on much more slender grounds—namely, that of thinking themselves the only polished and refined people on the earth.[19]

Throughout the nineteenth century, Tennessee's farmers maintained their piety toward Homer and Demosthenes, and Grecian architecture was as much a part of life as county seats named Sparta or Athens. There was a hint of the new Grecian style in the Bank of the United States (113), built in Nashville in 1827,[20] though its tenuous two-story columns also represented a late blooming Jeffersonian classicism. There was perhaps no proper example of the new style in Tennessee until 1831, when David Morrison remodeled President Jackson's Hermitage and built the garden monument.

The first Hermitage had been a squared-log house, but about 1819 Jackson employed Henry Reiff to build a brick dwelling.[21] The house was a plain, five-bay Federal block, brick, four rooms on each story (127). The only stylish details were a fanlight over the door and a plain one-story porch. There was, a visitor wrote in 1827, "no splendor to dazzle the eye but everything elegant and neat." To the right were two drawing rooms, to the left the dining room and the Jacksons' chamber.[22]

In 1828 Rachel Jackson died, and the general left the Hermitage for Washington. But three years later his adopted son married Sarah York of Philadelphia, and Jackson took that occasion to remodel the Hermitage, which the younger Jacksons would also make their home. David Morrison, perhaps brought to President Jackson's attention by Governor William Carroll, carried out the extensive project during 1831 and the spring of 1832. A projecting one-story wing containing dining room, pantry, and a separate but carefully aligned kitchen was built along the west side. The President's study was located in a wing placed symmetrically at the east of the main block, and a connecting one-story colonnade was built across the front between the projecting wings, with a temple-form second story at its center to give focus to the entrance and provide an upstairs porch. Jackson complained that his architect was slow, but he was satisfied and praised Morrison in a letter written in November 1831. Indeed, when the Hermitage was damaged by fire on October 13, 1834, Jackson was at first determined to rebuild it unchanged. That David Morrison had set out to give the President a Grecian plantation house is evident from the architect's description, and an engraving of the building made by Morrison and published on the 1831 Ayres's Map of Nashville illustrates his success (128). Unfortunately, all that remained after the fire of 1834 were the walls of the main block and the dining room "but little injured," in which the plaster frieze is perhaps the only distinctive remnant of Morrison's design.[23]

Morrison's Doric "temple and monument" is an even better example of the architect's competence in the Grecian style (4). The circular, domed tempietto, or monopteron, had been illustrated in eighteenth-century editions of Vitruvius. Thomas Jefferson used it for his well house at Monticello; Latrobe atop the Bank of Pennsylvania, and the form appeared frequently in belfries and cupolas throughout the South. Morrison employed it not only at the Hermitage, but at the penitentiary and the Methodist Church in Nashville. Morrison's monopteron in the Hermitage garden was, as Major Lewis wrote the president in April 1833, "quite tasty and appropriate," though, owing to the uneven, soft quality of local limestone, there were "many rough places and little holes in the columns themselves." Still, Morrison's stonecutter executed the design skillfully, and the expensive copper roof that Morrison mentioned to the President still serves. After Jackson's death in 1845, the Doric monopteron gained national significance as the burial place of a President and military hero. [24]

David Morrison's projects in Davidson County were partly the product of eighteenth-century neoclassicism, but the house and monument at Jackson's plantation and the Doric order at Nashville's McKendree Methodist church of 1833 make him Tennessee's first architect of the Greek Revival. During the three years it stood, the President's house made Grecian style fashionable, and the monopteron was perhaps the first local attempt to build an archaeologically correct work in stone. The Hermitage of 1831 probably inspired William Nichol's remodeling of nearby Belair (1838), the extant building that conveys most accurately the appearance of Morrison's Hermitage (129),[25] and the Doric style of the garden monument may have served as a model for another of the Hermitage's near neighbors.

Tulip Grove, originally named Poplar Grove, was built between 1832 and 1834 for Andrew Jackson Donelson on land immediately south of the Hermitage plantation, the President paying part of the cost.[26] The bold, clear use of the two-story Doric order makes

129

130

Tulip Grove the principal domestic monument of the local Greek Revival (130). Morrison was seeking commissions as far afield as Mississippi by 1833,[27] so it is not surprising that the work was given to Joseph Rieff and William Hume,[28] the former probably the son or nephew of Henry Reiff, who had built the Hermitage of 1819. Although one of the Donelsons may have brought the design for Tulip Grove's Doric porch back from Washington or Philadelphia, the house carpenters Reiff and Hume are also likely sources.[29] An apparent model for the Tulip Grove portico had perhaps already been built a few miles away in Lebanon, where the house of Judge Robert L. Caruthers, which should perhaps be dated as early as 1830, bears a stylistically identical porch (131).[30] Although the Caruthers house has only two, two-story Doric columns instead of the four found at Tulip Grove, the porticoes of both are archaeologically correct and in detail identical, the triglyphs, regulae and guttae, and palmettes in the corners of the soffit cut either from the same pattern or by the

131. The Doric porch of the Robert L. Caruthers house in Lebanon, Wilson County, was built, perhaps before 1830, from the pattern Reiff and Hume followed in 1835 at Tulip Grove.

same hand. Each house has a recessed porch, and the façades of both have pilasters with simplified capitals. The Caruthers house bears the scars of several remodelings, one of which gave it Eastlake millwork in the eaves and pediment and heavy caps above the windows; before these additions and changes were made, however, the similarities between the two buildings were obvious. This architectural relationship is perhaps to be explained by the proximity of the Reiffs,[31] who had settled on Spencer's Creek in Wilson County, about halfway between Tulip Grove and Lebanon. It might also be explained by the circumstance that Sarah Saunders, Robert Caruthers' wife, was Andrew Jackson Donelson's half-sister. Caruthers had won the plot on which his house was built in a lottery late in 1826. The next year he married Sally Saunders, and his house was probably built soon afterward.[32]

Thus before 1834 three archaeologically correct examples of the new Grecian style were begun or completed along the Hermitage Road from Nashville to Lebanon. Although it was the least bold of the three, Morrison's Hermitage was the house of the President, and Jackson's use of the Grecian style undoubtedly

129. Like the neighboring Hermitage, Belair was a plain Federal dwelling to which wings, a classic porch, and a gallery were added.

130. Tulip Grove, built across Lebanon Road from the Hermitage between 1832 and 1836, was given a Doric porch and frieze by the house carpenters Reiff and Hume.

132

133

made it popular. The architect had succeeded in leaving a fine impression on the beholder. When Featherstonhaugh visited the Hermitage a few weeks before the tragic fire in 1834, he wrote: "The mansion-house at the Hermitage . . . is built of brick, and is tolerably large; everything was neat and clean around it, the fences were well kept up, and it looked like the substantial residence of an opulent planter."[33]

The first Greek Revival building erected in Nashville was probably the Presbyterian Church, completed at the southeast corner of Spring and Summer streets in the autumn of 1833.[34] Although the building was crowned by a Federal clock tower and cupola, it faithfully reproduced the fluted columns, triglyphs, and metopes of the Doric order (6), and Eastin Morris commented that when completed it would be "one of the handsomest buildings in the city."[35] The new church was quite large with its capacity for about 1,300 and very expensive, having cost about $30,000.[36] The carpenter, Mason Vannoy, may also have been the architect,[37] though the Presbyterian Church was a fairly sophisticated Grecian design of the type David Morrison was then producing in Nashville. In 1833 David Morrison designed a banking house for the Union Bank of the State of Tennessee, a Doric hexastyle that stood at the northeast corner of Cherry (Fourth) and Union streets from 1834 until 1882 (132).[38] A sketch, probably made by W.A. Eichbaum, supports Morris's judgment that the bank was "a splendid house on the style of the United States Bank at Philadelphia,"[39] a building William Strickland had designed in 1818. This image of the proper Philadelphia banking house probably influenced in turn the design of the Union Bank (133), built on Knoxville's Main Street in 1836, and the Columbia branch, which Nathan Vaught built—but perhaps did not design—in 1839.

The Greek Revival came to Memphis soon after Morrison's Hermitage was completed. The Robertson Topp house (134), traditionally attributed to P.H. Hammarskold of Charleston,[40] was a stylish mansion that perhaps more than any other ever built in Tennessee displayed the influence of fashionable New York Grecian design. The George H. Whyett or Hunt-Phelan house,[41] built about 1828 at Lauderdale and

Beale streets, lacks the stylistic clarity of the Topp mansion, though its Ionic porch, probably added during the 1850s,[42] makes the building decidedly Grecian. The most important Greek Revival public building in Memphis was the Gayoso House (11) designed by James Dakin of New Orleans and begun in 1842.[43] The Gayoso, a stone building with a tall basement on which an elegant porch of six Corinthian columns stood, remained the local standard of Greek Revival elegance through war, neglect, and restoration until it was destroyed by fire on July 4, 1899.

During the forties Memphis had at least three resident architects capable of executing handsome Greek Revival designs. David Morrison had moved to Memphis before 1842 and was employed at the Navy Yard there as late as 1849. The main Navy Yard building, a large Doric octastyle surrounded by secondary structures also in the Grecian style (135), and the Baptist Church (136), begun on Second Avenue between

132. *Morrison's Union Bank of the State of Tennessee, completed at the northeast corner of Cherry (Fourth) and Union in Nashville in 1835, was a classic Doric hexastyle. After 1838 the building housed the Bank of the State of Tennessee.*

133. *Amateur architect Drury P. Armstrong, who was an officer of Knoxville's Union Bank, probably had some part in the designing of this neat but unprepossessing Grecian building.*

134. *Robertson Topp, a successful entrepreneur of Memphis, built this stylish Grecian house on the south side of Beale Street between Lauderdale and Orleans streets in 1841. The porch imitates Topp's Gayoso House hotel, begun in 1842, which suggests that James Dakin, architect of the Gayoso, may also have designed the house. The classic façade concealed an irregular plan, an early departure from the strict symmetry of traditional Federal design.*

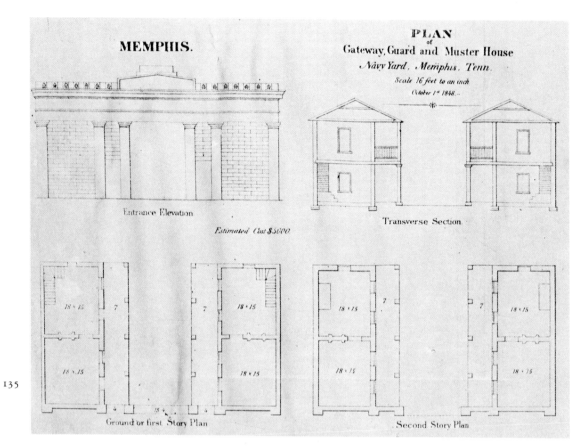

MEMPHIS.

PLAN
of
Gateway, Guard and Muster House
Navy Yard, Memphis, Tenn.
Scale 16 feet to an inch
October 1st 1848

Entrance Elevation

Estimated Cost $5000

Transverse Section

Ground or first Story Plan

Second Story Plan

135

136

Adams and Washington in 1846, resemble the banking house Morrison had built on Nashville's Union Street in 1834–1835,[44] imitating faithfully the example of Strickland's Bank of the United States in Philadelphia. Documentary evidence showing Morrison to have been the designer of these buildings has thus far not been discovered. William Crane came to Memphis before 1843 and worked in the city as late as 1859. During much of this period he was city engineer, but he persistently advertised his willingness "to draw plans and specifications of buildings of every description, estimate the cost and superintend the erection of any character of building."[45] The Greek Revival Second Presbyterian Church was designed by Crane in 1846. Built at the northwest corner of Main and Beale in south Memphis, Second Presbyterian boasted a tiered

135. *The important buildings of the Memphis Navy Yard were Grecian, such as this design for the Gateway, Guard, and Muster house.*

136. *The Memphis Baptist Church, begun in 1846, was a plain but elegant Doric design, the first building to signal the social importance of that denomination in West Tennessee.*

137. *The Presbyterian Church in Gallatin, Sumner County, was built about 1838. A comparison between this building, a columned temple form with pointed windows, and Immanuel Church in La Grange (120), where a Gothic design is given Ionic pilasters, illustrates the eclecticism which characterized nineteenth-century Tennessee church building outside the larger towns.*

cupola and a fine range of eight columns, each crowned by a simple capital of fronds (13).[46] Hugh Roland, who had designed a large hotel in Grecian style in Louisville about 1833, was in Memphis from the early 1840s until 1850, though nothing is known of his work in that city.[47] The Grecian style of Memphis and Nashville was widely imitated in the countryside, though often only in details like applied pilasters and simple pediments. The Presbyterian Church in Gallatin was a country builder's version of a fashionable distyle *in antis* Greek Revival design (137).[48]

Like Gothic, the Greek Revival came to East Tennessee somewhat later than to Nashville and Memphis. One of the first stylish Greek Revival buildings in the upper counties was the Rogersville branch of the Bank of the State of Tennessee, now the Masonic Hall, built in 1839 from "the plan and specifications designed and

138

139

140

141

made out by Thomas Jones."[49] Although the directors dispensed with the "frontispieces" over the windows and made the walls of the rotunda thinner and the pilasters shallower, the building's great wooden columns *in antis* and freely composed entablature made it a sophisticated local example of the Grecian style (138). In 1846 Jonesboro's Presbyterian Church employed a Sullivan County architect, W.H. Clyce, to provide plans for the new building.[50] Clyce furnished a well-drawn plan and an elevation featuring eight Doric columns, but he noted on his drawing that the number could be reduced to six should that arrangement be preferred. Jonesboro's Presbyterian Church (139) with its neatly proportioned entablature, triglyphs, and mutules remains one of Tennessee's outstanding Greek Revival buildings. The neighboring Methodist Church (140) was built at about the same time (1845–1847) in the Ionic order. The octagon with its Ionic columns, cupola, and spire is a vernacular reminiscence of the Georgian steeples of the seaboard.[51]

By 1840 architecture was becoming the province of the skilled professional. In an era when urban concentrations were rare and wealth derived from the land, architects often traveled, leaving behind a landscape dotted with examples of their skill. Thomas Blanchard, born in New York in 1814 or 1815, came to Tennessee about 1846 and built in or near the town of Madisonville at least three fine dwellings.[52] The most imposing was the Guilford Cannon house (141), still standing at the edge of Madisonville. The house has two superimposed single-story Doric porches and a generous plan

that follows the scheme Samuel McIntire had used at the John Gardiner house in Salem, Massachusetts, forty years earlier. Its distinctive features are the semicircular termination of the hall with a stair built to fit that shape, a secondary side entrance and stair hall, and a nugatory ell for dining and the kitchen. The nearby Robert Cooke house resembles the Cannon house, though additions have complicated the original design. The Coffin house, more Federal than Greek Revival, and built about two miles northwest of Madisonville, is also attributed to Blanchard. In 1850 he was at work in Blount County.

The relative scarcity of residential examples belonging unambiguously to the Greek Revival is partly owing to the regional conservatism which encouraged the building of simple, powerful Federal houses until 1840. Sometimes a one-story Greek Revival porch was given to these Federal blocks, as at the Whyett house in Memphis; the John Kincaid house (142) near Fincastle (Campbell County), probably built in the 1830s; the

138. *In Hawkins County the Rogersville branch of the Bank of the State of Tennessee, now the Masonic Hall, was a stylistically distinctive Grecian design by the otherwise unknown architect Thomas Jones.*

139. *The tower, spire, and fanlight of the Jonesboro Presbyterian Church (1850) in Washington County are Federal, but the temple form, Doric order, and basement make it a good example of the Greek Revival.*

140. *In 1847 Jonesboro's Methodists built a new structure with an Ionic portico and pilasters. Like the Gallatin Presbyterian Church (137), the design combined Grecian and Gothic elements.*

141. *Superimposed Doric orders and the plain pediment of the porch at the Cannon house in Madisonville, Monroe County, provide a reference to classic precedents strong enough to give the house a Grecian character. This Greek Revival porch should be compared with Palladian (41, 74) and Federal (75) examples.*

142. *The John Kincaid II house near Fincastle, Campbell County, in other respects a traditional central-passage house of the 1820s, is entered through a Doric temple.*

143

144

145

146

frame Frazer Titus house in Memphis; the Brazelton house near New Market (Jefferson County), built by Samuel Cleague in 1832; and Stockley Donelson's Cleveland Hall in Davidson County (1841).[53.] A few of the great plantation houses belong to the Greek Revival, notably Tulip Grove; the three Pillow houses in Maury County,[54] all nearly identical and all built with fine Ionic porches; and perhaps Josephus Conn Guild's Rosemont (188), though Rosemont, like the Topp house (134), is prophetic of the romantic classicism that became popular in Tennessee in the late forties and early fifties.

Many courthouses were built in the Greek Revival style. The Sumner County Courthouse of 1837 (143) represents the Greek Revival transformation of the hip-roofed Federal courthouse; and soon this distyle *in antis* scheme appeared in Knoxville (144), where John Dameron, superintended by Drury P. Armstrong, built the new courthouse in 1842.[55] Three years later a courthouse that imitated the Knoxville building was erected by Jefferson County authorities in Dandridge (145). The Roane County Courthouse (146) built in 1853 in Kingston, from the design of Frederick B. Guenther, is a strong vernacular Grecian design of the same type. The most stylish Greek Revival courthouse built in Tennessee was probably William Strickland's Wilson County Courthouse of 1848. If the sketch from Strickland's portfolio (33) is correctly identified, the building perpetuated the two-story Palladian porch and Strickland's favorite antique form, the Choragic

Monument of Lysicrates, into the late 1840s. The Williamson County Courthouse of 1858, a brick block with pillasters and portico, was planned in imitation of Strickland's Lebanon building, though the Franklin courthouse may have followed his design only loosely.[56] In 1857 James Hartley Strickland designed a courthouse for Davidson county (147), a Corinthian echo of the grander Ionic temple his father had erected on the hill above Nashville's Public Square.[57]

Morrison, Clyce, and Blanchard each brought to Tennessee something of the new Greek Revival that had swept Philadelphia, Boston, and New York between 1820 and 1830, but in 1845 an architect of national reputation came to Tennessee and gave Nashville a Greek Revival monument of distinction. William Strickland's name first appears in the minutes of the commissioners of the Capitol building on June 16, 1844. He was then a man of fifty-seven, behind whom lay successful practice in Philadelphia and several engineering achievements, notably the Delaware Canal. As the minutes of the Commissioners to Superintend

143. The Sumner County Courthouse, built in Gallatin in 1837, had a Grecian frieze, columns in antis, *and the ever popular monopteron.*

144. The dominant feature of the interesting but stylistically confusing Knox County Courthouse of 1842 was its distyle in antis *porch. The tower, built several years after the building was completed, was Federal; the window in the tympanum, Gothic. This form was imitated by the builder of the Jefferson County Courthouse and of Fairview (c. 1850), a plantation house east of Jefferson City.*

145. Although the Greek Revival character of the Jefferson County Courthouse (1845), Dandridge, is diffuse, the building is strong and dignified, dominating the valley which the town occupies.

146. The Roane County Courthouse at Kingston has the two-story portico popular in the 1850s and the Federal cupola that Tennesseans considered appropriate for public buildings.

147. After the Davidson County Courthouse burned in 1856, James Hartley Strickland designed this Grecian building for Nashville's Public Square. The brackets and pronounced verticality evince the weakening of the theory that designers should copy antique forms.

Construction of the Statehouse show, Strickland had first been invited to visit Nashville to discuss the proposed Capitol on June 16, 1844, but the architect apparently displayed no interest; on April 2, 1845, the commissioners wrote again. Perhaps Strickland agreed to build the Capitol because he had not had a prestigious commission since 1836, when he had designed the Philadelphia Exchange. He arrived in the provincial capital where he would spend his remaining nine years in May, and he thereafter devoted himself almost entirely to the construction of the statehouse. The building was completed in 1855, a few months after Strickland's death on April 6, 1854.

Nashvillians understood what Strickland had achieved. The editor of the *Nashville Directory* of 1860–1861 wrote: "The main idea of the elevation of the building is a Greek Ionic temple; erected upon a rustic basement, which in turn rests (in appearance) upon a terraced pavement... [the cupola is] a modified and improved re-production of the Choragic Monument of Lysicrates." The Capitol exemplified Greek Revival theory. An Ionic temple derived from the Erec-

theum, a building erected on the Acropolis about 420 B.C., was crowned by Strickland's interpretation of a delicate circular form the Athenians had built a century later as the base for the tripod on which some prize or trophy would rest. It seems appropriate to think of William Strickland studying the elegant four-volume version of Stuart and Revett's plates of Greek architecture, but he may have possessed only the one-volume edition, now in the State Library, that bears his signature. Whatever his source, the concept, a development of the scheme he had used at the Philadelphia Exchange, was Strickland's own, and the incontestable distinction of the building has given Nashville a central monument to which most of its subsequent architecture has aspired. The second-story hall remains perhaps the noblest space in Tennessee more than a century after its construction, and its Ionic porticoes, presiding over the city from Cedar Knob, represent an unexcelled architectural elegance (8).

With more than an ability to adapt Greek forms, Strickland brought to the design of the Capitol a sensitivity to its site which made the building great. Cedar Knob terminated a natural vista that began near the Cumberland with the Public Square and courthouse and extended along Cedar Street (Charlotte) to the foot of the hill on which the new statehouse stood. By raising the building on a basement, he lifted it above the brow of the hill so that the Capitol would dominate the city streets, as well as the distant view, and he gave it a certain lightness so that the Capitol has always seemed to float above the town. By arranging the axis of the building parallel to the Cumberland River, while at the same time locating a porch in the center of each side, Strickland made a building that caught and turned the axis established by the Square, the market house, and Cedar Street, echoing above Nashville the rectilinear pattern to which the city has always oriented itself (1, 9).

Apart from the Capitol, Strickland is known to have designed only two other public buildings in Tennessee, the Wilson County Courthouse of 1848, and the First Presbyterian Church, Nashville, which he designed in the Egyptian style the same year. Strickland had employed this style in his design for the Mikvey-Israel Synagogue, built in Philadelphia in 1822–1825, and in his proposal for the Laurel Hill Cemetery gate in 1837,[58] so the choice was not unprecedented. The decision to use the Egyptian style was apparently made, however, only after some study on the architect's part, for a surviving elevation probably drawn for the Presbyterian Church illustrates an Italianate alternative (148). While Strickland was at work on the Presbyterian Church and the Lebanon courthouse, he was also

148. *This drawing from the Strickland portfolios, a design for a church in the Renaissance style that John Notman's Philadelphia Athenaeum (1845–1847) had made popular, was probably a study for First Presbyterian, Nashville. The Nashville church was built in Egyptian Revival style in 1848–1851.*

149. *The Hugh Kirkman house, designed by William Strickland and built opposite the cathedral on Summer Street in 1848, belonged to the ring of opulent town houses which encircled the Capitol between 1845 and 1885.*

preparing plans for a hotel which would replace the aging Nashville Inn. Tannehill wrote that if completed, the building would "even throw into the shade the famous St. Charles of New Orleans," built by James Dakin in 1842. The new Nashville hotel, commissioned by James Walker's Nashville Insurance Company, was to have a central court 42 feet square; from this court stairs led to a mezzanine or ambulatory beneath the central dome. The building would have a portico of six columns on its 142-foot-long façade, and the dome stood 100 feet above the pavement.[59] Perhaps the cost—estimated by Strickland to be about $100,000—proved prohibitive, for Nashville had no elegant new hotel until the Maxwell House was completed in 1869.

Numerous residences in and near Nashville have been attributed to William Strickland, but only two are known to have been his work. In 1858 Francis W. Strickland sued to recover fees he believed were due him for acting as his father's assistant, and though he lost the case, testimony given produced a list of works

Strickland's Tennessee contemporaries considered his. Strickland, John M. Bass recalled, had designed his own residence and the Hugh Kirkman house, and when Samuel D. Morgan tried to expand this list he could add only the Lebanon courthouse.[60] The John M. Bass house was at 82 Spring Street, and Nashville tradition recounts that it was the first to have gas installed after the works were put in operation in 1851, but no photograph of the Bass house has yet been found. The Kirkman house at Summer and Cedar (149), is better documented.[61] The important features of the design were a stone basement, a full story high on the Summer Street side, and the long, severely rectilinear two-story Doric order of the Cedar Street façade. Despite its somewhat ponderous basement and columns, the building displays a richness and complexity not usually found in Strickland's earlier residential designs.

During the forties and fifties at least two other Nashville architects produced designs in the Grecian style. James M. Hughes built the Second Presbyterian Church (150) at College and Gay streets between 1844 and 1846.[62] With its handsome porch of six Ionic columns, Second Presbyterian was one of Nashville's most beautiful Greek Revival churches. In 1848 Hughes designed and built the James K. Polk house (151) near Vine and Union in Nashville. He had been recom-

150. Now a warehouse—its porch, spire, and tower removed—James M. Hughes's Second Presbyterian Church (1846) in Nashville was an elegant Grecian design.

mended to the President by Vernon K. Stevenson, an important Nashville commercial figure, after Polk rejected Strickland's proposal for remodeling the old Grundy house, which stood on the property. After a nearby explosion weakened the Grundy house structurally, Polk decided that most of it would be pulled down, and he employed Hughes to draw a plan and construct a substantially new building.[63] Hughes's design belonged more to the romantic classicism of the fifties than to the Greek Revival. Both porches of the Polk house had two-story "Tower-of-the-Winds" capitals, and pilasters were employed to give the appearance of symmetry to an irregular mass. Shortly after Hughes completed President Polk's house, he remodeled the old Nashville Theater at the northeast corner of Union and Summer for the Odd Fellows, completing it late in 1849. The two-story building was

divided into three bays, the center a distyle porch with pillars at the first floor and columns capped by simple fronds in the second. The Odd Fellows Hall had a belvedere on top. Although Wilkins Tannehill pronounced the building imposing, he noted that "to our eye the upper story—if it may be so called—looks like the cabin of a steamboat perched upon the roof and distracts from the architectural merit of the whole."[64] Hughes remained a popular designer. He worked for Andrew Polk in Maury County, perhaps remodeling Ashwood Hall in 1853, and shortly thereafter designed another Grecian building, Wesley Wheless's Bank of Nashville (19), erected on the west side of North

Cherry Street about 1853.[65] The bank had a handsome porch of Corinthian columns *in antis,* and Hughes was already using the arcuated windows characteristic of the Italianate style.

The other Nashville architect who sometimes used the Grecian style was Adolphus Heiman. Although Heiman usually preferred either his castellated variant of Gothic or a classical architecture that appealed directly to Renaissance precedents, he had offered Grecian designs for the Capitol in 1845 and for the asylum in 1849. Neither was built. Strickland won the commission for the Capitol, but the commissioners of the Hospital for the Insane preferred Heiman's castellated design. In 1851 Heiman found an opportunity to build his single monumental Grecian project, the Medical Department of the University of Nashville. The building, which stood on College Hill facing the city,

151.   The James K. Polk house (1848–1849), designed and built in Grecian style by James M. Hughes on the block bounded by Spring, Spruce, Vine, and Union in Nashville, was one of several mansions whose gardens formed islands in the city until 1900.

between Market (Second) and College (Third), was constructed in several stages. The trustees had given the Medical College a small building called the East Wing, and Heiman was engaged to add a "centre" building to it.[66] Construction was guided at first by the design that appeared in the *First Annual Announcement of the Medical Department* in 1851, a flat-roofed Grecian building, its bays defined by Ionic pilasters, having a portico of four columns (152). The entire building was placed on a rusticated basement, and this first design was crowned by a form derived from the Tower of the Winds, an element Heiman had perhaps borrowed from James Dakin's Louisiana Hose Company building

152(A)

152(B)

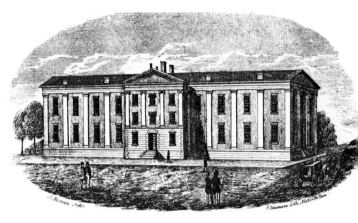

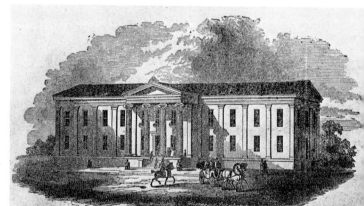

152(C)

in New Orleans (1841). By autumn 1851, the center building was completed.[67] In the summer of 1854 the west wing was added,[68] and the *Announcements of the Law, Literary and Medical Departments* for that year depicts a building with a pedimented entrance pavilion, a rusticated stone basement, and pilastered upper stories (152B), a design developed from the earlier scheme and influenced more by Heiman's Renaissance authorities than by American Grecian style. Beginning with the Medical Department catalog of 1858, yet a third version, presumably the Medical Department as actually built, is shown (152C).[69] The rusticated basement had been abandoned and the dominant feature was an open pedimented porch of four Ionic columns, crowned by a single anthemion, a detail Heiman subsequently used at the Masonic Lodge of 1860 and one which also appears at Belle Meade (1852–1853). In 1854 the *Nashville Journal of Medicine* called the building "a city ornament but little less imposing and certainly more classic and beautiful than the Capitol itself."[70] While the Medical College was under construction, Heiman remodeled Hugh Roland's Masonic Hall of 1818, giving it columns *in antis,* panels, and a balustrade; but like the 1854 scheme for the Medical De-

152. The Medical Department of the University of Nashville was, after the Capitol, the city's most imposing Grecian building. The first scheme Heiman proposed was not built (A), nor was the second (B), though its quoins, keystones, voussoirs, and basement borrowed from seventeenth-century Italy give this design interest as evidence of Heiman's use of European sources. The Medical Department as built (C) was typical of the regional Grecian of the 1850s.

partment, the Masonic Hall was influenced more by Renaissance precedents than by local Grecian style (31). The *Daily Evening Reporter* remarked on October 5, 1850, that the Masonic Hall would now "rank among the first in Nashville in point of beauty and correctness of architectural design."[71]

Several important Greek Revival buildings in Tennessee were designed by architects whose names have not yet been recovered. This list includes the Knoxville branch of the Union Bank of Tennessee (133); the main building at Cumberland University in Lebanon, built between 1842 and 1844 and remodeled in 1858–1859 (153);[72] the main building of the Memphis Navy Yard and the Memphis Baptist Church of 1846–1849 (136), both Doric designs reminiscent of

153. Cumberland University in Lebanon (Wilson County), built in 1844 and enlarged in 1859, illustrates the innovative Grecian image of the late 1850s. The building, destroyed during the Federal occupation, is attributed to Strickland, though construction and remodeling dates make it unlikely that he was the architect.

Morrison's Union Bank of the State of Tennessee (132); and the Nashville Christian Church of 1852 (154), which looks like a Heiman design.[73]

One important Grecian building of the 1840s usually attributed to Strickland was probably not his work. The Cathedral of the Blessed Virgin of the Seven Dolors was begun in April 1844 and dedicated June 6, 1847.[74] A few days after the cornerstone was laid on June 6, 1844, Richard Pius Miles, first bishop of Nashville, wrote to a friend: "Tell me, can Baltimore boast anything like it? Our foundation is gradually rising; and in a few years we hope to have a temple for worship in some degree worthy of the Great Being for whom we intend it."[75] Bishop Miles had in his mind's eye the building, now St. Mary's Church, that stands at Fifth and Charlotte (155). The editor of the *Nashville Union* probably knew the identity of the designer, for he wrote on the occasion of the dedication of the new cathedral, November 3, 1847: "It is a neat and chaste specimen of Grecian architecture, which reflects credit upon its architect."

Tennesseans have usually assumed that Strickland was the designer of St. Mary's, basing their judgment on the remark in Bishop Miles's biography, published in

1926, that Strickland was reported to have been the architect. Several articles about Strickland's work in Nashville had been published earlier, but none attributed the cathedral to him;[76] in 1858, only four years after Strickland's death, when John M. Bass and Samuel D. Morgan, both of whom had served as commissioners for the construction of the Capitol, enumerated the architect's works, they failed to mention it. The chronology of the building also makes it difficult to consider the cathedral Strickland's. After the lot was purchased by Bishop Miles, Strickland was seeking commissions in Washington.[77] In 1844 the journey from Philadelphia to Nashville took about a week, and letters often took two weeks. Before the cornerstone could be set in place on a footing or foundation wall, the removal of at least 1,000 cubic yards of Nashville soil and limestone was necessary. This would have taken several weeks and probably could not have been begun

154. *The new Christian Church was built in 1852 on the east side of Cherry Street, south of Spring in Nashville. The building should be compared with the Cathedral (155) and the Masonic Hall of 1851 (31).*

until the plans were complete. If the date on which the bishop took possession of the lot—March 30, 1844—accurately represents the date on which he began to seek architectural advice, it is difficult to believe that William Strickland was responsible for the foundations Bishop Miles saw rising early in June. Seven or eight weeks probably would not have allowed sufficient time for Strickland to be approached, agreement reached, plans provided, excavations completed, and foundations laid.

This chronology suggests that the designer was a Nashvillian, and in 1844 the best-known local architects were probably Heiman and Hughes. Heiman was almost certainly responsible for the belfry that was added to the cathedral in 1862 or 1863. An Eichbaum sketch, probably made during the 1850s, which shows the building without its belfry, exists (155A), and an engraving of the city published in 1860 omits it (9). The bell itself was probably not purchased until about 1863.[78] When the belfry was constructed, it was stylistically identical to the cupola of Heiman's Giles County Courthouse of 1859 (172). Both have octagonal bases

with composite columns at the angles, arcuated openings, and ribbed domical roofs accented by volutes. Of course it is possible that Heiman designed the belfry, Strickland or some other architect the building itself; but the attribution to Strickland remains unconvincing on grounds other than chronology. The cathedral was a brick building, stuccoed, with corner pilasters, a panel over the entrance, and ornamented lintels. None of this was typical of Strickland, but it is all reminiscent of Heiman's designs, especially the Masonic Hall of 1851 (31), which also had Ionic columns *in antis,* a stuccoed façade, and panels.

It is important to remember that the cathedral has been renovated more than once. It was repaired after its use as a hospital during the battle of Nashville, and in the nineties Bishop Joseph Rademacher undertook a renovation which gave the apse and ceiling new finishes.[79] On the occasion of the cathedral's golden jubilee in 1897, a reporter for the *Nashville American* wrote that the basilicas of Rome provided inspiration for the remodeling. Subsequently, in 1926, the building was again renovated, the architects perhaps proceeding on the newly published assumption that it was Strickland's and should therefore be made to resemble his other work as closely as possible. The building was faced with stone, and the Renaissance volutes and other details were removed from the belfry, obscuring its original character, and making the attribution to Strickland more believable.[80] Yet old photographs and notes made for the renovation of 1926 show that the cathedral, built of brick, wood, and stucco, neither adapted nor imitated classical precedents with the sophistication and seriousness characteristic of Strickland's Grecian designs but was, like much of Heiman's architecture, a combination of Grecian and Renaissance themes.

Although Strickland probably did not design all the buildings attributed to him by local tradition, he was the architect of Tennessee's greatest Greek Revival monument, and through articles published in the *Orthopolitan* and *Port Folio* he brought Greek Revival theory to the attention of literary Tennesseans. Strickland was committed to the academic principles of the revival and convinced that "art is a subject more of reason than imagination,"[81] agreeing with eighteenth-century aestheticians that a sense of order and proportion was innate in both human imagination and classical models. Strickland assured students that "whatever they may produce from principles and rules, in the exercise of their labors will be sure to lead them onward with an irresistible impulse to the perfection which it should be their desire at all times to attain."[82] The proportion and symmetry of Greek temples were "not

155 (A)

at all conventional" but were produced by "the innate sense of the propriety of these laws of order."[83] Professor Nathaniel Cross summarized the argument of the classicists before the alumni of the University of Nashville, observing that "as connected with Aesthetics, or taste, the Greek and Latin authors . . . occupy . . . a position very different from the productions of modern times; and which entitles them to be considered undoubted standards, from which there may be no rational appeal."[84]

But the foundations were not secure. It was unclear even to the most knowledgeable exponents of the revival whether Grecian architecture was to be preferred on rationalist grounds—because its orders and proportions followed certain immutable principles—or whether it was to be imitated because it was traditional, its rules and principles following from its inherent authority. In its American manifestation the Greek Revival was a kind of revolutionary conservatism, whose proponents advocated one final uprising against other

155 (B)

155. (A) The sketch of Nashville's Roman Cathedral was drawn by W. A. Eichbaum before the cupola was added. (B) The Cathedral of Our Lady of the Seven Dolors was stuccoed and painted contrasting shades. Heiman built the house to the immediate right of the cathedral about 1850 and occupied it until 1855.

historicist traditions and a firm resolve to follow only classical principles. Such arguments tacitly concede that the tradition they advocate is historical invention. By the time Strickland came to Tennessee, the Greek Revival was already succumbing to a local idea of its uses which had nothing to do with the theories and careful archaeological approach of its early practitioners.

The Greek Revival represented the single serious attempt of the American architects to develop a national style from the architectural inheritance of Greece and Rome. But by 1850 the classical temper which had formed imagination from Washington to Jackson was challenged by the contemporary interest in medieval styles, and despite the disapproval of the religious establishment, Tennesseans read Sir Walter Scott as avidly as Cicero. Thirty years before Strickland's Capitol was begun in Nashville, George Tucker had foreseen the difficulties that would arise if the appeal to precedent and rule lost its hold over imagination: "Whether the rules of art, must ever remain stationary, or whether an uncontrolable thirst for novelty, may not hereafter embody some of the infinite diversity of untried forms: and, having once overleaped the bounds, which have hitherto checked the luxuriant wanderings of taste, at length incessantly effect capricious novelties, it is for time only to show."[85]

The Maxwell House was a fitting symbol of the end of the local Greek Revival. Begun in August 1859, the hotel was the work of Isaiah Rogers, designer of a fabled succession of southern and western hotels: the Charleston Hotel, the second St. Charles in New Orleans, Burnet House in Cincinnati, and Galt House in St. Louis. When Tennessee left the Union in the spring of 1862, the Maxwell House was just closed against the weather, and in this unfinished condition the building saw service as Zollicoffer Barracks and, after the Federal occupation of Nashville, as a hospital. Henry J. Dudley of New York brought Rogers' design to completion four years after the war, and the Maxwell House was opened on September 22, 1869, with a memorable inaugural banquet.[86]

The Maxwell House effectively replaced the Nashville Inn and the City Hotel—both victims of fire during the 1850s—a task Strickland's elegant hotel project of 1848, intended for the site of the Nashville Inn, might have accomplished had it been built. But in the years immediately preceding the war Nashville had changed. The Public Square was no longer the center of a city rapidly expanding to the south and west, and taste had also changed since the completion of the Capitol. The Maxwell House greeted its guests with an imposing porch of six tightly composed, two-story Corinthian columns. Beyond this portico and up a flight of marble stairs were elegant public rooms, illuminated by chandeliers and (in the dining room) skylights, and surrounded by balconies carried on rich, pink-veined columns, from which opened handsome suites and parlors. A pullman-riding clientele entered this world of light and luxury through a Corinthian porch which summarized the regional architecture of the 1850s, but the building itself was an Italianate block, its plan sensitively shaped by Rogers' interpretation of function and by the exigencies of the compact site at the northeast corner of Cherry and Spring. Although it seemed classic, the Maxwell House was touched by a new fascination with that "infinite diversity of untried forms," those "luxuriant wanderings of taste" which George Tucker had prophesied.

IX. THE ROMANTIC EYE

Everything exhibited a highly cultivated taste, and a proper appreciation of the truly beautiful. May these grounds become a "Paradise restored."

The Naturalist, 1850

Palladio prefaced his *Four Books of Architecture,* the sixteenth-century Italian treatise which more than any other shaped English appreciation of classical design, with the observation that "the ancient Romans, as in many other things, so in building well, vastly excelled all those who have been since their time." Inigo Jones, Christopher Wren, the Adams, and Stuart and Revett brought classical inspiration and classical models home to England from their European travels, and for 200 years architecture was largely determined by loyalty to the orders. But the Renaissance, with its printed treatises praising the antique, had shown that living tradition could be set aside by romantic imagination, which, abetted by the press, could bring the remote past to life and immediacy. Architecture could be reshaped by historical research, nostalgia, and printing as easily as Gibbon could transform the English understanding of Rome and the Middle Ages. Although Strickland would rely on Stuart and Revett's *Antiquities of Athens* until his death, classicism was one of several styles after 1790. Augustus Welby Pugin posed an alternative understanding of England's architectural past in his *Contrasts* (1836), arguing in his treatises on medieval church architecture that Gothic was the only style suitable for Christian civilization. Rationalists from C.N. Ledoux (1736–1806) to Gottfried Semper (1803–1879) anticipated the moderns, suggesting that a new architectural theory could be founded on pure geometric form.

By 1840 the public, uncertain that any of the available histories should be considered authoritative and largely uncomprehending of rationalists' attempts to overcome history, willingly welcomed the new romantic styles to their streets and countryside, often without paying much attention to the theoretical foundations. Of these new styles, the most important were Gothic, an interpretation of medieval English architecture exemplified by the Gothic works of Lafever, Town and Davis, Richard Upjohn, and James Dakin; and Italian (later called Italianate), an architecture developed from the irregular, towered villas of the Italian hill country and from the polished palazzo style of Florence and Venice. Gothic was the style for romantic country houses like John Notman's residence for Bishop George W. Doane in Burlington, New Jersey (1857), and Italian was popular for public buildings like Notman's Philadelphia Athenaeum (1845–1847) and

Minard Lafever's Brooklyn Savings Bank (1846–1847). Gothic, born as an architecture of fantasy, was especially susceptible to ideologically inspired interpretation, and after 1840 Americans—architects like Richard Upjohn and Frank Wills, critics like John Henry Hopkins, and theologians like Charles Tomes—followed Pugin and the *Ecclesiologist* in ascribing serious social or religious implications to its revival. But while the revivalists urged principles, the American architectural public read Scott, and most—if they thought at all about architectural theory—probably concluded that styles were merely pleasing historical vignettes. Even Grecian, though often defended as an architecture embodying permanent principles, was in some respects a product of romanticism.

The new romantic styles came to Tennessee about 1823, when Franklin's Gothic Revival Masonic Hall (156)[1] was built in imitation of William Strickland's Philadelphia Masonic Hall of 1811.[2] The three-story building has a flat, symmetrical façade; and tall pointed windows encourage the association with ecclesiastical

156. *The Masonic Hall in Franklin (Williamson County), built in 1823, was probably the first important Gothic Revival building in Tennessee. Compare the castellations and pinnacles with similar details at Franklin's Episcopal Church (119).*

157

158

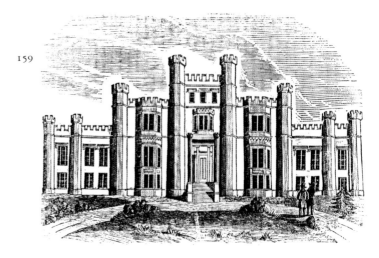

159

architecture that its designer probably intended. Although the architect's name has been lost, the building was clearly the work of a designer knowledgeable enough to follow the architectural fashions of Philadelphia. The first church building undertaken in the Gothic style was perhaps Christ Church, Nashville (7), designed by Hugh Roland and completed in 1831.[3] This stuccoed brick building, praised by Featherstonhaugh as "chaste" in 1834, stood at the northeast corner of High and Spring.[4] Like most Gothic buildings of the thirties, it employed nothing of the medieval structural system that Ruskin and Viollet-le-Duc later found praiseworthy, but the Gothic image was conveyed by the tower, pointed windows, pinnacles, castellations, and interior wooden arches.

In 1836 Tennessee's first Gothic Revival school, the pinnacled and crenelated building that Drummond and Lutterloh erected for the Female Institute, was built in Columbia (157).[5] Nathan Vaught recalled in 1871 that "It was built by Mr. Drummon"; and Caroline O'Reilly Nicholson recorded in her reminiscences that about 1836 or 1837 the Institute, the Roger Bradley Mayes house on West Sixth Street, and the Samuel Polk Walker house (158), later called the Athenaeum Rectory, were built, "all having been planned by the same architect, bearing the same characteristics of style and plan, and creating much interest by their novelty of structure."[6] The Institute was a "battlemented structure" with "Gothic turrets and Norman towers," originally stuccoed a grayish blue.[7] About 1848 J.H. Ingraham designed Tennessee's first Gothic college building for the Masonic College at Clarksville (159), and after his scheme was approved by the trustees of the college, working drawings were made by the young Nashville architect G. B. Vannoy.[8] The building took its place with James H. Dakin's Louisiana Capitol,[9] then under construction in Baton Rouge; the Columbia Female Institute; and the Georgia State Capitol in Mil-

ledgeville as one of the few monumental Gothic buildings in the South.

By 1850 most important towns had their Gothic churches. In 1844 the handsome Gothic Calvary Episcopal Church (12) was completed in Memphis. Calvary is usually attributed to its rector, Philip Alston, who Bishop Otey remembered "possessed no inconsiderable skill in limning and drawing"; however, a Memphis architect, perhaps Crane or Morrison, may have been the designer, or the undertaker, the enterprising W.A.

160. New York Architect Patrick C. Keely borrowed inspiration for St. Peter's, Memphis, from the twin towers of thirteenth-century English Gothic.

Bickford, may have furnished the plans.[10] The most imposing antebellum Gothic Revival building in Memphis was the work of the New York architect Patrick C. Keely, whose St. Peter's Church (160), a large stuccoed brick structure with martello towers, crenelations and pinnacles, and a finely detailed interior, was built between 1852 and 1858.[11] Keely, who described himself in the *Charleston Mercury* of August 1, 1850, as "a pupil (the only one in the United States) of the celebrated Pugin," had designed at least two dozen Gothic Revival churches during the forties and fifties, among them the Church of St. Peter and St. Paul, Williamsburgh

157. The castellated building of the Columbia Female Institute, advertised as resembling "the old castles of song and story," stood near Athenaeum Street between West Seventh and West Eighth.

158. The Samuel Polk Walker house built in Columbia about 1839 and the nearly contemporary Roger Bradley Mayes house, also in Columbia, were among the first Gothic Revival houses in Middle Tennessee, although the Walker house has also been called Moorish and is crowned by shapes reminiscent of the acroteria of a Greek temple.

159. J. H. Ingraham's Masonic College of 1848, Clarksville (Montgomery County), was conceived as a castle, complete with battlements and escutcheon.

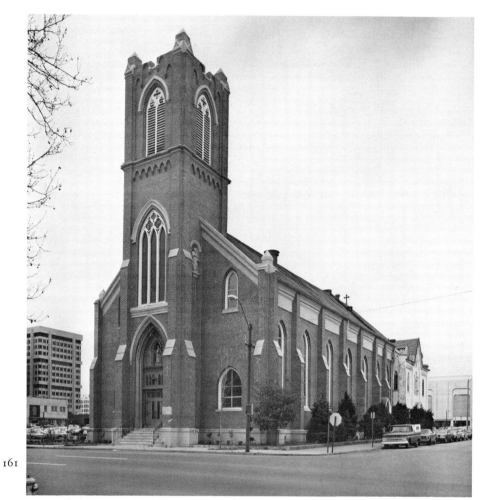

161

162

(Brooklyn); the Church of the Assumption (1848–1849) in Philadelphia; and the Cathedral of St. John and St. Finebar (1850–1854) in Charleston, built of Vermont sandstone in "Gothic or English ornamental" style. Keely's St. Peter's like Wills and Dudley's Church of the Holy Trinity in Nashville, was a good example of the stylish Gothic designs available from eastern architects. Memphis's little-known Presbyterian Church of 1852–1854, built on the northeast corner of Second and Poplar, also belonged to the revival. "The style of the architecture," wrote the editor of the *Whig*, "is Gothic, copied from the antique and sacred temples of the Middle Ages, and is unique and beautiful."[12] The next important Gothic Revival building in Memphis was James B. Cook's St. Mary's, begun in 1864 and still standing at 155 Market Street, which was completed after the war (161).[13]

The first Gothic church built in East Tennessee was Knoxville's St. John's Episcopal Church, begun in July 1844 under the leadership of Charles Tomes.[14] At Jonesboro the first signs of the Gothic Revival occurred in such details as the Gothic sash in the gable of the Snapp house (1830?) on Limestone Creek (87), and the pointed window in the tympanum of the Methodist Church (140), built in 1847, though these were as much survivals from eighteenth-century handbook practice as heralds of the Gothic Revival.

After 1810 Nashville, which in 1843 was designated the permanent capital of Tennessee, was the center of style as well as politics and commerce. One of the primary witnesses to the city's architectural importance is the beautifully embellished *Map of the City of Nashville and Edgefield*, which Haydon and Booth published in Philadelphia in 1860. The map located the city's important architecture and depicts in its border eighteen buildings or groups of buildings. The architect is named beneath ten of the buildings illustrated, and the authorship of many of these is documented elsewhere by contemporary sources. Of the works depicted, the Capitol (1845–1854) and the James K. Polk house (1848–1849) belong to the Greek Revival, only Strickland's building unambiguously. The other designs are all influenced heavily by the new Gothic or Italianate themes. The map depicts five Italianate build-

ings by Akeroyd: the Hicks and Ensley business blocks, Howard School, and the residences of J.B. Hayes and John D. Ewing. Also depicted are two Gothic Revival buildings, the Church of the Holy Trinity and the Church of the Advent, by the New York architect Frank Wills or his sometime partner Henry Dudley. The mapmakers included four of Adolphus Heiman's projects: Fatherland, the Italianate residence of General George Washington Barrow which Barrow's father-in-law, John Shelby, had built about 1857; the Gothic Revival Literary Department of the University of Nashville (1854); the Italianate Masonic Hall of 1860; and Colonel Joseph A.S. Acklen's Belmont, an 1859 villa designed in a sensitive combination of Grecian, Italianate, and Renaissance styles. Heiman and Akeroyd, clearly Nashville's leading architects in 1860, were largely responsible for the triumph of architectural romanticism in Tennessee's capital. They were very different men. Heiman was a Prussian artisan who distinguished himself in the Mexican War and died in the service of the Confederacy. He developed an extensive and fashionable practice designing in the Grecian, Gothic, and Italianate styles. Akeroyd, a young Englishman educated to the profession, came to Nashville with his bride Isabella about the time of Strickland's death in 1854. Akeroyd made a fine reputation as the master of Italian style; he fled before the Federals occupied Nashville in 1862.[15]

Heiman the stonecutter came to Nashville about 1837 "full of activity" and "desiring employment in cutting the finest variety of granite or marble."[16] He had been in the United States since the spring of 1834 and had spent some time first in New York and then in New Orleans.[17] In addition to his skill, his knowledge of architecture in Europe, New York, and New Orleans, and the recommendation of Humboldt, Adolphus Heiman brought with him a sixteenth-century copy of Giacomo da Vignola's *Regola delli Cinque Ordini d'Architettura*, a scholarly treatise that had been a standard reference work for architecture students for 200 years. Heiman's copy, probably published about 1590, was a family possession, and in his hands it symbolized an inherited interest in architecture and landscape. Heiman's father had been superintendent at Frederick the Great's Sans Souci,[18] so Adolphus Heiman had grown up amid an interest in buildings and gardens. He was working at his trade in 1841, when he was paid for repairing the stone steps at the University,[19] and at about the same time he completed his first known architectural commission, the Baptist Church on Summer Street, begun in 1837.[20] An engraving of the building made in 1857 for the *Baptist Family Visitor* (162) depicts a Gothic design with pinnacles and castel-

161. Begun in 1864, St. Mary's Catholic Church in Memphis perpetuated the central-tower Gothic image, a type first represented by Nashville's Christ Church (7) and perfected by the nearby Calvary Episcopal Church (12) in Memphis.

162. First Baptist Church, built on the east side of Summer Street (Fifth) north of Spring (Church) between 1837 and 1841, was Adolphus Heiman's first important commission in Nashville.

lations, the style Heiman would often use for churches and colleges. By 1843 Heiman was making technical drawings like the careful delineation of the apparatus for "Laning's Soda Fount" (which finally found its way to the State Library) and in the same year was admitted to the prestigious Cumberland Lodge of the Masonic Order. By 1845 he was competing, albeit unsuccessfully, with William Strickland for the Capitol commission.[21] Heiman's design for the Capitol has not been discovered, but commissioners knowledgeable enough to send away for Town and Davis' plans of the North Carolina statehouse and to solicit a design from James H. Dakin of New Orleans were not likely to give the most important commission in the history of the state to a young stonecutter who spoke with a German accent and worked with his hands.[22]

Almost nothing is known of Heiman's career between 1841 and 1848, so his progress from artisan to architect is obscure. Perhaps he ceased to be a craftsman and became a designer when his military skill and bravery came to the attention of a society that still considered valor and military rank prerequisites for public office and professional status. To Nashvillians, Strickland was always Major Strickland, and in Memphis David Morrison was Colonel Morrison. Adolphus Heiman was commissioned lieutenant in the First Regiment of Tennessee Volunteers when war was declared against Mexico in the spring of 1846. He served as adjutant to Colonel William B. Campbell, he fought valiantly, and he returned a hero. Heiman was praised by his commander and honored by Cumberland Lodge No. 8, whose members voted to confer on him "free of charge the orders of Knight of the Red Cross, Knight Templar and Knight of Malta."[23] After 1846 Heiman's skill and military distinction made him Strickland's peer to Nashvillians.

The first important commission Heiman undertook after his return was the suspension bridge across the Cumberland. Charles Ellet had spanned the Schuylkill near Philadelphia in 1842 and had begun his suspension bridge across the Ohio at Wheeling in 1847. The Nashville bridge, started in 1848, was to be another in this succession of technological triumphs. But soon after work was initiated, Heiman resigned because M.D. Field, the contractor who had employed him, ignored his advice regarding the location of the footings. Heiman's fears were justified. The bridge was strengthened in 1853 but gave way on June 16, 1855.[24] Despite the bad reputation of the suspension bridge, Heiman's part in its design was remembered favorably, and he continued to receive important commissions: the asylum in 1849, the Adelphi Theater[25] and the William Walton residence on Dickerson Pike in 1850,[26] and the Medical College in 1851.

In 1850 Heiman bought the lot immediately south of the Catholic cathedral, across the street from Strickland's monumental Kirkman house,[27] and soon afterward built a two-story town house for his own use (155). The move signaled Heiman's arrival in the best of Nashville's social and political circles. The *Daily Evening Reporter* commented on September 13, 1850, that the talents of the architect were "so well known, that a word of praise would be superfluous" and the next year Heiman's reputation was such that his former commander, Governor William B. Campbell, recommended him to sit with Major P.T. Beauregard, Major William H. Chase, Lewis E. Reynolds, and the Boston architect Ammi B. Young on a board convened by the Treasury Department to settle the dispute then raging around the half-completed New Orleans Custom House. Work had stopped because of differences between the architect James H. Dakin, Senator Pierre Soulé, protector of the interests of New Orleans' First Municipality, and A.T. Wood, the architect dismissed by the Treasury Department early in 1850 in Dakin's favor. Adolphus Heiman was in New Orleans from November 1851 until mid-January, remaining after the commission had recessed to assist Major Beauregard, a military engineer assigned to supervise the project, by producing the design the commissioners had recommended.[28] The earliest drawings in the voluminous file on the New Orleans Custom House retained in the National Archives were probably made by Heiman and his draftsmen in January 1852, but only Beauregard signed the finished sheets; therefore there is nothing to identify Heiman's work. In New Orleans, Adolphus Heiman met James H. Dakin, Ammi B. Young, and A.T. Wood as peers. Heiman was forty-one, and the visit to the city where he had begun his career in the South as a workman on the Pontchartrain Canal in 1837[29] probably influenced his subsequent development.

The first building Heiman had designed in Tennessee, the Baptist Church on Summer Street, was Gothic,

163. *Heiman's Hospital for the Insane, built near Nashville on Murfreesboro Road between 1851 and 1854, was a towered medieval castle.*

164. *Heiman's first scheme for the Literary Department of the University of Nashville called for an elaborate Gothic complex reminiscent of James Dakin's New York University building (1836). The chapel (left) was never built in Nashville, but Heiman used a similar design for the Huntsville, Alabama, Presbyterian Church in 1858, and the entire college scheme is nearly identical to Heiman's design for Southern University in Greensboro, Alabama.*

163

164

and he used that style frequently during the fifties, first at the new Hospital for the Insane (163), erected in 1851 to replace the asylum of 1831. During the winter of 1849–1850, Heiman had inspected hospitals in the eastern cities, and the plan he selected for Nashville was copied from the Butler Asylum in Providence, Rhode Island (1844), a building derived from the hospital for the insane in Maidstone, England. In his report to the trustees, Heiman described the asylum as "a structure erected in the castellated style: its extreme length from east to west is four hundred and five feet." "The building is constructed with twenty-four octagon towers... placed on the corners of the centre building and wings, rising eight feet above the battlements."[30] The building for the Literary Department of the University followed in 1852–1853 (164); Hume School in 1853–1854 (165);[31] the barracks for Western Military

165. *The Nashville Free School, named for Alfred Hume, was completed in 1854 at the northeast corner of Spruce (Eighth) and Broad in Nashville.*

Institute when it became part of the University the next year;[32] and both St. John's College, Little Rock,[33] and Southern University in Greensboro, Alabama,[34] in 1857–1859. In these castellated designs, Heiman usually subordinated Gothic details to symmetry, often by the use of centrally placed vertical elements. At the Hospital for the Insane, the University of Nashville, and Southern University, a dominant central block was crowned by a tower, a favorite design element of Heiman's which also appeared in his Italianate and Grecian designs of the late 1850s, at the remodeled Nashville city offices (166) of 1855 (if the attribution is

correct),[35] at Fatherland (167), at his own cottage in north Nashville (169), and at Belmont (171).

Of Heiman's castellated projects, the grandest was his scheme for the University of Nashville, a commission he was given after plans provided by Isaiah Rogers of Cincinnati proved too expensive,[36] but the same impecuniousness that had caused the trustees to reject Rogers' design prevented the completion of Heiman's. Originally conceived as a building containing not only classrooms but a dispensary, chapel, and museum, only the central portion was built. The building was constructed of limestone blocks in 1853 and 1854 at a cost of $45,000.[37] If the tower shown in engravings was ever constructed, it was removed before the University's grounds were photographed during the Federal occupation. The tower remains something of a mystery, for it appears in engravings and lithographs in several versions. One, published in the University's *Announcements* for 1854–1855, resembles the single square tower of Southern University (164); another, showing this square tower crowned with a graceful Gothic cupola, appeared in the *Medical Department Catalogue for the Session of 1857–58 and Announcements for the Session 1858–59*, as an embellishment on the Haydon and Booth map of 1860, and in the *Nashville City Directory* of 1860–1861. Yet a third, in which two secondary towers flank the central tower and the cupola is wanting, appeared in John Cornman's *The City of Nashville* (1888?). Perhaps these different representations depict successive additions and renovations, but no photograph showing the tower (or towers) has been found, leaving the single most persuasive piece of evidence the tower base, which is still in place.

From 1845 to 1854 Heiman designed in the contemporary popular styles, alternating between Gothic

166. *The towers, the shallow triangular pediment, the brackets or consoles at the window heads and sills, and stuccoed front all suggest that Adolphus Heiman may have been responsible for remodeling the Nashville City Hall about 1855. This office building was the south terminus of the market house that had occupied the west side of the square since 1829.*

167. *(A) As the lithograph shows, John Shelby's Fatherland, which by 1860 had been inherited by George W. Barrow, was a romantically classic Italian villa. Heiman's use of an identical porch at the William Law Murfree house and at Elmwood (173) suggests that he may have designed the Christopher H. Smith house in Clarksville (198). (B) The owner's failure to supply or maintain the delicate Grecian details and the stucco depicted in the lithograph of Fatherland deprived the building of the dramatic contrast between plain surfaces and rich detail which Heiman had intended.*

166

167 (A)

167 (B)

dling," cannot appear for
as not sent us his name,
postage.

ly will be ready for deliv-

yesterday prevented us
sertion to the communi-
respondent R., we give it
g so would tell the critic
quote correctly. He can-
t follows except in the
ing from his pen:—"Miss
quals and no superiors on

g Reporter of the 11th
—"As a correct reader,
no superior in this or any
an actress, she has few
e can assure the critic D.,
d up to the rack" and re-
tion as often as he chooses
nd we further assure him
been "pent up in the city
life," we have seen as
this country and Europe
e, critic. We should not

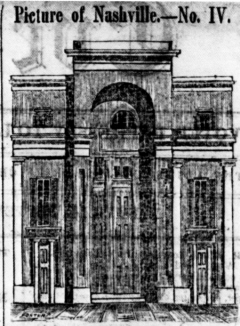

Picture of Nashville.—No. IV.

THE NEW ADELPHI THEATRE.

Our artist has been, as usual, very correct in the illustration for to-day's paper.—
The Adelphi Theatre was built by a joint
stock company, acting under a charter
from the Legislature of Tennessee.
The building is 142 feet deep and 65

A Good Story.

The following capital stor
from a letter to the Alabama
J. Hooper:
"Shall I tell you a bit of a
no connection with politics,
weather? By permission—
"Old Col. D——, of the
trict, was one of the most sin
ters ever known in Alabama.
ty and eccentric, but possess
qualities, which were fully a
the people of the district.
freaks are afresh in the memo
uns' of Mobile—and all of th
you, that the Colonel, though
was once terribly taken in b
legal tyros. It is George We
lieve, tells the story, but how
be, it is in keeping with oth
the old gentleman.
"It seems that Col. D——
misunderstanding with the tw
alluded to, and was not on s
with them, although all of th
professionally riding the circu
together. The young ones
aware of the Colonel's irasci
termined as they left one of
another, to have some sport
by the way. They accordin
half an hour's start in leaving
ly they arrived at a broad, da

168

169

and Grecian as the client and the work demanded. The third distinctive style Heiman employed was a carefully controlled combination of Italianate and classical themes determined partly by his own interpretation of the classical tradition, partly by his acquaintance with the Renaissance Revival designs of architects like Lafever, and partly by the pervasive popularity of the towered Italian or Tuscan style, with its tall ceilings, rich enframements, and irregular porches. The sumptuous Adelphi Theater (168), completed in 1850 on the west side of Cherry Street north of Cedar, was composed of a large entrance arch, "copied from the triumphal arches of Rome," which was buttressed by the lower mass of the auditorium. Finished in red damask and boasting a lyre-shaped dress circle, the Adelphi was proclaimed a triumph by the *Daily Evening Reporter* of September 20.

The house Heiman built for himself immediately south of the cathedral on Summer Street about 1850 foreshadowed this style (155 A), and the William Law Murfree house on Vauxhall Place (1854) represents its developed phase.[38] When the architect built his towered cottage on Jefferson Street (169), probably about 1855, he seemingly abandoned classical principles, adopting the irregular plan, porches, and cast iron of the Downing style;[39] but in most of Heiman's villas Italianate themes are subordinated to a formality that he seemed unwilling to abandon. Dr. John Shelby's Fatherland, built in Edgefield about 1857, illustrates his ability to create an Italianate villa in the contemporary manner which nevertheless remained controlled and traditional (167). Elmwood, begun on Thompson Lane near Nashville by W.W. Berry in 1861, was a large, suburban plantation house in which Italianate windows, the classical orders, and—at least in one façade—strict symmetry were combined (173). As the fifties wore on, Heiman used brackets, heavy lintels and enframements, and Italianate fenestration more frequently.

Belmont—or Belle Monte, which was the name Adelicia Acklen gave the house—belongs precisely to none of Heiman's familiar styles, though between it and

168. Nashville's new Adelphi Theater, a Heiman design completed on the west side of Cherry Street (Fourth Avenue) north of Cedar (Charlotte) in 1850, illustrates the architect's eclectic use of classical elements.

169. About 1855 Adolphus Heiman built this Italianate cottage at the northwest corner of Jefferson and McLemore (Ninth Avenue) in Nashville. The Eastlake window cap belongs to a later remodeling of the original arched opening.

the Nashville Masonic Hall of 1851 (31) there is a clear relationship. Built on the wooded, suburban plantation of Joseph and Adelicia Acklen southwest of Nashville, Belmont has a singular loveliness (17, 171). Although the building has often been considered William Strickland's, the Nashville map of 1860 attributes the "Residence of Col. Acklen" to "A. Heiman, Archt." An account written in 1867, shortly after Adelicia Acklen's marriage to W. A. Cheatham, names as Heiman's patron Joseph Acklen, who, "possessing refined taste and cultivation, made improvements in their large estate near Nashville, building a magnificent house, Italian in its style of architecture. It stands on the summit of a hill; the grounds surrounding it are highly ornamented, and the spacious greenhouses and conservatories are filled with choice flowers. This villa, called 'Bellemonte'—is said to be the most beautiful in the southwest."[40] Though Adelicia Acklen had a consuming interest in things European, the continental *mise en scène* was probably the work of Joseph Acklen's architect. Adelicia Acklen did not visit Europe until the summer of 1865, and she returned convinced that no place was as lovely as her villa in Nashville's suburbs. She wrote of Italian skies in February 1866: "I do not find them more bright than our own, nor have I seen a sun-set to equal many I have witnessed at Belle Monte." When she reached Newport on her journey home she wrote to her mother, "I have had (more especially when young) an ardent desire to visit Europe, and see something of the world on the other side of the great Ocean—now that wish is gratified, and I hope too to the benefit of my children."[41] In Adolphus Heiman, Colonel Acklen found an architect who knew something of Italian Renaissance architecture and who remembered the romantic European gardens of the early nineteenth century.

The development of the site was begun in 1853, when the Acklens built a summer villa on their estate. This was probably the house near Nashville that J.H. Ingraham described as "built after the plan of the Borghese Palace at Rome . . . furnished throughout with furniture made to order in Paris" and "adorned with European pictures and statuary."[42] Like the Roman original, the casino or summer house built near Porta Pinciana in 1632 by Cardinal Scipione Borghese, the Acklen villa consisted of a two-story central block with flanking belvederes and with wings extending down a pronounced slope to form a courtyard one story below the principal rooms. This Middle Tennessee version of the Borghese casino was remodeled in 1859 to provide a year-round residence of the Acklens.[43] Heiman enclosed part of the courtyard to create the ballroom, enclosed the second-story gallery at the rear of the

170

171

house, added the flanking wings and cast iron porches, and replaced the twin belvederes with the central belvedere presently in place. Before the house were elaborate gardens laid out with that fine combination of formality and irregularity that Downing approved. Statues, most of which still stand about the gardens, broke the skyline from plinths in the parapet; and stuccoed walls, struck in an ashlar pattern and painted ocher, provided a foil for Belmont's white columns and pilasters. Mother Frances Walsh of the Dominican Sisters remembered that Nashvillians had called Belmont "The Acklen Folly," and her description of visits to the house between 1860 and 1862 are the most complete surviving from the period before the fall of Nashville and the death of Joseph Acklen in 1863:

> On viewing the vista that opened up from the grand avenue thoughts of villas near the seven hilled city or gorgeous scenes in the vicinity of Paris arose in the mind. . . . A most gracious welcome was accorded the visitors, who were made to feel at home in the spacious reception hall, the surroundings suggestive of oriental luxury. The floor tessellated, a miniature fountain in the center sent up its misty spray. . . .
>
> Works of art, collected for the most part in Europe, adorned walls and niches. . . . On leave taking a scene of sylvan lovliness greeted the view; such a dazzling array of art and nature, commingling so as to beautify each other, was arranged as by the hand of a master artist. Here and there were statuary, marble and bronze, placed in groups or singly. Fountains, costly vases and flowers of the richest hues intermingled in endless profusion. There were summer houses and grottos of all devices, some so dainty that they might be the fitting haunts of wood-nymphs or water-sprites.[44]

Stylistically, Belmont is unique. Deference is shown the local and Renaissance love of symmetry and precedent, but the composition owes little to the direct inspiration of the Greek Revival, much to a romantic, somewhat Italianate, classicism of the type Lafever had depicted (170) in his *Architectural Instructor* and other works. The carefully modulated mass is surmounted by a belvedere, and wings are set behind the façade, a popular compositional scheme that reinforces the pronounced centrality which Heiman favored. The princi-

pal rooms open onto a terrace extending across the entire width of the main block. The façade is rather compressed and a trifle overly vertical. Pilasters at the corners bind the composition together. The second-story porch in the principal elevation is recessed, allowing the railing to finish flush with the façade. The columns, like those illustrated in Vignola's *Regola,* lack entasis, and the capitals are composite. Belmont has details that belong to Heiman's mature Italianate style: the interior cornices and brackets, colored glass and Italianate windows in the ballroom. However, the controlling image is the balustered Italian villa, its statuary silhouetted, with a complex mass that builds toward the belvedere (171).

Belmont was soon considered Nashville's finest estate, and its designer was clearly Middle Tennessee's master of elegant residential architecture. The Acklens' house was the single country villa depicted by Haydon and Booth in 1860, but it was only one of several, all resembling Belmont in important respects, built or remodeled in Tennessee during the forties and fifties. The others were Andrew Polk's monumental Ashwood Hall (191) in Maury County, remodeled in the 1850s; George Polk's Rattle and Snap (190), built near Columbia about 1845; Manor Hall (195) in Mount Pleasant, 1849; Belle Meade (196) in Davidson County, 1852–1853; and the Samuel Mayes house (194) in Columbia, 1858. Like Belmont, these buildings combine themes borrowed from the Greek Revival with influences deriving from the new Italianate style. The character that links these houses with the residential designs of James H. Dakin in New Orleans and Town and Davis in New York is a pronounced freedom in appropriating Greek forms and details, a spirit quite different from Morrison's Doric buildings of the 1830s. Other Tennessee examples of this romantic Grecian of the fifties include town houses like the William Batte house (*c.* 1848) in Pulaski, the Nathan Green house in Lebanon (1853), and the Littleton house in Memphis (1860?),[45] all buildings which illustrate the resonance between the stylish romantic conservatism of the South and the architecture of Lafever, Dakin, and Town and Davis.

Belle Meade, its stone portico derived from the Choragic Monument of Thrasyllus, a precedent followed at Bocage and Ashland in Louisiana as well,[46] is the only Middle Tennessee villa of the 1850s obviously influenced by an antique model. Although Belle Meade was built about seven years before Belmont, and thus the contemporary of Heiman's Grecian designs for the Masonic Hall (31) and the Medical Department of the University of Nashville (152c), it is nevertheless a highly romantic design, especially so in the context of

170. This design of a villa from Minard Lafever's Architectural Instructor *illustrates the romanticizing of the classical tradition which preceded its dissolution. Belmont (171) reflects this influence.*

171. Adolphus Heiman built Belmont (Belle Monte) in Nashville for Colonel Joseph A. S. Acklen in 1859. The projecting porches are developments of a feature Heiman often used, and the distyle in antis porch had appeared in his repertoire with the Masonic Hall of 1851 (31). The statues originally stood on the plinths of the parapet.

its gardens, which, like Belmont's, had auxiliary buildings—at Belle Meade a Grecian crypt and a Gothic gardener's cottage.[47] Adolphus Heiman remains a likely source for this design. Even the carefully detailed stone porch at Belle Meade does not quite show the finesse Strickland had displayed at the Hugh Kirkman house five years earlier, and by 1853, the date traditionally given Belle Meade, Strickland was already partly incapacitated.[48]

Rattle and Snap, the George Polk plantation house in Maury County (190), could be a plate from Minard Lafever's *Modern Builder's Guide* (1833). Letters written at Rattle and Snap in 1845[49] exist, but if the present house was completed as early as 1844, it was the most advanced Grecian design in the state. There are arcuated secondary openings, and its compact, attenuated proportions give the house an Italianate flavor. The broken range of rich Corinthian columns is unique in Tennessee architectural history. The plan resembles that of Hamilton Place, the nearby Lucius Polk house (41), built in 1832, having a large central hall with a secondary, transverse stair hall leading from it at the rear. Rattle and Snap, its ten white columns thrown against the blue-grey stucco of the façade, presents one of the grandest architectural images in Tennessee.

Three other romantic Grecian houses in Maury County are remarkable for their beauty and are strikingly similar. Both Andrew Polk's Ashwood Hall (191) and nearby Mercer Hall[50] are remodeled versions of houses built in the 1830s. In 1853 Andrew Polk employed James M. Hughes "to erect some buildings" and Hughes tried, unsuccessfully, to secure the services of Francis Strickland as architect.[51] Whether Hughes found another architect for Andrew Polk or drew the plans himself, he was still at work on a job "for one of the Polks in Maury County" in 1857, when, in Nicholas Hobson's opinion, Hughes's employment in Maury and Giles counties had caused him to neglect his duties at Wesley Wheless's house in Nashville. So between 1853 and 1857 Hughes may have remodeled Ashwood Hall from the house built by Andrew's brother Leonidas Polk about 1837. Certainly a comparison between Ashwood Hall and James M. Hughes's Bank of Nashville (19), built in 1853, makes their common authorship a possibility. Mercer Hall, originally the William Leacock house, was remodeled either shortly before Bishop James Henry Otey moved to Memphis in 1853 or soon afterward by the new owner Narcissa Martin. The segmental window heads and paired brackets at Mercer Hall occur again in the third house belonging to this group, the Samuel Mayes house in Columbia (194). These Middle Tennessee villas are all

examples of the romantic classicism that Adolphus Heiman's Belmont epitomized. They do not belong precisely to the Greek Revival and are too stylish to be quite typical of the plantation architecture of the 1850s. Except for the suggestive but obscure connection between Francis Strickland, James M. Hughes, and Andrew Polk, nothing is known of their architects.

During the twenty-five years Heiman practiced in Nashville, his work was subject to the influences that guided the development of style on the eastern seaboard, and in the late fifties he retained command of the entire current vocabulary of styles. In 1857 he built the chapel originally designed for the University of Nashville for the congregation of the First Presbyterian Church, Huntsville, Alabama.[52] The Nashville Masonic Hall, begun in 1858 after a fire destroyed the building he had remodeled in 1852, was a symmetrical four-story Italianate block, its parapet crowned by an acroterium which provided the single clear allusion to the classical tradition. The next year in his design for the new courthouse in Pulaski, Heiman returned to Renaissance classicism. The two-story brick building had a hipped roof, and porches with the shallow pediment the architect preferred were centered on the principal axes (172). The building carried an octagonal cupola with Corinthian columns at the angles and a ribbed dome, a sixteenth-century form Heiman could have derived from many sources, among them Vignola's domes at St. Peter's.[53] Heiman was so pleased with the Pulaski cupola that he used it on the greenhouse and the art gallery at Belmont soon afterward. Heiman's development in 1861 is illustrated by Elmwood, the Berry house built on the Middle Franklin Pike near Nashville (173). There the tight, central composition that Heiman preferred is attained by projecting the center of the main block forward, as at the house on Summer Street (1850), the Murfree house (1854), and Fatherland (1857). At Elmwood the porch is but one story tall, topped with a balustrade, and there are numerous Italianate features—the elaborately decorated window caps, each crowned with a cartouche, quoins, and the asymmetrically placed tower.

172. The Giles County Courthouse was designed and built by Adolphus Heiman in 1858–1859. The two-story entrance arch repeats the theme of the Adelphi (168), and the cupola was later used at Belmont and the Cathedral.

173. Elmwood, the Berry house built near Nashville in what is now the suburban city of Berry Hills, was designed by Heiman about 1861. By then he had mastered the Italianate system of details: decorated caps, brackets, quoins, and arcuated windows.

172

173

174. The Bryce Stewart house in Clarksville (Montgomery County), designed by Adolphus Heiman about 1861, was a princely mansion in the Italiante style.

Heiman's architectural career was ended by the war. On April 21, 1861, he wrote his old mentor, former Governor W.B. Campbell, asking Campbell's advice and deploring "the destruction of this great Republic for which the world will have to mourn." But while Heiman wrote, a delegation interrupted to invite him to command a company "composed of gentlemen of education and standing, who were as strong as myself for the preservation of the Union as long as there was a shadow of hope." Carpenters and bricklayers working at Elmwood laid aside their tools. The enormous Italianate villa Heiman was building for Bryce Stewart on a hilltop near Clarksville, then only a few miles behind the Confederacy's northern frontier, would remain unfinished (174). The architect took command of the Tennessee Tenth in May 1861. When the forts on the lower Tennessee fell in February 1862, Colonel Heiman was captured and imprisoned at Fort Warren in Boston Harbor. In the autumn he was exchanged, and the Tennessee Tenth was reorganized at Clinton, Mississippi, under Heiman's command. But his health was

broken, and early in December Adolphus Heiman died peacefully at Jackson, Mississippi, having been promoted to brigadier only a few weeks before.[54]

By 1869 Nashvillians had recovered from their defeat enough to begin to remember the fallen in the bloody war as heroes, and Heiman's body was located, disinterred, and transported to Nashville, where the men of his old regiment, the north Nashville Germantown community, and the Masons met the train bearing his remains. The obituaries suggest that in 1869 Tennesseans were more interested in Heiman's military distinction than in his buildings, and soon his prodigious architectural career was mostly forgotten. By 1920 William Strickland's reputation as an important architect of the Greek Revival was well established, and Tennesseans willingly speculated that, besides the Capitol and the Presbyterian Church, Strickland might have built many fine residences in Middle Tennessee. Yet to Nashvillians, Heiman, as the *American* noted on November 6, 1850, had been "our tasteful and elegant architect," while Strickland was the prototypical architect from Philadelphia, the masterful designer from the acknowledged capital of fashion who journeyed to the Old Southwest to erect stylish buildings. When Strickland died, obituaries published in Nashville routinely described him as architect of the State Capitol. Heiman was remembered in 1869 as an architect who furnished "plans for many churches and private residences."

The years between Strickland's death in 1854 and the war witnessed local acceptance of the national movement toward irregularity, informality, and the integration of architecture and landscape. In *Cottage Residences* (1842) Downing recommended "an irregular villa in the Italian style" that resembled Heiman's towered cottage on Jefferson Street to "persons who have cultivated an architectural taste, and who relish the higher beauties of art growing out of variety."[55] Such designs, Downing wrote, were "capable of awakening more strongly emotions of the beautiful or picturesque, as well as the useful or convenient." The house on Jefferson Street may have been Heiman's first experiment in planning such an irregular cottage, but soon elements from the Italianate vocabulary began to appear in his designs. The window that is frequently associated with the Italianate style, two tall, narrow arcuated shapes surmounted by a circular element, appears frequently in his later works, and Elmwood (1861–1867), though it had a classic porch and symmetrical façade, was Italianate (173). Despite the success of villas like Fatherland and Kingsley,[56] Nashvillians did not relish irregularity in design, and the traditional imagination of the eighteenth century did not fade until after 1865. Adolphus Heiman considered himself a disciple of Vignola, writing of the five orders on June 1, 1857, that any man, "great as his genius as an Architect may be, could "lay hands on their fair proportions" only at the risk of punishing himself.[57] The orders were the standards "to which Architects in all civilized countries have adhered," and this loyalty to the classical tradition gave Heiman's designs a seriousness that antebellum architecture often lacked. Castellated, Gothic, Italianate, the architecture of Vignola, the local preference for symmetry and apparent order, and his own education as an artisan in early nineteenth-century Prussia were sources from which Heiman took themes which recur in his work. His Italicisms, the belvederes, arched fenestration, and romantic gardens are not simply borrowed from A.J. Downing but are sensitive combinations of Renais-

sance, Grecian, and American Italianate themes.

The English-born architect Harvey M. Akeroyd—his name was difficult for Tennesseans, appearing sometimes as Ackroyd, Ackeroyd, and Ackeroid—deserves mention not only for his handsome Italianate designs, but because he was the first of the new professionals, men like Edward Culliat Jones and James B. Cook who brought highly developed romantic styles from Europe and the seaboard on the eve of the war. Akeroyd's designs were usually Italianate, with the windows, ornament, and enframements that mark that style. He was also partly responsible for popularizing the new commercial blocks, much in the manner of Field's *City Architecture*, that began to encircle the Nashville Public Square about 1855. Akeroyd practiced in Nashville about six years. After Francis W. Strickland, who had inherited his father's post as architect of the Capitol, was dismissed in May 1857, Akeroyd was employed. Two years later he was commissioned to build Howard School (175) on the east side of College Street (Third Avenue) near the University.[58] About 1860 Akeroyd designed St. Peter's Episcopal Church in Columbia,[59] and the Haydon and Booth map attributes the Hicks and Ensley blocks on

175. *The tower and arcuated windows of Howard School, Nashville, designed by Harvey M. Akeroyd about 1859, make the building an advanced Italianate design.*

176. *The house second from right, built about 1860 on South Spruce (Eighth Avenue, North) was the Italianate town house of William P. Bryan. The house was occupied by Ward's Seminary from 1866 until its merger with Belmont College in 1912. The building at the left margin of the photograph, the residence and office of Dr. Christopher Giles Savage, is the only private house remaining in downtown Nashville.*

Nashville's Public Square, buildings in which the new cast-iron store fronts were used, to the English architect. The interior of the State Library in the Capitol, cast-iron shelving set on delicate iron balconies to which a graceful spiral stair leads, was designed by Akeroyd in 1859 and ordered from the Philadelphia works of Wood and Perot. Laid over Strickland's classic pilasters, Akeroyd's cast-iron scheme, adapted from Sir Walter Scott's library at Abbotsford, signified the turn imagination had taken since the Capitol was begun in 1845.[60] Harvey M. Akeroyd disappears from Tennessee architectural history in the winter of 1861–1862, when he departed for the North, leaving unfinished the school and convent of the Dominican Sisters in north Nashville, perhaps his only work remaining in Davidson County.[61] Several other buildings in an Italianate style similar to Akeroyd's were constructed in Nashville during the late fifties: the George W. Cunningham house on High Street (Sixth Avenue),[62] the William P.

Bryan house (176) on Spruce (Eighth Avenue) just south of Spring Street,[63] and the Spring Street Baptist Church at Spring and Polk Avenue.[64]

Just as most architects had learned the Grecian style during the thirties, most learned during the forties to design in the Gothic and Italianate styles. James M. Hughes, who is first known in 1844 as the architect of Nashville's Greek Revival Second Presbyterian Church, was at work by 1856 on Wesley Wheless' large Gothic mansion (177), a building in the style of Alexander Jackson Davis's Blithewood (1834) at Fishkill, New York, which Davis included in his *Rural Residences*

(1837). George Spencer built not only the Episcopal Church but several other Italianate buildings in Greeneville.[65] Several important Italianate or Gothic buildings were the work of designers not yet identified, among them the Elisha Johnson house (178) in Monroe County (c. 1845)[66] and the Gothic Revival house that Charles McClung McGhee built in Monroe County about 1857 (179), a design sufficiently stylish to recall the plans for the rectory at St. Andrew's Church (furnished perhaps by Richard Upjohn), which were mentioned in the correspondence engendered by the church's controversial liturgical furnishings. The Reverend Charles Tomes, English-born rector of Christ Church, came to Nashville from New York in 1848 and about 1854 began Glenoak (180) on a hilltop southwest of the city. Glenoak has many cousins, dwellings like the G.M. Wellons house in Bolivar (181), Oakley near Gallatin,[67] and the Matthew Aiken house in Jonesboro.[68] There was seemingly no institutional

177. The Wesley Wheless house, designed and built by James M. Hughes in 1856–1857, was an imposing mansion in the Gothic style Alexander Jackson Davis had popularized in the North. The house stood on the north bank of the Cumberland about two miles east of Nashville.

178. The Elisha Johnson house near Tellico Plains in Monroe County, built about 1845, was a romantic villa of the type recommended by A.J. Downing. ▶

179. Built about 1857, the Charles McClung McGhee house in Monroe County is a stylish residential example of Gothic.

180. Charles Tomes, rector of Christ Church, Nashville, who employed Frank Wills to design the Church of the Holy Trinity, built his own Glenoak in Gothic style.

181. The G.M. Wellons house, built in Bolivar (Hardeman County) about 1860, is a stylish Gothic cottage designed by Fletcher Sloan, a brother of Samuel Sloan of Philadelphia, the architect of Longwood, a famous Moorish fantasy built near Natchez at about the same time.

178

179

180

181

182

183

use for which Gothic was considered inappropriate. The railroad depot in Nashville was a Gothic Revival building of the early 1850s,[69] and before 1861 Knoxville had an imposing castellated jail and three Gothic Revival churches: William Homer's St. John's Episcopal (1845–1846); the tiny stone Catholic church on Summit Hill (182), built in 1852; and Second Presbyterian (13), built on the north side of Clinch Street in 1860.[70]

182. Knoxville's first Catholic Church, a tiny stone building erected in 1852, was an academically correct Gothic design, probably the work of an eastern architect. The building was razed about 1886 to make room for the apse of the church, which still stands on Summit Hill (214).

183. The residence of the Reverend David H. Pise was built in Columbia (Maury County) about 1858 in a Swiss chalet style, another of the romantic modes encouraged by Downing's horticultural romanticism.

184. Now called Annesdale after the wife gets second owner, this towered Italianate villa may have been built Samuel Mansfield, a successful Memphis druggist. The porch at the right and the second-story window trim are later replacements or additions.

A few houses were built in the chalet style, among them the David H. Pise house in Columbia (183), Hillcrest in La Grange, and, shortly after the war, General Josiah Gorgas' house in Sewanee.[71]

The first unambiguously Italianate plantation house completed near Memphis before the war was probably the Samuel Mansfield house (184), built about 1859.[72] The Mallory house on Adams Street was built between 1849 and 1861 but in its present form is the result of a subsequent renovation.[73] At least two important Italianate mansions were built in Knoxville before 1861: John J. Craig's Lucknow,[74] which stood on a hill overlooking the Tennessee River near the University,

185

186

187

and Bleak House (1858), the Robert H. Armstrong house still standing on Kingston Pike. Several plantation houses were designed in the complex, highly developed Italianate style of the late fifties, among them Samuel Graham's Pinewood in Hickman County; James Hoggatt's Clover Bottom (185) and David H. McGavock's Two Rivers, both in Davidson County; and Oaklands near Murfreesboro.[75] The Frank Cossitt house (186) in La Grange is a wooden bracketed villa, complete with belvedere, of a type common in the Lower South, especially along the banks of the Mississippi, in the 1850s. Although the type was never so popular in Tennessee, it was represented during the decades preceding the war by the William S. Campbell house in Franklin (c. 1840?), Isaac W.R. Franklin's Riverview (c. 1850) in Jefferson County, and the Christopher H. Smith house (198), built about 1859 in Clarksville.[76] Indeed Belmont, though more classic, owes much to this hip-roofed, belvedered house type.

Before 1860, romantic images, when they appeared, were usually tempered by traditional themes. The McNeal house in Bolivar (187) is a good example of the inability of local imagination to follow romantic theory to its conclusion. Even during the early fifties Heiman's castellated style had been composed symmetrically, and his clients probably construed these castellated buildings as allusions to the Middle Ages that Scott had written about, not to the exotic images which such Gothic fantasies as Fonthill Abbey or Strawberry Hill embodied. The *Clarksville Jeffersonian* described the new Masonic College as "built in the handsomest style of Elizabethan architecture,"[77] and a building like Belmont was probably valued for its columns more than for its romantic massing and colored glass. A Northern soldier, who had perhaps seen more of the Gothic Revival than most Nashvillians, remarked with some justice that Colonel Acklen's buildings were "gothicified and starched and bidizened to perfection,"[78] but Tennesseans have usually praised Belmont as an example of the classicism that William Strickland practiced so successfully. Gothic was very rarely chosen for important residences before the war. The Wesley Whe-less mansion in Nashville was an exception to this apparent rule, but Wheless was an Englishman, accustomed to the use of Gothic in country villas. Tennesseans liked the romantic styles even less than their neighbors in Alabama, Mississippi, and Louisiana, who generally joined Tennesseans in disregarding the reiterated advice of the press that their farmhouses should be towered, bracketed, and pinnacled. Despite the favor that Adolphus Heiman's castellated designs finally earned, many Tennesseans would probably have shared Henry Ruffner's opinion that the Baptist Church he saw going up in Nashville in 1838 was "deformed, externally, with a superfluity of corrupt Gothic appendages."[79] Ruffner preferred the "generally neat" style of Nashville's other buildings, by which he meant Federal and Greek Revival. During the forties Gothic was generally reserved for schools and for Episcopal and Catholic churches. Irregular plans and affective surface textures did not appear in domestic architecture until about 1855, and only after the war did Gothic gain respectability as an architecture of progress. It was considered eminently suitable for the utopias that inhabited postwar imagination, for Sewanee, to which Confederate generals and gentlemen students retired, or Rugby, where Thomas Hughes proposed to build his ideal community.

Perhaps the most interesting aspect of the romantic revivals was their failure as revivals and their success as the medium through which architectural romanticism gradually permeated the Upper South. When the Embrees built Samuel Jackson's town houses in 1820, the chief detail the contract settled was the width of the house, for given that dimension both undertaker and client knew what a house must be. None of the theories of the 1830s was able to replace this tradition successfully. The followers of A.W. Pugin had been men of principle, who taught that Gothic was not a fashion but a social necessity. Strickland insisted that Grecian architecture embodied permanent principles. But once the tradition had been destroyed by alternative historiographies, there could be no certain ground. Even at their best the charming styles of the 1850s were fashions.

185. *With its two-story porch, the James Hoggatt house at Clover Bottom in Davidson County, built in 1858, is an Italianate development of the Federal plantation house.*

186. *The Frank Cossitt house in La Grange (Fayette County) illustrates the adaptation of the nationally popular bracketed villa to the uses of southern plantation life.*

187. *The McNeal house in Bolivar, Hardeman County, has a traditional character despite a tower and cast iron porches borrowed from the Italian style.*

X. THE ARCHITECTURE OF SOUTHERN NATIONALISM

And we shall have among us too, greater historians, finer painters, and more skillful musicians, than the world has ever known, or our knowledge has taught us to believe in. We shall have our troubadours, and our minstrels—and the banks of our Mississippi will become in song as classic as the Tiber, and in romance as famous as the Danube.

J. TOMLIN, *The Guardian*, COLUMBIA, 1842

Southern plantation architecture of the forties and fifties is the darling of historical novelists and the stepchild of American architectural history. Tennessee plantation architecture is no exception. Although Belle Meade and the Hermitage are famous, only one book, Gifford Cochran's *Grandeur in Tennessee*, and a chapter in J. Frazer Smith's *White Pillars* have ever been devoted to the interpretation of Tennessee plantation houses. Neither offers a satisfactory critical history, and the attempt to provide such a history is hampered not only by the absence of documentation but by literary and sociological interpretations which confuse the study of a regional architectural type with the praise or blame due antebellum southern civilization. The task is to disentangle Belle Meade and Rattle and Snap from the emotion-laden context of Confederate historiography, remembering always that these indisputably beautiful buildings are, for better or worse, an architecture specifically expressive of the regional culture of the Upper South.

Because the plantation houses of the forties and fifties were the obvious symbols of the antebellum agrarian order, historical interpretations have often been colored by attempts to defend or reform southern civilization. Frederick Law Olmsted journeyed across the South in the 1850s, and the accounts of his travels became a primary source for theorists who wished to prove that southern plantation life was brutalizing and southern plantation architecture either undistinguished or showy. Meticulously fair in praising those aspects of southern civilization he found progressive, Olmsted was troubled by the sight of countless dirty and poorly constructed cabins, and he was convinced that slavery and the plantation system were the causes. The solution was to be abolition, the abandonment of the plantation system, and factories because Olmsted was convinced that "the mass of men must have in their minds the idea and hope of a comfortable home as the starting point of respectable industry."[1] George Rogers, a Universalist preacher who visited West Tennessee in 1830 and found only log huts, suggested different reasons for the untidiness: "Now if this state of

things was unavoidable, if it resulted from poverty, I should hold myself inexcusable in remarking upon it; but such is not the fact; it holds with regard to all, poor and rich, with slaves and without, with large and small plantations, with fertile or with sterile lands. It results either from an inordinate cupidity, or a want of refinement; possibly from a union of both these causes."[2] Perhaps George Rogers was closer to the mark than Olmsted, who neither pointed out that a quiet evening with *Harper's Weekly* was the reward most readily accessible to those engaged in "respectable industry" nor understood southern neglect of these improved social arrangements. Certainly the want of refinement George Rogers found was a factor, for as settlement moved west from Nashville, memories of the old civilization faded. Although the architectural history of antebellum West Tennessee is full of exceptions, the result was generally a landscape less lovely than the early nineteenth-century villages and farms of Washington, Sumner, and Davidson counties. Olmsted's interpretation of this widespread architectural failure was essentially sociological. He was quick to condemn the refusal of slave holders to make "the slightest concession to the spirit of the age," or to acknowledge "the principles of social science under which we live and must live."[3] James C. Bonner, author of the first scholarly discussion of the plantation architecture of the Lower South, used a similar descriptive method and reached a similar conclusion.[4] When the few architecturally distinguished plantation houses are enumerated among the countless lesser examples, the type itself seems unremarkable and the great examples meaningless exceptions. The paradox is familiar. Art is not typical but ideal, epitomizing the essential images of place and habitation belonging to the culture in which it appears. There is only one Belmont.

Paralleling this sociological critique is the literary interpretation that stretches from Thomas Nelson Page to the novels and stories of Faulkner and the popular epic of Margaret Mitchell. In this literature the architecture of the two decades before the war symbolized an order of agrarian opulence, dignity, and permanence. These writers proposed no critical interpretation, for they were novelists and critics following their art, but their romantic image of the pillared mansion was a permanent legacy to the first generation that had no living access to memories of the antebellum South. Colonel Sartoris' pillared mansion is an indispensable symbol of agrarian order in Faulkner's stories; the real heroine of *Gone With the Wind* is Tara; and though Margot's perfervid restoration of Belle Isle in *Lancelot* is no piety, the house is still the warm-blooded carcass on which the wraiths who inhabit Walker Percy's plot must feed their own impoverished sensibilities. The literary tradition, in which the mansion is always inhabited by demons or glories, has made architectural interpretation difficult.

Rattle and Snap, Ashwood Hall, and Belle Meade were farm houses, monuments to the agricultural boom of the forties and fifties which was centered in the Lower South, where the best cotton lands lay. In 1818 the Indians had been removed from West Tennessee, in 1831 the Choctaws from Mississippi. Texas had begun to encourage immigration in 1836, and on April 25 of that year Colonel Robert Love wrote Jackson that the Hermitage had not been completed because "workmen are not to be had, all gone and going to Mississippi and Louisi." Sometimes the new agrarian adventurers were not southerners. In 1839 J.H. Ingraham wrote, "If a farmer from the neighborhood of Pittsburgh or Cincinnati, sees a piece of land on the lower Mississippi, on one of his boating expeditions, which pleases him, he returns home, sells out, builds an ark, embarks with his family, committing himself to the waves, after a voyage of five or six weeks arrives at his new home, ties his ark to a tree . . . commences chopping down the forest, opens a wood-yard, becomes thrifty, buys negroes, grows rich, and is at last a planter."[5]

These were among the new planters Bishop Otey had in mind when he wrote: "The instances are almost without number, of men who came hither a few years ago, nearly penniless, whose incomes are now reckoned by thousands and tens of thousands."[6] Two years later Olmsted quoted the letter a South Carolina lawyer had published in *Harper's Weekly* in February 1859. "The sudden acquisition of wealth in the cotton-growing region of the United States . . . is miraculous. . . . The result is, in a few years large estates, as if by magic, are accumulated. The fortunate proprietors then build fine houses,—and surround themselves with comforts and luxuries to which they were strangers in their earlier years of toil and care."[7] Olmsted's "Southern lawyer" wrote at the end of a five-year period during which cotton had commanded the highest prices it would ever bring and on the eve of the largest crop that southern planters would ever produce. The boom had in fact begun almost thirty years earlier and had never abated completely despite such setbacks as the depression of 1837. Tennessee participated in that boom, and her architectural celebration of it has a unique distinction.

To become a successful planter, a southern capitalist did not need a great house like Ashwood Hall or Belle Meade. A few cabins for slaves, a log house for the overseer, and a neat villa in town for himself and his family would suffice. These town houses, built mostly during the 1840s and 1850s, were symbols of the successful exploitation of labor and land by absentee owners. Natchez is perhaps the clearest example of a town where architectural character was determined by the construction of urban dwellings for absentee plantation owners. Clement Eaton notes correctly that "classic houses in the country were relatively rare, except in favored regions like the Bluegrass sections of Kentucky and Tennessee, the black belt of Alabama, and the delta counties of Louisiana and Mississippi."[8] There is very little architectural evidence of the existence of an urban, absentee planter class in Tennessee. A few Greek Revival town houses were built in Memphis, where the Richardson house still stands, though the Hugh Rice Austin house and the H.A. Littleton house[9] survived the war and Federal occupation only to be destroyed by twentieth-century urban redevelopment. Other examples are to be found in La Grange and Bolivar, villages which functioned briefly as the centers of large-scale West Tennessee plantation life.

The distinctive excellence of Tennessee's plantation architecture is probably the result, at least in part, of the willingness of many members of its relatively small planter class to live on the land, occupying themselves with the management of their plantations during much of the year. The mixed agricultural economy of Tennessee did not yield the bonanzas of sudden wealth as liberally as did the new cotton lands of Mississippi, Texas, and Louisiana, but neither did it support the absentee ownership of large, single-crop plantations. Slavery was widespread in Tennessee, but "the institution had neither the grandeur nor the harshness that it has been portrayed as possessing for the South as a whole."[10] Although the builders of the greatest plantation houses were often the largest slave owners—an inventory of Isaac Franklin's estate taken September 28, 1847, listed 137 slaves at Fairvue—the typical planter had far fewer, and in 1860 only one in 45 heads of farming families owned the labor of as many as 30 slaves.[11] Tennessee's plantations were not great agricultural factories but complex operations involving corn, wheat, cattle, and the breeding of horses as well as the culture of cotton and tobacco. Perhaps Tennessee planters lived on the land because the successful management of the farms required their presence. Certainly a country house in Maury County, Williamson County, or Giles County was more pleasant than attempting to live graciously in the sweltering heat of the Lower South. Caroline O'Reilly Nicholson remembered driving home from Nashville to Columbia about 1838 with McCord Williamson in his "elegant carriage behind four beautiful clay bank horses, with white manes and tails." Williamson had moved from Maury County to Mississippi but, "like many others from that state . . . would come back in style and lavish his riches among us during the summer months."[12] And perhaps the reasons the apologists for the plantation system urged were partly correct.

It is tempting to discover in the willingness of Tennessee planters to live on the land, among their fields and slaves, the agrarian idealism which characterized the southern apologia both before and after the war. The evidence is ambiguous. Tennessee planters were apparently divided as a class between the notion of a fixed and aristocratic order which exercised patrician responsibilities and the immense opportunities for gain through the impersonal exploitation of land and slaves which existed after 1830. James K. Polk was the absentee owner of a plantation in Mississippi which he clearly considered chiefly an investment. A surviving correspondence between Polk and a succession of overseers which spans twenty-five years offers no evidence that Polk ever displayed concern (beyond that dictated by his fair-minded and prudent character) for his slaves or for the Mississippi community in which his plantation was located. Sometimes the heirs to great estates were merely ineffective planters. Frederick Ross wrote of the loss of Rotherwood: "As I never had a particle of knowledge or taste for farming, I left everything to my overseer; and he, worthy man, made all the money. In this way one of the most beautiful landed estates in Tennessee went with the rest."[13] Often the tradition that the planter was deeply attached to the land is belied by accounts of their frequent travels and removals. Isaac Franklin divided his time between his plantations in Louisiana and in Sumner County, Tennessee, and fashionable springs in Virginia, and the trial which resulted from Adelicia Hayes Franklin's attempt to set aside certain provisions of her husband's will was concerned in part with the difficult question of establishing Isaac Franklin's place of residence. Franklin was respected by his neighbors; he was certainly not cruel or unfeeling and was sufficiently philanthropic to leave the bulk of his vast estate to found a college. Yet Isaac Franklin was a driving executive, exercising sole control over four plantations in Louisiana and Tennessee, unable either to secure competent managers or to divest himself of his empire. And there is the smell of fear in house carpenter Lewis T. White's refusal of the position of overseer at Fairvue because no sum could persuade him to take his wife into Franklin's quarters.[14] Planters were not sentimental Cavaliers, but capitalists whose funds were invested in land and slaves and whose attachment to the land—or lack of it—was roughly that of their contemporaries. It would be dif-

ficult to show that Tennesseans were less devoted to profit-taking than mill owners in Massachusetts; and each spring the Gayoso House was crowded with plantation families going north for the summer.

But plantation life had another face. John Robinson, sometimes considered Tennessee's first writer of fiction, expressed in 1833 the native conviction that attachment to the land was praiseworthy and the commercial spirit somehow detrimental to the best interests of mankind: "Will the nation be great and happy because 'merchants becomes princes' surrounded by crowds of menials and mercenary dependents? Does the nation become powerful because its citizens are continually subjected more and more to the influence of men who are destitute of local attachments?"[15] This conviction that men properly have obligations to the land, and to an agrarian order, was sometimes echoed in Tennessee plantation life. Throughout Jackson's correspondence there runs, beneath his incessant concern for the health of the horses and the price of cotton, a thread of genuine attachment to "my Hermitage . . . There rest my thoughts, when disengaged from the constant business with which I am summoned. Could I with honor, and a duty I owe my country, I would fly there."[16] The Polk plantations in Maury County seem to have been planned and operated as conscious attempts to create an ideal and profitable agrarian community. An idyllic account of Sunday at St. John's, Ashwood, the chapel built where the Polk plantations joined, survives. There slaves and masters were instructed and received Holy Communion together.[17] Life at Belle Meade was likewise marked by the implicit commitment of the Hardings to the perpetuation of an ideal agrarian order. The letters that Elizabeth McGavock Harding wrote to her husband during his imprisonment at Fort Mackinac Island are full of descriptions of the crops and greetings which the slaves wished forwarded to General Harding.[18] Elizabeth Harding's letters fill out the picture which made the apologia for the plantation system credible. The Polks and Hardings were not agricultural profiteers, and the identification with the classical past which Belle Meade, Ashwood Hall and Rattle and Snap symbolize was undoubtedly both intentional and serious. Perhaps the typical planter, like his twentieth-century descendants, was not always able to discern his desire for gain in his high-minded defense of the economically successful plantation system, mistakenly identifying his economic interests with classical notions of a fixed order that were in fact inimical to them. The architecture itself would suggest as much, for it is a distinctive and beautiful attempt to combine an appeal to classic precedent with innovation and progress.

188. Rosemont, the Josephus Conn Guild house, built near Galla-
tin in Sumner County, anticipated the free use of classic orders. The
plan, central parlors divided from the dining room at the right and
bedrooms to the left by open passages, was also novel.

The title "white pillars" was invented by J. Frazer Smith in his attempt to show that the architecture unerringly identified as southern by popular imagination was not simply colonial, or Greek Revival, or Georgian.[19] Smith's epithet was appropriate because it served to isolate a moment in the architectural history of the South when society, its forms, and style were undergoing dramatic transformation. Popular imagination had completed its migration through neoclassicism, had abandoned its fascination with the Greek Revival, and finally had settled upon a style, the theme of which was columns. Grecian had passed quickly, and in Tennessee few examples had been properly archaeological. Suddenly the carefully proportioned Greek Revival mansions, typified by Blanchard's houses in Monroe County (141) and Tulip Grove (130), passed, and the new architecture of the forties and fifties appeared. Although this new style used a classical vocabulary, it was not a revival. It had precedents, but no obvious principles. Its advent was marked

in Tennessee by the building of the fourth Hermitage (189) in 1834–1836, by Josephus Conn Guild's Rosemont (188) near Gallatin (1835),[20] and by the new portico its owners gave the Whyett house in Memphis, probably in the early 1850s.[21] Although these houses employed the vocabulary of classicism, they ignored its images, exemplifying a transition that was occurring across the South. Austerlitz, built in 1832,[22] and Rosedown, built in 1835,[23] still maintained in Louisiana the French colonial tradition of galleries with dominant horizontals, but as early as 1825 the Cottage (West Feliciana Parish)[24] had been given a two-story Doric order. Shadows-on-the-Teche (Iberia Parish), which boasted eight tall columns beneath a Greek Revival frieze, was built in 1830,[25] and Oak Alley was built with a two-story order in 1839.[26] Bocage near Burnside (1840),[27] Ashland (1841),[28] and Belle Alliance (1846)[29] established the new style in Louisiana.

In Mississippi the two-story order appears at Gloucester and Auburn, both designed by Boston architect Levi Weeks soon after 1808,[30] and at Arlington in 1816.[31] These early Natchez examples, however, are not the architecture of southern nationalism but were constructed in imitation of such late neoclassical models as Mount Vernon or Hampton in Berkeley County, South Carolina (1780).[32] The great examples of the new architecture in Mississippi are D'Evereux (1850)[33] and Staunton Hall (1851)[34] at Natchez. In Alabama, columns first ranged across the front of Belle Mina (Limestone County)[35] and the Forks of Cypress (Lauderdale County)[36] during the 1820, but these houses were also inspired by late Federal models, and it is rather Rosemont (1832–1839) near Forkland in Greene County[37] and Gaireswood (1842–1861) in Demopolis,[38] both of which belong to the thirties, which typify the new architecture there. In Georgia the Hugenin-Proudfit-Birdsey house (1843) in Macon[39] and the Hoxey-Cargill house in Columbus[40] (c. 1850) are important monuments of the new, free classicism. Walnut Hall (1842) near Lexington marks its advent in the Kentucky bluegrass.[41]

The transition is aptly illustrated by the Polk houses in Maury County. Lucius Polk built Hamilton Place (41), a fine example of late-blooming Palladianism, in 1832. About 1844 Rattle and Snap (190), which belongs decisively to the new romantic Grecian style of Minard Lafever, was built.[42] Ashwood Hall (191), the Andrew Polk plantation house,[43] combining columns and brackets in a grand display that has no obvious precedent either in classical tradition or in handbooks, probably belongs to the 1850s. Beginning about 1840, Federal and Grecian country houses gave way to a highly self-conscious architecture that combined classical principles of symmetry and proportion with disregard for antique precedents and a baroque assertiveness. The plain, Federal columns of the Bank of the United States in Nashville (1827), and the Greek Revival porticoes at Tulip Grove (1834–1836) and the Caruthers house (c. 1830) had undoubtedly been influential, but the architecture of the forties and fifties had other themes. It was the work of a culture which for the first time had conceived for itself goals that were regional and agrarian. The depression of 1837 had passed. Soon Texas would be won for the South by events in which Tennesseans would play an important part. In 1850 Tennessee stood midway in the ranks of the cotton-growing states, after Alabama, Georgia,

Mississippi, and South Carolina but ahead of Louisiana, Kentucky, North Carolina, Texas, and Virginia. In 1850, 200,000 bales were grown in Tennessee; in 1860 nearly 300,000 were produced. The development of West Tennessee, where the richest cotton lands lay, had linked the cultures of Middle Tennessee and the lower Mississippi Valley. The first assembly of southern delegates at which secession was proposed took place in 1850 at Nashville, and in 1854 John Shelby, a distinguished resident of Nashville, served as vice president of the Convention of Charleston. Frederick A. Ross, the proud builder of Rotherwood, was of the opinion that "he who sits on the throne of the cotton-bag has triumphed at last over him who sits on the throne of the wool-sack."[44]

With the flowering of an agrarian culture, Tennesseans began to develop institutions that reflected the interests of their own civilization. As early as 1849, Ashbel Smith, one of the founders of the University of Texas, advised the trustees of the University of Memphis that "the mind of our people must be cultivated, educated, disciplined to turn back the onslaught made on us by the North."[45] In 1850 the University of Nashville succeeded in opening a Medical College, and by 1857 Leonidas Polk, James Hervey Otey, and Stephen Elliot had agreed that a university, "an institution of conservatism," should be founded in Tennessee because the South was "a region whose urgent necessity can be met only by an institution set up within its own borders."[46] Gideon Pillow warned at the Columbia fair on October 24, 1855: "Let the people of Tennessee change their system—resuscitate their lands—adopt labor-saving machinery—build up manufactures. . . . The impulses of self-interest should prompt this course; but the instincts of self-preservation may soon demand it . . . ."[47] *DeBow's* proclaimed, "Light up the torches of industry [for] the cup of endurance is full."[48] In 1855 the University of Nashville became a military school. The South was developing national institutions and a national architecture.

The architecture of southern nationalism appeared suddenly, unheralded by evolutionary precursors. Both Gifford Cochran in *Grandeur in Tennessee* and J. Frazer Smith in *White Pillars* have suggested that houses like Rattle and Snap may have been the result of a process that began with the pioneer's one-room cabin and progressed through several clearly defined stages.[49] This is true in only the most limited sense. While it is the case that eighteenth-century log houses displayed the symmetrical themes which determined eighteenth-century architecture generally in Tennessee, this regular character was the result of a highly traditional folk aesthetic which was reinforced by and reflected in traditional

building techniques. Log cabins, as distinguished from neat squared-log houses, were the dwellings of the poor in 1850 as well as in 1780, and fine houses like the Watauga stone houses were built from the first years of settlement. Architectural imagination did not evolve through one-room and "dog-trot" cabins to a crude version of the single house, and finally to the columned mansion, though some settlers may have lived successively in such a series of buildings. Frequently, the families that built well in the eighteenth century maintained a high standard of architectural excellence in the nineteenth, as an architectural history of the dwellings of the descendants of the first Polks, Carters, or Gillespies would show. Many planters had, of course, run the gamut from poverty to riches, from ignorance of architecture to a desire for showy architectural finery almost overnight, but more frequently genealogy was the father of architectural ambition.

The buildings which resulted from the maturing of plantation society were produced through the combined efforts of educated owners, skilled carpenters, and professional architects. General Pillow of Maury County, for example, determined for himself the main architectural features of the plantation house he built in

189. When the rebuilt Hermitage was completed in 1836, its dominant feature was a range of six two-story columns, spaced asymmetrically to acknowledge the fenestration of the original Federal block, the walls of which withstood the fire of October 13, 1834. In the foreground is the one-story dining room that survived the fire intact—this room was the only one not rebuilt in 1835–1836.

1838 and employed carpenters like Nathan Vaught to construct it. The result was a high vernacular very different from the pristine architecture of Rattle and Snap. The tradition that buildings such as Rattle and Snap were built by their first owners without architectural advice is probably erroneous, for such houses possess an excellence that only a well-trained and talented architectural imagination could have conceived. Belle Meade (196), Manor Hall (195), and Ashwood Hall (191) were almost certainly the work of skilled designers, but whether owners, house carpenters, or architects determined the designs, these buildings possess characteristics constituting a distinct type.

In Tennessee the prototypical work of the architecture of southern nationalism was, fittingly, the fourth Hermitage (189), the building that stands today, the result of a remodeling undertaken after the Morrison

190

191

Hermitage of 1831 was destroyed by fire in 1834.[50] The Hermitage had followed the succession of American styles. Jackson had abandoned his log house and built a Federal dwelling that was considered quite impressive in Davidson County in 1819. Twelve years later he had employed David Morrison to remodel the Hermitage in the Greek Revival style. When Morrison's Hermitage was destroyed by fire only three years later, Jackson was determined to rebuild it. The result was the first monument of the architecture of southern nationalism in Tenessee, though the President had clearly not intended to encourage an architectural revolution when he employed Reiff and Hume on January 1, 1835.

Jackson had at first intended to rebuild the Morrison Hermitage unchanged. When news of the fire reached him in Washington, he wrote to Andrew Jackson, Jr.: "I will have it rebuilt. Was it not on the site selected by my dear departed wife, I would build it higher up on the Hill, but I will have it repaired."[51] The contract executed between Jackson and Joseph Reiff and William C. Hume required that the house be "rebuilt in the same order as it was before," and it is clear from the list of materials appended that the south front was again to have the long, one-story gallery, this time with the number of columns reduced from ten to six, crowned with the same small second-story portico. Before the contract was drawn, Colonel Robert Armstrong passed on to Jackson Mr. Lewis' advice that "the Stories of the House should be made Higher,"[52] and this was presumably among the improvements Jackson authorized in a letter to Andrew Jackson, Jr., on November 12. Increasing the height of the Hermitage's ceilings was itself an important step toward bringing the President's house into line with the architectural ideals of the late thirties, but the main feature of the fourth Hermitage, the full range of two-story columns, is not mentioned until August 2, 1836. When building costs were tallied,

$750 was included for "the full length two story Porch added [the carpenters] finding every thing."[53] The six tall columns, made of boards planed to imitate fluting and crowned with cast-iron acanthus leaves, with their porch, had cost more than a tenth of the entire sum spent on the rebuilding and had made the Hermitage a premier example of the new architecture that would soon sweep plantation society. A few houses built at the same time hint at the solution exemplified by the Hermitage of 1836. Yet the Whyett house in Memphis was originally Federal, and the Robertson Topp mansion in Memphis belongs properly to Greek Revival; and though the plan of Josephus Conn Guild's Rosemont, built near Gallatin in 1834 or 1835, displays the new sense of spatial freedom, Rosemont's columns and galleries draw their power from antique precedents (188). The Hermitage of 1836 was the home of the nation's first citizen, and an unambiguous example of the new romantic use of classical tradition.

The source of the design remains unclear. Reiff and Hume could have copied the Doric order of David Morrison's garden monument, or even their own fine porch, then under construction or contemplated at Tulip Grove. They, or their clients, chose instead to give the Hermitage a dramatic range of columns that referred to classical precedents only obliquely. The remodeled building was given a temple form, but in the principal façade the pediment was concealed behind the tall architrave and frieze. At some time after 1836 the Hermitage was given its two-story rear porch, for the statement showing the sum payable on completion,

192. *The temple form and Ionic porch of Beechlawn, the A.W. Warfield house in Maury County, are Grecian, but the decorated lintels, brackets, and segmental arch are Italianate. The type, a two-story temple form with one-story wings, has a history in Georgian Palladianism and was illustrated in Lafever's* Modern Builders' Guide. ▶

190. *Rattle and Snap, Maury County, built in the early 1840s, exemplifies the free use of Grecian orders and details to create a dramatic fusion of classical allusions and romantic spirit. Of all the Tennessee houses of its type, stylish Rattle and Snap stands closest to the work of Minard Lafever and the New York Greek Revival, the national movement to which the architecture of southern nationalism had close but ambivalent affinities.*

191. *Andrew Polk bought Ashwood Hall, Maury County, from his brother Leonidas in 1841, later remodeling the house to bring it into line with the regional notion of plantation architecture. The architrave was about 25 feet above the porch floor, and the Corinthian capitals were about 3 feet tall. If the remodeling took place between 1853 and 1856, James M. Hughes was probably the carpenter and architect.*

193. *The Nathaniel Cheairs house in Maury County, built about 1855, had a two-story porch on each of its two principal façades, one having the locally popular Tower-of-the-Winds capitals and the other paneled columns with simplified capitals.*

194. *Although it belongs in the countryside, the Samuel Mayes house was built in Columbia (Maury County) about 1859. The segmental lintels and arcuated mutins are Italianate. The staircase at the Mayes house, a freestanding run that divides and returns at the landing, was used by Adolphus Heiman at Belmont in 1859.*

195. *Manor Hall, the Martin Luther Stockard house at Mount Pleasant, Maury County, was built about 1849. The composition of the arcuated doorway and its flanking lights recalls Rattle and Snap.*

192

193

194

195

drawn August 2, 1836, mentions only one "full length two story porch," the extant portico of six columns, freely composed, lacking entasis, and supporting the heavy architrave and parapet. In the late 1830s James H. Dakin would make similar designs for the Bringier plantations, Bocage and Ashland, but when Reiff and Hume built in 1835 the only precedents were the remote works of architects like Alexander Jackson Davis and Ithiel Town of New York, though even Town and Davis seldom dealt as freely with classical precedent as the builders of the new Hermitage did.

It has been suggested that Jackson himself may have ordered the new porch, taking as his inspiration the presidential residence in Washington, which had also been painted white to efface the marks of fire and had been given an impressive north portico during the first years of Jackson's administration. The changes, however, as the President's letter of May 16, 1835, to his son shows, had originated in Tennessee. The White House porch displays a spirit utterly different from the Hermitage, conveying a disciplined image of the antique that the Hermitage of 1836 lacks. The Roman

196. At William Harding's Belle Meade near Nashville, a stone porch adapted from the Choragic Monument of Thrasyllus fronts a traditional central-passage plan.

Empire of the second and third centuries had abandoned the staid forms inherited from the Greeks in favor of a new architecture which, though it used orders, arches, and moldings, lacked precise references to classical precedents. Again, in the seventeenth century the classical tradition exploded into the exuberant forms of baroque. Between 1835 and 1860 southern architects displayed on a provincial scale a similar ability to create a powerful synthesis of classical form and romantic movement. Eaton, commenting on antebellum architecture, noticed that in the South "even classic culture was viewed in an unhistorical light,"[54] though he overlooked the differences between the Greek Revival, still an architecture of principle and precedent, and the romantic classicism of the period after 1845, concluding that the progress from the classicism of Monticello to Belle Meade and Rattle and Snap represented only a weakening of tradition. But the romantic

197. *Wealthy tobaccoman J.P. Williams built Tip Top at the edge of Clarksville, Montgomery County, in 1859. The capitals crowning the six massive columns are an expressionist commentary on the richness of the orders.*

classicism of the forties was more innovative than imitative. Symmetry was preserved, but the simple masses of older Federal and Greek Revival forms were complicated by the addition of secondary wings and porches which were developed around the axes of central and secondary halls. Sometimes, as at Belle Meade, the familiar plan of the four-room central-passage house is still evident. At Belmont tradition was adapted to create a new spatial scheme combining classic and Italianate ideals. Although the new architecture usually included at least some Greek details, the architecture of southern nationalism took columns and porches as its principal subject; Italianate and Gothic variants were built alongside more numerous Grecian examples.

The Columbia house carpenter Nathan Vaught wrote in his autobiography: "We also in 1860 put up a large fine Front Portico the whole length of the house and Remodelled all the Front windows of Mr. Ben Harlan's old house 7 miles west from Town on the Williams Port Road. This was quite a heavy job." The result of Vaught's labor was the transformation of Skipwith Place, a Federal house built about 1800,[55]

into a pillared plantation house of the type planters preferred during the fifties. Porticoes and columns sprang up wherever cotton grew, from the Davie Place in Brownsville and Edgewood in Jackson to Riverview and Fairview,[56] which stood in rich pockets of plantation land in Jefferson County and the tiny pillared Carter house north of Greeneville. The heartland of the new, columned style was Middle Tennessee, where rich soil and well-watered land had created a broad band of prosperous agricultural communities. There were built the Polk houses (190, 191), the Pillow houses, Beechlawn (192), and the Nathaniel Cheairs house (193), all in Maury County.[57] The Samuel Mayes house was built in Columbia (194), Manor Hall in Mount Pleasant (195),[58] Westview and Everbright in Williamson County,[59] Riverwood and Belle Meade (196) near Nashville,[60] Tip Top (197) and the Chris-

198

199

200. *Everbright, the John D. Bennett house, built in Williamson County about 1838, was a fine example of the free use of Grecian detail to create a Palladian image of agrarian grandeur.*

topher Smith house (198) in Clarksville,[61] Melrose in Davidson County south of Nashville, the Davis house near Gallatin, the Crest in Murfreesboro,[62] and the John Junius Pulliam house, Hancock Hall, in La Grange (199).[63] Four, Everbright, Rattle and Snap, the Davis house, and Westview, serve to illustrate this single new image whose subject was columns.

Everbright (200) was built between 1838 and 1840 by John D. Bennett, and though the house can hardly have been constructed without architectural assistance, the name of the designer has been lost. The architectural subject of Everbright was the square columns that supported its two-story porches. These massive columns, decorated with panels bearing a single anthemion at the top, are crowned by capitals composed of a single row of smaller palmettes, and the plain, deep cornice is denticulated. The largest of the porches breaks forward from a portico extending the length of the front, and openings leading onto the porches have shouldered, Grecian frames. The roof is hipped, and the main block was originally symmetrical in both its

principal elevations. There is in Everbright something of Palladio's Villa Rotunda, set in its fields, commanding the land along the axes its porches establish. Although Everbright relied upon classical elements and themes, columns, anthemia, dentils, and palmettes, the house has very little to do with Greek Revival. Despite its delicate details, it is Palladian in its boldness and baroque in its freedom.

Rattle and Snap (190), built on the extensive Polk holdings in Maury County before 1845, is a pristine example of the architecture of southern nationalism derived from the romantic Grecian of Lafever's *Modern Builders' Guide*. The porch is supported by ten two-story Corinthian columns, of which four are set forward beneath a rather shallow pediment. The porch extends across five of seven bays. The mass is baroque, having a strong extended axis around which reiterative forms that decrease in width and weight with their distance from the center are arranged symmetrically. The plan is Palladian in inspiration—a large central hall flanked by parlors, with stairs in a secondary hall at one side. The porch and steps are carefully worked limestone, the porch paved in a diagonal pattern. Although the imposing columns are Corinthian, an Italianate theme— evident in the shallow pitch of the pediment and hipped roof, overly vertical proportions, and the arcuated windows flanking the entrance—dominates the composi-

198. *The Christopher H. Smith house in Clarksville, built about 1859, has the porch and entrance Adolphus Heiman used at Elmwood about two years later (173). The center bay of the Italianate house penetrates a hexastyle porch like that of Tip Top (197).*

199. *Hancock Hall, the John Junius Pulliam house in La Grange, Fayette County, built about 1850, has two porches, the west porch combining the Doric order and a Gothic doorway.*

201

202

tion. One of Rattle and Snap's secondary porches is cast iron; the other, like the central hall, has Tower-of-the-Winds capitals. Doors open onto the porch from the principal rooms. Although the house is symmetrical and although it was undoubtedly considered Grecian by its owner and perhaps its architect, Rattle and Snap is a highly affective and romantic building. Its graceful mass meets the land in a series of gentle transitions effected by its portico, porch, and steps. The façade was stuccoed and originally painted yellow, setting its white columns in startling contrast.

The James Harvey Davis house (201), probably built only a few years before the war, stands south of Gallatin on a knoll overlooking Spencer's Creek. The house was the high vernacular of a competent house carpenter and a knowledgeable owner. Ceilings in Tennessee had increased in height as southern fortunes prospered. Jackson's friends had warned him that the ceilings of the building destroyed by fire in October 1834 had been unfashionably low, and he had raised them when the fourth Hermitage was rebuilt from the ruins of David Morrison's 1831 design. The ceilings of the Davis House are among the tallest in antebellum Tennessee. The house is, however, at heart nothing other than the old Tennessee single house grown grand. Its central hall now has a curved end, much in the manner of the Blanchard houses in Monroe County, and its size is enormous. But the house is essentially the same central-passage house with ell that Daniel Smith had begun a few miles to the west in 1784. Six white plank columns guard the façade, and full-length windows open onto the porch. The single clear allusion to the classical tradition that the Davis house offers is its oblique reference to the columned porches of Greek and Roman tradition.

Unlike the Davis house, Westview (202), built in Williamson County by Samuel Perkins about 1854, was a decidedly stylish design. The subject of the architecture was the same six columns that Jackson had used at the Hermitage twenty years earlier, but the idiom was Italianate. There is almost nothing Grecian about the house, but it has the essentials of the type—columns, the overpowering scale, the conquest of both the essential classical element and the new Italianate

style by the distinctive image proper to the architecture of southern nationalism. This single image and the foundations are all that remain of Westview now, but it is still possible to sense that the builders must have been pleased with a building that was thoroughly modern and satisfyingly traditional.

Everbright, Rattle and Snap, the Davis house, and Westview each expresses the architectural ideal of the agrarian South of the forties and fifties—an ideal that prevailed nowhere else in the American republic and which endured for only two short decades. The new architecture was intended to express the mind and sentiments of an agrarian society. The subject of the architecture was columns, symbols that defy the dust on which they stand. The vocabulary was often romantic, though the architectural syntax was usually classical. Just as southern intellect adhered unvaryingly to a unique intellectual succession that included Aristotle and Witherspoon, and just as the folk philosophy of the period insisted upon orthodoxy—as determined by private judgment—architectural imagination required a romantic, individualistic classicism. Neither member of the paradox could be abandoned without courting imaginative failure. The land of cotton was both conservative and progressive, committed both to tradition and to a proto-Darwinian struggle, principles which may not be peaceably conjoined in ethics and politics. Revolution, with its inescapable subjectivist bias, could not be reconciled with the classical imagination, with a policy of authority and command, with the classicism of the academies, or with the regular early-nineteenth-century aesthetic. During the fifties the quiet conflict between the South that based itself upon its constitutional rights to independence, its moral presumptions, and its institutions on tradition and antiquity and the South that claimed racial and economic superiority continued apace. When Tennessee seceded, it did so on an ultimately satisfying combination of these themes. Tennessee, alone among the southern states, spurned constitutional arguments, asserting revolution to be the most ancient and self-evident of human traditions. The essays which most satisfactorily combined the two great themes of the fifties were not written but built. The anthemia that grace the great square stone columns of Belle Meade; the Corinthian colonnade that breaks into the pediment of Rattle and Snap; the variegated columns and porches of Cheairs Place; the gigantic columns of the George Thomas Lewis house,[64] with their free capitals; the seven columns of Carnton's back porch;[65] and the delightful mass of Everbright are visual testimonies to the restless attempts of the forties and fifties to combine classical precedent and agrarian triumphalism.

201. *The builder of the James Harvey Davis house (c. 1860) in Wilson County was not a master of Grecian or Italianate style, but he interpreted successfully the local conviction that the house of a prosperous planter had columns.*

202. *Built about 1854, Westview in Williamson County was an Italianate transformation of the columnar architecture of southern nationalism.*

Photographs of crumbling, vine-encrusted columns are often prominently displayed in the picture books and films which perpetuate the romantic interpretation of antebellum southern architecture, and this representation has suggested to casual readers that great numbers of pillared plantation houses were damaged or burned during the war of 1861–1865. Certainly the destruction was significant. Gilmore recalled that as he had approached Nashville in 1863, "Its beautiful suburbs, though covered with the early foliage of spring, wore a most desolate appearance. Magnificent villas were heaps of ruins; splendid plantations and charming gardens overgrown with weeds."[66] Mother Frances Walsh reflected that after the northern victory, "a blight passed over the land. All things felt its withering touch." At Belmont "grass grew on walks and avenues, gold fish died in ponds and basins, green houses remained unkept. . . . The broad acres were mostly cut up for city lots."[67] But granting that the state suffered much and that the Tennessee governed by Parson Brownlow was very different from the antebellum world of Jackson and the Polks, it is important to remember that the plantation architecture of the forties and fifties was not destroyed in its full flower by Buell's invading army. That architecture had died on the eve of the war, and its demise was among those minor prophecies of the fate of southern civilization which a knowledgeable critic might have read. After nearly a century during which romantic architectural themes had been controlled and rejected, the years between 1855 and 1860 suddenly witnessed the abandonment of the familiar classical images. Houses like the McGhee mansion (179), Clover Bottom (185), Pinewood, Oaklands in Murfreesboro, the McNeal Place (187), and Elmwood (173), all Gothic or Italianate, appeared in the countryside, compelling indications that national fashions could invade the most conservative art of a highly traditional American region. If the war had been delayed for a decade, it would have become clear that the architecture of southern nationalism was a brilliant, imaginative survival, a transitional architecture that pointed to the abandonment of traditional images and the triumph of American styles. To the degree that architectural images are significant, this suggests that, alongside those values we usually identify as prototypically southern—the love of precedent, order, and regularity—there were at work progressive, romantic tendencies which would have assimilated the imagination of the Upper South to the modern experience of the nation even without the violent defeat of 1865.

For civilizations there comes a time for dying, and it is important that the time not be missed or delayed unduly, for defeat has a way of fixing the best in memory and providing justification for the abandonment of the worst. From the point of view of architectural history, southern civilization picked the right time for dying. After the collapse of southern nationalism, Tennessee plantation architecture was interpreted as a permanent witness to the best of the agrarian order. Had plantation society survived for fifty years, its architecture might not have been memorable.

XI. AMERICAN STYLES

If American architecture has any distinctive features, it may be paradoxically stated to consist of a lack of features, or rather the combination and adaptation of various styles.

CHARLES HITE-SMITH
Chattanooga Times, DECEMBER 8, 1892

Tennessee temporized until the newly elected President called for troops whose duty it would be to fight against the soldiers of the Lower South, and then, on June 8, 1862, cast its lot with the Confederacy. Tennessee soon became, after Virginia, the most ravaged of the southern states. The fall of Fort Henry and Fort Donelson early in February 1862 left Middle Tennessee defenseless. Nashville was occupied on February 25; Memphis fell on June 6; Chattanooga, in September. Ironically, Knoxville, metropolis of a region in which sentiment had always been with the Federals, remained in Confederate hands until the bloody battle of Fort Sanders in November 1863. Federal control of Middle Tennessee was seriously contested only once, by the magnificent campaign of Hood, who, despite the heroism of his badly outnumbered army, was not able late in 1864 to recapture Nashville.

There was very little continuity between the antebellum civilization of Tennessee and the era of reconstruction and industrialization which followed the war, and very little continuity between the architectural profession of the fifties and postwar practice. If Hugh Roland or David Morrison survived the war, they were too far advanced in age to influence the local development of style. The younger Stricklands had left Tennessee before 1861, and Akeroyd had fled before the Federal invasion. Of the important antebellum architects only W.H. Clyce and James M. Hughes continued to design after the war, and in 1866 Hughes was still the only native Tennessean prominent in the profession. A.C. Bruce was almost a native son. He had come to Tennessee with his parents as a boy of twelve in 1847 and had been educated there by his house-carpenter father and by being in the office of Harvey M. Akeroyd. In 1866 Bruce opened an office in Knoxville, remaining there until 1879 when he moved to Atlanta. There he formed partnerships first with William H. Parkins and on Parkins's death in 1882 with Thomas H. Morgan.[1]

Several architects who would become important after the war had come to Tennessee during the boom days of the late fifties. English-born James B. Cook came from the Cincinnati office of Isaiah Rogers to Memphis in 1857, in time to take part in the war as chief of submarine batteries in New Orleans.[2] Joseph Willis moved from Cincinnati to Memphis in 1858;[3]

and Mathias Harvey Baldwin (1827–1891) from New York[4] and P.H. Hammarskold from Charleston in 1859.[5] Henry J. Dudley, who came south in 1866 to complete the Maxwell House, thereafter divided his long career between Nashville and New York.[6]

Defeat made possible a migration of men and ideas more important than the invasion of armies, opening the Upper South, still a new land, to settlement by pioneers who might otherwise have remained in the Midwest or the eastern cities; among the pioneers were the architects who would build Tennessee's houses, churches, and commercial blocks in the new styles of the postwar period. Edward Culliatt Jones, born in Northampton, Massachusetts, in 1822, came to Memphis from Charleston after serving four years in the Confederate Army,[7] and William C. Smith had served in the Army of Virginia before opening his architectural practice in Nashville in the early 1870s. Peter J. Williamson, who had come south in 1862 with the First Wisconsin Cavalry, stayed to practice architecture in Nashville. The architect-developer John W. Adams moved south from Ohio to Chattanooga in 1871,[8] and H.L. Huntington came to Chattanooga from New York state in 1875.[9] George W. Thompson, (1831–1910), English by birth, moved to Nashville from Cleveland before 1882.[10] Samuel McClung Patton came to Chattanooga in 1888 to supervise construction of the Richardson Building for the New Orleans firm of Sully, Toledano, and Patton; he stayed to become the city's most fashionable designer.[11] In the same year George F. Barber moved to Knoxville from De Kalb, Illinois, where he had begun to practice architecture about 1884.[12]

The new architects were drawn to the profession from apprenticeship, carpentry, and horticulture. Henry J. Dudley had come from England as a lad and had learned his profession in New York.[13] W.K. Dobson, born in Ireland about 1839, appears in the catalog of the Nashville Mechanics' Institute Exhibition of 1856 as a carver. In the *Tennessee State Gazetteer* of 1860–1861 Dobson advertised as a "Sculptor, Architectural and Fancy Wood Carver, Modeller, and Ornamental Designer," and by 1868 he was P.J. Williamson's partner in a Nashville architectural practice. Joseph F. Baumann of Knoxville had learned house carpentry from his father and had taught himself to draw.[14] Hugh C. Thompson began at the lowest rung of the ladder, working as a carpenter from 1854 until 1874, at least once on a job Heiman had designed,[15] and then as a draftsman and designer under P.J. Williamson before opening his own architectural office in Edgefield in 1878. M.H. Baldwin "before adopting this profession was a practical builder" in New York.[16]

Some had apprenticed under distinguished masters. James B. Cook had studied at King's College and had worked as one of the supervisors of construction at Joseph Paxton's Crystal Palace before coming to the United States. R.Z. Gill, born in Urbana, Illinois, had studied architecture under Professor N.C. Ricker at the University of Illinois and had worked for the famous Chicago firm Holabird and Roche before moving to Knoxville about 1889.[17] J.E.R. Carpenter, who came to Nashville in 1890, was a graduate of M.I.T. and a pupil of H.H. Richardson; and Henry Gibel, who also practiced in Nashville, had graduated from the Polytechnic School of Zurich before coming to the United States.[18] Between 1865 and 1900 study in a collegiate school of architecture became a common avenue into the profession, and the self-taught designer became a rarity.

After the war, architecture was an organized profession. The American Institute enjoyed a continuous existence after 1857; in 1870 the Western Association of Architects was formed; and on February 24, 1887, the Tennessee State Association of Architects was organized at Nashville, with W. C. Smith as president, James B. Cook, P. J. Williamson, and J. F. Baumann as vice-presidents.[19] Architects no longer worked with their hands as Thomas Hope had a century before; nor were architects itinerant like Blanchard or gentlemen-designers like Heiman or Strickland. In a world in which technology and commerce were increasingly important, reputable architects became businessmen. The designing house-carpenter vanished, as did the individual genius of the Gothic and Greek Revivals. The architectural partnership, the firm in which architects combined to increase their profits and supplement individual strengths dominated practice after 1865.

Postwar architects, formed by new educational and professional ideals and presiding over new materials and techniques, revolutionized design in Tennessee. Sentimental references to the Greek Revival (203) would never cease entirely, but the stable architectural images of the forties had been irretrievably lost. Even the Gothic Revival did not come through the war unaltered. Heiman's castellated style was replaced by an exuberant, unhistorical expressionism that employed Gothic details and themes playfully and affectively. The new design theories were to varying degrees developments of the popular romanticism that had begun to dominate American life after the war. In prewar theory precedent and principle had been important authorities, but the designs of the period between 1865 and the Centennial were full of weak, oblique references to the orders and to Gothic and Romanesque detail. Postwar architectural images displayed man not as the creature of some reasonable and regular order but as master of space, matter, and the historical past, capable of effecting whatever might please. Between architects like Joseph F. Baumann, Mathias Harvey Baldwin, and Peter J. Williamson and their antebellum predecessors there was an impassable theoretical gulf. Although Strickland's attempt to state his Grecian theory clearly was never entirely successful and although Heiman might have had difficulty explaining the relation between his Jefferson Street cottage and Vignola, both were convinced that architecture proceeded according to imaginative rules and followed historical precedents. Most postwar architects were innocent of historical understanding: Gropius and Wright, coming as they did on the heels of the Renaissance Revival of the nineties, thought historicism a beast worth slaying, but as a source of theory and precedent history had in fact been dead since 1865, destroyed by the eclectic architects of the seventies and eighties whose works the moderns so roundly despised. An obituary published in the *Nashville Tennessean* on July 25, 1919, praised Hugh C. Thompson as an architect who had "developed several styles in vogue before the Civil War." Thompson himself called his design for the McKendree Church of 1879, "the Thompsonian style, as there is nothing like it anywhere."[20]

Despite the conviction of postwar architects that tradition and precedent were dead, architectural images coalesced into several fashions. Second Empire was a style developed in France after 1854, when the *Nouveau Louvre* was begun by J. T. Visconti and Hector Martin Lefuel; the Paris Expositions of 1855 and 1867 spread the style. Although there were strong allusions to the architecture of the French Renaissance, Second Empire was not a traditional style but was rightly described by writers of the period as modern. Steep mansard roofs broken by richly enframed dormers, elongated openings, roofs crowned with heavy, ornate, and untraditional pediments, as well as the extensive use of iron railings and balustrades typified the new fashion; and details were free, often exotic, treatments of highly mannered classical elements: arches, brackets, fanlights, and pediments. The James D. Cowan residence (204) built by J. F. Baumann near the University in Knoxville in 1879,[21] and the towered

203. *The Hardeman County Courthouse in Bolivar, designed by Joseph Willis and Fletcher Sloan, illustrates the persistence of Grecian themes into the late sixties.*

204. *Joseph F. Baumann designed this Second Empire mansion for James D. Cowan of Knoxville in the late 1870s. Every movement of the beholder's eye brought variety and surprise.*

203

204

205

206

mansions E. C. Jones built in Memphis during the 1870s—the Amos Woodruff house (1871), the Charles W. Goyer house (1873) on Adams Street, and the H. A. Montgomery house on Poplar (205), built about 1875[22]—were imposing townhouses erected in this style. The Oaks (206), John Roper Branner's elegant mansion near Jefferson City, designed by W. H. Clyce about 1868, is perhaps the grandest Second Empire country house remaining in Tennessee. The east side of Nashville's Public Square, where John L. Smith's Methodist Publishing House and P. J. Williamson's City Hotel Block stood from the early 1870s until 1974,[23] illustrated the use of the style in commercial designs (207). Among the most successful Second Empire public buildings were the courthouses built by

205. The H.A. Montgomery house on fashionable Poplar Avenue was the palace of the general manager of the Memphis Cotton Exchange and Storage Company, a firm which compressed and forwarded much of the cotton shipped through the port of Memphis.

206. The Oaks, John Roper Branner's Second Empire villa, overlooked the tracks of his railroad, the East Tennessee and Virginia, from a hilltop near Jefferson City.

207. On August 8, 1872, the Nashville Union and American wrote of John L. Smith's Methodist Publishing House (left): "There is a contagion in the very look of this and similar buildings on the east side of the Square, and it is to be hoped that the disease will spread until our capitalists are fever hot in advocacy of such improvements." P. J. Williamson's City Hotel Block (on the right), the publishing house, and other nearby buildings formed the most impressive group of Second Empire buildings in Tennessee.

A. C. Bruce during the years of his Knoxville practice, in Loudon (1871–1872), Morristown (1874), Athens (1875), and Chattanooga (1879);[24] and the handsome Smith County Courthouse at Carthage (1871) by a still unidentified architect.

The Italianate of the 1850s seldom reappeared after the war, except in combination with the new Second Empire style. Originally touted by A. J. Downing in the archetypal version that usually included brackets, the tower, porch, and asymmetrical, irregular volumes, a type exemplified by Heiman's house on Jefferson Street in Nashville (169), Italianate bequeathed to postwar architecture its tower, massing, overly vertical fenestration, heavy moldings, and a fascination with the

208

209

fifteenth-century Italian window, but these devices were used throughout a wide range of Italianate-Second Empire styles (often called simply Italian) in which pure types, if such were possible, were exceptions. Residences in Nashville like the tiny towered frame house at 913 Fatherland (208) are vernacular adaptations of pervasive Italianate themes, which had survived the war in such designs as M. H. Baldwin's residence for Judge William M. Randolph (209), built at Beale and Lauderdale in Memphis in the late 1860s,[25] and achieved monumental expression in buildings like W. C. Smith's Robertson County Courthouse (1879) at Springfield, where Italianate arcades and towers, Second Empire mansards, and Renaissance balusters and pilasters were stylishly combined.

During the seventies Gothic style was transformed by an expressionism in which traditional details were reinterpreted as elements in complex, abstract designs. W. K. Dobson's Moore Memorial Presbyterian Church (210),[26] begun in Nashville in 1872; Hugh C. Thompson's McKendree Methodist (211) in the same city;[27] and A. C. Bruce's Church Street Methodist (212), built in Knoxville in 1879[28] illustrate the development of this expressionist Gothic style. The most spectacular example was perhaps Central Baptist in Memphis (213), begun by E. C. Jones about 1868 but not completed until 1885,[29] which was hardly Gothic at all. As the seventies waned the nervous expressionism of McKendree and Church Street Methodist passed into the superficially historicist Ruskinian style of J. F. Baumann's Immaculate Conception Catholic Church (1883–1887) on Knoxville's Summit Hill (214)[30] and J.W. Adams' First Methodist Church at McCallie and Georgia in Chattanooga (215).[31] After 1880 there was more concern for historical correctness, and churches like Nashville's First Baptist (1884–1886), by George W. Thompson and William S. Matthews,[32] Christ Episcopal Church (1888–1892) in the same city, designed by Francis H. Kimball of New York; and First Methodist, Memphis (1887–1891)[33]; were built.

Beginning about 1885, the neo-Romanesque architecture developed by the New York designer H. H. Richardson became popular in Tennessee. The towers and arcades that characterized this style were probably derived in part from antebellum Italianate architecture,

210. *Moore Memorial Presbyterian Church, built on Broad Street opposite Fifteenth Avenue in Nashville, was designed by W. K. Dobson. The building was a good humored example of the abstract geometrics of the 1870s.*

211. *The McKendree Methodist Church, built on Nashville's Church Street in 1877–1878, was an engaging collage of borrowed historical details, interpreted in the vertical imaginative matrix which the eye preferred during the seventies.* ▶

208. *The house at 913 Fatherland Street, Nashville, is a carpenter's version of Italianate, the dwelling of a prosperous clerk or mechanic.*

209. *Mathias Harvey Baldwin's house for Judge William M. Randolph, built about 1870 at the northeast corner of Beale and Lauderdale in Memphis, was an expressionist version of Second Empire and Italianate themes.*

212. *Knoxville's Church Street Methodist Church, built on the north side of Church between Market and Walnut in 1879, was a masterful essay in Gothic expressionism by architect A. C. Bruce.*

213. *Central Baptist Church, built on Second Street north of Beale in Memphis, illustrates the tendency of designs of the 1870s to lapse into an unhistorical and profoundly modern concern for form and texture.*

211

212

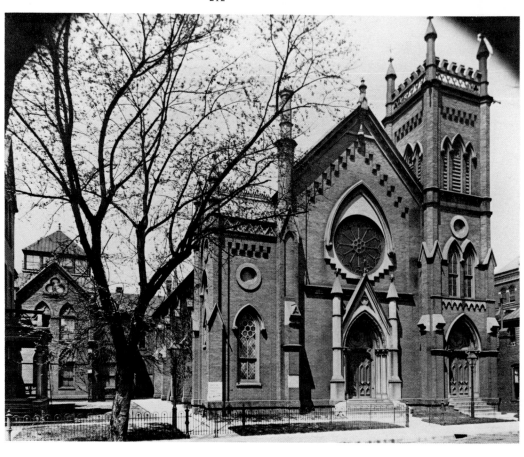

213

214. *Joseph F. Baumann's Immaculate Conception Catholic Church, built in a Ruskinian Gothic style, still dominates downtown Knoxville from atop Summit Hill.*

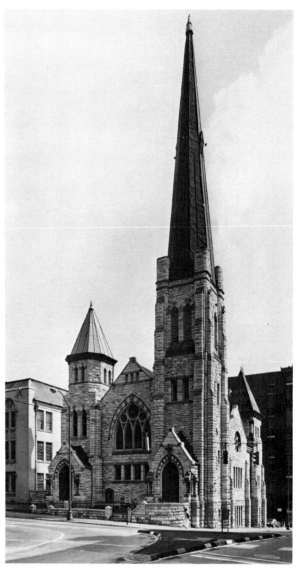

215. *By 1885, when John W. Adams' First Methodist Church was completed in Chattanooga, Gothic was becoming more traditional, but the design still displays greater interest in textures and tensions than in imitating the style of the Middle Ages.*

but in the hands of Richardson and his followers Romanesque became an architecture of rough stone textures, massive arches, and interesting, irregular masses. Richardson Romanesque, like the Gothic of the postwar period, adapted medieval themes without paying much attention to the principles which shaped the originals. The European architecture of the twelfth century inspired, albeit obliquely, S. M. Patton's Mountain City Club (216), built in 1890 at Seventh and Cherry in Chattanooga; Reuben Harrison Hunt's Second Presbyterian Church (217) in the same city, completed in 1891;[34] and the Adams Block at Seventh and Georgia, also in Chattanooga. The style was at its best in the stonework of the Nasville YMCA (218), by G. W. Thompson (1887);[35] and the Second Presbyterian Church in Memphis (219), built from a design of Frederick Kees and Francis B. Long of Minneapolis in

1891–1892.[36] Memphis' Cossitt Library (220), built at the northwest corner of Front and Monroe between 1890 and 1893 by L. B. Wheeler, was, as the *Commercial* pronounced it on April 13, 1893, a handsome Romanesque building unsurpassed "in all the south and west." One of the most sensitively executed Romanesque churches was Thomas Lynch Dismukes' Tulip Street Methodist Church (221), built in Nashville in 1893,[37] and remarkable for its beautifully finished oak interior. These brick and stone Romanesque buildings were rarely without touches of the delicate, interesting curvilinear ornament Louis Sullivan made famous after 1880. Occasionally, as with Knoxville's St. John's Episcopal Church, built by J. W. Yost of Columbus, Ohio, in 1892,[38] and First Methodist (222), built in 1894 at Clinch and Locust by Kramer and Weary of Akron, Romanesque became an architecture of clean, almost

216. *The Mountain City Club in Chattanooga, designed in 1890 by S. M. Patton, shows the influence of the Romanesque of H. H. Richardson.*

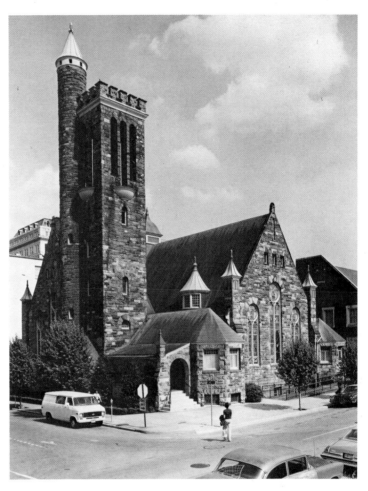

217. *In his 1891 design for Second Presbyterian Church, Chattanooga, Reuben Harrison Hunt used Romanesque themes to create an architecture of bold, dynamic forms.*

modern masses and clear, dynamic geometry. Nashville's Union Station (223), built in 1900, in frank imitation of the Allegheny County (Pennsylvania) Courthouse of 1888, was one of the last great Richardsonian buildings in the United States.[39]

Designers were challenged by the new technology and often used it with remarkable success. Cast iron had been manufactured in Tennessee before the war, and in the seventies there was still some use of iron for architectural details; and although Romanesque and other new styles made cast-iron store fronts unpopular after 1880, cast and wrought iron continued to be used structurally until the riveted steel frame came into local use in the 1890s. Glass was also used in greater quantities after 1865. The Glass Building, a four-story block built by P. C. Wilson in 1879 at the southeast corner of Eighth and Broad in Chattanooga, had walls of glass set

218. *(A) Nashville's* YMCA, *on the south side of Church between College and Cherry, was a sensitive, sophisticated, Romanesque design. (B) This rendering illustrates the development of architectural drawing during the 1880s.* ▶

219. *Second Presbyterian Church, Memphis, completed in 1813, was a late-blooming Richardson Romanesque design by Kees and Long of Minneapolis. When the photograph was made, the windows had not been set.*

220. *The Cossitt Library was the Memphis version of Richardson's Crane Memorial Library (1880–1883) at Quincy, Massachusetts, or Billingsley Library (1883–1886) in Burlington, Vermont.*

221. *Tulip Street Methodist Church in Nashville is an expressionist Romanesque masterpiece in which molded brick replaced the delicately carved banding of stone examples.*

218(A)

219

218(B)

220

221

222

223

in delicately worked iron frames (224), a use anticipating twentieth-century practice.[40] In Tennessee the commercial buildings of the seventies were four- and five-story blocks, often vaguely Italianate, like the Tennessee Block (225) in Memphis, designed by Jones and Baldwin,[41] or the commercial rows erected on Second Avenue, South and around the Public Square in Nashville.[42] Tenants and clients would walk four flights (but not much higher) to the top of these buildings, but the elevator, first used in an office building in 1871, soon made possible six- and seven-story office buildings like S. M. Patton's Richardson Building, built on Seventh Street between Broad and Market in Chattanooga (1888), and E.C. Jones's six-story office for the *Memphis Appeal* (1890), built at Jefferson and Main in 1890. The Eastlake style, named, perhaps inappropriately, for the English architect Charles Eastlake (1833–1906), who in his *Hints on Household Taste* (1868) proposed a simplified system of ornament, was an attempt to turn

224. P. C. Wilson's glass store in Chattanooga (1879) anticipated the twentieth-century curtain wall.

technological mastery over wood and iron to good account by creating a system of architectural detail that utilized the rectilinear patterns that steam carpentry machines could easily produce (226). Industrial processes permitted a proliferation of metal castings, composition tiles and shingles, and cast-iron mantels and railings. The machine was used precisely as Wright was later to demand, to demonstrate the supremacy of the human imagination, though those who employed it sometimes confused the proliferation of exuberant detail with good design.

An interest in innovation, effect, and technique made architects daring and experimental. The work of Peter J. Williamson typified the postwar development of a new architecture of pure design. After a brief Italianate and Second Empire phase—represented by the City Hotel Block (1870) on the east side of Nashville's public square; the proposed Nashville Markethouse of 1871, "designed after the Rococo or Italian style" with a "superbly decorated dome" and "four handsomely ornamented turrets of elaborate and unique finish";[43] and the "Norman style" Charles J. McClung mansion in Knoxville (1875–1876)[44]—Williamson adopted a manner which combined geometrical forms and masses without serious reference to any discernible stylistic

222. First Methodist, Knoxville, built in 1894, was Richardson Romanesque at its best—powerful, carefully composed, full of dramatic contrasts between rough and smooth, randomness and rectilinearity, and light and dark.

223. Nashville's Union Station, the hub of the industrial city of the early twentieth century, is an urban monument second in importance only to the Capitol.

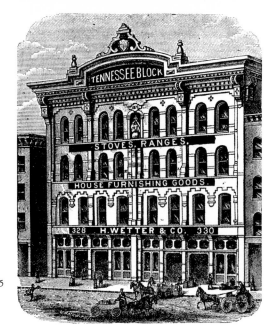

225

226

227

228. *The St. Luke's Episcopal Church, Cleveland, Bradley County (1887), designed by Peter J. Williamson, is a composition of bold forms which, given clues like pointed windows and buttresses, seems Gothic.*

precedent. The Blind School (227) in Nashville (1873–1881);[45] and St. Luke's Episcopal Church, Cleveland (228), built in 1877,[46] illustrate Williamson's ability to transcend historicism with design. Although the school seems at first to be a Second Empire building because of its mansards and St. Luke's Church seems Gothic because of its mass and tower, both are free compositions of shapes and details evoking reminiscences of past architectural types. Williamson found an apt disciple in Hugh C. Thompson, a carpenter who learned to design while working in Williamson's office in 1874. The "Thompsonian style" of McKendree

225. *The Tennessee Block, which stood on Main between Monroe and Union streets in Memphis, was a good example of the postwar business block.*

226. *The staccato rectilinearity of Chattanooga's Central Block (1883) on the northeast corner of Broad and West Ninth was characteristic of Eastlake designs in brick.*

227. *As P. J. Williamson's design for the Tennessee School for the Blind (1874) in Nashville shows, the neoclassical manner of his City Hotel Block of 1871 (207) had quickly given way to more exciting geometries.*

Church (1879), described by one writer as "Norman-Gothic," was a concatenation of lancet windows, bulls-eyes, buttresses, and rusticated voussoirs, as well as spires, the center one an impressive 230 feet tall.[47] McKendree Church was prophetic of Thompson's architectural career. Hugh C. Thompson of Nashville later designed the Fourth National Bank (1884),[48] a miniature version of Richard Morris Hunt's Second Empire-Eastlake Tribune Building (1873–1875); the famous Union Gospel Tabernacle, best remembered as the Ryman Auditorium, in a flat, mannered Gothic in 1889;[49] and the Glen Leven Presbyterian Church in a fanciful combination of Gothic and Flemish styles (1891).[50] Nashville's new Vine Street Christian Church (229), designed by Bruce and Morgan of Atlanta, was typical of this innovative spirit.[51] There were arches and gables, two nugatory pinnacles, and overstated curvilinear dentils. With or without the steeple presumably intended by the architect to dominate the right corner of the building, the church remains an asymmetrical exercise in affective surfaces and free design elements. The staggered windows and bull's-eye on the right are transitional to Louis Sullivan and Frank Lloyd Wright. The pediment on the left, taken alone, is almost worthy of Mackintosh. Although the building refers to Richardson's Trinity Church, Boston, the architect's theory was that there is no theory, only form and materials. A similar analysis could be offered of

229. *Nashville's Vine Street Christian Church, built on the west side of Vine near Church in 1889, combined stylistic elements usually identified as Romanesque (arches), Queen Anne (the gable treatment), Gothic (pinnacles), and Art Nouveau (the tower base).*

W. C. Smith's Main Building at Vanderbilt (230), built in 1874.[52] It is an interesting marriage of themes borrowed from Second Empire (the mansards, dormers, and metal finials), and from expressionist Gothic (the lancets, trefoils, quatrefoils, and gabled porch). The building displays no historical commitments, only a series of engaging images which allude in passing to various historical styles.

In the year before the World's Columbian Exposition of 1893, Charles Hite-Smith, in an article describing the new office tower the New York firm of De Lemos and Cordes had designed for the *Chattanooga Times* (238), traced the course architecture had taken since the war: "The first departures from the old forms were but the copies of other buildings abroad, the next step a combination of selected features, until now, no important building is erected in which may be found what a student would class as a 'pure' type."[53] Very little in the recent architectural history of Tennessee would have

230. Main Building, at Vanderbilt University, Nashville, was a Second Empire villa enlarged, with Gothic fenestration.

called Hite-Smith's judgment in question. W. K. Dobson had completed the new temple for Ohavaj Sholom congregation (231) on Nashville's Vine Street in 1877, in what one critic called "Byzantine style."[54] W. A. Potter of Washington had begun the Gothic Custom House at Spruce and Broadway in Nashville in 1875,[55] and five years later William C. Smith had completed the building for the Nashville Centennial in a style that combined medieval details and Eastlake millwork in the southwest corner of the same intersection.[56] The most imposing commercial building completed in Memphis during the eighties was the new Cotton Exchange, designed in an expressionist Renaissance manner (232). Vine Street Christian Church, Nashville, had been occupied in 1889, and in 1890 West End

231. *Nashville's Vine Street Temple is another example of W. K. Dobson's irrepressible imagination.*

Methodist Church, a "modern" design combining Romanesque and Byzantine details, the work of Pohl and Simeon of Washington, D.C., was completed at the northeast corner of Broadway and Belmont (Sixteenth Avenue) in the same city.[57] T. L. Dismukes' Romanesque Tulip Street Church had been dedicated in Nashville a few months before Hite-Smith wrote. Thompson and Zwicker were at work on the new Warner School, a Romanesque-Queen Anne design built in 1893 at the southwest corner of Russell and South Seventh; and the towered Victor E. Shwab Building, which still stands in Nashville on the corner of Second and Broad.[58] In Knoxville George Barber was becoming famous as a designer who could supply Queen Anne designs by mail throughout the world (233, 234). A conservative estimate would suggest that

10,000 residences were built from his plans in the United States, Canada, and Japan, and his pattern books, with titles like *Modern Artistic Cottages* (1891) and *New Model Dwellings* (1894), circulated widely. George Barber was following the practice of such eastern firms as Palliser and Palliser of New York, who had published books like *Palliser's Courthouses, Village, Town and City Halls* in which the design for Knox County's own Queen Anne courthouse (1884–1886) appeared in 1889 (235).

In the centennial year two other monumental courthouses, both extant, were completed in Queen Anne style: the Henry County Courthouse at Paris, by Reuben Harrison Hunt of Chattanooga, and the Sevier County Courthouse at Sevierville, designed by the McDonald Brothers of Louisville.[59] Although its bay windows, gables, dormers, cantilevers, and intricate detailing partly justified the association with English domestic architecture of the early eighteenth century, the title Queen Anne was used comprehensively to refer to a wide variety of free classical types and designs.

Most critics viewed this profusion of trivialized historical themes with approval. Reviewing the development of American architecture in his *Chattanooga Times* article, Charles Hite-Smith remarked, "The departure from the Greek and Gothic path is hardly noticeable in the architecture of this country until in the more expensive public buildings which have been erected by private capital in the years succeeding the war." What did not disturb the critic, who wrote only a few months before the designs for the Chicago fair would popularize the classical tradition once more, was the evidence that imagination, uninformed by tradition or theory and presiding over the almost magical resources of a new technology, threatened to degenerate into an empty architectural rhetoric.

There is more than one analysis of late-nineteenth-century architecture. One theme often reiterated is that

232. *The Memphis Cotton Exchange, built at Madison and Second streets between 1883 and 1885, was composed of fancifully imagined classical elements.* ▶

233. *The Isaac Ziegler house, Knoxville, probably designed by Charles F. Barber, illustrates the playful richness of the Queen Anne style.*

234. *This Queen Anne dwelling, built by Baxter Smith just south of Gallatin in Sumner County about 1894, was probably constructed from plans provided by Charles F. Barber's Knoxville drafting room.*

235. *Knox County's Queen Anne courthouse was designed in 1884 by Palliser, Palliser and Company of New York, perhaps at the request of the Knoxville contractors Stephenson and Getaz.*

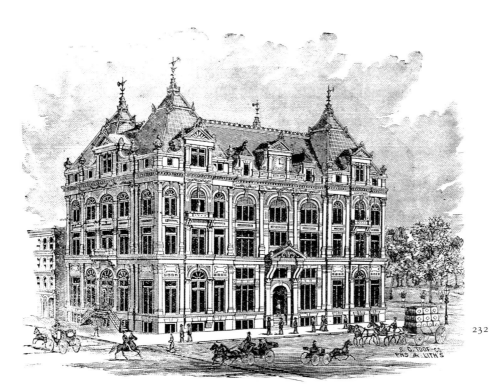

232

233

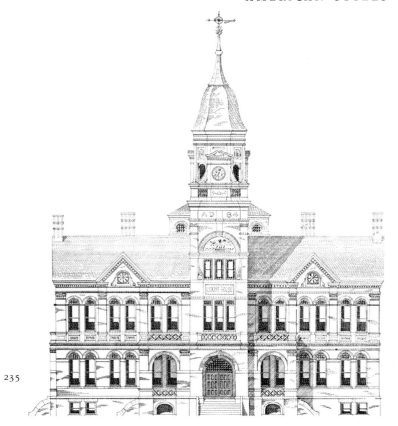

235

234

236. *The Memphis Custom House, begun on the west side of Front Street at Madison in 1877, was a dignified and successful essay in Italianate classicism.*

237. *The architect's attempt to use classic forms in his design for this twelve-story skyscraper, the Duncan Building in Nashville, illustrates the late-nineteenth-century liason between architectural historicism and the new technology.*

the revivals of the postwar period were corrupt and derivative, imitative and unauthentic. This analysis was sometimes offered by defenders of the various modern movements, who saw in the works of Wright, Le Corbusier, and Gropius some cause for believing that architecture had returned to a reasonable, coherent, theoretical foundation. More recently, late-nineteenth-century architecture has been praised for its rich variety and playful, humane character. Both appreciation and criticism are in order. From 1865 to 1890 there was an abandonment of the appeal to precedent and traditional principles that had determined design and theory since the fifteenth century. The architecture that resulted was fanciful, generous, and interesting but usually only remotely related to the technological rationalism that inspired postwar industrial development.

When the architects of the Chicago exhibition met to discuss their task in 1892, it became clear that an architecture of whimsy was not suited to the development of a vast unified scheme for the Grant Park site. The alternative that appealed to Richard Morris Hunt

and Charles McKim, easterners who dominated the committee, was a return to the classicism Americans like Richardson had learned at the Ecole des Beaux-Arts. During the seventies and eighties Beaux-Arts Classicism, which combined an appeal to Renaissance tradition with a sweeping, rationalistic theory of design, influenced not only individual architects, but the curriculum of M.I.T., which under William Rotch Ware and W. Francis Chandler often appointed instructors educated in Paris to its faculty. Classicism carried the day, and the buildings for the Chicago fair, with the famous exception of the Transportation Building, were designed in that style.

The classical tradition had never died. It was the source from which the fantastic details of Second Empire were developed, as well as the careful Italianate of Alfred B. Mullet, whose Knoxville Custom House (1871–1874) displays a classic restraint. In the late 1880s this ambivalent classicism gave way to a new academic style. Although the Memphis Custom House (236) was completed in this same chastened Italian manner in 1885,[60] by the late 1880s Italianate

classicism was giving way to the studied refinements of a more academic style. The premier American monument of Beaux-Arts Classicism was the Boston Public Library, designed by Charles McKim in 1888. The building's classic character was established by the great glazed arcade, a form summarizing western architecture from the aqueducts to Henri Labrouste's Bibliothèque Sainte-Geneviève (1844–50), which faced Copley Square. The style had the advantage of at least seeming to reinstate precedent as a source for design, and in the minds of those who had actually attended the École des Beaux-Arts or one of the American schools influenced by it, Renaissance classicism was associated

238. The Chattanooga Times Building, built in 1891–1892 by De Lemus and Cordes of New York, anticipated the classical revival in Tennessee. Without the bull's eye, the monopteron, and the entrance arch, the building might have passed for Romanesque, though the treatment of the arches was Palladian rather than medieval. The building in the foreground is Reuben Harrison Hunt's Carnegie Library (1904).

with a consistent design methodology. The year after McKim's design for the Boston Library was accepted, George W. Thompson of Nashville produced a design for an office building, commissioned by William Duncan, which had Renaissance elements: pilaster, pedi-

ments, a heavy cornice, and balusters (237). The new style was evident in the *Chattanooga Times* building of 1892 (238), where the arcading and corner tower belong ambivalently to the fading Romanesque while the dome and other details are derived from Renaissance precedents; and there is more than a hint of the new classicism in W.C. Smith's design for Colemere, the handsome residence E. W. Cole built on Murfreesboro Pike six miles southeast of Nashville in 1893.[61] These were attempts, varying widely in their success, to appropriate the classic image McKim and Hunt had grasped quite clearly.

The Chicago fair was the sign, not the cause, of the victory of Beaux-Arts Classicism, and through the exposition the style was popularized across the country. The pages of the *American Architect and Building News* and the *Architectural Record* suggest that most architects of the 1890s saw the new classicism as a reprieve from the imaginative chaos of the Reconstruction era and the beginning of a reformed architecture based on sound theoretical and traditional norms. By 1895, when George W. Thompson and his partner Julius G. Zwicker designed the Vanderbilt Medical School in the

239. The Vanderbilt University Medical Department building was constructed in 1895 by Thompson and Zwicker at the southeast corner of Summer (Fifth Avenue, South) and Elm in Nashville.

new style (239),[62] Beaux-Arts Classicism had captured the imaginations of provincial architects, providing an irresistible precedent for the executive committee of the proposed Tennessee centennial celebration.

On September 12, 1895, Director General E.C. Lewis announced a scheme that made a copy of the Parthenon the central building in a carefully designed park, and on October 8 Lewis solicited plans for the Parthenon, the Transportation Building, and the Auditorium. The scheme adopted at Nashville imitated Frederick Law Olmsted's design for the Chicago exposition site, a triangular plot with buildings grouped around canals and lakes. A committee composed of Director General Lewis, H.W. Buttorff, J.W. Thomas, and W.L. Dudley recommended that the Parthenon be entrusted to W.C. Smith, that G.W. Thompson's classic design for the Auditorium be accepted, and that J.G. Zwicker be given the commission for the Transporta-

tion Building.[63] The choice of Smith was fitting, for he had designed the building for the Nashville Centennial of 1880, and had been among the first to propose a celebration of the state's centennial as a means of overcoming the depression of 1893. Smith had been an active local member of the A.I.A. before 1885, when he was present at the first of two meetings the institute would hold in Nashville before the centennial.[64] When Smith presented his proposal to the Commercial Club of Nashville in a letter dated November 13, 1893, he already appreciated both the architectural character of the Chicago fair and its economic success. The official history of the centennial notes that it was "more than passing strange" that in two thousand years no one had attempted to reproduce the Parthenon. Perhaps the willingness of Tennesseans to undertake what the world had left alone was significant, representing simultaneously a failure of imagination of which the age was naïvely unaware, an innocent presumption about Tennessee's place in history, a half-conscious nostalgia for the classic past, and a fascination with the new transcendence over time and place that technology made possible.

240. The Transportation Building which Louis Sullivan designed for the World's Columbian Exposition at Chicago in 1893 is usually ranked among the major monuments of the modern movement in America. The building was an innovative development of themes found within the Romanesque revival.

If the Parthenon was to be the central building on the centennial site, it followed that the other important structures would be built in the new classical revival style. George W. Thompson's Auditorium and B.J. Hodge's Commerce Building were collages of the architecture of Chicago's white city, most strongly reminiscent of the Agriculture Building by Van Brunt and Howe. So thoroughly had the architecture of the Chicago fair captured imagination that Zwicker's Transportation Building (241) was designed in imitation of Louis Sullivan's famous building in Chicago (240) and, like Sullivan's, was the single important building on the site not built in classical style. Indeed the entire spatial conception, the arrangement of buildings around a water garden, was borrowed from Frederick Law Olmsted's design for the Chicago site. Tennessee followed Chicago in importing gondolas; there

241

242

was a Chinese Village, and Nashville's Streets of Cairo would undoubtedly have compared favorably with Chicago's Javanese Village and Ruins of the Yucatán. When the exposition opened on May 1, 1897, William C. Smith's Parthenon and James B. Cook's Shelby County pyramid stood outlined in electric lights above a lovely man-made lake where a little more than a century before there had been wilderness (242).

Beaux-Arts Classicism had triumphed in Tennessee before the American Institute of Architects held their thirtieth conference in Nashville on October 20–22, 1896.[65] William C. Smith, James B. Cook of Memphis, and S.M. Patton of Chattanooga were prominent hosts. J.W. Yost of Columbus, Ohio, who had recently designed Knoxville's Romanesque St. John's Episcopal Church, read a brilliant analysis of the effects of steel and glass, observing that steel "should not be concealed in the design, and that the surface of the building should take the form of a covering of continuous posts, and a covering of horizontal members between posts, and the filling in of the panels which intervene."[66] Dankmar Adler, the engineer who had made Sullivan's steel-framed Wainwright Building (1891) a reality, was absent, perhaps because the straitened circumstances which had followed upon the breakup of Adler and Sullivan the preceding year had nearly impoverished him, but a paper in which Adler urged the use of steel as a development of modern life and a necessity in business buildings was read by the secretary. At the Nashville meeting the A.I.A. voted to locate its permanent headquarters in Washington, and first empowered a committee to investigate the opinions of the chapters regarding licensing laws. In the closing session the members voted to contribute at least $500 toward the cost of Daniel French's memorial to the institute's past president, Richard Morris Hunt, the architect who, perhaps more than any other, was responsible for the Beaux-Arts phase of the Renaissance Revival.

After the centennial, buildings in the new style were constructed across Tennessee and the regional tradition ended. Tennessee had never been isolated from the major trends in American architecture; the first dwellings had been as much products of tradition as the exposition buildings were of national fashion. But the

241. The Transportation Building at the Tennessee Centennial, Nashville, lacked the magnificence of Sullivan's original (240), but Julius G. Zwicker's building was obviously designed with the Chicago building in mind.

242. The brilliant light of electric lamps silhouetted the Parthenon and Pyramid at Nashville's Centennial Exposition, symbolizing Tennessee's ambivalent reappropriation of the classic past.

Beaux-Arts Classicism of the 1890s marked the deliberate assimilation of regional architecture to American style. The Carnegie libraries in Nashville and Chattanooga, both built in 1904—the first by A.R. Ross of New York[67] and the second by Reuben Harrison Hunt[68]—represent the style in its maturity, and New York architect James Gamble Rogers' Shelby County Courthouse, built in 1909,[69] and Hunt's Hamilton County Courthouse (1913)[70] set fashions that were followed until the forties.

Tennesseans understood in 1897 that the local flavor of their civilization was fading. As late as 1891, F.W. Kreider, editor of the only issue of the *Southern Builder and Decorator* that ever came off the presses of its Nashville publisher, wrote: "Beauty and utility will be both best advanced by rendering Southern homes and business houses more surely in touch with Southern tastes and requirements than by merging their distinctiveness in types chosen by those more interested in other sections than our own." But the process of assimilation was nearly completed. At the opening of the centennial, H.W. Carmack had warned Tennesseans that "the wise thing is to move forward with the moving world" and suggested that education "needs to have a little less reference to Greece and Rome, and a little more to the United States of America." The regional architecture that Kreider called for was no longer possible, though, ironically, the modern style that marked the end of local architectural traditions had a good deal to do with Greece and Rome.

During the last decade of the nineteenth century movements that would determine design in the twentieth century matured: the failure of the old cities under the pressures of increasing population; industrialization; the construction of tall, high-density buildings; and the inevitable flight from this unsatisfactory urban environment to the suburbs and new industrial towns. Because tall, riveted-steel buildings became technically and economically feasible twenty years before the automobile, the first attempts to renew the urban environment encouraged concentration rather than the dispersion which theorists like Frank Lloyd Wright proposed and new trasnportation systems soon made possible. The form of urban work (factories and stores) also encouraged the concentration of population, and made tall buildings the dominant form. H.C. Thompson's Baxter Court (243), built in 1887,[71] and Henry J. Dudley's Jackson Building (244), completed three years later,[72] were symbols of Nashville's success as a modern city. When S.M. Patton's Richardson Building burned on April 3, 1897, a Chattanooga newspaper asked, "When will we have another six story building?"

243. When Hugh C. Thompson designed Baxter Court, for the southeast corner of Church and College (Third Avenue, North), Nashville, in 1887, the form of the modern skyscraper was already evident. This photograph shows the building as it was reconstructed after the fire of Christmas Eve, 1888.

244. The Jackson Building (1896) in Nashville was derived from H. H. Richardson's Marshall Field Wholesale Store in Chicago (1885).

These six- and seven-story buildings, however, were still built with the technology of the 1850s, perfected by the better iron and steel new processes made possible and by elevators. But in 1895 Tennessee's first skyscraper, the Continental Building (245), a tower of skeleton-steel construction, twelve stories high with two high-speed electric elevators, was begun in Memphis. The architects were E.C. Jones, whose career had begun when buildings were joined and cast iron a rarity, and his partners Henderson J. Hain and Marion A. Kirby. The *Appeal* for February 24, 1895, interpreted the new bank's significance correctly: "This building marks a new era in structural architecture in the south, being the only large, fire-proof edifice built on first-class modern principles south of the Ohio River."

Railroad stations and freight yards, built at the heart of most of Tennessee's large towns, drove out wealthy residents and made city centers desirable sites for factories. Industrialization, rising population density, and the consequent deterioration of the cities reinforced visually the message of the romantic poets: the good life could best be found outside town walls. Inspired by the ideal of a cooperative agrarian existence, Thomas Hughes, the famous author of *Tom Brown's School Days,* came from England to establish Rugby in Morgan County in October 1880, and the chapel and Kingston Lisle (246), Hughes's own residence, are remnants of a grand scheme meant to turn a corner of the Cumberland Plateau into a Ruskinian paradise. The plateau, the wilderness or barrens through which the eighteenth-century traveler had hurried on his way from Southwest Point to the Cumberland Settlements, was poor land, and Rugby soon failed, but the Cumberlands were rich in minerals and often beautiful. Stephen F. Tracy had opened his Sewanee Mining Company about 1854 and in 1857 had given land to the trustees of the proposed University of the South in order to encourage them to choose the Franklin County site for their new school. In 1859 Bishop John Henry Hopkins came from Vermont to provide the plans that would determine the development of the campus and village until his design was superseded in 1886.[73] The war delayed construction, but afterward the university was given several distinguished buildings. St. Luke's Memorial Hall (247), designed by Henry Hudson Holly in 1878,[74] and the library with its Breslin Tower, probably inspired by Oxford's Magdalen and built from a design of W. Halsey Wood in 1886–1888,[75] were soon surrounded by Gothic and Queen Anne cottages.

The grandest resort on the plateau was Beersheba Inn, founded at Beersheba Springs in Grundy County in 1833 and enlarged by John Armfield in 1857.[76] After the war the Beersheba Inn no longer resounded to "the merry jingle of violins and castenets" that a novelist described in the 1850s,[77] but the plateau gained the attention of a group of Middle Tennessee businessmen who were interested in establishing a suitable summer site for a local Chautauqua, the adult education movement that had captured the imagination of the liberal middle class of the postwar period. The Monteagle Assembly Grounds, its Children's Temple and Hall of Philosophy set among woodland paths, was a monument to the postwar conviction that temperance, liberal religion, and education would result in permanent betterment. In the summer of 1883, Monteagle residents could have heard lectures on bacteria and education, as well as attending sermons and prayer meetings.[78] And for the wealthy there was Lookout Mountain with its famous inn, the huge shingle-style resort hotel designed by S.M. Patton in 1889 (248),[79] where billiards and miniature golf replaced the uplifting entertainments of Monteagle.

The conviction that the good life could best be found in the countryside does much to explain why suburbs flourished as soon as streetcar lines and automobiles made them accessible. By 1900 the middle class was in full flight to the first subdivisions and the wealthy to the English style and classical revival villas that ringed the cities. The mere possession of land, not as a necessity for the agrarian way of life or even as a productive asset but as a means of gaining control over social space and distance from urban life, determined new patterns of land use. The middle-class dwellings of the 1880s and 1890s were separated from street and neighbors by small (and often useless) green spaces; and the villas of

245. *The Continental Building in Memphis, the first skeleton-steel building in Tennessee, heralded urban density, suburbs, and automobiles. The building stood at the southeast corner of Main and South Court, its twelfth-floor observatory providing a spectacular view of Memphis and the Mississippi.*

the rich, no longer farms but the homes of bankers and entrepreneurs, were set amid carefully designed gardens.

The abandonment of the cities was accompanied by the first attempts to develop towns especially suited to the new industrial organization of life, and in Tennessee these attempts were often associated with mineral discoveries and the attendant land speculation. Tracy City was as much a child of the search for southern coal and iron as Birmingham, but the Alabama city became a successful manufacturing center while Tracy City, Altamont, and Coalmont remained mining villages. Early in the 1890s a dozen new towns were founded in the Cumberlands and the Tennessee Valley. Harriman was

246

247

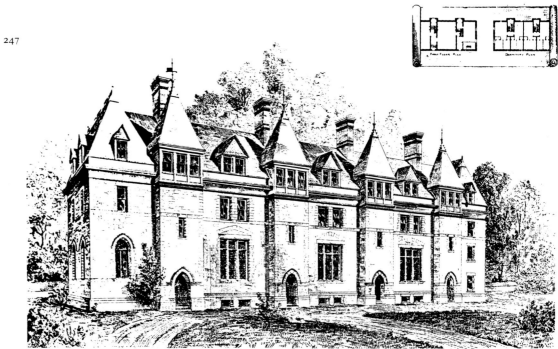

a scheme combining the popular zeal for the temperance movement with the interest of the Harriman Manufacturing Company, both projects of the railroad magnate E.S. Harriman. Rockwood, Kimball, and Cardiff were land speculations grander than the wildest dreams of Overton or Winchester, and the sale of lots at Cardiff brought ten railroad cars of northern speculators to the scene to participate in the ritual of the lottery that had begun in Nashville and Knoxville a

246. Kingston Lisle (1880), the Thomas Hughes house at Rugby, Morgan County, the work of carpenter Cornelius Orderdonk, was in the Gothic style that late-nineteenth-century social critics often preferred.

247. St. Luke's Memorial Hall, built to house the seminary at the University of the South in Sewanee (Franklin County), was designed about 1878 by Henry Hudson Holly of New York. Without the pointed architraves and lintels, the building, while conveying the overall impression of a towered castle, would have been quite modern, and Holly's stairwells are a contemporary commonplace.

248. The initial impression of symmetry gives way to a rich variety as the eye moves into the ambiance of S. M. Patton's Lookout Mountain Inn (1889). The right-hand tower harks back to Second Empire; the left-hand, to Romanesque; and the overall roof treatment and composition derive from the New England shingle style. Tradition had been tamed.

century earlier.[80] Cardiff and Kimball failed and Harriman abandoned the idealistic vision of its founders, but the land schemes of the 1890s were dim prophecies of the prosperity bound to come to the well-watered and mineral-rich Tennessee Valley. Harriman and Rockwood were anticipations of Morristown, Clinton, Norris, and Oak Ridge.

Men of affairs, taught by the successes of their enterprises and the aphorisms of popular philosophy, understood that the world into which they had been born—Polk in the White House, men of substance mostly planters, Washington a week away by stage—was changing. At the formal opening of the centennial on June 1, 1896, H.W. Carmack noted that for "the vast, deep, and rapid changes going on in the world of matter and of mind . . . history has no parallel." Of course, Carmack did not quite mean what he said, for about the only thing history does provide parallels for is the fascinating account of man's successes in overcoming unforeseen and apparently unprecedented problems, often of his own making. But Carmack, like other poets and politicians, was much taken with the Hegelian pieties which taught that "the silent, bloodless, but stupendous revolution toward which the ages have been moving with unwearied purpose is at last upon us. . . . We are approaching the grand climax of history."

Carmack's oratory was applauded by an audience who could not have understood it entirely, but his questionable metaphysics included one indisputable truth: "The civilization of the future will be different in kind and not only in degree from the civilization of the past." If by civilization we mean the subtle, coherent transformation of technique by vision, manners, ethics, and style that has distinguished the European past, Carmack was right, for when technique changes, so must the mode by which it is transformed. Almost exactly a year after Carmack's speech, President McKinley rode from the Maxwell House to the centennial grounds in an open carriage with glistening brightwork, drawn by four gray horses, preceded by two footmen and escorted by an honor guard of Confederate veterans; but on March 10 of the preceding year Preston Dorris had driven his automobile down Nashville's Broadway, and it was Dorris's automobile as much as the centennial exposition that marked in local history the beginning of a new era. The romantic historiography of the Renaissance had begun in the sixteenth century to make the past an object of popular study and imitation. In the 1840s Daguerre had taught the camera's eye to capture and hold the images of time. In 1843 the human intellect was transmitted bodiless, "mind in close contact with mind" as Wilkins Tannehill put it,[81] over Thomas H. Allen's telegraph line from Memphis to New Orleans, and by the end of 1851 Tennessee's cities were part of the nation's first electronic system. On September 1, 1877, Mrs. James K. Polk heard a distant voice from a small electromagnetic box in her Greek Revival house on Nashville's Vine Street hill. By 1890 electric light companies had finally broken the determinate rhythm of day and night that oil and wax had been able to moderate but never to abolish. When Preston Dorris drove his motorized trap down Nashville's streets, the old relations between man and place were moot.

Standing less than a century from Preston Dorris's historic ride, it is hard to know whether we are succeeding as well as Hope, David Morrison, and Strickland in the graceful transformation of space that is the business of architecture, whether our present works are mere essays in the beginnings of a new spatial order, or how the images of place will be determined when the forms of nature that guided man's hand and imagination when Watauga was founded have been broken by technique. Perhaps if Colonel John Carter could ride his bay horse Darby out of the eighteenth century into the world of systems, skyscrapers, and interstates he would find us lacking more in courage than in skill, and remind us that if he could build a tall house paneled like Tuckahoe or Marmion in the nearly empty wilderness with Virginia 100 miles to his back, we ought not allow our own uncertain situation to keep us from stamping our time with the human image of design.

Location and Ownership Catalog

Extant Tennessee architecture built before the end of 1897 and mentioned in the text and notes is included in the following catalog. Many other Tennessee buildings belonging to this period deserve study, and the catalogs of the Historic American Buildings Survey and the National Register of Historic Places, as well as surveys published by the Tennessee Historical Commission and the East Tennessee Development District, should be consulted. The list following is arranged by county and city or town, with town names taken to refer to both incorporated places and their vicinities.

The names given to public buildings and churches by their first owners or tenants are retained, with some historically important names derived from subsequent uses and ownerships supplied in brackets. Houses were usually called after their owners, and in this catalog, as in the text, the original owners' names have been preferred. The few instances in which the name of the original owner is lost or known only through local tradition are designated with an obelisk (†). Houses were sometimes given names suggested by their sites, as at Fairview, Fairvue, Meridian Hill, Rural Mount, State's View, and Stony Point. Trafalgar and Lucknow were named for British victories, and Windsor for a royal palace, while Rokeby, Melrose, and Rotherwood attest the popularity of Scott, and Sabine Hall and Tusculum the lingering authority of classical tradition.

The locations given often imply directions, but further inquiry may be necessary. Distances from cities and towns are taken from the city center, usually the courthouse, unless otherwise indicated. Buildings designated with an asterisk (*) are routinely open to the public, and many public and commercial buildings can be viewed during business hours. Most of the buildings listed are privately owned, and the majority are the residences of their owners. With a few exceptions, ownerships are given, but since these were collected over a period of several years, this information may be anachronistic.

BLEDSOE COUNTY
Pikeville, the county seat
†Harvey Greening house. Town center; Spring Street opposite the courthouse. *Mrs. Georgiana Swafford*

BLOUNT COUNTY
Friendsville, 11 miles west of Maryville
Levi Parkins house. 2.1 miles west of town center on Big Springs Road, south side. *Mr. and Mrs. Jack E. Russell*

Louisville, 4 miles northwest of Maryville
James Gillespie house. West of Louisville, 1.7 miles east of intersection of Lowe's Ferry Road on Holston College Road, north side. *Mrs. Max Sherrill*

BRADLEY COUNTY
Cleveland, the county seat
St. Luke's Episcopal Church. Town center; 320 Broad Street.

CAMPBELL COUNTY
Fincastle, 5 miles north of LaFollette on highway 25 W
John Kincaid II house. 4 miles north of Fincastle on highway 25W, east side. *Claiborne Construction Company*

CARTER COUNTY
Elizabethton, the county seat
Alfred Moore Carter house. Town center; 824 East Elk Ave. *Mrs. Carrie Hunter*
*John Carter house [The Mansion, Landon Carter house]. Northeast of town center; east of highway 321 on Broad Street Extension (old highway 91), north side. *Tennessee Historical Commission*
Sabine Hall [Watauga Point], the Mary Patton Taylor house. 2.4 miles east of town center on highway 67 (West G Street), south side. *Mr. and Mrs. James Reynolds*

CLAIBORNE COUNTY
Speedwell, 20 miles west of Tazewell
Thomas McClain house. 1 mile west of Speedwell, north of highway 63 on Ellison Lane. *Mr. and Mrs. Earl Hobson Smith*

Tazewell, the county seat
William Graham house. Town center; southeast corner of Main Street and Old Knoxville Road. *Mrs. Inez Kivette*

DAVIDSON COUNTY
Antioch, 9 miles southeast of Nashville on Antioch Pike
John Hays house. ½ mile east of Antioch Pike at 834 Reeves Road. *Mr. and Mrs. John Kiser*

Donelson, 11 miles east of Nashville on highway 70
Belair, the Harding-Nichol house. 1½ half miles west of town center; 2250 Lebanon Road (highway 70), north side; northeast corner of Lebanon Pike and Briley Parkway. *Mr. and Mrs. Harry H. Chitwood*
Clover Bottom, the James Hoggatt house. ½ mile east of the Donelson post office; 275 Stewart's Ferry Pike. *Tennessee State School for the Blind*

Two Rivers, the David H. McGavock house. 1 mile north of Lebanon Pike on McGavock Pike, west side. *Metropolitan Government of Nashville and Davidson County*

Hermitage Hills, 15 miles east of Nashville on Lebanon Pike (highway 70), north of I-40
Cleveland Hall, the Stockley Donelson house. North of Lebanon Pike, 4041 Old Hickory Boulevard. *John Donelson VII, Leonard Donelson, Mary Hooper Donelson Stevens*
*The Hermitage, the Andrew Jackson house. 1 mile north of Lebanon Pike on Rachel's Lane. *Ladies' Hermitage Association*
*Tulip Grove [Poplar Grove], the Andrew Jackson Donelson house. Lebanon Pike at Rachel's Lane. *Ladies' Hermitage Association*

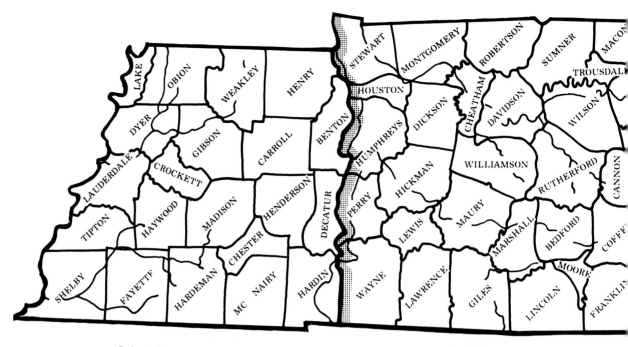

West Tennessee

Middle Tennessee

Nashville, the county seat

*Belle Meade, the William G. Harding house. 6½ miles west of the city center on Harding Pike (highway 70– 100), south side. *Association for the Preservation of Tennessee Antiquities*

*Belmont [Bellemonte, Belle Monte], the Joseph A.S. Acklen house. 2½ miles south of city center near Twenty-first Avenue, South (Hillsboro Pike, highway 106– 431); on Belmont College campus. *Belmont College*

The Cathedral of Our Lady of the Seven Dolors [St. Mary's Catholic Church]. City center; southeast corner of Charlotte Avenue and Fifth Avenue, North.

Christ Episcopal Church. City center; northwest corner of Broadway and Ninth Avenue, North; 900 Broadway.

Church of the Holy Trinity. South of city center; Sixth Avenue, South and Lafayette Street; 615 Sixth Avenue, South.

Custom House. City center; southeast corner of Broadway and Eighth Avenue, South.

First Baptist Church. City center; southeast corner of Broadway and Seventh Avenue, South. Only the tower of the building of 1886 remains.

First Presbyterian Church [Downtown Presbyterian Church]. City center; southeast corner of Church Street and Fifth Avenue, South.

Glenoak [Glen Oak], the Charles Tomes house. 3 miles southwest of city center near Twenty-first Avenue, South (Hillsboro Pike, highway 431); 2012 Twenty-fifth Avenue, South. *Mrs. Eleanor F. Morrisey.*

Glen Leven Presbyterian Church. 2½ miles south of city center near Eighth Avenue, South (highway 31); southeast corner of Douglas and Elliot Avenues. *The Way Ministry, Inc.*

House on Fatherland Street. East of city center; 913 Fatherland Street. *Carrie Sissom*

House on Second Avenue, South. South of city center; 908 Second Avenue, South. *Burkhalter-Hickerson Associates*

Main Building [Kirkland Hall], Vanderbilt University. On the campus 2 miles southwest of city center, near West End Avenue (highway 70S– 100).

Riverwood, the Alexander James Porter house. 5½ miles northeast of city center; on Welcome Lane near Porter Road. *Mr. and Mrs. James High*

Saint Cecilia Convent and Academy for Young Ladies [St. Cecilia Motherhouse]. 1.8 miles northwest of city center; Eighth Avenue, North at Clay Street. Only the center building was designed by Harvey M. Akeroyd. *Dominican Sisters of St. Joseph's Province*

Second Presbyterian Church. City center; southeast corner of Second Avenue, North and Gay Street. *Standard Candy Company*

†Giles Christopher Savage house. City center. 167 Eighth Avenue, North. *Dr. Kate Savage Zerfoss*

Tennessee State Capitol. Charlotte Avenue between Fifth Avenue, North and Sixth Avenue, North.

Tennessee State Hospital for the Insane [Farmer Building, Central State Psychiatric Hospital]. East of city center; 1501 Murfreesboro Road (highways 41– 70), south side.

Travellers' Rest, the John Overton house. 6.7 miles southwest of city center near I-65 (Harding Place exit) on Farrell Parkway. *National Society of the Colonial Dames of America in Tennessee*

Tulip Street Methodist Church. East of city center; 522 Russell Street.

*Union Gospel Tabernacle [Ryman Auditorium, Grand Ole Opry House]. City center; 116 Opry Place. *National Life and Accident Insurance Company*

Union Station. Broadway at Tenth Avenue, South. *Metropolitan Government of Nashville and Davidson County.*

University of Nashville Literary Department Building [Tennessee State Normal College; Main Building, Peabody College; Childrens' Museum]. 1 mile southeast of city center; 724 Second Avenue, South. *Metropolitan Government of Nashville and Davidson County.*

Victor E. Shwab building [Silver Dollar Saloon]. City center; northeast corner of Broadway and Second Avenue,

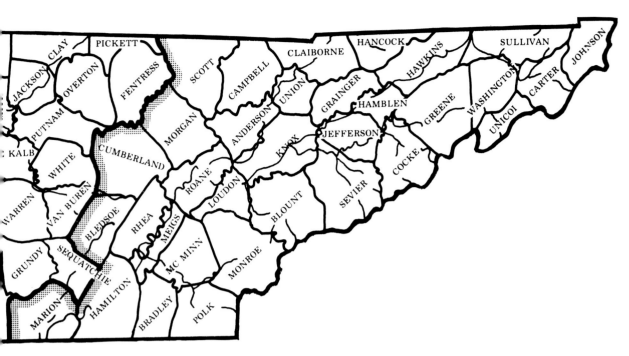

East Tennessee

North. *Metropolitan Government of Nashville and Davidson County.*
Woodlawn, the John Nichols house. 4.7 miles southwest of city center, near Harding Road (West End Avenue, highway 70– 100); 127 Woodmont Boulevard. *Mrs. Howard A. Moore*

DICKSON COUNTY
Charlotte, the county seat
John McRae house [Leech and Dixon Store]. Court Square (west side) and Dunning Street. *Mr. and Mrs. William Marion Adcock*
Dickson County Courthouse. Court Square.

FAYETTE COUNTY
La Grange, 14 miles south of Somerville on the La Grange Road
Frank Cossit house [Tiara]. Northeast corner of Third Street (highway 57) and Main Street (Somerville Road). *Mrs. Edna Jones*
Hancock Hall, the John Junius Pulliam town house. East of town center; .4 mile east of Main Street (Somerville Road) on Third Street (highway 57), north side. *Mrs. Peter Beasley*
Hillcrest. West of town center; .4 mile west of Main Street (Somerville Road) on Third Street (highway 57), north side. *Mr. and Mrs. Barry Saunders*
Immanuel Episcopal Church. Town center; southeast corner of Second and Chestnut Streets.
Westover of Woodstock, the Beverley La Fayette Holcombe house. Pine street north of Third Street (highway 57), north of the Louisville and Nashville Railroad. *Mr. and Mrs. Stanley Allen*

Somerville, the county seat
St. Thomas Episcopal Church. Town center; southwest corner of Market and West Streets.

FRANKLIN COUNTY
Sewanee, 13 miles east of Winchester on alternate highway 41
Breslin Tower and the University Library. Near the center of the University of the South campus on south side. *University of the South*
Josiah Gorgas house. West of Breslin Tower on north side. *University of the South*
St. Luke's Memorial Hall. East of Breslin Tower on south side. *University of the South*

GILES COUNTY
Pulaski, the county seat
William Batte house [Colonial Hall]. Town center; 318 West Madison Street. *Mr. and Mrs. James K. Blackburn, III*

GREENE COUNTY
Afton, 6 miles east of Greeneville, north of highway 11E-411
Thomas Ripley house. South of Afton; .7 mile south of highway 11E-411 on Sinking Creek Road (east side). *Mr. and Mrs. William Saylor*

Chucky, 11 miles east of Greeneville, south of highway 11E-411
Felix Earnest house. 1 mile south on the Chucky-Horse Creek Road (west side), at Nolichucky River. *Mr. and Mrs. Claudius G. Clemmer, Mr. and Mrs. J.W. Massengill*
Henry Earnest house. On south bank of Nolichucky River about 1 mile east of Chucky-Horse Creek Road. *Robert Broyles, Jr.*

Greeneville, the county seat
*Andrew Johnson house (c. 1836). Northeast corner of College and Depot Streets. *National Park Service*
Robert Carter house. 6 miles northwest of Greeneville on highway 70, north side. *Mr. and Mrs. Floyd Castlow*
St. James Episcopal Church. Town center; 105 West Church Street.

Valentine Sevier house [Sevier Place]. Town center; 214 North Main Street. *Dr. and Mrs. Robert G. Brown*

Tusculum, 4 miles west of Greeneville on highway 107
*Tusculum, the Samuel Doak house. Village center; west of Tusculum College on highway 107, south side. *Tusculum College*
Tusculum Academy, 1841. *Tusculum College*

GRUNDY COUNTY
Beersheba Springs, 6 miles northeast of Altamont on highway 106
Beersheba Springs Hotel. Village Center. *United Methodist Church*

Monteagle, I-40 at alternate highways 41–64
Monteagle Assembly grounds and buildings. Village center. *Monteagle Sunday School Assembly.*

HAMBLEN COUNTY
Lowland, on highway 160 south of I-81
Rural Mount, the Alexander Outlaw house. 1.9 miles south of I-40 near highway 160, east side. *James Neuhoff*

Morristown, the county seat
Hamblen County Courthouse. West of town center; 511 West Second North Street.

HAMILTON COUNTY
Chattanooga, the county seat
Adams Block. City center; between Georgia and Cherry Avenues on East Eighth Street, south side. *Building Corporation*
Carnegie Library. City center; northeast corner of Georgia Avenue and East Eighth Street. *North American Royalties, Incorporated*
Chattanooga Times Building [Dome Building]. City center; northwest corner of East Eighth Street and Georgia Avenue. *North American Royalties, Incorporated*
First Methodist Church. City center; northwest corner of East Ninth Street and Georgia Avenue. Only the tower of the building of 1888 remains. *North American Royalties, Incorporated*
Second Presbyterian Church. City center; northeast corner of West Seventh Street and Pine Street.

HARDEMAN COUNTY
Bolivar, the county seat
Hardeman County Court house. Town center.
Ezekiel Polk McNeal house. Southwest of town center; southeast corner of Bills and Union Streets. *Mrs. Irene Bond McDonnell*
G.M. Wellons house [Presbyterian Manse]. Town center; 503 Main Street. *Mr. and Mrs. Sam W.L. Thompson*
Presbyterian Church and Masonic Hall. Town center; northeast corner of North Water and East Market (highway 64) Streets.

HAWKINS COUNTY
Rogersville, the county seat

Thomas Amis house. Town center; 2.1 miles south of East Main Street (highway 11W) on Burem Road, east side. *Jack Amis*
Bank of the State of Tennessee, Rogersville Branch [Masonic Temple]. Town center; northeast corner of Main and Depot Streets. *Overton Lodge, No. 5, F.–A.M.*
Hawkins County Courthouse. Town center; southeast corner of Main and Depot Streets.

Surgoinsville, 12 miles east of Rogersville on highway 11W
†Looney house. 6 miles north of Surgoinsville, on Hickory Cove Road. *William L. Jenkins*
Stony Point, the William Armstrong II house. East of town center; southeast corner of highway 11W and Stony Point Road. *Mr. and Mrs. Alex Armstrong, Miss Jane Armstrong*

HAYWOOD COUNTY
Brownsville, the county seat
Christ Episcopal Church. Town center; southeast corner of North Washington and East College Streets.
Davie Place. Northeast of Brownsville, 5.6 miles from highway 19 on Fulton Road. *Mr. and Mrs. David Evans*

HENRY COUNTY
Paris, the county seat
Henry County Courthouse. Town center.

HICKMAN COUNTY
Centerville, the county seat
Pinewood, the Samuel M. Graham house. 6 miles south of I-40 on highway 48; southeast corner of highway 48 and Lyle Road. Pinewood is an unroofed ruin. *William Boyce*

JACKSON COUNTY
Gainesboro, the county seat
†Sally Reed Davis house. Town center; southeast corner of Cox and Main Streets. *Mrs. Sally Reed Davis*

JEFFERSON COUNTY
Dandridge, the county seat
John Fain house. North of town center; northwest corner of highway 92 (Gay Street) and highway 25W–70. *Mr. and Mrs. James Nicely*
Hickman House [Dandridge City Hall]. Town center; Main Street, south side, east of Gay Street. *Town of Dandridge*
Jefferson County Courthouse. Town Center; northwest corner of Main and Gay Streets.
†Vance Building. Town center; southwest corner of Main and Gay Streets. *Mrs. Henry Vance*

Jefferson City, 11 miles north of Dandridge on highway 92
Fairview, the Stockley Donelson Williams house. 1.9 miles east of town center on the Old Morristown Road, south side. *Mr. and Mrs. Larry Musick*
*The Oaks [Glenmore], the John Roper Branner house. .4 mile east of town center on Old Morristown Road, south side. *Association for the Preservation of Tennessee Antiquities*

White Pine, 12 miles east of Dandridge, on highway 113 at highway 25E

Lawson D. Franklin house. 2 miles south of White Pine, ½ mile east of highway 25 on the Leadvale Road, north side. *Kenneth Smith*

Riverview [Fairfax], the Isaac W.R. Franklin house. 4.2 miles southeast of White Pine on highway 25E. *H.C. Jessee, Thomas J. Green, Richard C. Jessee, Jim Baker*

KNOX COUNTY

Campbell's Station (Concord), about 5 miles southwest of Knoxville city limits on Kingston Pike (highway 11–70)

David Campbell house. Northwest corner of Kingston Pike and Campbell's Station Road. *Albert Russell*

Ebenezer, about 2 miles southwest of Knoxville city limits, south of Kingston Pike (highway 11–70)

State's View [States View, Statesview], the Charles McClung house. 1.7 miles south of Kingston Pike on Peters Road, east side. *L.R. Allee*

Knoxville, the county seat

James Armstrong house. East of Knoxville, southwest corner of Asheville Highway (highway 11E–25W–70) and Governor John Sevier Road. *Mr. and Mrs. Ben Maloy*

Bleak House [Confederate Memorial Hall], the Robert H. Armstrong house. 3 miles west of the city center; 3148 Kingston Pike Southwest (highway 11–70). *United Daughters of the Confederacy*

*William Blount house [Blount Mansion]. City center; southwest corner of West Hill Avenue and State Street. *Blount Mansion Association*

*John Craighead house [Craighead-Jackson house]. City center; southeast corner of West Hill Avenue and State Street. *Blount Mansion Association*

*Crescent Bend [Longueval, Longview], the Drury P. Armstrong house. 2.2 miles west of the city center; 2728 Kingston Pike Southwest (highway 11–70). *Toms Foundation*

Custom House [U.S. Post office; Tennessee Valley Authority offices]. City center; southeast corner of Market and Main Streets. *Knoxville-Knox County Public Library*

Immaculate Conception Catholic Church. City center; 414 West Vine Avenue.

Knox County Courthouse (1886). City Center; southwest corner of Main and Gay streets.

St. John's Episcopal Church. City center; northeast corner of Walnut Street and Cumberland Ave.

Tennessee Institution for the Deaf and Dumb [Asylum for the Deaf and Dumb, Knoxville City Hall]. Northeast corner of Western Avenue and Broadway.

James White house. City center; northwest corner of Hill Avenue and Mulvaney Street. *James White's Fort Association*

John Williams house. East of city center; 5335 Dandridge Avenue. *Sunshine Learning Center*

Isaac B. Ziegler house. City center; 712 North Fourth Avenue. *Chris MacDowell and Vicky Baker*

Marbledale, 3 miles east of Knoxville city limits near the fork of the French Broad and Holston rivers

Francis A. Ramsey house. East of Governor John Sevier Highway East on Thorngrove Pike, north side. *Association for the Preservation of Tennessee Antiquities*

LOUDON COUNTY

Loudon, the county seat

George Bowman house. East of Loudon; 7 miles east of highway 72 near the end of Davis Ferry Road, on TVA reservation. *Tennessee Valley Authority*

Loudon County Courthouse. Town Center.

Greenback, northwest of highway 411 on temporary highway 95

†Griffith house. South of Greenback; 4.9 miles northwest of highway 411 on New Axel's Chapel Road, north side. *Larry S. Benson*

Moses Hughes house. South of Greenback; 4.7 miles northwest of highway 411 on New Axel's Chapel Road, north side. *Roger Denis*

McMINN COUNTY

Athens, the county seat

Samuel Cleague house. North of town center on highway 11 by-pass, east side; ½ mile south of intersection of the by-pass and highway 11 business route. *Mrs. R.A. Davis*

Niota, 7 miles northeast of Athens on highway 11

Elijah Cate house. 1 mile south of town center on west side. *Dr. John Cate*

MAURY COUNTY

Columbia, the county seat

Annoatuck, the John Brown house. 1.3 miles north of town center on North Garden Street (highway 31), west side. *Ben Looper*

Beechlawn, the A.W. Warfield house. 3.1 miles south of the courthouse on Pulaski Highway (highway 31), west side. *Dr. and Mrs. William G. Fuqua*

Bank of the State of Tennessee, Columbia Branch. Town center; southwest corner of South Garden and West Seventh Streets. *John R. Neal*

Clifton Place, the General Gideon J. Pillow house. 4.3 miles southwest of town center on Mt. Pleasant Pike (highway 43), east side. *Mr. and Mrs. John R. Neal*

Leacock-Otey-Martin house [Mercer Hall]. Southwest of town center, east of Trotwood Avenue (highway 43); 902 Mercer Court. *Mr. and Mrs. Wally S. Beasley*

Roger Bradley Mayes house. Town center; 305 West Sixth Street. *Mr. and Mrs. Walter A. Lowe*

Samuel Mayes house. Town center; 306 West Sixth Street. *Thomas Lee Wilson*

Jerome Pillow house [Bethel Place]. 5 miles southwest of town center on Mt. Pleasant Pike (highway 43), east side. *Mr. and Mrs. J.B. Jewel*

Pillow Place, the Granville Pillow house. 2.6 miles south of by-pass on Campbellsville Road, west side. *Mr. and Mrs. W.P. Halliday*

David H. Pise house [Parsons Place]. West of town center; 909 West Seventh Street. *Mr. and Mrs. Clifford Parsons*

*Samuel Polk house. Town center; 301 West Seventh Street.

James K. Polk Association, Nashville, and the James K. Polk Auxiliary, Columbia

Rattle and Snap [Oakwood Farm], the George Polk house. 7.8 miles southwest of town center on Mt. Pleasant Pike (highway 43), east side. *Mr. and Mrs. William B. Allen*

St. Peter's Episcopal Church. Town center; 311 West Seventh Street.

*Samuel Polk Walker house [Athenaeum Rectory]. Town center; northwest corner of West Eighth Street and Athenaeum Street. *Association for the Preservation of Tennessee Antiquities*

*Skipwith Place [Oakwood Farm, Skipwith Hall, the Skipwith-Harlan house]. 7 miles west of town center on Williamsport Road (highway 50), north side. *Mr. and Mrs. H.L. Harlan*

Mt. Pleasant, 11 miles southwest of Columbia on highway 43

Hamilton Place, the Lucius Polk house. 3 miles northeast of town center on highway 43, west side. *Mr. and Mrs. Leslie Whitley*

Manor Hall, the Martin Luther Stockard house. West of town center; southwest corner of Pleasant Street and Adams Avenue. *Mr. and Mrs. W.R. Young*

Spring Hill, 12 miles north of Columbia on highway 31

Nathaniel Cheairs house [Houston Hall Farm, Rippavilla]. 2 miles south of town center on highway 31, east side. *Mrs. Hesta Petty Munn*

Grace Episcopal Church. Town center; southwest corner of North Main and East Beachcroft Streets.

MONROE COUNTY
Madisonville, the county seat

Guilford Cannon house [Cannon-Stickley house]. Town center; southwest corner of Monroe and Warner Streets. *Mr. and Mrs. Joe Stickley*

Coffin house. 1.7 miles west of town center on Old Sweetwater Road (Old Highway 68), south side. *Mr. and Mrs. Paul Turner*

Robert Cooke house. South of town center; .2 mile east of highway 411 by-pass on Tellico Road (highway 68), east side. *Diana Kefauver, Gail Kefauver, Lynda Kefauver, Dr. D.E. Kefauver*

†Mary Thomas house. West of Madisonville, 1.6 miles west of highway 411 on highway 68, north side. *Mrs. Mary Thomas*

Tellico Plains, 16 miles south of Madisonville on highway 68

Elisha Johnson house [The Mansion]. 1.7 miles east on Riverside Road, north side. *Mr. and Mrs. James Williams*

Vonore, 9 miles northeast of Madisonville on highway 411

Charles McClung McGhee house. Northeast of Vonore, .9 mile north of New Citico Road on the River Road. *Tennessee Valley Authority*

MONTGOMERY COUNTY
Clarksville, the county seat

Christopher H. Smith house. South of town center; northeast corner of Spring and McClure Streets. *Mr. and Mrs. Russell Rives*

Tip Top, the J. P. Williams house. South of town center; Trahern Place north of Madison Street. *Mr. and Mrs. William G. Patch*

MORGAN COUNTY
Rugby, 7 miles west of highway 27 on highway 52

Christ Episcopal Church. Village center.

Kingston Lisle, the Thomas Hughes house. Village center. *Rugby Historical Association*

RHEA COUNTY
Washington, 7 miles east of Dayton on highway 30

The Aspens, the Darius Waterhouse residence. West of town center; north of highway 30. The Aspens is an unroofed ruin. *Guy Denton*

ROANE COUNTY
Kingston, the county seat

Roane County Courthouse, 1853. Town center.

ROBERTSON COUNTY
Springfield, the county seat

Robertson County Courthouse. Town center.

Wessyngton, the Joseph Washington house. 5 miles southeast of Springfield near Kinney's Road. *The Wessyngton Company*

RUTHERFORD COUNTY
Murfreesboro, the county seat

*Oaklands, the James Maney house. West of town center; North Maney Avenue at Roberts Street. *Oaklands Association*

SEVIER COUNTY
Boyd's Creek, 6 miles northwest of Sevierville on the Old Knoxville Highway

Thomas and Ephraim Buckingham house. 6.2 miles west of highway 441 on the Old Knoxville Highway, north side. *Mrs. Lena Catlett, Mrs. Anna Kate Ellis, Mrs. Paul Hammer, Miss Stella Trundle, B.M. Trundle, P.R. Trundle*

Sevierville, the county seat

Sevier County Courthouse. Town center.

SHELBY COUNTY
Memphis, the county seat

Calvary Episcopal Church. City center; southeast corner of Adams Avenue and North Second Street.

Continental Building [Dr. D.T. Porter Building]. City center; southeast corner of Court Street and Mid-America Mall. *Philip Belz*

First Methodist Church. City center; northeast corner of Poplar Avenue and North Second Street.

*Charles W. Goyer house [James Lee, Jr. house]. East of city center; 690 Adams Avenue. *City of Memphis*

*Eugene Magevney house. City center; 200 Adams Street. *City of Memphis*

*Mallory-Neely house. East of city center; 652 Adams Avenue. *Daughters of the American Revolution*

†Samuel Mansfield house [Annesdale]. 2 miles east of city

center; south corner of Lamar Street and Central Avenue. *Mr. and Mrs. Thomas, H. Todd, Jr.*

†Richardson house [Peter McIntyre house, Pillow-McIntyre house]. East of city center; 707 Adams Avenue. *Margie Vanlandingham, Inc.*

St. Mary's Catholic Church. City center; southwest corner Market Avenue and North Third Street.

St. Peter's Catholic Church. City center; northeast corner of Adams Avenue and North Third Street.

Second Presbyterian Church. South of city center; northeast corner of Hernando and Pontotoc streets. *Claiborne Temple*

George Whyett house [Hunt-Phelan house]. East of city center; 533 Beale Street. *George R. Phelan*

*Amos Woodruff house [Noland Fontaine house]. East of city center; 680 Adams Avenue. *City of Memphis*

SMITH COUNTY
Carthage, the county seat
Smith County Courthouse. Town center.

Dixon Springs, 12 miles northwest of Carthage on highway 25
David Burford house [Beechwood]. .4 mile east of village center on highway 25, north side. *Estate of George Allen Webster*

SULLIVAN COUNTY
Blountville, 14 miles east of Kingsport on highway 126
Elkanah Dulaney house [Anderson Hall]. Town center; Central Avenue, east side. *Miss Birdie Anderson*
William Deery Inn, house and store. Town center; Central Avenue and Courthouse Lane. *Mrs. Joseph Caldwell*

Kingsport, the county seat
Aaron Hoffman house. Southwest of town center; 2 miles west of highway 23 on Netherland Inn Road. *Mr. and Mrs. Jacob Zachary*
Richard Netherland Inn. Southwest of town center; 1.7 miles west of highway 23 on Netherland Inn Road. *Association for the Preservation of Tennessee Antiquities*

Piney Flats, 13 miles south of Bristol (8 miles north of Johnson City, Washington County) on highway 11E
Rocky Mount, the William Cobb house. 5 miles south of Piney Flats on highway 11E, east side. *Association for the Preservation of Tennessee Antiquities.*

SUMNER COUNTY
Castalian Springs, 6 miles east of Gallatin on Hartsville Pike (highway 25)
John Bearden house. East of village center; ½ mile east of Corum Hill Road on old highway. *Mr. and Mrs. William McLaughlin*
*Alfred R. Wynne Inn [Castalian Springs Inn, Wynnewood]. West of village center on old highway. *Tennessee Historical Commission*
*Cragfont, the James Winchester house. 2 miles west of Castalian Springs, 1 mile north of Hartsville Pike. *Association for the Preservation of Tennessee Antiquities*

Gallatin, the county seat

Samuel K. Blythe house [Blythewood]. East of town center; 814 Hartsville Pike, north side. *Mrs. Sarah P. Woodward*
David Chenault house [Greenfield]. East of Gallatin, 3 miles north of Hartsville Pike on Rock Springs Road, west side. *Dr. and Mrs. Thomas F. Parish*
Fairvue, the Isaac Franklin house. 4 miles west of town center on Nashville Pike (highway 31E), south side. *Mr. and Mrs. William Hatch Wemyss*
James B. Jameson house. 5 miles east of Gallatin on Hartsville Pike (highway 25), north side. *Mr. and Mrs. Nathan B. Harsh*
Daniel Wade Mentlo house [Oakland]. 4 miles east of Gallatin on Hartsville Pike, north side. *Mr. and Mrs. Billy Hale*
Oakley, the John W. Franklin house. 4.2 miles west of town center on Nashville Pike (highway 31E), south side. *Mr. and Mrs. Louis A. Green*
Presbyterian Church. Town center; southwest corner of West Main and South Foster Streets.
Rosemont, the Josephus Conn Guild house. South of town center; 810 South Water Street (highway 109), west side. *Mr. and Mrs. Josephus Conn Guild*

Hendersonville, 13 miles southeast of Gallatin on highway 31E
*Rock Castle, the Daniel Smith house. 1 mile east of town center on Indian Lake Road. *Tennessee Historical Commission*
William Bowen house. Northwest of town center; 1.7 miles west of Center Point Road on Caldwell Road, west side. *Mrs. J.L. Rogers*

Shackle Island, about 13 miles west of Gallatin on Long Hollow Pike
Daniel Montgomery house [Greystone]. .4 mile north of Long Hollow Pike on New Hope Road, east side. *Colonel Haynie S. Bastian, III*
William Montgomery house. .4 mile north of Long Hollow Pike on New Hope Road, west side. *Mr. and Mrs. J.D. Scott, Jr.*
Robert Taylor house. .4 mile south of Long Hollow Pike on Longview Drive, west side. *Herbert Stone*

TIPTON COUNTY
Covington, the county seat
St. Matthew's Episcopal Church. Town center; southwest corner of Washington and Munford Streets.

WARREN COUNTY
Viola, 13 miles south of McMinnville on highway 108
David Ramsey house. 3 miles north of Viola, west of highway 108, on the old Viola-Vervilla Road. *Robert S. Ramsey*

WASHINGTON COUNTY
Johnson City, 10 miles east of Jonesboro on highway 11E–411
Martin Kitzmiller house. North of Johnson City, .7 mile north of Boone's Creek on highway 23, west side. *Mr. and Mrs. Howard J. Steed*
Jacob Range house. North of city center; southwest corner of Oakland Avenue and Twin Falls Road. *M.B. Morton*

Jonesboro, the county seat

Matthew Aiken house. South of town center; 104 Third Avenue South, west side. *Mrs. Mary Gunther*

Chester Inn. Town center; between Cherokee Street and North First Avenue on Main Street, north side. *Mrs. Charles M. Bennett*

†Green house. Town center; east of the courthouse on Woodward Avenue, north side. *E.S. Dillow*

Samuel Jackson townhouses [Sisters' Row]. Town center; between South First Avenue and South Second Avenue on Main Street, south side. *Jonesboro Methodist Church, Mr. and Mrs. Burgin Dossett, Dr. George A. Byrd*

†Samuel Lyle house. South of Jonesboro on Old Highway 34, east side, near Hall Road. *Ralph Susong*

Methodist Church. Town center; between South First Avenue and South Second Avenue on Main Street, south side.

Presbyterian Church. Town center; between Cherokee Street and North First Avenue on Main Street, north side.

Christopher Taylor house. Town center; between Cherokee Street and North First Avenue, on Main Street, north side. [The house has been moved to its present location from a site south of Jonesboro.] *Town of Jonesboro*

†B.G. Young house. 7 miles northeast of Jonesboro at the northwest corner of highway 137 and Boone's Creek Road. *Mr. and Mrs. B.G. Young, Jr.*

Limestone, 10 miles west of Jonesboro, south of highway 11E–411 on Limestone Road

George Gillespie house. South of village center. *Mr. Wayne Jeffers, Mr. James F. Jeffers, Jr.*

†Snapp house. 3 miles south of Limestone on John Smith Road, overlooking Limestone Creek. *U.S. Keebler, Jr.*

Leesburg, west of Jonesboro; 6 miles west of highway 81 on the Old Stage Road

Frederick DeVault house. Village center; Old Stage Road, south side. *Mrs. Edward Guerant DeVault*

Telford, 7 miles southwest of Jonesboro, 3 miles south of highway 11E–411 on highway 81

Thomas Embree house. East of Telford; .2 mile north of Old Highway 34 on Matthews Mill Road, north side. *Mrs. J.L. Bell*

Watauga, 5 miles northeast of Johnson City on Watauga Road

Jeremiah Dungan house. Between the Watauga River and Austin Springs Road on Watauga Road, west side. *Mrs. J.T. St. John, George W. St. John*

WILLIAMSON COUNTY

Franklin, the county seat

William S. Campbell house [Magnolia Hall]. 1 mile north of town center, on highway 96, west side. *Mr. and Mrs. Mark Garrett*

Carnton, the Randall McGavock house. Southeast of town center, .6 mile west of Lewisburg Pike (highway 431) on Carnton Lane. *The Carnton Association, Inc.*

*Fountain Branch Carter house. South of town center; 1140 Columbia Avenue. *Carter House Association of the Association for the Preservation of Tennessee Antiquities*

Clouston Hall, the Edward G. Clouston house. Town Center; 202 Second Avenue South. *Bunn Gray*

Eaton house. Town center; 125 Third Avenue North. *Cletus McWilliams, DeWees Berry, James T. Oglesby*

Masonic Hall. Town center, Second Avenue South *Hiram Lodge, No. 7, F & A.M.*

Poplar Grove [Two Rivers], the Nicholas Tate Perkins house. West of Franklin; 3.5 miles west of highway 431 on Del Rio Pike, north side. *Mr. and Mrs. H.L. Buford Martha Perkins Trousdale, Mrs. Leighla Perkins Carroll*

St. Paul's Episcopal Church. Town center; northeast corner of Sixth Avenue and West Main Streets.

Saunders-Marshall house. Town center; 224 Third Avenue South. *Mr. and Mrs. James T. Farrell*

Poplar Grove [Two Rivers], the Nicholas Tate Perkins house. West of Franklin; 3.5 miles west of highway 431 on Del Rio Pike, north side. *Mr. and Mrs. H.L. Buford*

Williamson County Courthouse. Town center; southwest corner of Third Avenue and the Public Square.

Thompson's Station, 10 miles south of Franklin near highway 31

John Neely house [Hilltop Manor]. East of Thompson's Station on Sedberry Road. *Mr. and Mrs. George Burlein*

Triune, 11 miles east of Franklin at the intersection of alternate highways 31–41 and highway 96

Newton Jordan house. South of Triune, 1.1 miles east of alternate highways 31–41 on Possum Trot [Patterson] Road, north side. *Mrs. Leroy Pierce*

WILSON COUNTY

La Guardo, 6 miles northwest of Lebanon, on highway 109

James Harvey Davis house. 9 miles north of I–40 on highway 109, west side. *Alfred Adams*

Lebanon, the county seat

Robert L. Caruthers house [Ligon-Bobo Funeral Home]. Town center; 241 West Main Street. *C.H. Ligon, Alex Bobo*

Glossary

Ashlar — Masonry of squared stones laid in regular courses.

Attic — A low story directly below the roof; a garret.

Arcade — A series of arches supported on piers or columns.

Architrave — A lintel or beam resting on columns, the lowermost member of a classical entablature.

Acroterium (pl. Acroteria) — On classical buildings, one of the ornamented angles of a pediment; a statue or other ornament placed at the angle or apex.

Anthemion (pl. Anthemia) — An ornament of floral forms in a flat, radiating cluster.

Baluster — The upright support, often decoratively carved or turned, in a handrail or balustrade.

Battlement — A parapet consisting of a series of embrasures or indentations, between which are raised portions called merlons.

Belvedere — A structure designed and situated to look out upon a pleasing view and therefore often placed atop a building.

Blind arcade — An arch or arches infilled, with the infilling recessed so as to preserve the outline of the arch and its jambs.

Boxed staircase — Stairs built in a wood enclosure, sometimes of cabinetwork; a sealed or cabinet staircase.

Bull's eye — A circular or oval opening for air or light.

Butt hinge — A hinge designed to be fastened to the surface of a door's edge, or butt.

Cabinet staircase — See boxed staircase.

Cantilever — Any rigid construction extending horizontally well beyond its vertical support.

Capital — The uppermost portion of a column, pillar, or shaft, usually characteristic of an order, supporting the entablature.

Cartouche — A rounded, convex surface, usually surrounded with carved ornamental scrollwork, for receiving a painted or low-relief decoration.

Castellated — Built like a castle, especially with turrets and battlements.

Cella — In a classical temple, the enclosed area containing a statue of a deity.

Chamfer — A beveled edge.

Colonnette — A small column, in Federal architecture often flanking a doorway.

Common bond — Sometimes called American bond. Brickwork in which headers recur every fifth or sixth course. In Tennessee, headers often recur every eighth course.

Console — An ornamental bracket, especially one high in relation to its projections.

Corinthian order — See Orders.

Cornice — The uppermost section of a classical entablature.

Corona — The projecting, slablike member of a classical cornice.

Course — In brickwork, a single horizontal row of bricks.

Cupola — A light structure on a dome or roof, serving as a belfry, lantern, or belvedere.

Curtain — A screen; in fortifications a wall of puncheons set vertically and connecting bastions or gates; also used to refer to a screened connecting passageway.

Cusps — The points formed by the intersection of curvilinear shapes or foils in Gothic tracery.

Dentil — One of a series of small projecting rectangular blocks, especially under a cornice.

Diapering — In brickwork, a diagonal pattern, often made of bricks burned until the headers are vitrified and very dark.

Distyle — Ordered porch of two columns, usually recessed between antae. See *In antis*.

Doric Order — See Orders.

Embrasure — The openings between merlons in a battlement.

Entablature — The upper section of a wall or story that is usually supported on columns or pilasters and consisting in classical orders of architrave, frieze, and cornice.

Entasis — A slight convexity given to columns.

Fanlight	A semicircular or elliptical transom widow, often having radiating muntins.		joists or studs so as to leave narrow interstices, thereby providing a groundwork for plaster.
Fenestration	The design and disposition of windows and other exterior openings of a building.	Merlons	See Battlement.
		Metope	Any of the square spaces between triglyphs in the Doric frieze.
Flemish bond	Brickwork having alternate stretchers and headers in each course, each header being centered above and below a stretcher.	Millwork	Work produced by a mill, such as wooden doors and window sashes, as distinguished from cabinetwork.
Foil	A texture or feature which sets off another by contrast.	Modillion	The enriched block or horizontal bracket generally found beneath the cornice of the Corinthian and Composite entablature and in a simplified form in other orders.
Frieze	The part of a classical entablature between the architrave and the cornice.		
Garret	The room or rooms directly below the sloping roof of a house; an attic.	Monopteron	A structure having a single ring of supporting columns, without a cella.
Grade	Ground level.	Mortise and tenon	A tenon, the shaped projection on a piece of wood, is set in a mortise, a hole or slot of identical size made in another to receive it. A treenail is driven in a drilled hole which passes through the mortise and tenon to join the two pieces.
Gutta(e)	One of a series of cone-shaped ornaments set in the bottom of mutules. In Tennessee guttae are sometimes simulated by holes drilled in the bottom of the mutule block.		
Header	The two sides of a brick having the smallest area.	Mullion	A vertical member, as of stone or wood, between the lights of a window, the panels in wainscoting, or the like.
Hexastyle	In classical architecture, a porch of six columns.		
Hipped roof	A roof having sloping ends and sloping sides.	Muntin	A bar for holding the edges of window panes within the sash.
In antis	Antae are piers produced by thickening a wall at its termination, treated architecturally as a pilaster, with capital and base. In a portico with columns standing between two antae, the columns are said to be in antis.	Mutule	A projecting flat block beneath the Doric cornice, corresponding to the modillion of other orders.
		Newel post	A post supporting one end of a handrail at the top or bottom of a flight of stairs.
Interstice	A space or interval between things or parts.	Octastyle	In classical architecture, a porch of eight columns.
Ionic Order	See Orders.	Orders	A column with its base and capital, together with the entablature which is supports. The Greek orders are Doric, distinguished by a capital consisting of a plain curved molding, triglyphs in the frieze, and the absence of a base; Ionic with its scroll-like capital; and Corinthian, in which the capital consists of stylized acanthus leaves. The Composite order, in which the capitals com-
Joist	A small beam laid horizontally to support a floor or ceiling.		
Keystone	A wedge-shaped stone at the summit of an arch.		
Lancet arch	An acutely pointed arch.		
Lancet window	A high, narrow window with an acutely pointed head.		
Lintel	A horizontal architectural member supporting the weight above an opening.		
Laths	Strips of wood nailed to ceiling		

bine Ionic scrolls and the acanthus leaves of Corinthian; and the Tuscan order, a simplified Doric, were added by the Romans.

Palladian window
A three-part window consisting of an arched center window and smaller flanking windows.

Palmette
An ornament consisting of radiating fronds or petals arranged in a palm-like pattern, closely related to the Egyptian lotus and Greek anthemion, in the Doric order often applied to the soffit at its corners.

Parapet
A low wall at the circumference of a roof or elevated terrace.

Pediment
A low gable or gable-like feature, typically triangular and outlined with cornices, usually placed over a door, window, or porch.

Pilaster
A shallow rectangular feature projecting from a wall, having a capital and base and usually imitating the form of a column.

Pinnacle
A small, upright structure, capping a tower, buttress, or other projecting architectural member; common in nineteenth-century Gothic Revival buildings.

Pitch
In the seventeenth and eighteenth centuries the clear vertical distance from the floor to the ridge of the roof; later commonly used to refer to the inclination or slope of the sides of a roof expressed by the ratio of the height to the span; as, a pitch of 5 inches to a foot, or 5 in 12.

Plate
Either of the horizontal members at the top and bottom of a framed partition, between which the studs are placed. The member on the top is called the top plate and the lower member, on which the studs rest, is called the bottom plate or soleplate.

Plinth
The square base of a statue or turning; the base, usually rectangular in cross section, from which vertically placed trim or molding rises.

Portico
A structure consisting of a roof supported by columns or piers, usually attached to a building as a porch.

Puncheon
A log roughly dressed, often planed on one side, from which palisades were constructed; sometimes used as floorboards, in which case the puncheon rests directly on the ground.

Quatrefoils
In Gothic architecture a window or open shape with four cusps or points.

Quoin
Dressed, oversized, or otherwise specially treated or patterned stone laid up the corner of a building.

Reveal
The side of an opening (as for a window) between the front or forwardmost face of the frame and the outer surface of a wall.

Ridge
The line of intersection at the top of a roof between the opposite slopes or sides.

Riser
The vertical face of a stairstep.

Rustication
Masonry deliberately rough and laid up in oversized and crude blocks, usually in basements.

Scantling
Small sawed members, commonly sized for studs, used in frame construction.

Segmental window head
Window head laid out on the circumference of a circle, but, unlike an arched opening, intersecting the window jambs at an angle.

Sill
A horizontal timber, block, or the like, usually resting immediately on the foundation wall of a house; the horizontal piece beneath a window, door, or other openings.

Sleeper
A horizontal timber with which the floor is framed; a floor joist.

Soffit
The underside of a subordinate part or member of a building, such as a staircase, entablature, archway, cornice, or the like.

Stretcher
The two longest, narrowest surfaces of a brick.

Stud
The uprights (not corner posts or braces) in the framing of the wall of a building to which clap-

Stringcourse
boards, paneling, or laths are fastened.

A horizontal band projecting from a wall or differentiated by material or color.

Tenon
See Mortise and tenon.

Tower-of-the-Winds-capital
A capital of the Corinthian type consisting of simple fronds overlaid with a lower ring of acanthus leaves.

Tracery
Architectural ornamental work with branching lines; especially, decorative openwork in a Gothic window.

Treenail
A small wooden peg made of dry compressed timber so as to swell in its hole when moistened and used to join timbers and attach shingles.

Trefoils
In Gothic architecture an open shape with three cusps or points.

Triglyph
A member of a Doric frieze, separating two consecutive metopes, and consisting of three incised vertical elements.

Truss
A framework of wood designed to carry roof loads, and usually spanning from wall to wall.

Tympanum
The recessed triangular face of a pediment within the frame made by the upper and lower cornices.

Vernacular
The common building style of a period or place.

Volute
A spiral ornament, found especially on the capitals of the Ionic, Corinthian, and Composite orders.

Voussoir
Any of the pieces, in the shape of a truncated wedge, that form an arch or vault.

Water table
A stringcourse or similar member when projecting so as to throw off the water; especially in the United States, the first table above the ground, at the top of the foundation and beginning of the upper wall.

Weatherboarding
Boards nailed or pegged horizontally to the exterior of a house frame, the top of each set beneath the overlapping board above.

Window head
The line of the top of the window frame or bottom of the lintel or architrave.

Welch chimney
A chimney constructed of wattles or laths daubed with clay or plaster.

Abbreviations

AMN   J.P. Ayres, *A Map of the City of Nashville.* Copy in TSLA.

AMT   Thomas B. Brumbaugh, ed., *Architecture of Middle Tennessee.*

BJC   John Spencer Bassett, ed., *Correspondence of Andrew Jackson.*

CCJ   Charles Coffin, MS Journals, 1800–1822. McC.

CHD   W.W. Clayton, *History of Davidson County Tennessee.*

CSR   *Commercial and Statistical Review of the City of Memphis.* Copy in Memphis Room, Memphis-Shelby County Public Library and Information Center.

DPA   Drury P. Armstrong, Diary. McC.

ETHSP   *East Tennessee Historical Society Publications.*

ETT   Samuel C. Williams, ed., *Early Travels in the Tennessee Country.*

HABS   Historic American Buildings Survey.

HBM   Haydon and Booth, *City of Nashville and Edgefield, Davidson County, Tennessee.* Copy in National Archives.

HHG   Roberta Seawell Brandau, ed., *History of Homes and Gardens of Tennessee.*

HWC   Virginia McDaniel Bowman, *Historic Williamson County.*

JCD   Juliana Margaret Conner, Diary from June 10 to Oct. 17, 1827. Typescript in North Carolina State Archives.

JSAH   *Journal of the Society of Architectural Historians.*

LTH   William T. Alderson and Robert M. McBride, eds., *Landmarks of Tennessee History.*

MAT   Michael A. Tomlan photograph.

McC   Calvin M. McClung Historical Collection, Lawson-McGhee Library, Knoxville.

MLT   Robert M. McBride, ed., *More Landmarks of Tennessee History.*

MTG   Eastin Morris, *The Tennessee Gazetteer.*

MTW   F.A. Michaux, *Travels to the Westward of the Allagheny Mountains.*

NCCR   Colonial Records of North Carolina

NCSR   State Records of North Carolina

NST   Samuel C. Williams, ed., "Nashville As Seen by Travelers, 1801–1821."

THM   *Tennessee Historical Magazine.*

THQ   *Tennessee Historical Quarterly.*

TSLA   Tennessee State Library and Archives.

TVA   Tennessee Valley Authority.

WTHSP   *West Tennessee Historical Society Publications.*

WHN   John Woolridge, ed., *History of Nashville, Tennessee.*

Notes

CHAPTER I

1. *ETT*, 508; CCJ, Feb. 7, 1801.

2. *MTW*, 254.

3. NST, 192, 194.

4. Anne Newport Royall, *Letters from Alabama on Various Subjects* (Washington, D.C.: The author, 1830), 19.

5. JCD, Sept. 1, 1827.

6. Quoted in *CHD*, 208–9.

7. Robert Baird, *View of the Valley of the Mississippi; or, the Emigrant's and Traveller's Guide to the West*, 2d ed. (Philadelphia: H.S. Tanner, 1834), 209.

8. George W. Featherstonhaugh, *Excursion Through the Slave States, . . .* (New York: Harper, 1844), 52.

9. *Nashville Republican Banner*, May 26, 1847.

10. "Nashville and her Manufactures. Number I.," *Tennessee State Farmer and Mechanic* 1 (1856), 170.

11. James Roberts Gilmore [Edmund Kirke], *Down in Tennessee and Back by Way of Richmond* (New York: Carleton, 1864), 64.

12. J.H. Ingraham, *The Sunny South; or, The Southerner at Home* (New York: G.G. Evans, 1860; rpt. Negro Univ. Press, 1968), 130.

13. John Fitch, *Annals of the Army of the Cumberland* (Philadelphia: Lippincott, 1864), 596.

14. *Memphis American Eagle*, Nov 18, 1842, Nov. 13, 1843.

15. *Memphis Appeal*, May 17, 1844; *Memphis Semi-Weekly Appeal*, Jan. 7, 1845.

16. Hugh Jones, *Present State of Virginia* (London: J. Clarke, 1724; rpt. New York: Joseph Sabin, 1865), 35.

17. *Succession of Isaac Franklin*. Prepared by Mrs. Joseph A.S. Acklen's counsel for use of the Supreme Court (n.p., 1851), 284, 299.

18. Fitch, 603.

19. Featherstonhaugh, 52.

20. *Nashville Daily Orthopolitan*, Nov. 28, 1845.

21. J. Fowler Smith, "American Literature," *Naturalist* 1 (1846), 410.

22. William Strickland [S.], "The Three Orders of Architecture—Wisdom, Strength, and Beauty," *Port Folio* 1 (1847–48), 321–23; [Wilkins Tannehill], "The Greek and Roman Order of Architecture—Their distinctive Characters," *Port Folio* 3 (1849–50), 325–26; "Orders of Architecture," *Port Folio* 2 (1848–49), 194–95, 239.

23. William Strickland [S.], "Sketches of Roman Architecture," *Nashville Daily Orthopolitan*, 11 articles, May 22-June 24, 1846; [Tolbert Fanning], "Architecture," *Naturalist*, ser. 2, no. 1 (1850), 47.

24. William Prichard to A.J. Downing, May 30, 1848, "Domestic Notices," *The Horticulturist and Journal of Rural Art and Rural Taste* 3 (1848–49), 49–50; *Acts of the State of Tennessee . . . for the years 1845–6* (Knoxville: James C. Moses, 1846), ch. CIV.

25. Robert W. Weathersby II, "J.H. Ingraham and Tennessee: A Record of Social and Literary Contributions," *THQ* 34 (1975), 264, 270.

26. [Wilkins Tannehill], "Masonic College of Tennessee," *Port Folio* 2 (1848–49), 270–71.

27. [J.H. Ingraham], "A Letter from Nashville," *Port Folio* 1 (1847–48), 276–79; J.H. Ingraham [I.] "Rural Taste," *Naturalist*, ser. 2, no. 1 (1850), 185; J.H. Ingraham, [Visitor], "The Nashville Horticultural Society and Garden," *Naturalist*, ser. 2, no. 1 (1850), 85–86.

28. Prichard to Downing, 49.

29. Fanning, 50; Andrew J. Downing, *The Architecture of Country Houses* (1850; rpt. New York: Dover, 1969), 30.

30. A.G. Stacey, "Piety and Beauty," *Home Circle* 1 (1855), 364–66; "Rural Architecture," *Southern Lady's Companion* 1 (1847–48), 78.

31. James F. White, *The Cambridge Movement: The Ecclesiologists and the Cambridge Revival* (Cambridge: Cambridge Univ. Press, 1962), 1–47.

32. TSLA.

33. Ingraham, "The Nashville Horticultural Society and Garden," 86; Prichard to Downing, 50. Prichard purchased the garden in 1850 and in 1853 was bankrupt. See John G. Frank, "Adolphus Heiman, Architect and Soldier," *THQ* 5 (1946), 46–47.

34. J.G.M. Ramsey, *Annals of Tennessee to the End of the Eighteenth Century* (Charleston: The author, 1853), 715.

35. Thomas Nelson Page, *The Old South: Essays Social and Political* (New York: Scribners, 1892), 253.

36. [Telfair Hodgson], review of *The Old South: Essays Social and Political*, by Thomas Nelson Page, *Sewanee Review* 1 (1892), 90.

37. Mary Poppenheim and Others, *The History of the United Daughters of the Confederacy* (Richmond: Garrett and Massey, 1938; rpt. Raleigh: Edwards and Broughton, 1958), 26.

38. Mary Currey Dorris, *Preservation of the Hermitage, 1889–1915; Annals, History, and Stories* (Nashville: Smith and Lamar, 1915), 35.

39. Page, *The Old South*, 211–32.

40. *Nashville Daily American*, Oct. 22, 1896.

41. (New York: Appleton, 1930), 279.

42. Thomas Nelson Page, "Jamestown, the Cradle of American Civilization," *Century Magazine* 74 (1907), 141–50.

43. *Journal of the American Institute of Architects* 7 (1919), 159.

44. *HHG*, 357, 439, 475.

45. Frances Archer Christian and Susie Williams Massie, *Homes and Gardens of Old Virginia* (Richmond: The authors, 1931); Lorraine Meeks Cooney, comp., *Garden History of Georgia* (Atlanta: Peachtree Garden Club, 1933); Archibald Henderson and Bayard Wooten, *Old Homes and Gardens of North Carolina* (Chapel Hill: Univ. of North Carolina Press, 1939).

46. John Crowe Ransom et al., *I'll Take My Stand; the South and the Agrarian Tradition* (New York: Harper, 1930), 1.

47. Allen Tate, "The Profession of Letters in the South," *Reactionary Essays on Poetry and Ideas* (New York: Scribners, 1936), 156.

48. John Haywood, *The Civil and Political History of the State of Tennessee* (Knoxville: Heiskell and Brown, 1823; rpt.

New York: Arno Press and the *New York Times*, 1971), 16.
49. *ETT*, 398.
50. Ibid., 422.

CHAPTER II

1. Capt. Paul Demere and other officers to Mr. De Brahm, Dec. 23, 1756, William L. McDowell, ed., *Colonial Records of South Carolina*, ser. 2, *Documents Relating to Indian Affairs, 1754–1765* (Columbia: South Carolina Dept. of Archives and History, 1970), 284–86; Demere to Lyttleton, Dec. 27, 1756, Jan. 31, Mar. 1, Nov. 24, 1757, ibid., 287, 327, 345, 417.
2. Charles E. Peterson, "The Houses of French St. Louis," John Francis McDermott, ed., *The French in the Mississippi Valley* (Urbana; Univ. of Illinois Press, 1965), 35–38; Samuel Wilson, Jr., "Colonial Fortifications and Military Architecture in the Mississippi Valley," ibid., 115, figs. 9, 20.
3. Robert D. Stoner, *A Seed-Bed of the Republic*, 2d ed. (Roanoke: Roanoke Historical Society, 1962), 233–35.
4. *HHG*, 90, 117.
5. *MTW*, 280.
6. Charles Coffin Ross, ed., *The Story of Rotherwood from the Autobiography of Rev. Frederick A. Ross, D.D.* (Knoxville: Bean, Warters, 1923), 15.
7. *Davidson County Court Minutes*, I, 9; *Davidson County Will Books* I, 156.
8. Beatrice St. Julien Ravenel, *Architects of Charleston*, 2d ed. (Charleston: Carolina Art Assoc., 1964), 89. *South Carolina Historical and Genealogical Magazine* 37 (1936), 160.
9. NCCR VII, 431.
10. Agreement between John Steele and John Langton, Mar. 13, 1800, in H.M. Wagstaff, ed., *The Papers of John Steele* (Raleigh: Edwards and Broughton, 1924), II, 785.
11. *Tennessee Gazette*, Feb. 11, July 8, 1801; July 13, 1803. Although no references to carpenters' companies have been found in Tennessee, John Overton's contract with Cummins and Pinkley, dated Nov. 7, 1799 (Claybrook-Overton Collection, TSLA), gives responsibility for valuing the work to a list of house carpenters (presumably inclusive or nearly so) then working in Nashville. A similar procedure was required by George Augustus Suggs in his contract with the stonemason William Erwin in 1784 (*Davidson County Will Books* I, 156). The notion that artisans acting as a company were the final authority in the valuing and pricing of work persisted. See CCJ, May 9, 1805.
12. *Williamson County Court Minutes* I, 372. See also the suit of 1713 (NCCR II, 42) which recites the duty of an apprentice to learn "ye trade and mistery of a Carpenter and house Joiner."
13. Charles E. Peterson, ed., *The Rules of Work of the Carpenters' Company of the City and County of Philadelphia* (New York: Bell Publishing, 1971), XV; Louis Hall, "Founding of the Company: Loxley's Provocative Note," *JSAH* 20, no. 4 (Dec. 1956), 26–27.
14. Wendell Holmes Stephenson, *Isaac Franklin: Slave Trader and Planter of the Old South* (Baton Rouge: Louisiana State Univ. Press, 1938), 157, 159, 160.
15. *Tennessee Gazette*, Mar. 29, 1811; CCJ, Sept. 13, 1805, Feb. 26, 1806.
16. *Tennessee Gazette*, Mar. 29, 1811.
17. Articles of agreement made and concluded this seventh day of November, 1799 Between John Overton of the one part and Frederick Pinkley and David Cummins of the other part, Claybrook-Overton Collection, TSLA.
18. Ellen Beasley, "Tennessee Cabinetmakers and Chairmakers Through 1840," *Antiques* 100 (July-Dec. 1971), 621; Contract between Robert Taylor and William Montgomery, Feb. 20, 1804, in Walter T. Durham, *The Great Leap Westward* (Gallatin: Sumner County Library Board, 1969), following p. 140.
19. *Wilson's Knoxville Gazette*, Apr. 21, 1810; *Knoxville Register*, June 25, 1828; Apr. 14, 28, 1830; *Knoxville Register*, Feb. 22, 1820; Jan. 16, 1824.
20. *Nashville Daily Orthopolitan*, May 6, 1847.
21. *Knoxville Gazette*, Mar. 20, 1797.
22. *Davidson County Will Books*, II, 205.
23. Sally Smith to Daniel Smith, July 20, 1793, T100, Tennessee Historical Society Collection, TSLA.
24. Ingraham, "Rural Taste," 186.
25. Henry Chapman Mercer, *Ancient Carpenters' Tools*, 5th ed. (Bucks County Historical Society, 1975), 25–32.
26. Draper Collection 3XX18(6); *ETT*, 507.
27. Chambers to John Steele, Nov. 5, 1799, Wagstaff, ed., I, 182; CCJ, June 5, 11, 12, 21, 22, 1805.
28. William Douglass, *A Summary, Historical and Political, of the first planting, progressive improvements and present state of the British Settlements in North-America* (London: R. and J. Dudsley, 1760), II, 54; *Davidson County Will Books* II, 133.
29. Thomas Jefferson Werthenbaker, *The Old South: The Founding of American Civilization* (New York: Scribners, 1942; rpt. Cooper Square, 1963), 206–8.
30. *ETT*, 454; *WHN*, 452–53; *CHD*, 325.
31. *Davidson County Will Books* I, 156.
32. Alexander von Humboldt to the Citizens of the United States, Apr. 4, 1834, TSLA, published in Stanley F. Horn, ed., "A Von Humboldt Letter," *THQ* 4 (1945), 232–33.
33. *MTW*, 255.
34. John D. DeWitt, ed., "Journal of Governor John Sevier," *THM* 6 (1921), 24–25.
35. Joseph Arnold Foster, ed., *Contributions to a Study of Brickmaking in America*, 6 pts. (Claremont, Calif.: The author, 1968–1971), pt. 5: *Accounts of Brickmaking in America Written before 1850*, 1–7, 59–60, 69–74; pt. 6: *Accounts of Brickmaking in America Published between 1850 and 1900*, 24.
36. *MTW*, 73; *Tennessee Gazette*, Nov. 20, 1801.
37. Harriette Simpson Arnow, *Flowering of the Cumberland* (New York: Macmillan, 1963), 292.
38. CCJ, Nov. 1, 1805.
39. *BJC* V, 316.
40. Articles of Agreement between Adam Lowry on Behalf of Samuel Doak of the One Part and John Squibb of the Other, Sept. 26, 1802, Samuel Doak Papers, TSLA; CCJ,

July 4, 1805.

41. *John Smith* v. *Elijah Embree*, Records of the Washington County First Judicial Circuit Court, March Term 1822.

42. DeWitt, ed., 32.

43. *Virginia Gazette* (R), Oct. 22, 1772; (P), Oct. 31, 1777; Kathleen Bruce, *Virginia Iron Manufacture in the Slave Era* (New York: Century, 1931), 63–64, 77.

44. NCSR XVIII, 302–3, 787; William Tatham to Thomas Jefferson, Aug? 1791, *William and Mary Quarterly*, ser. 2, 16 (1936), 176; *Knoxville Gazette*, May 5, 1792.

45. Raymond F. Hunt, "The Pactolus Ironworks," *THQ* 25 (1966), 180; William Blount to James Robertson, Apr. 24, 1797, *American Historical Magazine* 4 (1899), 342.

46. *ETT*, 33; Samuel C. Williams, "Early Ironworks in the Tennessee Country," *THQ* 6 (1947), 43–44.

47. Werthenbaker, 185; *ETT*, 333; CCJ, July 25, 1806.

48. James M. Swank, *History of the Manufacture of Iron in All Ages* (Philadelphia: American Iron and Steel Assoc., 1892), 86–99, 288–92.

49. Klaus G. Loewald, Beverly Starika, and Paul S. Taylor, trans. and eds., "Johann Martin Bolzius Answers a Questionnaire on Carolina and Georgia," *William and Mary Quarterly*, ser. 3, 15 (1958), 246.

50. George S. McKearin and Helen McKearin, *American Glass* (New York: Crown, 1941), 100ff.

51. *Davidson County Will Books*, I, 255.

52. William Blount to John Sevier, Jan. 2, 1792, Philip M. Hamer, ed., "Letters of William Blount," *ETHSP* 4 (1933), 127; Albert C. Holt, "The Economic and Social Beginnings of Tennessee," *THM* 7 (1921), 292.

53. CCJ, Oct. 3, 1805; *Tennessee Gazette*, Feb. 11, 1801; *Nashville Clarion*, Feb. 18, 1811.

54. *Davidson County Will Books* I, 255.

55. Ibid., II, 133.

56. CCJ, June 4, 1806.

57. *Davidson County Will Books*, I, 63.

58. CCJ, Dec. 26, 1805; Jan. 29, 31, 1806.

59. Ibid., May 6, 1806.

60. *Tennessee Gazette*, Feb. 15, 1811.

61. Stephenson, 281–83.

62. *Nashville Daily American*, Feb. 13, 1882; *BJC* V, 399; Mechanics' Institute of Tennessee, *Report of the Third Annual Exhibition* (Nashville: Bang, Walker and Co., 1857), 36–37.

63. William B. Sprague, *Annals of the American Pulpit* (New York: R. Camter, 1857–59), IV, 225.

64. "Nashville and her Manufactures," *Tennessee State Farmer and Mechanic* I (1856), 170; *AMN*.

65. "The First Heat," *Naturalist* 1 (1850), 160.

66. "Nashville and her Manufactures, New Series—Number IV," *Tennessee State Farmer and Mechanic* 2 (1857), 269.

67. "Hatcher's Rotary Shingle Machine," *Tennessee State Farmer and Mechanic* 2 (1857), 269.

68. Mechanics' Institute of Tennessee, *Report of the First Annual Exhibition* (Nashville: John F. Morgan, 1855), 50.

69. *AMT*, 5–6; 22–25; HBM; Mrs. John Trotwood Moore, "The Tennessee State Library in the Capitol," *THQ* 12 (1953), 10–11.

70. Federal Writers' Project, *Tennessee: A Guide to the State* (New York: Hastings House, 1939), 215; Charles W. Crawford, *Yesterday's Memphis*, Seemann's Historic Cities Series No. 25 (Miami: E.A. Seemann, 1976), 38.

71. *Illustrations of Architectural Iron Made by the Architectural Iron Works of the City of New York* (New York: Baker and Godwin, 1865), 33.

72. Horace Greeley, Leon Case, et al., *The Great Industries of United States* (Hartford, Conn.: J.B. Burr, 1872), 1070.

73. *Commercial Review of the South and West* 1 (1846), 505; *Nashville Daily Orthopolitan*, Dec. 20, 1845.

CHAPTER III

1. Marcus Whiffen, *The Public Buildings of Williamsburg*, (Williamsburg Va.: Colonial Williamsburg, 1958) 140–41; John Fitzhugh Millar, *The Architects of the American Colonies, or Vitruvius Americanus* (Barre, Mass.: Barre Publishers, 1968), 43–57.

2. *South Carolina Historical and Genealogical Magazine* 37 (1936), 160; *South-Carolina Gazette*, Aug. 18, 1769; Apr. 15, 1785; Oct. 6, 1797.

3. CCJ, July 30, Aug. 6, Sept. 11, 1806; Ravenal, 89. Ralph Izard, Sr., South Carolina statesman and senator, died in May 1804, so the visitor whom Charles Coffin welcomed to Knoxville was Ralph Izard, Jr., whose residence in Charleston, probably the house then standing at 99 Broad Street, Thomas Hope had designed.

4. *Knoxville Gazette*, Nov. 14, 1796; Mar. 20, 1797.

5. U.S. Census, Botetourt County, Va. 1820, McMinn County, Tenn. 1850; Anne Lowry Worrell, comp., *Early Marriages, Wills, and Some Revolutionary Records of Botetourt County, Virginia* (Roanoke, Va.: The author, 1958), 11; J.M. Sharp, *Recollections & Hearsays of Athens: Fifty Years and Beyond* (Athens, Tenn.: The author, 1933), 6.

6. U.S. Census, Davidson County, 1820, 1830; Shelby County, 1850; *Nashville Clarion and Tennessee Gazette*, June 20, 1820; *The Louisville Directory for the Year 1832* (Louisville,: Richard W. Otis, 1832), 70, 154. Governor William Carroll to Governor Lynch, Sept. 13, 1833, Mississippi Archives; *Memphis Appeal*, May 10, 1844.

7. U.S. Census, Wilson County, 1820; Davidson County, 1830; Shelby County, 1850; Theodore Laist, "Two Early Mississippi Valley State Capitols," *Western Architect* 35 (1926), 56; D. Morrison to James K. Polk, Nov. 12, 1845, Polk Papers.

8. E. Alexander to T.A.R. Nelson, Apr. 12, 1845, T.A.R. Nelson Papers, McC; DPA, May 21, 1842. Thomas U. Walter, Joseph M. Wilson, and Frederick Graff, "Obituary—John C. Trautwine," *Journal of the Franklin Institute* 116 (1883), 392.

9. *HHG*, p. 97; U.S. Census, Blount County, 1850.

10. *South-Carolina Gazette*, Aug. 18, 1769.

11. Ingraham, "Rural Taste," 186.

12. *Nashville Republican*, Dec. 6, 1831; D. Morrison to Andrew Jackson, Dec. 6, 1831, Historic Hermitage Properties Collection; published in Mary French Caldwell, *Andrew Jackson's Hermitage* (Nashville: Ladies' Hermitage Assoc., 1933), 78–79. An elevation rendered in the style of the Ayres's map perspective was also published. See Stanley F. Horn, *The Hermitage, Home of Old Hickory* (Richmond: Garrett and Massie, 1938; 2d ed. New York: Greenberg, 1950; rpt. Nashville: Ladies' Hermitage Assoc., 1960), following p. 10.

13. Mechanics' Institute of Tennessee, *Report of the First Annual Exhibition*, 67, 69.

14. Washington County Court of Quarter Sessions and Pleas, *Minutes*, Nov. 3, 1784, TSLA.

15. Washington County First Judicial Circuit Court, *Records*, March Term, 1822.

16. *Tennessee Gazette*, Mar. 29, 1811.

17. Contract between the Directors of the Bank of Tennessee and William Fields and H.M. Ledbetter, Oct. 10, 1839, copy in McC.

18. *Virginia Gazette*, (PD), Mar. 23, 1769.

19. *Virginia Gazette* (R), Mar. 31, 1774.

20. Articles of agreement between Adam Lowry . . . and John Squibb, Sept. 26, 1802, Samuel Doak Papers, TSLA.

21. Rosamund Randall Bierne and John Henry Scarff, *William Buckland (1738–1774), Architect of Virginia and Maryland* (Baltimore: Maryland Historical Society, 1958), 30.

22. *Virginia Gazette* (P), Aug. 15, 1777.

23. Memorandum of an agreement made and entered into between William Strickland of Philadelphia Architect of the first part and The Commissioners to Superintend the Construction of the State house, June 18, 1845, Capitol Construction Records, Record Group 7, Series 4, TSLA.

24. Deposition of G.B. Vannoy, Nov. 19, 1860, in *James M. Hughes* v. *Wesley Wheless*, Docket No. 2277, filed Nov. 22, 1858, Davidson County Chancery Court.

25. Articles of Agreement . . . Between John Overton . . . and David Cummins and Frederick Pinkley, Claybrook-Overton Collection, TSLA.

26. Memorandum of Agreement . . . Between Joseph Reiff and William C. Hume of the One Part and Andrew Jackson Jr. of the Other Part, Jan. 1, 1835, *BJC* V, 317.

27. An article of agreement between Wesley Wheless of the first part, and Smith & Hughes of the Second, July 18, 1856, copy in *Hughes* v. *Wheless*.

28. DPA, Sept. 28, 1842; June 6, 24, July 25, 1843; June 24, 1845.

29. *South-Carolina Gazette*, Feb. 2, 1734.

30. *Constitution and By-Laws of the American Institution of Architects* (Philadelphia, 1837). Copy in the Metropolitan Museum of Art Library, New York.

31. DPA, July 13, Sept. 25, 26, 1842; June 6, 7, 24, July 25, Aug. 1, 1843.

32. Deposition of G.B. Vannoy, Nov. 19, 1860, *Hughes* v. *Wheless*.

33. *Davidson County Will Books*, I, 156.

34. DPA, May 23, Mar. 12, 1842.

35. [Tannehill], "Masonic College of Tennessee," 270–71.

36. Deposition of Nicholas Hobson, Nov. 19, 1860, *Hughes* v. *Wheless*.

37. "Library of John Carter of Lancaster County," *William and Mary Quarterly*, ser. 1, 8 (1899–1900), 18.

38. Helen Park, "A List of Architectural Books Available in America Before the Revolution," *JSAH* 20 (Oct. 1961), 117.

39. "A Catalogue of Books in the Westmoreland County, Va., Library of Councillor Robert Carter, at Nomini Hall," *William and Mary Quarterly*, ser. 1, no. 10 (1901–2), 232–41; Bierne and Scarff, 149–50.

40. *Virginia Gazette* (P), Aug. 15, 1777.

41. Adolphus Heiman to A.W. Putman, June 1, 1857, TSLA.

42. *The Antiquities of Athens; and other Monuments of Greece; as Measured and Delineated by James Stuart, F.R.S. and F.S.A., and Nicholas Revett, Painters and Architects* (London: Charles Tilt, 1837).

43. Prichard to Downing, 49–50.

44. Michael A. Tomlan, "George Franklin Barber (1854–1915), Carpenter, Architect, and Publisher," *JSAH* 35 (1976), 261–62.

45. *Records of Maury County: St. Peter's Episcopal Church, Columbia, Tennessee*. Copied under the WPA, June 15, 1938.

46. *Knoxville Register*, May 31, 1848.

47. Joseph Jackson to T.A.R. Nelson, May 29, 1845, T.A.R. Nelson Papers, McC; Washington County Court Minutes, Sept. 6, 1847.

48. *Nashville Whig*, Apr. 27, 1844.

49. William Strickland to James K. Polk, Nov. 12, 1846; Agreement between J.M. Hughes and J.K. Polk, Oct. 18, 1847; Contract between James M. Hughes and James K. Polk, Apr. 22, 1848; Polk Papers; *Nashville Daily Evening Reporter*, Sept. 24, 1850; Deposition of Nicholas Hobson, Nov. 19, 1860, *Hughes* v. *Wheless*.

50. Jesse E. Wills, "An Echo from Egypt: A History of the Building Occupied by the First Presbyterian Church, Nashville, Tennessee," *THQ* 11 (1952), 66; Contract between James M. Hughes and James K. Polk, Apr. 22, 1848, Polk Papers.

51. Bierne and Scarff, 30; *South-Carolina Gazette*, Aug. 18, 1769; *Virginia Gazette* (P), Aug. 15, 1777.

52. Walter, Wilson, and Graff, 392–96.

53. *Memphis Tri-Weekly Appeal*, Jan. 10, 1846; *Memphis Daily Appeal*, July 6, Nov. 22, 1856.

54. *Memphis Commercial-Appeal*, Feb. 22, 1909; *Memphis News-Scimitar*, Feb. 22, 1909.

55. Quoted in H.M. Pierce Gallagher, *Robert Mills, Architect of the Washington Monument, 1781 to 1855* (New York: Columbia Univ. Press, 1935), 170.

56. Ingraham, "Rural Taste," 186.

57. James Marston Fitch, *American Building*, vol. 1: *The Historical Forces That Shaped It*, 2d ed. rev. (Boston: Houghton Mifflin, 1966), 172.

58. *ETT*, p. 52; *Nashville Journal of Medicine and Surgery* 7 (1854), 250.

CHAPTER IV

1. William Penn, *Information and Direction to Such Persons as are inclined to America, more Especially Those related to the province of Pennsylvania* (n.p., 1684), quoted in Harold R. Shurtleff, *The Log Cabin Myth: A Study of the Early Dwellings of the English Colonists in North America* (Cambridge, Mass.: Harvard Univ. Press, 1939), 125–26.

2. Henry Glassie, *Folk Housing in Middle Virginia: A Structural Analysis of Historic Artifacts* (Knoxville: Univ. of Tennessee Press, 1975), 78–79, 168; Sara Sprott Morrow, "The William Bowen House," *THQ* 32 (1973), 63–64.

3. Henry Chandlee Forman, *The Architecture of the Old South: The Medieval Style, 1585–1850* (Cambridge, Mass.: Harvard Univ. Press, 1948), 40–48, 86–89. The Magevney house on Adams Avenue in Memphis, built in 1831, is among the oldest frame story-and-loft houses in Tennessee.

4. Walter Muir Whitehead, *Palladio in America* (Milan: Electa Editrice, 1976), 27–28; Eleanor Graham, ed., *Nashville: A Short History and Selected Buildings* (Nashville: Historical Commission of Metropolitan Nashville-Davidson County, 1974),179; *HHG*, 229, 268–69.

5. Glassie, 20.

6. Ibid., 41.

7. Ibid., 57–65.

8. *HHG*, 197.

9. Ibid., 109–10.

10. Glassie, 94, 95, 191.

11. Ibid., 88–101. The "I" house was identified and named by Fred Kniffen in "Folk Housing: Key to Diffusion," *Annals of the Assoc. of American Geographers* 35 (1965), 549–87.

12. Marcus Whiffen, *Eighteenth-Century Houses of Williamsburg* (Williamsburg: Colonial Williamsburg, 1960), 56–59.

13. Thomas Tileston Waterman, "The Bay System in Colonial Virginia," *William and Mary Quarterly*, ser. 2, no. 15 (1935), 117–22.

14. Sprague, III, 370.

15. William Henry Foote, *Sketches of Virginia Historical and Biographical*, ser. 1 (Philadelphia: William S. Martien, 1850), 462.

16. Charles Coffin, *A Discourse Preached Before the East Tennessee Bible Society at Their Annual Meeting in Knoxville, April 30th, 1817* (Knoxville: Heiskell and Brown, 1817), 22.

17. Philip Lindsley, *Baccalaureate Address, October 3, 1827* (Nashville: John S. Simpson, 1827), 5.

18. Frederick A. Ross, Scrapbook [p. 10], McC.

19. Douglas Sloan, *The Scottish Enlightenment and the American College Ideal* (New York: Teachers College Press, 1975), 113–17, 122–24; E. Brooks Holifield, *The Gentlemen Theologians: American Theology in Southern Culture 1795–1860* (Durham: Duke Univ. Press, 1978), 110–54.

20. Foote, 460–61.

21. Samuel Doak, *Lectures on Human Nature* (Jonesborough: F. Gifford & Co., 1845), 3.

22. *HHG*, 102, 118.

23. Doak, 65–66.

24. Sprague, III, 292.

25. John Witherspoon, *Lectures on Moral Philosophy*, ed. Varnum Lansing Collins (Princeton: Princeton Univ. Press, 1917), 17.

26. Ibid., 16.

27. Francis Hutcheson, *An Inquiry into the Original of Our Ideas of Beauty and Virtue*, 2d ed. (London, 1726; rpt. New York: Garland Publishing, 1971), 12, 13.

28. Ibid., 10.

29. Ibid., 38.

30. Ibid.

31. Henry Home, Lord Kames, *Elements of Criticism* (London: A. Millar, 1762; rpt. New York: George Olms, 1970), III, 328.

32. Thomas Reid, *Lectures on the Fine Arts*, ed. Peter Kivy (The Hague: Martinus Nijhoff, 1973), 41–42.

33. Quoted in John Fleming, *Robert Adam and His Circle* (Cambridge, Mass.: Harvard Univ. Press, 1962), 34, 43–44.

34. Royall, 19.

35. Quoted in Fleming, 34.

36. "Diary of a French Traveller in the Colonies, 1765," *American Historical Review* 27 (1921–22), 72.

37. *Knoxville Gazette*, Apr. 6, 1793.

38. Emil Kaufmann, *Architecture in the Age of Reason* (1955; rpt. New York: Dover, 1968), 62–71.

39. "Architecture in the United States," *American Journal of Science* 17 (Jan.-June 1830), 254.

40. "Transcendentalism," *Southern Quarterly Review* 2 (1842), 438.

41. Frederick A. Ross, Scrapbook [p. 10], McC.

CHAPTER V

1. William A. Klutts, "Fort Prudhomme: Its Location," *WTHSP* 4 (1950), 28–40.

2. Wilson, 106–8.

3. J.F.H. Claiborne, *Mississippi as a Province, Territory, and State, With Biographical Notices of Eminent Citizens* (Jackson, Miss.: Power and Barksdale, 1880), I, 71, 82; Wilson, figs. 10, 20.

4. Wilson, fig. 10.

5. Charles Pinckney to the Lords Commissioners for Trade and Plantations, June 27, 1754, quoted in P.M. Hamer, "Anglo-French Rivalry in the Cherokee Country, 1754–1757," *North Carolina Historical Review* 2 (1925), 305–6. In 1755 Gov. Dinwiddie anticipated a French attempt to fortify the Susquehanna. See Dinwiddie to Sir Robert Thompson, Nov. 15, 1755, *Collections of the Virginia Historical Society*, vols. III and IV: *The Official Records of Robert Dinwiddie, Lieutenant Governor of the Colony of Virginia, 1751–1758* (Richmond: Virginia Historical Society, 1933–34), II, 267.

6. Capt. Raymond Demere to Gov. Lyttleton, July 10, 1756, McDowell, ed., 132–33; Gov. Dinwiddie to Maj. Andrew Lewis, Apr. 24, 1756, Dinwiddie Papers, II, 389–90.

7. William Gerard De Brahm, "History of Three Provinces: South Carolina, Georgia, and East Florida," MS, in

Harvard Library, quoted in Hamer, "Anglo-French Rivalry in the Cherokee Country, 1754–1757," p. 316. A lunette was a field-work forming a salient angle; a hornwork, a single-fronted outwork, the head of which consists of two demi-bastions connected by a curtain and located outside the main wall to serve as an advantageous outpost. The cavalier was a raised platform within and commanding the fortified area. In accordance with contemporary practice, the bastions at Fort Loudoun were named King George, Queen, Prince of Wales, Duke of Cumberland. The fortifications also included Lyttleton's Ravelin and Glen's Fort, named for the governors who had financed and supplied the fort building expeditions. See McDowell, ed., 285–86; *HHG,* 25.

8. Capt. Raymond Demere and other officers to De Brahm, Dec. 23, 1756, McDowell, ed., 285; Council of War held by Capt. Raymond Demere, Dec. 26, 1756, ibid., 287; Demere to Gov. Lyttleton, Aug. 26, 1757, ibid. 407; Capt. Paul Demere to Lyttleton, Nov. 24, Dec. 30, 1757, Jan. 5, 1758, ibid., 417–18, 428, 437. For the number and skills of the soldiers and artisans at Fort Loudoun see McDowell, ed., 291–92, 345, and for a catalog of the tools used in the building of back country forts, see ibid., 343–44, 482.

9. Ellsworth Brown, "Archaeology of Fort Loudoun, Field Investigations, 1956–57, for the Fort Loudoun Association." Vonore, Tenn.: 1958. Copy in McC.

10. Raymond Demere to Gov. Lyttleton, Sept. 12, 1756, McDowell, ed., 200. See also Demere to Lyttleton, Oct. 26, Nov. 8, 1756, ibid., 230, 243.

11. Wilson, fig. 20; Norman W. Caldwell, "Fort Massac During the French and Indian War," *Journal of the Illinois State Historical Society* 43 (1950), 100–19. Caldwell (106, n.27) discovered no mention of Fort Massac before Aug. 30, 1759.

12. The French prisoner John Charles Vain, captured near Fort Loudoun late in 1757, had been stationed at Fort Assumption, "a square fort with four bastions," which Vain located on the Mississippi just above the Ohio, noting that repairs undertaken three years earlier had been completed in May of that year (McDowell, ed., 442). Gov. Kerlérec reported to Paris in the summer of 1760 that Fort Ascension on the Cherokee [Tennessee] River had been rebuilt (Wilson, 121). Fort Ascension had been the original name of Fort Massac. Gov. Dobbs of North Carolina assumed that Fort Assumption was on the Tennessee (Dobbs to the Lords Commissioners for Trade and Plantations, ?Feb. 1761, NCCR VI, 617). When Haywood wrote (before 1823), he followed (26) a map locating one French fort at the fork of the Mississippi and Ohio, another on the Ohio near the Tennessee (Fort Massac), and another a few miles up the Tennessee. For other references to the French fort on the Tennessee see McDowell, ed., 472–77.

13. McDowell, ed., 439.

14. Demere to Lyttleton, May 2, 15, 1759, McDowell, ed., 483–84, 492–93; William Shorie to Demere, May 8, 1759, ibid., 493–94.

15. Thomas Hutchins, Notes, quoted in Harriette Simpson Arnow, *Seedtime on the Cumberland* (New York: Macmillan, 1960), 74; Haywood, 33–34; John Donelson's

journal, Apr. 1, 1799, *ETT,* 241.

16. Ramsey, 54. The date given by Ramsey is 1758, but nothing in Byrd's correspondence suggests that he built a fort at the Long Island of the Holston during the journey he made through Cherokee country in February and March 1758 or during his futile attempt to relieve Fort Loudoun and pacify the Cherokees in the summer and fall of 1760. Byrd recommended that "a respectable fort be built at the Big Island" in June or July 1760. See Governor and Council (Minutes), July 11, 1760, in Marion Tinling, ed., *The Correspondence of the Three William Byrds of Westover, Virginia 1684–1776* (Charlottesville: Virginia Historical Society and Univ. of Virginia Press, 1977), II, 695; Byrd to Jeffry Amherst, Sept. 18, 1762, ibid., 760–61. Fort Robinson was built in the summer and fall of 1761 by Lt.-Col. Adam Stephen and Virginia troops and artisans. See Samuel C. Williams, ed., *Lieut. Henry Timberlake's Memoirs 1756–1765* (Johnson City, Tenn.: Watauga Press, 1927), 38.

17. McDowell ed., 418.

18. Quoted in P.M. Hamer, "Fort Loudoun in the Cherokee War, 1758–1761," *North Carolina Historical Review* 2 (1925), 446. Dr. Thomas Walker noted in his journal on March 24, 1750, that he "went to Stalnaker's, helped him raise his house" (*ETT,* 169). Samuel Stalnaker's house was a few miles northeast of the site of Bristol, but others were built south of the colony line in the 1750s. Cornelius Dougharty's house was at Hiwassee town on the Hiwassee River in 1757, and his establishment included slaves, hogs, and horses. See Dougharty to Capt. Paul Demere in McDowell, ed., 432–33.

19. Haywood, 45. There was also a French trading post at Muscle Shoals on the Tennessee. See Peter J. Hamilton, *Colonial Mobile* (rev. ed., Boston: Houghton Mifflin, 1910; rpt. University: Univ. of Alabama Press, 1976), 203.

20. "John Redd's Reminiscences," *Virginia Magazine of History and Biography* 7 (1899–1900), 2.

21. Haywood, 98.

22. Featherstonhaugh, 55. On the brick blockhouse at Fort Pitt see Charles Morse Stotz, *The Architectural Heritage of Early Western Pennsylvania* (Pittsburgh: Univ. of Pittsburgh Press, 1966), 262–63. See also the discussion of this building type in Arnow, *Seedtime on the Cumberland,* 267, 271. Other references to blockhouses occur in *ETT,* 278, 360, 381, 434, 436; and in Clarence Edwin Carter, ed., *Territorial Papers of the United States:* Vol. 4. *The Territory South of the River Ohio, 1790–1796* (Washington, D.C.: Government Printing Office, 1936), 313, 323. The two-story log structures Paul Demere built in Fort Loudoun served as blockhouses (McDowell, ed., 345).

23. Henry Hartwell, James Blair, and Edward Chilton, *The Present State of Virginia, and the College* (London: John Wyat, 1727; rpt. Charlottesville: Dominion Books, 1964), 12, 14.

24. *ETT,* 452.

25. *Knoxville Gazette,* Dec. 17, 1791; Samuel C. Williams, "The South's First Cotton Factory," *THQ* 5 (1946), 212–21.

26. *Tennessee Gazette and Mero District Advertiser,* Mar. 20., Feb. 13, Apr. 10, 1805; Lealand D. Baldwin, *The Keelboat Age on Western Waters* (Pittsburgh: Univ. of Pittsburgh

Press, 1941), 164–65. *MTW*, 110–11; John R. Bedford, Tour in 1807 Down the Cumberland, Ohio, and Mississippi Rivers from Nashville to New Orleans," *THM* 5 (1919), 50.

27. *ETT*, 412.

28. [Wilkins Tannehill], "The Town We Live In," *Port Folio* 2 (1848–49), 82.

29. *MTW*, 245.

30. Royall, 21. Clayton's source counted four brick houses in Nashville in the same year (*CHD*, 197).

31. Abashai C. Thomas to John Gray Blount, Oct. 26, 1794, Alice Barnwell Keith, ed., *The John Gray Blount Papers, II: 1790–1795* (Raleigh: State Dept. of Archives and History, 1959), 447.

32. *ETT*, 454.

33. Ibid.

34. *MTW*, 272.

35. NCSR XXIV, 310.

36. Frederick Emory, *Queen-Anne's County, Maryland; Its Early History and Development . . .* (Baltimore: Maryland Historical Society, 1950), 315; William Hande Browne, ed., *Archives of Maryland*, vol. 19: *Proceedings and Acts of the General Assembly of Maryland, Sept. 1693–June, 1697* (Baltimore: Maryland Historical Society, 1899), 112; Whiffen, *Eighteenth-Century Houses of Williamsburg*, 53. The dimensions required by eighteenth-century legislation reflect late medieval conventions regarding the sizes of ground plans, and these sizes are in turn related to the bay system which governed building. This system was conventional and intuitive. See Forman, *Architecture of the Old South*, 15–16.

37. Forman, *Architecture of the Old South*, 20–21. Clay chimneys were mentioned in the Fincastle, Virginia, tax list of 1784 (Stoner, 233–35). Welch chimneys were still occasionally built in mid-nineteenth-century Tennessee. See Oliver P. Temple, *Notable Men of Tennessee from 1833 to 1875; Their Times, and Their Contemporaries* (New York: Cosmopolitan Press, 1912), 153n; Knox Co. Minute Book A, 7.

38. Whiffen, *Eighteenth-Century Houses of Williamsburg*, 54.

39. NCSR XXIV, 616.

40. Paul M. Fink, *Jonesborough: The First Century of Tennessee's First Town* (Springfield, Va.: National Technical Information Service, 1972), 17–18.

41. *Knoxville Gazette*, Apr. 6, 1793.

42. *ETT*, 454.

43. *Davidson County Court Minutes*, I, 3.

44. *WHN*, 454.

45. M.W. Barley, *The English Farmhouse and Cottage* (London: Routledge and Kegan Paul, 1961), 70–71, 95–97, 104, 123, 133, 201; Forman, *Architecture of the Old South*, 37–46. On the nomenclature of interior spaces see Barley, 14, 28–29.

46. Durham, *Great Leap Westward*, 146–48; Morrow, "William Bowen House," 63–64.

47. Glassie, 24, 78–79, 168.

48. *HHG*, 117. This house stood in the countryside south of Jonesboro until it was moved to a site near the Jonesboro Presbyterian Church in 1975.

49. *HWC*, 164–65.

50. *AMT*, 102–5.

51. Ibid., 106–9.

52. *Beloved Landmarks of Loudon County, Tennessee* (n.p.: Hiwassee Chapter, Daughters of the American Revolution, n.d.).

53. Penn, *Information and Direction to Such Persons as are Inclined to America*, quoted in Shurtleff, 125–26.

54. Stotz, 46–49, 72, 93, 97; James D. Trump and Arthur P. Ziegler, Jr., *Landmark Architecture of Allegheny County, Pennsylvania* (Pittsburgh: Pittsburgh History and Landmarks Foundation, 1967), 230, 250, 218; Alan Gowans, *Architecture of New Jersey* (New York: D. Van Nostrand, 1964), 24; Henry Chandlee Forman, *Maryland Architecture; A Short History from 1634 Through the Civil War* (Cambridge, Md.: Tidewater Publishers, 1968), 51–55; Wesley I. Shank, "Eighteenth-Century Architecture of the Upper Delaware River Valley of New Jersey and Pennsylvania," *JSAH* 31 (1972), 137–44; Frances Benjamin Johnston and Thomas Tileston Waterman, *The Early Architecture of North Carolina* (Chapel Hill: Univ. of North Carolina Press, 1941).

55. *HHG*, 119–20.

56. The mat of photograph (34) dated Mar. 24, 1909, is inscribed "Built in 1791 by Tom Edmond."

57. *HHG*, 120.

58. Forman, 78–79, 102; Jones, 36; William Priest, *Travels in the United States of America; Commencing in the year 1793, and ending in 1797 . . .* (London: J. Johnson, 1802), 42.

59. Benjamin Rush, *An Account of the Manners of the German Inhabitants of Pennsylvania* (Philadelphia: Samuel P. Town, 1875), 12n; *HHG*, 60–61.

60. *HHG*, 86–87. The Collins Mansion in Westchester, Pa., is a stone house with regular pent eaves. See Alan Gowans, *Images of American Living: Four Centuries of Architecture and Furniture as Cultural Expression* (Philadelphia: Lippincott, 1964), 85.

61. *Washington County, Tennessee Records*, transcribed by Mary Hardin McCown (Johnson City, Tenn.: The author, 1964), 23–24.

62. *HHG*, 38–40. Washington County tax records for 1779 call John Carter's land on the Watauga his "manor plantation," a description probably intended to signify that his house stood on this tract. There were buildings there by Dec. 23, 1776, when the North Carolina Assembly voted to place gun powder at Colonel Carter's in Washington District as a public magazine (NCCR X, 998; NCSR XII, 103–4), and Carter's dwelling was a mustering place in the fall of 1780 (Draper Collection, 16DD12). Landon Carter inherited the house about 1780, and his residence at Watauga was noticed (though not described) during his lifetime by William Tatham (*Knoxville Gazette*, Sept. 22, 1792), and during the lifetime of Landon Carter's widow, Elizabeth McLin Carter, by Charles Coffin (CCJ, Feb. 16, 1803). On the nineteenth-century identification and location of the house see William B. Carter's letters to Lymon C. Draper (Draper Collection, 4DD41, 45). See also *ETT*, 342. On the use of "manor" see *Virginia Magazine of History and Biography* 24 (1932), 188–90.

63. The William Blount house is difficult to interpret. See J. Everette Fauber, "Research Report and Proposal for Resto-

ration, the Governor William Blount Mansion, Knoxville, Tennessee" (Lynchburg, Va.: The author, 1968). Copy in McC. For the date of the house see Blount to James Robertson, Jan. 2, 1792 (Carter, ed., 109), where Blount notes: "My houses there [Knoxville] are not yet done," and Blount to the Secretary of War, May 24, 1793 (ibid., 261), in which Blount refers to "my house" in Knoxville. Glass was ordered on Jan. 2, 1792. See Hamer, ed., 127.

64. The history of the central-passage house in the colonial South is still incomplete. The pattern Glassie identifies, though dominant only after the formalizing tendencies of the eighteenth century had done their work, is anticipated by the medieval cross plan and appears as early as 1680 (Forman, *Architecture of the Old South*, 47–51, 75).

65. *Beloved Landmarks of Loudon County*.

66. Maxwell Chambers to John Steele, Nov. 5, 1799, Wagstaff, ed., I, 183.

67. *HHG*, 58–59.

68. *AMT*, 96–101; Gifford A. Cochran, *Grandeur in Tennessee* (New York: J.J. Augustin, 1946), 23–26; *HHG*, 277–79; Sally Smith to Daniel Smith, July 20, 1793, Tennessee Historical Society Collection, TSLA.

69. *AMT*, 110–15; Cochran, 28–30; *HHG*, 280–83; Ward Allen, "Cragfont: Grandeur on the Tennessee Frontier," *THQ* 23 (1964), 103–20.

70. *HHG*, 72–74; Susan Douglas Tate, "Thomas Hope of Tennessee, c. 1757–1820," M.S. thesis, Univ. of Tennessee, Knoxville, 1972, pp. 90–95. Wessyngton (1819), like State's View and the Lawson D. Franklin house at Leadvale, Jefferson County, was a large brick plantation house that, while displaying Federal influence, was conceptually an eighteenth-century building. See *AMT*, 130–33.

71. Talbot Hamlin, *Greek Revival Architecture in America* . . . (New York: Oxford Univ. Press, 1944; rpt. Dover, 1966), 235.

72. James Parton, *Life of Andrew Jackson* (New York: Mason Brothers, 1860; rpt. Johnson Reprint, 1967), II, 645.

73. Jack D.L. Holmes, "Some French Engineers in Spanish Louisiana," in McDermott, ed., 130.

74. *ETT*, 349. Collot's map is reproduced in *HHG*, 19.

75. Mary Wallace Crocker, *Historic Architecture in Mississippi* (Jackson: Univ. Press of Mississippi, 1974), 13–14.

76. Jack D.L. Holmes, "Fort Ferdinand of the Bluffs: Life on the Spanish-American Frontier, 1795–1797," *WTHSP* 13 (1959), 50; Folch to Carondelet, Oct. 9, 11, 1795, *ibid.*, 46; Abraham P. Nasatir, *Spanish War Vessels on the Mississippi 1792–1796* (New Haven: Yale Univ. Press, 1968), 60, 116–17, n. 59.

CHAPTER VI

1. [Wilkins Tannehill], "Cumberland Lodge," *Port Folio* 1 (1847–48), 73.

2. *AMT*, 102–5.

3. DeWitt, ed., 32.

4. *HHG*, 85–86.

5. Ibid., 117.

6. Graham, ed., 179.

7. *AMT*, 144–49; *HHG*, 268–71.

8. *HHG*, 229.

9. Ibid., 88, 130, 187–90; *HWC*, 106–7.

10. *HHG*, 86–87.

11. Tate, 32–43; vertical file, McC.

12. Millar, 87, 90, 132, 133.

13. Thomas Hope to Elizabeth Large Hope, Jan. 29, 1820, McC.

14. Charles Coffin Ross, ed., 15–16, 27–28.

15. Millar, 20, 31, 34, 65.

16. *HHG*, 72–74; Tate, 92–95; vertical file, McC.

17. CCJ, Aug. 11, 1806; Nannie Lee Hicks, *Historic Treasure Spots of Knox County, Tennessee* (Knoxville: Simon Harris Chapter, Daughters of the American Revolution, 1964), 45–47.

18. Tate, 103–10.

19. Palladio's Basilica at Vicenza (1549) is sometimes considered the source of the Palladian, or Venetian, window, which William Kent and Robert Adam popularized in England. Diocletian's palace at Split (Yugoslavia), where an arch breaks into the tympanum of the pediment, studied by Adam in 1757, is also a source.

20. *Succession of Isaac Franklin*, 277, 286.

21. E. Bruce Thompson, "Reforms in the Penal System of Tennessee, 1820–1850," *THQ* 1 (1942), 296–301.

22. Thompson, 301; *MTG*, 220–21; *AMN*.

23. Gilmore, 63.

24. Fleming, see IV, 33, plates 81, 84.

25. *MTG*, 221.

26. Ibid., 213–14.

27. Morrison to Jackson, Dec. 6, 1831, in Mary French Caldwell, 78–79.

28. J.M. Keating, *History of the City of Memphis and Shelby County, Tennessee, with Illustrations and Biographical Sketches of Some of Its Prominent Citizens* (Syracuse, N.Y.: D. Mason, 1888), I, 236–38; David Morrison to James K. Polk, May 12, 1845, Polk Papers.

29. *HHG*, 226–28.

30. Ibid., 109–10.

31. Ibid., 41–42.

32. Richard Harrison Doughty, *Greenville: One Hundred Year Portrait, 1775–1875* (Greenville: The Author, 1975), 275–79.

33. Ibid., 118; Records of the Washington County First Judicial Circuit Court, March Term, 1822.

34. *HHG*, 96.

35. *HWC*, 123–25. The Saunders house on Third Avenue in Franklin, traditionally dated before 1805, is nearly identical to the Samuel Polk house, Columbia. See *HWC*, 133; *HHG*, 187–88; Herbert Weaver and William G. Eidson, "The James K. Polk Home," *THQ* 24 (1965), 3–19.

36. *HWC*, 98.

37. *HHG*, 239.

38. Ibid., 130.

39. *HWC*, 96–98.

40. Ibid., 8–9.

41. Walter T. Durham, *Old Sumner: A History of Sumner County, Tennessee* (Gallatin: Sumner County Library Board, 1972), 298–300.

42. *HHG*, 63; Sharp, 6.

43. Graham, ed., 179. The horizontal ellipse was a prominent feature of the "Design for a large building," plate 37 in Owen Biddle's *Young Carpenter's Assistant* (1805).

44. G.R. Dempster, "History and Houses: Craighead-Jackson House," *Antiques* 98 (July-Dec. 1970), 110-14.

45. *HWC*, 106-7. On the nearly identical Carter house, also in Franklin, see *HHG*, 285; *AMT*, 138-43.

46. Durham, *Old Sumner*, 17-18.

47. Ibid., 18.

48. Marcus Whiffen, "The Early Courthouses of Virginia," *JSAH* 18 (1959), 2-10; Morris L. Radoff, *The County Courthouses and Records of Maryland. Part One: The Courthouses* (Annapolis: Hall of Records Commission, 1960), 10, 54, 82, 126, 146.

49. *Impartial Review and Cumberland Repository*, Nov. 8, 1806.

50. *Tennessee Gazette*, Mar. 29, 1811.

51. *Tennessee Gazette*, Feb. 25, 1800; NST, 192; *Nashville Tennessean Magazine*, Oct. 4, 1936.

52. NST, 194.

53. Herbert L. Harper, "Antebellum Courthouses of Tennessee," *THQ* 30 (1971), 3-5.

54. James W. Rogan, "Hawkins County," typescript in McC.

55. Stoner, 179-82.

56. Doughty, 277; *American Economist and East Tennessee Statesman*, Apr. 17, 1824.

57. CCJ, Nov. 27, 29, 1805; Doughty, 156, 174.

58. Pryor Lea to Charles Coffin, Nov. 3, 1826, Special Collections, Univ. of Tennessee Library.

59. *Knoxville Register*, Oct. 22, 1828; John C. Gunn cited in Moses White, *Early History of the University of Tennessee* (Knoxville: The author, 1879), 27-28; Henry Ruffner, "Notes of a Tour from Virginia to Tennessee in the Months of July and August, 1838," *Southern Literary Messenger* 5 (1839), 270.

60. White, 27, 23; DPA, June 23, 29, July 13, Sept. 24, 25, 28, 1842; June 6, 24, July 25, 1843.

61. *Catalogue of the Officers and Graduates of the University of Nashville, With an Appendix Containing Sundry Historical Notices, Etc.* (Nashville: A. Nelson, 1850), 22-29.

62. Parton, I, 391-92.

63. *MTG*, 220. The Nashville Branch of the Bank of the United States having been closed in 1836, the building was used after about 1838 by the Bank of the State of Tennessee and subsequently, about 1843, was purchased by the Planters' Bank of Tennessee. See *Nashville Daily Evening Reporter*, Oct. 10, 14, 1850; *WHN*, 284, 286.

64. JCD, Sept. 1, 1827.

65. Parton, I, 391.

66. *National Banner and Nashville Whig*, Jan. 24, 1829; *MTG*, 214; *WHN*, 116. This building was remodeled about 1856, probably by Adolphus Heiman (166).

67. *Fort-Pickering American Eagle*, July 22, 1842; *Memphis American Eagle*, Aug. 12, 1842.

68. *Memphis American Eagle*, Aug. 12, 1842; *Memphis Appeal*, May 17, 1844; *Daily Memphis Enquirer*, May 13, 1847; *Memphis Semi-Weekly Appeal*, Jan. 7, 1845; DPA, May 23, 1842.

69. DPA, May 23, 1842.

CHAPTER VII

1. *MTW*, 304.

2. *ETT*, 455.

3. Lewis Preston Summers, *Annals of Southwest Virginia, 1769-1800* (Abingdon, Va.: The author, 1929; rpt. Baltimore: Genealogical Publishing, 1970), 653, 954.

4. S.W. Tindell, *The Baptists of Tennessee* (Kingsport: Southern Publishers, 1930), 24-26.

5. J. Burnett, *Sketches of Tennessee's Pioneer Baptists* (Nashville: Marshall and Bruce, 1919), 311-12; Tindell, 40-43.

6. J.G.M. Ramsey, *History of Lebanon Presbyterian Church "in the Fork," Five Miles East of Knoxville* (Knoxville: The author, 1918), 8, 20.

7. *Beloved Landmarks of Loudon County.*

8. CCJ, Apr. 19, 1801; May 12, Dec. 29, 1805; Feb. 9, 1806; Aug. 10, Sept. 5, 1807. Harmony Meetinghouse in Greeneville, perhaps a frame building, may have been an exception. It was sufficiently well finished to encourage the building of box pews by members of the congregation. See Charles Coffin, Memoir of Samuel Doak and Hezekiah Balch, Coffin Papers, McC.

9. *WHN*, 453-54; *CHD*, 325.

10. *WHN*, 476.

11. Ibid., 454.

12. NST, 194-95.

13. *WHN*, 454. *CHD* (325) gives the date 1812.

14. NST, 194.

15. *WHN*, 466; A.W. Putnam, "Further Reminiscences of Davidson County," *Port Folio* 3 (1849-50), 157-58; *CHD*, 196; Mary U. Rothrock, ed., *The French Broad-Holston Country* (Knoxville: East Tennessee Historical Society, 1916), 281.

17. Fink, *Jonesborough*, 211.

18. Quoted in J.E. Perkins, "Highlights in the Life of the First Methodist Church of Memphis, Tennessee, 1826-1963," *WTHSP* 18 (1964), 137; James D. Davis, *The History of the City of Memphis* (Memphis: Hite, Crumpton & Kelley, 1873), 233-35.

19. J.H. Ingraham, "Dots and Lines," *Ladies Companion* 11 (1839), 196.

20. George Rogers, *Memoranda of the Experiences, Labors, and Travels of a Universalist Preacher* (Cincinnati: J.A. Gurley, 1845), 321.

21. JCD, Aug. 16, 1827.

22. *WHN*, 476.

23. *ETT*, 309.

24. Ingraham, "Rural Taste," 185-86.

25. John D. Blair, *Sermons Collected from the Manuscripts* (Richmond: Shepherd and Pollard, 1825), 292-93.

26. Richard D. Beard, *Lectures on Theology. Third Series* (Nashville: Board of Cumberland Presbyterian Church, 1870), 150, 162.

27. Timothy Dwight, *Theology Explained and Defended in a Series of Sermons* (New York: Harper, 1850), IV, 303.

28. Thomas Hawkeis, *An Impartial and Succinct History of the Rise, Declension and Revival of the Church of Christ . . .* 2d ed. (Baltimore: Abner Neal, 1807), I, 542.

29. *National Banner and Nashville Whig*, July 8, 1830; quoted in *Christ Church, Nashville, 1829–1929* (Nashville: The Vestry, 1929), 66–67. *MTG*, 215–61.

30. Sara Sprott Morrow, "St. Paul's Episcopal Church, Franklin," *THQ* 34 (1975), 7.

31. Records of Maury County: St. Peter's Episcopal Church History. Copied under the WPA, June 14, 1938.

32. *WHN*, 499; *AMN*; JCD, Sept. 1, 1827. Eastin Morris (*MTG*, 219) noted in 1834 that the building was in a state of dilapidation.

33. DPA, July 22, 1845.

34. Doughty, 141–46.

35. "The Consecration; St. John's Chapel, Maury County," *Guardian* 2 (1842), 153; "St. John's Church, Maury County, Tennessee," *Guardian* 2 (1842), 143; David C. Page (Rector of Calvary Church, Memphis), "St. John's Church, Maury County, Tennessee," *Guardian* 8 1848), 200. Ingraham's description of a plantation church (*Sunny South*, 66–70) is probably drawn from St. John's.

36. *Nashville Union*, May 21, 1844.

37. *Calvinist Magazine* 1 (1846), 2.

38. *New York Ecclesiologist* 2 (1849–50), 25, 26.

39. Frank Wills, *Ancient Ecclesiastical Architecture and Its Principles, Applied to the Wants of the Church at the Present Day* (New York: Stanford and Swords, 1850), 9. For Wills's biography see Phoebe B. Stanton, *The Gothic Revival and American Ecclesiastical Architecture* (Baltimore: Johns Hopkins Univ. Press, 1968), 127, 148, 196, 321.

40. Wills announced his partnership with Dudley in the *New York Ecclesiologist* (3 [1850–51], 161), commenting on June 3, 1851 in a letter to Bishop Whittingham of Maryland that Dudley had been "for twenty years past engaged in the erection of many of our best churches in England" (Stanton, 286). He came to the United States about 1851 and disappears from city directories about 1893. His contribution to the American Institute of Architects is mentioned by Everard, M. Upjohn, *Richard Upjohn, Architects and Churchman* (New York: Columbia Univ. Press, 1939), 159, 161, 164, 165.

41. Church of the Nativity, Huntsville, Ala., Parish Register, Entry for Easter Even, 1859.

42. Stanton, 293–95.

43. *Address Delivered at the Laying of the Corner Stone of the Church of the Holy Trinity by the Rector of Christ Church, Nashville, May 29, 1852* (Nashville: South Western Monthly Office, 1852), 6.

44. CHD, 336–38; *Nashville Daily American*, Apr. 11, 1887; *Nashville Union and American*, Apr. 17, 1870; *Mechanics' Journal* 1 (Mar. 17, 1860), 191.

45. Upjohn, 82–86.

46. "Troubles in Episcopacy," *Christian Review* 2 (1845), 52; *Memphis Appeal*, Jan. 24, 1845.

47. "Is He a Churchman? Then He's Fond of Power," *Churchman* 27, No. 44 (Dec. 24, 1857), 346.

48. Bishop Otey to the editor, Feb. 2, 1858, *Episcopal Recorder* 35, No. 47 (Feb. 20, 1858), 185; "The Riverside Case," *Episcopal Recorder* 35, No. 52 (Mar. 27, 1858), 205; "Stringent Episcopacy," *Episcopal Recorder* 35, No. 44 (Jan. 30, 1858), 174; *Churchman* 27, No. 44 (Dec. 24, 1857), 346. *Natchez Weekley Courier*, May 12, 1857; Feb. 10, 1858.

49. *Episcopal Recorder* 35, No. 42 (Jan. 16, 1858), 167; *Churchman*, n.s., 8 (1874), 59, 411.

50. "The Riverside Case," *Episcopal Recorder* 35, No. 52 (Mar. 27, 1858), 205. The substance of this article is a letter from Bishop Otey.

51. *Calvinistic Magazine* 1 (1846), 2.

CHAPTER VIII

1. Morrison to Jackson, Dec. 6, 1831, in Mary French Caldwell, 78–79.

2. George Tucker, *Essays on Various Subjects of Taste, Morals, and National Policy . . .* (Georgetown, D.C.: The author, 1822), 124.

3. Benjamin Henry Latrobe, *The Journal of Latrobe; Being the Notes and Sketches of an Architect, Naturalist, and Traveler in the United States from 1801 to 1820* (New York: Appleton, 1905), 139.

4. Frank, 36.

5. Agnes Addison Gilchrist, *William Strickland: Architect and Engineer, 1788–1854* (Philadelphia: Univ. of Pennsylvania Press, 1950; 2d ed. New York: Da Capo Press, 1969), 5, 15.

6. *Southern Literary Journal* 1 (1837), 481–92.

7. Tucker, 110, 122–23.

8. *Southern Literary Messenger* 1 (1834–35), 214.

9. Ibid., 2 (1835–36), 233.

10. Ibid., 677–84.

11. Tucker, 90.

12. G. Cook, "Commerce and the Fine Arts," *Commercial Review of the South and West* 1 (1846), 271.

13. "Transcendentalism," *Southern Quarterly Review* 2 (1842), 431–71.

14. Richard M. Gummere, *The American Colonial Mind and the Classical Tradition* (Cambridge, Mass.: Harvard Univ. Press, 1963), 13. Col. Robert Armstrong to Jackson, May 27, 1836, *BJC* V, 400; Bill for Wall-paper, May 30, 1836, *BJC* V, 401. The paper put up in 1836 replaced "a very splendid French paper—beautiful scenery, figures, &c," which Juliana Conner had seen Sept. 1, 1827.

15. *Knoxville Gazette*, Dec. 1, 1792.

16. *WHN*, 383–84.

17. Aaron M. Boom, ed., "A Student at the University of Nashville, Correspondence of John Donelson Coffee, 1830–1833," *THQ* 16 (1957), 150–52.

18. Enoch L. Mitchell, ed., "College Life in Antebellum Tennessee," *WTHSP* 12, (1958), 8, 20, 23.

19. James Silk Buckingham, *The Slave States of America* (London: Fisher, Son and Co., 1842; rpt. New York: Negro Univ. Press, 1968) II, 252.

20. *MTG*, 220.

21. Mary Currey Dorris, *The Hermitage, Home of General Andrew Jackson* (Nashville: Ladies' Hermitage Assoc., 1913), 1; Parton, II, 643–44; Jackson to William B. Lewis, 1819, *BJC* II, 408.

22. JCD, Sept. 24, 1827; Auguste Levasseur, *Lafayette in America in 1824 and 1825; or, Journal of a Voyage to the United States,* trans. John D. Goodman (Philadelphia: Carey and Lea, 1829), II, 170. Another engraving of the Hermitage of 1819 was published by S.B. Hall and is reprinted in Marquis James, *Andrew Jackson, The Border Captain* and in John Spencer Basset, *The Life of Andrew Jackson.* For a history of the misleading engraving first published in *The Jackson Wreath* (Philadelphia, 1829), and reprinted in *Harper's* (Jan. 1855) and Mary French Caldwell, see Horn, 24–27.

23. Robert Armstrong to Jackson, Oct. 14, 1834, *BJC* V, 295. The remodeling of the Hermitage and building of the garden monument were begun late in 1831 and continued through the summer of 1832. The house was apparently completed by December 6 because Morrison sent the President a description of the remodeled building. This letter was written in answer to a letter of Jackson's praising Morrison, since the architect replied, "I return you thanks for the expressions of kindness it contains . . . ." See Mary French Caldwell, 78–79. Work on the monopteron sheltering Rachael Jackson's tomb continued into the summer of 1832. See Jackson to Graves W. Steel, Feb. 4, 1832, *BJC* IV, 403–4; Memorandum for Andrew Jackson, Jr., *BJC* IV, 431–32; Jackson to Andrew Jackson, Jr., May 19, 1832, *BJC* IV, 441–42. Morrison's remodeling moved the dining room to the wing added at the west (left) of the main block. Jackson suggested that the old dining room, on the left at the rear (?) of the house, become the younger Jackson's chamber (JCD, Sept. 4, 1827). On the right of the passage were the portrait room (at the front) and the parlor. The kitchen was relocated at the rear of the new dining room and the President's study and an overseer's office at the east side of the house. The location of the kitchen before 1831 is much disputed. After the remodeling occasioned by the fire of Oct. 14, 1834, both rooms to the left of the central passage became parlors and the front chamber on the right became Jackson's bedroom.

24. "Andrew Jackson," *Harper's New Monthly Magazine* 10 (1855), 172.

25. Cochran, 42–46; *HHG*, 195.

26. Stephen S. Lawrence, "Tulip Grove: Neighbor to the Hermitage," *THQ* 26 (1967), 3–22; Tulip Grove, Itemized Statements, Receipts, and Estimates, TSLA; Col. Robert Armstrong to Andrew Jackson, Oct. 14, 1834, *BJC* V, 295.

27. Laist, 56.

28. Col. Robert Armstrong to Andrew Jackson, Oct. 14, 1834, *BJC* V, 295–96.

29. The Stockley Donelson House, Cleveland Hall, built near the Hermitage and Tulip Grove, with a one-story porch which is stylistically similar to the porches of Tulip Grove and the Caruthers house in Lebanon, has also been attributed to Reiff and Hume. See *HHG,* 157.

30. Ibid., 291.

31. Dixon Merritt, *History of Wilson County* (Lebanon: Wilson County Court, 1961), 28; U.S. Census, Wilson County, 1820; U.S. Census, Davidson County, 1830.

32. Caruthers described his Lebanon house as "my homestead since 1828." See *Wilson County Will Book* A, 1878–84, p. 474.

33. Featherstonhaugh, 50.

34. *MTG*, 216; *WHN*, 466. Accounts for finishing the church were still being paid in 1836.

35. *MTG*, 218.

36. Ibid.; *Seven Early Churches of Nashville* (Nashville: Charles Elder, 1972), 28.

37. Records of First Presbyterian Church, Nashville, TSLA.

38. *Nashville Daily Evening Reporter,* Sept. 9, 1850; *WHN,* 281. The building was purchased in 1843 by the Bank of the State of Tennessee.

39. *MTG*, 220; *Nashville Daily American,* Feb. 13, 1882.

40. Federal Writers' Project, *Tennessee,* 224; [William Gilmore Simms], "Charleston, the Palmetto City," *Harper's New Monthly Magazine* 15 (June-Dec. 1857), 16, 18; Ravenel, 241–43.

41. *HHG,* 316–17.

42. James Cole, "Admiral Guards His Home With Historical Passion," *Memphis Commercial-Appeal,* July 26, 1971.

43. Arthur Scully, Jr., *James Dakin, Architect: His Career in New York and the South* (Baton Rouge: Louisiana State Univ. Press, 1973), 105–6; *Memphis Appeal,* Mar. 1, 1844; *Memphis Evening Scimitar,* Oct. 1, 1900.

44. A.U. Boone, *History of First Baptist Church* (The author, n.d.), 9–10. A photograph of the Navy Yard building was published in Benjamin La Bree, ed., *The Confederate Soldier in the Civil War* (Louisville: *Courier-Journal* Job Printing, 1895; rpt. n.p.: Fairfax Press, 197?), 402.

45. *Memphis Tri-Weekly Appeal,* Jan. 10, 1846; *Memphis Daily Appeal,* Nov. 24, 1857.

46. Albert B. Curry, *History of the Second Presbyterian Church of Memphis' Tennessee* (Memphis: Adams Printing and Stationery, 1937), 8.

47. *Memphis Appeal,* Feb. 16, 1844; U.S. Census, Shelby County, 1850; Samuel W. Thomas, ed., *Views of Louisville Since 1766* (Louisville: *Courier Journal, Louisville Times,* 1971), 94. Another Memphis architect of the 1850s whose work remains unknown was Thomas Crider. Crider appears in the Shelby County census of 1850 and in the city directories for 1850, 1855–1856, 1856–1857, 1859, and 1860.

48. Durham, *Old Sumner,* 328.

49. Contract between the directors and William Field and H.M. Ledbetter, Oct. 10, 1839. Copy in McC. No other work by this talented architect has been discovered in Tennessee.

50. Judith Haws Hash, "A History of the First Presbyterian Church of Jonesboro," M.A. thesis, East Tennessee State Univ., 1965, pp. 103–4; Letters in the collection of Paul M. Fink, Jonesboro, Tenn.; *Calvinistic Magazine,* n.s., 5 (1850), 288.

51. Fink, *Jonesborough,* 187; *HHG,* 118.

52. *HHG,* 97; Hamlin, 15, 16, 236; A.W. Ogden, "Madisonville . . .," *Knoxville News-Sentinel,* Feb. 25, 1935.

53. Sharp, 6; *HHG,* 63, 156–57, 314.

54. *HHG*, 223–28.
55. DPA, Feb. 1, 11, 28, Mar. 1, 5, 12, June 16, 17, 1842; Jan. 2, 28, 1843; Knox County Minute Books XVII, 177–78.
56. Harper, 19; *HWC*, 130–31.
57. *CHD*, 309.
58. Jesse E. Wills, 63–67. This building has been studied extensively. See *WHN*, 467; *AMT*, 64–66; Gilchrist, 62–63, 91, pl. 32A.
59. [Tannehill], "The Town We Live In," *Port Folio* 2 (1848–49), 155; *Nashville Republican Banner*, Oct. 5, 1848.
60. Testimony of Samuel D. Morgan, James M. Hughes, Feb. 19, 1859, in *Francis W. Strickland v. The State of Tennessee*, Capitol Construction Records, Record Group 7, Series 10, TSLA.
61. *Nashville American*, Aug. 29, 1909; *Nashville Tennessean*, May 9, 1976.
62. *Nashville Whig*, Apr. 27, 1844; Sept. 3, 1846.
63. Contract between James M. Hughes and James K. Polk, Oct. 18, 1847; Contract between James M. Hughes and James K. Polk, Apr. 22, 1848; James Walker to James K. Polk, Oct. 30, 1847; James K. Polk to Vernon K. Stevenson, Feb. 12, 1848, Polk Papers. Donald MacDonald-Millar, "The Grundy-Polk Houses, Nashville," *THQ* 25 (1966), 281–86; Cochran, 87.
64. [Tannehill], "The Town We Live In," *Port Folio* 2 (1848–49), 242; *Nashville Daily Evening Reporter*, Sept. 24, 1850; *WHN*, 560.
65. Deposition of Nicholas Hobson, Nov. 19, 1860, in *Hughes v. Wheless*; Nell Savage Mahoney, "An Early Nashville Banker," *Nashville Tennessean Magazine*, Apr. 19, 1953.
66. *Catalogue of the Officers and Graduates of the University of Nashville*, 28; Minutes of the Trustees of the University of Nashville, Nov. 11, 1850, TSLA; *Nashville American*, Nov. 6, 1850; *Tennessee Whig*, Nov. 12, 1850. Heiman's first two designs for the Medical Department were influenced by the large hip-roofed block he had erected for Union University, Murfreesboro, a three-story brick building with a stone basement, pilasters, and pedimented entrance pavilion. See the frontispiece of *Eleventh Annual Catalog of the Officers and Students of Union University, Murfreesboro . . .* (Nashville, Tenn.: Graves, Marks 1860).
67. *First Annual Announcement of the Medical Department of the University of Nashville* (Nashville: John T.S. Fall, 1851), frontispiece; *Nashville True Whig*, Nov. 15, 1850; *Nashville Daily American*, Nov. 6, 1850; Sept. 16, Nov. 4, 1851.
68. *Announcements of the Law, Literary, and Medical Departments of the University of Nashville. Session of 1854–55.* (Nashville: *Nashville Medical Journal*, 1854), 16.
69. *University of Nashville, Medical Department, Catalogue for the Session of 1857–58 and Announcement for the Session 1858–59* (Nashville: John T.S. Fall, 1858), frontispiece.
70. *Nashville Journal of Medicine and Surgery* 7 (1854), 250.
71. *Nashville Daily Evening Reporter*, July 30, Oct. 5, 1850.
72. *Banner of Peace and Cumberland Presbyterian Advocate*, Feb. 24, Mar. 10, July 28, Sept. 8, 1843; Feb. 2, 1844; Winstead Paine Bone, *A History of Cumberland University* (Lebanon: The author, 1935), 37–38.

73. *WHN*, 494–95.
74. *Davidson County Deed Books VI*, 675–76; *Catholic Advocate*, June 22, 1844; Nov. 20, 1847.
75. Bishop Miles to Mrs. Emilie Sanders, June 13, 1844, quoted in V.F. O'Daniel, *The Father of the Church in Tennessee* (Washington, D.C.: The Dominicana, 1926), 398.
76. O'Daniel commented of St. Mary's, "Strickland is reported to have considered it his finest ecclesiastical structure" (p. 426), and the next year Elizabeth Porterfield Elliot echoed O'Daniel in her article "Legacy of Architectural Beauty Left to City by Strickland," published in the *Nashville Tennessean* on May 29, 1927. St. Mary's was not attributed to Strickland by Wilkins Tannehill, who knew Strickland and praised his designs in "Nashville—Retrospective, Present, and Prospective," *Port Folio* 1 (1847–48), 178, and in "The Town We Live In," *Port Folio* 2 (1848–49), 242, 337; by B. Leslie Gillams in "William Strickland, A Pioneer Architect," *Architectural Record* 23 (Jan.-June 1908), 123–35; or by "The Architecture of Nashville," *Journal of the American Institute of Architects* 7 (1919), 159–70.
77. Gilchrist, 102–5.
78. *Seven Early Churches of Nashville*, 78.
79. *Nashville Banner*, Oct. 23, 1897; *Nashville Daily American* Oct. 24, 1897.
80. *AMT*, 58–61.
81. Strickland, "Three Orders of Architecture," 322.
82. Ibid., 321.
83. Ibid.
84. Nathaniel Cross, *An Address Delivered Before the Alumni Society of the University of Nashville. Oct. 7, 1846* (Nashville: Burton and Billings, 1846), 29.
85. Tucker, 125.
86. *Nashville Union and American*, Sept. 23, 1869.

CHAPTER IX

1. *HWC*, 104–5.
2. Gilchrist, 16.
3. *National Banner and Nashville Whig*, July 8, 1830, quoted in *Christ Church, Nashville, 1829–1929*, 66–67. Hugh Roland left Nashville before the summer of 1830 for Louisville, where he designed St. Louis Catholic Church, begun late in June in Gothic style. See Clyde F. Crews, *Presence and Possibility: Louisville Catholicism and Its Cathedral* (Louisville: The author, 1973), 20–21.
4. Featherstonhaugh, 52.
5. *First Annual Catalogue and General Advertisement of the Female Institute* (Columbia, Tenn.: J.H. Thompson, 1838), 9–12.
6. Caroline O'Reilly Nicholson, "Reminiscences of an Octogenarian," *Maury Democrat*, Mar. 15, 1894, in Jill K. Garrett, ed., *Tennessee Historical Sketches* (Columbia: The editor, 1967), 247.
7. Ingraham, *Sunny South*, 187.
8. [Tannehill], "The Masonic College," 271.
9. Scully, 127–46.
10. Sprague, V, 757; Ellen Davies-Rodgers, *The Great*

Book: Calvary Protestant Episcopal Church 1832–1972 (Memphis: Plantation Press, 1973), 187–90.

11. *Memphis Daily Appeal,* Jan. 19, 1858; June 6, 1867. On Keely's other works see *American Architect and Building News* 53 (1896), 58; 55 (1898), 333; H.L. McGill Wilson, "Preserving a Forgotten Heritage," *Catholic Historical Review* 38 (1952–53), 23–24; J.J. O'Connell, *Catholicity in the Carolinas and Georgia* (1879; rpt. Westminister, Md.: Ars Sacra, 1964), 114; [Sims], "Charleston," 15; Ravenel, 255–57.

12. *Memphis Daily Appeal,* Nov. 24, 29, 1854; *Memphis Commercial-Appeal,* Jan. 1, 1940.

13. *Memphis Daily Avalanche,* Oct. 30, 31, 1870; George J. Flanigen, *Catholicity in Tennessee* (Nashville: Ambrose, 1937), 76–77.

14. Rothrock, ed., 294; DPA July 23, 1845.

15. *Mechanics' Institute of Tennessee, Report of the First Annual Exhibition,* 69; Frances Walsh, *The Annals of St. Cecilia Convent, 1860–81* (Nashville: The Dominican Sisters, 1969), 17.

16. Horn, ed., 232–33.

17. *Nashville Republican Banner,* Nov. 17, 1869.

18. Frank, 44.

19. Frank, 45.

20. *Nashville Republican Banner,* Nov. 17, 1869; *WHN,* 477–78; *Seven Early Churches of Nashville,* 61.

21. Gilchrist, 16; Frank, 35.

22. Nell Savage Mahoney, "William Strickland and the building of Tennessee's Capitol, 1845–1854," *THQ* 4 (1945), 105, 113; Scully, 112; James H. Dakin to Samuel D. Morgan, June 15, 1846; Gideon Shryock to John M. Bass, Nov. 26, 1846; Capitol Construction Records, Record Group 7, Series 11, TSLA.

23. Adolphus Heiman, "Concise Description of the services of the first Regiment of the Tenn. Volunteers Commanded by Col. W.B. Campbell in the war with Mexico in 1846 & 7—presented to the Historical Society by A. Heiman. Adjut. of the Regiment— Nashville, May 1, 1858," TSLA; *Nashville Republican Banner,* May 5, 1858; Cumberland Lodge No. 8, Minutes, Oct. 18, 1843, TSLA.

24. Copy of A. Heiman's report about the Construction of the Suspension Bridge Across the Cumberland at Nashville, Dec. 29, 1857, TSLA; [Tannehill], "The Town We Live In," *Port Folio* 2 (1848–49), 242, 305; *Nashville Union,* Apr. 18, 1849; *Nashville True Whig,* June 16, 1855; *WHN,* 327.

25. [Tannehill], "The Town We Live In," *Port Folio* 3 (1849–50), 82; *Nashville Daily Evening Reporter,* Sept. 17, 1850; John Cornman, *Nashville: An Illustrated View of Its Progress and Importance* (Nashville: Enterprise Publishing, 1886), 23.

26. *HHG,* 201.

27. *Davidson County Deed Books* XIII, 313; XXII, 608.

28. Adolphus Heiman to W.B. Campbell, Dec. 26, 1851, Campbell Family Papers, Manuscript Dept., William R. Perkins Library, Duke Univ.; Report of Maj. W.H. Chase to the Secretary of the Treasury, Dec. 15, 1851, National Archives; Scully, 182–84; *Nashville Republican Banner,* Nov. 17, 1869.

29. Copy of A. Heiman's report about the Suspension Bridge, Dec. 29, 1857, TSLA.

30. *CHD,* 304; Frank, 36–39; "Tennessee Hospital for the Insane," *Tennessee State Farmer and Mechanic* 1 (1856), 77.

31. *Nashville Daily Union and American,* May 21, 1853.

32. Minutes of the Trustees of the University of Nashville, Apr. 4, July 15, 1855; June 9, 1857, TSLA.

33. *Hinkle & Guild Co.'s Plan of Buildings, Moldings, Architraves, Base, Brackets, Stairs, Newels, Ballusters, Rails, Cornice, Mantles, Window Frames, Sash, Doors, Columns, &c. for the Use of Carpenters and Builders, Adapted to the Style of Building in the United States* (Cincinnati: Hinkle, Guild & Co., 1862), 44; Grand Lodge, F.&A. Masons of Arkansas, *Proceedings* XIV, no. 5 (1949), 154–68.

34. Joseph C. Parks and Oliver C. Weaver, Jr., *Birmingham-Southern College, 1856–1956* (Nashville: Parthenon Press, 1957), 23, 30, 39.

35. Charles E. Röbert, *Nashville and Her Trade for 1870* (Nashville: Roberts and Purvis, 1870), 371–73.

36. Minutes of the Trustees of the University of Nashville, Nov. 7, 1851; Mar. 4, Apr. 30, 1852; Mar. 19, Oct. 22, 1853, TSLA.

37. *Announcements of the Law, Literary, and Medical Departments of the University of Nashville. Session of 1854–55,* frontispiece; *Nashville Gazette,* Apr. 17, 1853; *AMT,* 78–81.

38. *Davidson County Deed Books* XXII, 608; *HHG,* 255.

39. HBM; *AMT,* 154–55; *Davidson County Deed Books* XVI, 474.

40. Elizabeth Fries Ellet, *The Queens of American Society* (Philadelphia: Porter and Coates, 1873), 418.

41. Adelecia Hayes Acklen to Sarah Hightower Hayes, Feb. 25, July 22, 1866, Lawrence Family Papers, TSLA; *Nashville Daily American,* May 31, 1888.

42. Ingraham, *Sunny South,* 73–74.

43. *Nashville Daily American,* May 30, 1880. May Winston Caldwell attributed Belmont to Strickland about 1911, and this attribution was repeated by the author of "The Architecture of Nashville," *Journal of the American Institute of Architects* 7 (1919), 159. *HHG* avoids it in favor of "plans drawn by an Italian architect," but *AMT* accepts it.

44. Walsh, 31–32.

45. *HHG,* 204–5, 294, 321; Ingraham, *Sunny South,* 196.

46. Scully, 87, 98–99.

47. *HHG,* 124–29; *Nashville Daily American,* June 7, 1884.

48. Gilchrist, 18, 117.

49. Sally Leah Polk, Nov. 20, 1845, Tennessee Historical Society Collection, TSLA.

50. *HHG,* 231, 235.

51. Testimony of James M. Hughes, Feb. 19, 1859, in *Francis W. Strickland v. The State of Tennessee,* Capitol Construction Records, Record Group 7, Series 10, TSLA.

52. Charlotte Forgey Shenk and Donald Hugh Shenk, *History of the First Presbyterian Church, Huntsville, Alabama* (Huntsville: Paragon Press, 1962); *Nashville Republican Banner,* Nov. 17, 1869; *AMN.*

53. James McCallum, *A Brief Sketch of the Settlement and Early History of Giles County, Tennessee* (1876; rpt. Pulaski,

Tenn.: *Pulaski Citizen*, 1928), 110.

54. Lewis R. Clark, "Tenth Tennessee Infantry," *Picturesque Clarksville, Past and Present: A History of the City of Hills* (Clarksville: S.P. Titus, 1887), 139.

55. Andrew J. Downing, *Cottage Residences; or, A Series of Designs for Rural Cottages and Cottage Villas, and their Grounds and Gardens*, pt. 1, 2d ed. (New York: Wiley and Putnam, 1844), 124.

56. *HHG,* 167.

57. Heiman to A.W. Putnam, June 1, 1857, TSLA.

58. *HBM.*

59. *Records of Maury County: St. Peter's Episcopal Church, Columbia, Tennessee;* Garrett, ed., 88.

60. *AMT,* 6; Moore, 11; *Nashville City and Business Directory for 1860–61* (Nashville: L.P. Williams, 1860), 39–41.

61. Walsh, 117. The J.B. Hayes residence, Ensworth, built by Akeroyd on Hayes Street near the site later occupied by St. Thomas Hospital, stood until the 1930s. See *HBM; HHG,* 137.

62. *HHG,* 149.

63. *WHN,* 435.

64. Ibid., 484; *HBM.*

65. Doughty, 269, 285, 291, 295.

66. Z. Cartter Patten, "A History of the Mansion on the Tellico River," *THQ* 10 (1951), 366–69.

67. Cochran, 125.

68. Paul M. Fink, "The Rebirth of Jonesboro," *THQ* 31 (1972), 236.

69. Edwin M. Alexander, *Down at the Depot: American Railroad Stations From 1831–1920* (New York: Clarkson N. Potter, 1970), 251.

70. Called Castle Fox in deference to its style and keeper, R.P. Fox, the Knox County Jail of 1857 is visible at the left margin of the panoramic photograph of Knoxville made about 1865 (14). See Rothrock, ed., 66–67, 132. On Knoxville's early Gothic churches see St. John's Episcopal Church, Parish Register, TSLA; Flanigen, 100–5; W. Russell Briscoe and Kathleen Boles Buehler, *Her Walls Before Thee Stand: History of the Second Presbyterian Church, 1818–1968* (Knoxville: The authors, n.d.), 18.

71. John H. De Berry, "La Grange–La Belle Village," *THQ* 30 (1971), 152; *HHG,* 296–97.

72. *HHG,* 325–26.

73. Ibid., 320; Terry B. Morton, "Victorian Mansions in Memphis," *Antiques* 100 (July-Dec. 1971), 411–12.

74. *HHG,* 84; Lucile Deaderick, ed., *Heart of the Valley: A History of Knoxville, Tennessee* (Knoxville: East Tennessee Historical Society, 1976), 417.

75. James L. McDonough, "Forgotten Empire: Sam Graham's Pinewood," *THQ* 27 (1968), 40–49; *HHG,* 180, 196, 303; *AMT,* 164–67.

76. De Berry, 153; *HWC,* 150–51; John Halliburton, *Clarksville Architecture* (Nashville: The author, 1971), 23–30. The popularity of the bracketed Italian villa is attested by *Hinkle, Guild and Co.'s Plans of Buildings,* 44, 46, 51, 54.

77. Quoted in Waller Raymond Cooper, *Southwestern at Memphis, 1848–1948* (Richmond: John Knox Press, 1949),

10. Heiman's Hospital for the Insane was also considered Elizabethan. See the *Nashville Daily Evening Reporter,* Sept. 13, 1850.

78. Fitch, 633.

79. Ruffner, 208.

CHAPTER X

1. Frederick Law Olmsted, *A Journey in the Back Country* (New York: Mason Brothers, 1861), 305.

2. Rogers, 323.

3. Olmsted, 451.

4. James C. Bonner, Plantation Architecture of the Lower South on the Eve of the Civil War," *Journal of Southern History* 11 (1945), 370–88.

5. Ingraham, "Dots and Lines," *Ladies Companion* 11 (1839), 69.

6. James Hervey Otey, "Address on the Subject of a Proposed Southern University," *Proceedings of a Convention of the Trustees of a Proposed University for the Southern States . . .* (Atlanta: R.C. Hanleiter, 1857), 32.

7. Quoted in Olmsted, 27.

8. Clement Eaton, *The Growth of Southern Civilization* (New York: Harper, 1961), 121.

9. *HHG,* 313, 320, 321.

10. Chase C. Mooney, "Some Institutional Aspects of Slavery in Tennessee," *THQ* 1 (1942), 208.

11. Ibid., 224.

12. Nicholson, *Maury Democrat,* Apr. 19, 1894, in Garrett, 248.

13. Charles Coffin Ross, ed., 20.

14. *Succession of Issac Franklin,* 294.

15. John Robinson, *The Savage, by Piomingo, a Headman and Warrior of the Muscogulgee Nation* (Knoxville: Scrap Book Office, 1833), 168.

16. Jackson to John Coffee, May 13, 1831, *BJC* IV, 283.

17. "St. John's Church, Maury County, Tennessee," *Guardian* 8 (1848), 200.

18. Randall M. Miller, ed., "Letters from Nashville, 1862, II: 'Dear Master,'" *THQ* 33 (1974), 85–92.

19. J. Frazer Smith, *White Pillars: Early Life and Architecture of the Lower Mississippi Valley Country* (New York: William Hellburn, 1941), 213–17.

20. *HHG,* 270–71.

21. Ibid., 316–17; *Memphis Commercial-Appeal,* July 26, 1971.

22. *Plantation Homes of Louisiana* (Gretna, La.: Pelican Publishing, 1972), 89.

23. J. Frazer Smith, 123–25.

24. *Plantation Homes of Louisiana,* 99–100.

25. J. Frazer Smith, 161–63.

26. Ibid., 190–91.

27. Scully, 98–99.

28. Scully, 98.

29. *Plantation Homes of Louisiana,* 44.

30. Crocker, 17–22.

31. Ibid., 22.

32. Thomas Tileston Waterman, *The Dwellings of Colonial America* (Chapel Hill: Univ. of North Carolina Press, 1950).

33. J. Frazer Smith, 118, 121, Crocker, 32–33.

34. Reid Smith and John Owens, *The Majesty of Natchez* (Montgomery, Ala.: Paddle Wheel Publications, 1969); Crocker, 38–41.

35. J. Frazer Smith, 80–82; Ralph Hammond, *Ante-Bellum Mansions of Alabama* (New York: Architectural Book Publishing, 1951), 33–35.

36. J. Frazer Smith, 76–78; Hammond, 48–51.

37. Hammond, 114–26.

38. Ibid., 104–8.

39. Frederick Doveton Nichols, *Early Architecture of Georgia* (Chapel Hill: Univ. of North Carolina Press, 1957), 119, 208.

40. Ibid., 118–19, 132–33, 135, 225.

41. J. Frazer Smith, 54–55; Rexford Newcomb, *Architecture in Old Kentucky* (Urbana: Univ. of Illinois Press, 1953), 141, pl. 62–B.

42. *HHG*, 232–34; *AMT*, 150–53; Cochran, 82–89.

43. *HHG*, 230–32.

44. Frederick A. Ross, *Slavery Ordained of God* (Philadelphia: Lippincott, 1857; rpt. New York: Negro Univ. Press, 1969), 75.

45. Jack D.L. Holmes, ed., "On the Practicability and Advantages of a First-Class University in Memphis: A Letter from Dr. Ashbel Smith in 1849," *THQ* 19 (1960), 67.

46. Otey, "Address . . . on the Subject of a Proposed Southern University," 38–39.

47. Gideon J. Pillow, *Address Delivered Before the Maury Agricultural and Mechanical Society, at the Annual Fair, October 24, 1855* (Columbia: *Democratic Herald*, 1855), 20.

48. *De Bow's Review* 10 (1851), 106.

49. Cochran, 6–14; Smith, *White Pillars*, 23–27.

50. Col. Robert Armstrong to Andrew Jackson, Oct. 14, 1834, *BJC* V, 295–96.

51. Andrew Jackson to Andrew Jackson, Jr., Oct. 23, 1834, *BJC* V, 302.

52. Col. Robert Armstrong to Andrew Jackson, Nov. 4, 1834, *BJC* V, 305.

53. Estimates for Rebuilding the Hermitage, Aug. 2, 1836, *BJC* V, 414–15.

54. Clement Eaton, *The Mind of the Old South* (rev. ed.; Baton Rouge: Louisiana State Univ. Press, 1967), 299.

55. *HHG*, 236–37.

56. Ibid., 64.

57. Ibid., 216–17, 223–26, 242–43.

58. Ibid., 221, 240.

59. On Westview see *HWC*, 6–8. The sensitive Grecian details of Everbright's cornice and columns, not evident in the extant nineteenth-century photograph (200), are visible in *HHG*, 284. On Everbright see also *HWC*, 142–44.

60. *HHG*, 124–29, 146–48.

61. Halliburton, 23–30. Tip Top is nearly identical to the George Thomas Lewis house, Clarksville, which was remodeled from an older dwelling in the 1850s. See *HHG*, 244.

62. *HHG*, 141, 257.

63. De Berry, 147–48.

64. *HHG*, 244.

65. *HWC*, 61–63; *HHG*, 286–87.

66. Gilmore, 55.

67. Walsh, 31–32.

CHAPTER XI

1. *National Cyclopaedia of American Biography* III, 361.

2. *Memphis Commercial-Appeal*, Feb. 22, 1909.

3. *CSR*, 86.

4. Ibid., 87.

5. *Memphis City Directory for 1859* (Memphis: Hutton and Clark, 1859), pl. 183, facing p. 84; Ravenel, 241–43.

6. Morrison, *City of Nashville*, 74; *Nashville Union and American*, Sept. 23, 1869.

7. *CSR*, 95–96; [Simms], "Charleston," 9, 10, 12, 15; Ravenel, 203–19; *Memphis Commercial-Appeal*, Feb. 13, 1902.

8. *Chattanooga Times*, Dec. 3, 8, 1892.

9. *Pen and Sunlight Sketches of Chattanooga* (n.p.: American Illustrating Co., n.d.), 133.

10. *Nashville American*, Feb. 23, 1910.

11. Kay Gaston, "Chattanooga's First Famous Architect," *Chattanooga News-Free Press*, Apr. 3, 1977.

12. Michael A. Tomlan, "George Franklin Barber," 261–62.

13. Morrison, *City of Nashville*, 73–74.

14. Michael A. Tomlan, "Joseph F. Baumann (1844–1920), Architect of the First Knoxville," B. Arch. thesis, Univ. of Tennessee, 1973, p. 9.

15. Morrison, *City of Nashville*, 74–75; Cornman, 111; H.C. Thompson to Andrew Johnson, Apr. 28, 1862, *Papers of Andrew Johnson*, Vol. 5 (Knoxville: Univ. of Tennessee Press, 1979), 346–47; *Nashville Daily American*, Nov. 21, 1875.

16. *CSR*, 87.

17. Andrew Morrison, *The City of Knoxville*, The Englehardt Series: American Cities, vol. 25 (St. Louis: Englehardt Publishing, 1892), 46.

18. Morrison, *City of Nashville*, 73.

19. *Nashville Daily American*, Feb. 25, 1887.

20. *Nashville Daily American*, Aug. 11, 1878.

21. *Knoxville News-Sentinel*, June 24, 1954. The Cowan house was a close copy of the Charles J. McClung house, built on Knoxville's Main Street in 1875–1876 by Peter J. Williamson of Nashville in collaboration with Baumann.

22. *CSR*, 96.

23. *Nashville Union and American*, Aug. 8, 1872; *Tennessee State Directory*, 1871–72, facing p. 86.

24. *Loudon County Court Minutes*, I, 381; *National Cyclopaedia of American Biography*, III, 361. The Chattanooga building burned in 1909, and the Morristown building was remodeled extensively in 1968.

25. *CSR*, 87.

26. *Nashville Union and American*, Mar. 22, 24, 1874.

27. *Nashville Daily American*, Aug. 11, 1878.

28. *Knoxville Daily Journal*, Feb. 3, 1878.

29. *CSR*, 96.

30. *Knoxville Daily Journal*, June 1, 1884.

31. *Chattanooga Times,* July 1, 1928; *Chattanooga Free Press,* June 28, 1936.

32. *Nashville Daily American,* May 11, 1884.

33. Ibid., Nov. 13, 1883; Jan. 10, 1888.

34. *Chattanooga Star,* Aug. 31, 1907.

35. *Nashville Daily American,* June 24, 1887; Morrison, *City of Nashville,* 73.

36. Curry, 27.

37. Morrison, *City of Nashville,* 75; *Nashville Daily American,* Sept. 19, 1892.

38. Morrison, *City of Knoxville,* 44.

39. Henry-Russell Hitchcock, *The Architecture of H.H. Richardson and His Times,* 2d ed. (Cambridge, Mass.: M.I.T. Press, 1966), 258–62; Thomas B. Brumbaugh, "The Architecture of Nashville's Union Station," *THQ* 27 (1968), 3–12.

40. *Chattanooga Times,* Dec. 31, 1880.

41. *CSR,* 87, 96.

42. *AMT,* 28–33.

43. *Nashville Union and American,* June 18, 1871.

44. *Knoxville Daily Press and Herald,* Feb. 7, 1875; *Knoxville Daily Chronicle,* Aug. 11, 1875; *Knoxville Daily Tribune,* Apr. 5, 1876.

45. *Nashville Union and American,* Oct. 28, 1878; *Nashville Daily American,* Nov. 21, 1875; Jan. 15, 1881.

46. Frank Cummings and Katherine L. Trewitt, *History of St. Luke's Episcopal Church, Cleveland, Tennessee, 1867–1967* (Cleveland: St. Luke's Episcopal Church, 1967), 29. The Vanderbilt Gymnasium, usually attributed to Williamson, is another good example of the neglect of precise historical reference on behalf of form. See *AMT,* 86–87.

47. *Nashville American,* Nov. 21, 1875; *Nashville Daily American,* Aug. 11, 1878; *WHN,* 456.

48. Morrison, *City of Nashville,* 46, 74; *Nashville Daily American,* Mar. 2, 1884.

49. *Nashville Daily American,* July 5, 1889; *Nashville Banner,* Sept. 27, 1889; Morrison, *City of Nashville,* 74.

50. Richard S. Reynolds, "History of Glen Leven," MS in possession of Glen Leven Presbyterian Church, Nashville.

51. *Nashville Daily American,* Dec. 11, 1887; Jan. 10, 1888; Dec. 1, 1890.

52. *Nashville Union and American,* Apr. 29, 1874.

53. *Chattanooga Times,* Dec. 8, 1892.

54. *CHD,* 343.

55. *Nashville Daily American,* July 21, 1878; July 24, 1881; Oct. 26, 1882.

56. *CHD,* 360–61.

57. *Nashville Daily American,* Feb. 13, 1887; *WHN,* 456.

58. George W. Thompson and Julius G. Zwicker, *Selections from Executed Work and Sketches* (Louisville: Southern Publishing and Advertising Co., 1896); *Inland Architect and News Record* 22 (Aug. 1893), pl. 1.

59. *Chattanooga Times,* Dec. 8, 1892.

60. *Memphis Daily Appeal,* Sept. 1, 1885. The architect was Maj. G.H. Sease.

61. *HHG,* 455.

62. Thompson and Zwicker.

63. Herman Justi, ed., *Official History of the Tennessee Centennial Exposition . . .* (Nashville: Brandon Printing, 1898),

33; Wilbur Foster Creighton, *Building of Nashville* (Nashville: The author, 1969), 138–51.

64. *Nashville Daily American,* Oct. 21, 22, 23, 1885.

65. Ibid., Oct. 21, 22, 1896.

66. J.W. Yost, "The Influence of Steel Construction and of Plate Glass upon the Development of Modern Style," in Lewis Mumford, ed., *Roots of Contemporary American Architecture* (New York: Reinhold, 1952), 158.

67. Paul H. Beasley, comp., "Ninety-nine Landmark Buildings," Typescript in the Nashville Room, Public Library of Nashville and Davidson County.

68. Zella Armstrong, *The History of Hamilton County and Chattanooga, Tennessee* (Chattanooga: Lookout Publishing, 1940), II, 151.

69. Federal Writers' Project, *Tennessee,* 217.

70. *National Cyclopaedia of American Biography* XXVIII, 178.

71. *Nashville Daily American,* Mar. 16, 1889.

72. *Centennial Album of Nashville, Tennessee* (Nashville: J. Prousnitzer, 1896).

73. George R. Fairbanks, *History of the University of the South at Sewanee, Tennessee* (Jacksonville: A. and W.B. Drew Co., 1905), 252–55; David Green Haskins, *A Brief Account of the University of the South* (New York: Dutton, 1877), 15–18.

74. "St Luke's Hall, University of the South, Tennessee," *American Architect and Building News* 3 (1878), 165.

75. Fairbanks, 245.

76. *Nashville Union and American,* Apr. 1, 1855; *Nashville Republican Banner,* Apr. 20, 1856; Blanche Spurlock Bentley, *Sketch of Beersheba Springs and Chickamauga Trace* (Chattanooga: The author, 1928).

77. Ingraham, *Sunny South,* 313.

78. *Nashville American,* July 18, 1883; Aug. 1, 4, 1885; *Memphis Commercial-Appeal,* Aug. 1, 1885.

79. Gaston.

80. *Chattanooga Daily Times,* Apr. 23, 26, 1890; July 30, 1891.

81. [Tannehill], "The Town We Live In," *Port Folio* 2 (1848–49), 154.

Selected Bibliography

Although the notes to the text frequently refer to other works, this bibliography is limited to printed sources and manuscripts about Tennessee architecture and those general works which contain important architectural information. City and county histories, as well as the institutional histories of churches, schools, and hospitals should also be consulted. See also Sam B. Smith, ed., *Tennessee History, A Bibliography* (Knoxville: Univ. of Tennessee Press, 1974). Where appropriate the first edition and the most recent have been included in the entries.

ARCHITECTURAL HISTORIES AND RELATED SOURCES

Alderson, William T., and Robert M. McBride. *Landmarks of Tennessee History*. Nashville: Tennessee Historical Society and Tennessee Historical Commission, 1965.

"The Architecture of Nashville," *Journal of the American Institute of Architects* 7 (Apr. 1919), 159–70.

Bass, Neil. "Second Avenue North, Nashville—A Personal View," *Tennessee Valley Historical Review* 1, no. 1 (Spring 1972), 32–34, 36–38.

Beasley, Paul H., comp. "Ninety-Nine Nashville Landmark Buildings." Typescript in Nashville Room, Nashville Public Library.

Beloved Landmarks of Loudon County, Tennessee. N.p.: Hiwassee Chapter, Daughters of the American Revolution, 1962.

Bonner, James C. "Plantation Architecture of the Lower South on the Eve of the Civil War," *Journal of Southern History* 11 (1945), 370–88.

Bowman, Virginia McDaniel. *Historic Williamson County: Old Homes and Sites*. Nashville: The author, 1971.

Brandau, Roberta Seawell, ed. *History of Homes and Gardens of Tennessee*. Nashville: Garden Study Club of Nashville, 1936: 2d ed., Friends of Cheekwood, 1964; rpt. 1974.

Brumbaugh, Thomas B., ed. *Architecture of Middle Tennessee*. Nashville: Vanderbilt Univ. Press, 1974.

Caldwell, May Winston. *Historical and Beautiful Country Homes Near Nashville, Tennessee*. Nashville: Brandon Printing, 1911?

Carberry, Michael. *Historic Sites in Blount, Cocke, Monroe, and Sevier Counties*. Knoxville: East Tennessee Development District, 1973.

Chandler, Walter. "The Court House of Shelby County," *WTHSP* 7 (1953), 72–78.

Clayton, W.W. *History of Davidson County, Tennessee, with Illustrations and Biographical Sketches of its Prominent Men and Pioneers*. Philadelphia: J.W. Lewis, 1880; rpt. Nashville: Charles Elder, 1971.

Cochran, Gifford A. *Grandeur in Tennessee: Classical Revival Architecture in a Pioneer State*. New York: J.J. Augustin, 1946.

Crane, Sophie, and Paul Crane. *Tennessee Taproots*. Old Hickory, Tenn.: Earle-Shields Publishers, 1976.

Creighton, Wilbur Foster. *Building of Nashville*. Rev. and enlarged by Wilbur F. Creighton, Jr., and Leland R. Johnson. Nashville: The author, 1969; 2d ed., 1975.

Crouch, Arthur Wier, and Harry Dixon Claybrook. *Our Ancestors Were Engineers*. Nashville: Nashville Section, American Society of Engineers, 1976.

Crutchfield, James A. "Pioneer Architecture in Tennessee," *THQ* 35 (1976), 162–74.

Davant, Madge Hardin. "Historical Buildings in Knoxville," *Taylor-Trotwood Magazine* 11 (1910), 554–60.

De Berry, John H. "La Grange—La Belle Village," *THQ* 30 (1971), 133–53.

Deaderick, Lucille, ed. *Heart of the Valley: A History of Knoxville, Tennessee*. Knoxville: East Tennessee Historical Society, 1976.

Doughty, Richard Harrison. *Greeneville: One Hundred Year Portrait (1775–1875)*. Greeneville, Tenn.: The author, 1975.

Durham, Walter T. *The Great Leap Westward*. Gallatin, Tenn.: Sumner County Library Board, 1969.

———. *Old Sumner: A History of Sumner County Tennessee*. Gallatin: Sumner County, Library board, 1972.

Fink, Paul M. *Jonesborough: The First Century of Tennessee's First Town*. Springfield, Va.: National Technical Information Service, 1972.

———. "The Rebirth of Jonesboro," *THQ* 31 (1972), 223–39.

Graham, Eleanor, ed. *Nashville: A Short History and Selected Buildings*. Nashville: Historical Commission of Metropolitan Nashville-Davidson County, 1974.

Halliburton, John. *Clarksville Architecture*. Nashville: The author, 1977.

Hamlin, Talbot. *Greek Revival Architecture in America: Being an Account of Important Trends in American Architecture and American Life prior to the War Between the States*. New York: Oxford Univ. Press, 1944; rpt. Dover, 1964.

Harper, Herbert L. "Antebellum Courthouses of Tennessee," *THQ* 30 (1971), 3–25.

Hicks, Nannie Lee. *Historic Treasure Spots of Knox County, Tennessee*. Knoxville: Simon Harris Chapter, Daughters of the American Revolution, 1962.

Justi, Herman, ed. *Official History of the Tennessee Centennial Exposition, Opened May 1, and Closed October 30, 1897*. Nashville: Brandon Printing, 1898.

Lathrop, Elsie. *Early American Inns and Taverns*. New York: Tudor, 1937.

McBride, Robert M., ed. *More Landmarks of Tennessee History*. Nashville: Tennessee Historical Society and Tennessee Historical Commission, 1969.

McNabb, William Ross. *Architecture of Knoxville, Tennessee, 1790–1940*. Knoxville: Dulin Gallery of Art and McClung Historical Collection, 1974.

Mathews, Maxine. "Old Inns of East Tennessee," *ETHSP* 2 (1930), 22–33.

"The Memphis Churches," *Fort-Pickering American Eagle*, Aug. 12, 1842.

Moran, Ann. "Hotels and Taverns of Williamson County," *Williamson County Historical Journal* (Spring 1975), 53–59.

Morton, Terry B. "Victorian Mansions in Memphis," *Antiques* 100 (Sept. 1971), 408–12.

Noll, Arthur Howard. "Tennessee Centennial Exposition," *American Architect and Building News* 58 (Oct. 23, 1897), 31–32.

Official Catalogue of the Tennessee Centennial and International Exposition, Nashville, Tennessee, May 1 to October 31, 1897. Nashville: n.p., 1897.

"Picture of Nashville, Nos. I-IX," *Nashville Daily Evening Reporter,* Sept. 9, 13, 17, 20, 24 [pt. 6 date ?], Oct. 5, 10, 14, 1850.

Priddy, Bennie Hugh, Jr. "Nineteenth-Century Architecture in Memphis: Ten Surviving Structures," M.A. thesis, Vanderbilt Univ., 1972.

Putnam, Albigence Waldo. *History of Middle Tennessee: The Life and Times of James Robertson.* Nashville: The author, 1859; rpt. Knoxville: Univ. of Tennessee Press, 1971.

Rogan, James W. "Hawkins County." Published in the *Rogersville Review,* Dec. 19, 1889, to Nov. 27, 1890. Typescript in McC.

Rothrock, Mary U., ed., *The French Broad-Holston Country.* Knoxville: East Tennessee Historical Society, 1946; rpt. 1976.

Ryan, Arthur Frank, ed. *Historical Forts and Houses in Knoxville and Nearby Vicinity.* Knoxville: Knox County Library, 1972.

Scofield, Edna. "The Evolution and Development of Tennessee Houses," *Journal of the Tennessee Academy of Science* 11 (1936), 229–39.

Seven Early Churches of Nashville: A Series of Public Lectures Presented at the Public Library of Nashville and Davidson County. Nashville: Charles Elder, 1972.

Shell, William S., ed., *Historic Jonesboro.* Knoxville: School of Architecture, Univ. of Tennessee, 1972.

Smith, J. Frazer. *White Pillars: Early Life and Architecture of the Lower Mississippi Valley Country.* New York: William Helburn, 1941; rpt. Bramhall House, n.d.

Spoden, Muriel C., comp. *Historic Sites of Sullivan County.* Kingsport: Sullivan County Court, 1976.

Winters, Ralph L. *Hospitality Homes and Historic Sites in Western Robertson County, Tennessee.* Clarksville: The author, 1971.

Woolridge, John, ed. *History of Nashville, Tenn.* Nashville: Publishing House of the Methodist Episcopal Church, South, 1890; 2d ed., Charles Elder, 1970.

Young, J.P. *Standard History of Memphis, Tenn.* Knoxville: H.W. Crew, 1912; rpt. Evansville, Ind.: Unigraphic, 1974.

STUDIES AND DESCRIPTIONS OF INDIVIDUAL BUILDINGS (BY PERIOD)

The following sections contain studies and descriptions, institutional histories which include descriptions, and selected newspaper articles. The vertical files of local libraries should also be consulted.

Eighteenth Century

Allen, Ward. "Cragfont: Grandeur on the Tennessee Frontier." *THQ* 23 (1964), 103–20; rpt. *LTH,* 135–54.

Bowman, Elizabeth Scaggs. "Swan Pond: Francis Alexander Ramsey's Stone House," *ETHSP* 27 (1955), 9–18.

Brown, Elsworth. "Archaeology of Fort Loudoun, Field Investigations 1956–57, for the Fort Loudoun Association." Vonore, Tenn., 1958. Copy in McC.

Cates, Alice Smith. "Blount Mansion—'The Cradle of Tennessee,'" *D.A.R. Magazine* 69 (1935), 344–49.

Davis, Louise. "Travellers' Rest," *Nashville Tennessean Magazine,* Apr. 8, 1956.

DeFriece, Pauline Massengill, and Franklin B. Williams, Jr. "Rocky Mount: The Cobb-Massengill Home, First Capitol of the Territory South of the River Ohio," *THQ* 25 (1966), 119–34; rpt. *MLT,* 247–64.

Delaney, Joseph D. *A Historical Study of Rock Castle.* Nashville: Tennessee Historical Commission, 1969.

Dickenson, Margaret S. *Travellers' Rest.* Boston: Chrisopher, 1944.

Fauber, J. Everette. "Research Report and Proposal for Restoration, The Governor William Blount Mansion, Knoxville, Tennessee, for the Blount Mansion Association, Knoxville, May 13, 1968." Copy in McC.

Fink, Paul M. "Jonesboro's Chester Inn," *ETHSP* 27 (1955), 19–38.

Folmsbee, Stanley J., "The Ramsey House: Home of Francis Alexander Ramsey," *THQ* 24 (1965), 203–18; rpt. *MLT,* 229–46.

———, and Susan Hill Dillon. "The Blount Mansion, Tennessee's Territorial Capitol," *THQ* 22 (1963), 103–22; rpt. *LTH,* 47–66.

Garrett, W.R., ed., "Rock Castle," *American Historical Magazine* 5 (1900), 291–94.

Kelley, Paul. *Historic Fort Loudoun.* Vonore, Tenn.: Fort Loudoun Assoc., 1958.

Lawson, Dennis T. "The Tipton-Haynes Place: I. A Landmark of East Tennessee," *THQ* 29 (1970), 105–25.

Morrison, A.J. "Fort Loudoun and Its Author," *Virginia Magazine of History and Biography* 32 (1924), 88–89.

Morrow, Sara Sportt. "The William Bowen House," *THQ* 32 (1973), 59–66.

Orr, Mary T. "John Overton and Travelers' Rest," *THQ* 15 (1956), 216–32.

Porter, Matilde A. "Swan Pond, the Ramsey Home," *THM,* ser. 2, no. 3 (1932), 283–86.

"Rock Castle," *American Historical Magazine* 10 (Oct. 1900), 293; 11 (July 1901), 213–35.

Rose, Norvell Sevier. "John Sevier and Marble Springs," *THQ* 29 (1970), 205–26.

Swint, Henry Lee. "Travellers' Rest: Home of Judge John Overton," *THQ* 26 (1967), 119–36; rpt. *MLT,* 327–46.

Tomlan, Michael. "The Stone Houses of Watauga." Typescript in McC.

Williams, Samuel C. "Fort Robinson on the Holston,"
ETHSP 4 (1932), 22–31.

Young, S.M. "The Old Rock House," *THM*, ser. 2, no. 3
(1932), 59–64.

Federal

Arnold, James E. "The Hermitage Church," *THQ* 28
(1969), 113–25; rpt. *MLT*, 169–84.

*Catalogue of the Officers and Graduates of the University of
Nashville . . ., With an Appendix Containing Sundry Historical Notices, etc.* Nashville: A. Nelson, 1850.

Clayton, LaReine Warden. "The Irish Peddler-Boy and the
Old Deery Inn," *THQ* 36 (1977), 149–60.

Connally, Ernest Allen. "The Andrew Johnson Homestead
at Greeneville, Tennessee," *ETHSP* 29 (1957), 118–40.

Crawford, Charles W. and Robert M. McBride. "The
Magevney House, Memphis," *THQ* 28 (1969), 345–55.

"Davidson County's 'Lost' Courthouse," *Nashville Tennessean
Magazine*, Oct. 4, 1936.

Davis, Louise Littleton. "House on a Haunted Hillside,"
Nashville Tennessean Magazine, Sept. 18, 1949.

Dempster, G.R. "History and Houses: Craighead-Jackson
House," *Antiques* 98 (Aug. 1970), 110–14.

"Drury P. Armstrong House," *Echoes from the East Tennessee
Historical Society* 21, No. 1, (Mar. 1975) 720, 723.

Durham, Walter T., "Wynnewood," *THQ* 33 (1974), 127–
56.

Laist, Theodore. "Two Early Mississippi Valley State Capitols," *Western Architect* 35 (May 1926), 53–58.

Lewis, J. Eugene. "Cravens House: Landmark of Lookout
Mountain," *THQ* 20 (1961), 203–21; rpt. *MLT*, 155–75.

McGann, Will Spencer. "The Old Carter House at Franklin,
Tennessee," *THM*, ser. 2, no. 3 (1932–37), 40–44.

Meredith, Owen N. "The Sam Davis Home," *THQ* 24
(1965), 303–20; rpt. *MLT*, 99–118.

Morris, Betsy. "Old Strong House Has Concerned Admirers," *Knoxville News-Sentinel*, Mar. 27, 1971.

"The Presbyterian Church," *Fort-Pickering American Eagle*,
July 22, Aug. 12, 1842.

Preston, Thomas Wilson. "The Netherland Inn at Old
Kingsport," *ETHSP* 4 (1932), 32–34.

Robison, Dan M. "The Carter House, Focus of the Battle of
Franklin," *THQ* 22 (1963), 3–21; rpt. *LTH*, 69–87.

Ross, Charles Coffin, ed., *The Story of Rotherwood* from the
*Autobiography of Rev. Frederick Augustus Ross, D.D., in Let-
ters Addressed to a Lady of Knoxville, Tennessee, Mrs. Juliet
Park White, Huntsville, Alabama, 1882–3.* Knoxville:
Bean, Warters and Co., 1923.

Succession of Isaac Franklin. Prepared by Mrs. Acklen's Counsel for the use of Supreme Court, of that part of the record
applicable to the questions now on appeal, arranged according to the proper order of the proceedings in the
Lower Court. Copy in Special Collections, Joint University Libraries, Nashville.

Tannehill, Wilkins. "Cumberland Lodge," *Port Folio* 1
(1847–48), 73.

Thruston, Gates P. "The Nashville Inn," *American Historical
Magazine* 7 (1902), 174–77.

Weaver, Herbert, and William G. Eidson, "The James K.
Polk Home," *THQ* 24 (1965), 3–19; rpt. *LTH*, 279–97.

White, Moses. *Early History of the University of Tennessee.*
Knoxville: Board of Trustees, 1879.

Greek Revival

Adams, Malcolm. "Mansion, Once a Show Place, To Be
Torn Down Next Week," *Memphis Commercial Appeal*,
Apr. 23, 1939.

*Annual Announcement of the Law, Literary and Medical De-
partments of the University of Nashville. Session of 1854–5.*
Nashville: John T.S. Fall, 1854.

Barr, Daniel F. *Souvenir of St. Mary's Cathedral, Including the
Century's Annals of the Roman Catholic Church in Nashville.*
Nashville: Burton and Fick, 1897.

"A Beautiful Piece of Sculpture—An Honor to our Own
Mechanics," *Nashville Republican Banner*, May 26, 1847.

Capitol Construction Records, Record Group 7, TSLA.

Carr, Margaret Thompson. *History of the Tennessee School for
the Deaf.* N.p., n.d. Copy in McC.

"The Christian Church," *Nashville Daily American*, June 2,
1852.

"City Intelligence: Medical College," *Nashville Daily American*, Nov. 6, 1850.

"The Corner Stone of the Second Presbyterian Church,"
Nashville Whig, Apr. 27, 1844.

Dardis, George. *Description of the Plan, Structure, and Apartments of the State Capitol of Tennessee.* Nashville: G.C. Cor-
bett, 1855.

Dekle, Clayton. "The Tennessee State Capitol," *THQ* 25
(1966), 213–68; *LTH*, 3–30.

"The East Wing of Our Medical College Edifice," *Nashville
Journal of Medicine.* 7 (1854), 249–50.

"Famous 'Little Greek House' Gives Way to Wrecking
Crews," *Memphis Commercial Appeal*, June 27, 1937.

"The Fiftieth Anniversary," *Nashville Banner*, Oct. 23, 1897.
(St. Mary's Cathedral.)

*First Annual Announcement of the Medical Department of the
University of Nashville.* Nashville: John T.S. Fall, 1851.

Hash, Judith Haws. "A History of the First Presbyterian
Church of Jonesboro." M.S. thesis, East Tennessee State
Univ., 1956.

"History and Cost of the New Church Edifice." Minutes of
the Session of the Jonesborough Presbyterian Church,
Oct. 1, 1845–Oct. 19, 1962.

Kelton, Allen. "The University of Nashville, 1850–1875."
Ph.D. diss. George Peabody College for Teachers, 1969.

Lawrence, Stephen S. "Tulip Grove: Neighbor to the Hermitage," *THQ* 26 (1967), 3–22; rpt. *MLT*, 347–68.

MacDonald-Millar, Donald. "The Grundy-Polk Houses,
Nashville," *THQ* 25 (1966), 281–86.

McNabb, William Ross. "The Knoxville City Hall," *THQ* 31 (1972), 256–60.

"Medical College," *Nashville Daily American*, Sept. 16, 1851.

"Nashville Medical College," *Nashville True Whig*, Nov. 15, 1850.

Old St. Mary's: An Historical Sketch of St. Mary's Church, Nashville, Tennessee, 1847–1947. Nashville: Cullom and Ghertner, 1947.

"The Oldest Church," *Nashville Daily American*, Feb. 16, 1890. [First Presbyterian]

"Opening of the New Medical College," *Nashville Daily American*, Nov. 4, 1851.

Patton, Charles. "Century-Old Mansion Holds Fond Memories for Writer," *Knoxville Journal*, Aug. 15, 1948. [Guilford Cannon house]

"Religious Affairs: Second Presbyterian Church," *Nashville Whig*, Sept. 3, 1846.

"St. Mary's Will Celebrate Its Golden Jubilee Today," *Nashville Daily American*, Oct. 24, 1897.

Second Annual Announcement of the Medical Department of the University of Nashville. Nashville: A. Nelson, 1852.

"The State Bank Building: The Recollections of a Venerable Citizen of Nashville" [Samuel P. Ament to the Editor, Feb. 10, 1882], *Nashville Daily American*, Feb. 13, 1882.

Strickland, William. "State Capitol," *Nashville Daily Orthopolitan*, Dec. 2, 1845.

University of Nashville, Medical Department. Catalogue for the Session 1857–8, and Announcement for the Session of 1858–59. Nashville: John T.S. Fall, 1858.

Gothic

Cooper, Raymond Waller. *Southwestern at Memphis, 1848–1948*. Richmond: John Knox Press, 1949.

First Annual Catalogue and General Advertisement of the Female Institute, Columbia, Tenn. Columbia, Tenn.: J.U. Thompson, 1838.

Garrett, Jill K. "St. John's Church, Ashwood," *THQ* 29 (1970), 3–23.

James, Lena Graham. *Historic St. Luke's Episcopal Church, Jackson*. Jackson, Tenn.: The author, 1962.

Mahoney, Nell Savage. "A Story-Book House: Nashville's Gothic Mansion," *Nashville Tennessean Magazine*, Apr. 26, 1953.

Morrow, Sara Sprott. "The Church of the Holy Trinity: English Countryside Tranquility in Downtown Nashville," *THQ* 34 (1975), 333–49.

———. "St. Paul's Church, Franklin," *THQ* 34 (1975), 3–18.

"Nashville Free High School," *Nashville Daily Union and American*, May 21, 1853.

Polk, George W. "St. John's Church, Maury County, Tennessee," *THM* 7 (1921), 147–53.

St. James Episcopal Church, Greeneville, Tennessee, 1850–1950, ed. Haskell W. Fox, Sr. Greeneville: Vestry of St. James' Parish, 1950.

[Tannehill, Wilkins]. "Masonic College of Tennessee." *Port Folio* 2 (1848–49), 270–71.

Templeton, Lucy. "Some Recollections of 'Old' St. John's on the Occasion of Its Centennial," *Knoxville News-Sentinel*, Oct. 27, 1946; rpt., Charles M. Seymour, ed., *A History of One Hundred Years of St. John's Episcopal Church in Knoxville, Tennessee, 1846–1946*. Knoxville: Vestry of St. John's Parish, 1947, pp. 193–99.

"Tennessee Hospital for the Insane: Architect's Report," *Tennessee State Farmer and Mechanic* 1, (1856), 77–78.

Woods, Mary. "The Building of the First Christ Church," *Christ Church, Nashville*. Nashville: The Vestry, 1929, pp. 64–72.

Yeatman, Trezevant Player, Jr. "St. John's—A Plantation Church of the Old South," *THQ* 10 (1951).

Italianate

Graham, Eleanor. "Belmont: I. Nashville Home of Adelicia Acklen," *THQ*, 30 (1971), 345–68.

Hubbard, Louise. "Journeys to Great Homes: 'Bleak House' Withstood Union Artillery Shells," *Washington Post*, Mar. 12, 1960.

McBride, Robert M. "Oaklands: A Venerable Host; A Renewed Welcome," *THQ* 22 (1963), 303–22; rpt. *LTH*, 257–78.

McDonough, James L. "Forgotten Empire: Sam Graham's Pinewood," *THQ* 27 (1968), 40–50.

" 'Melrose,' Home of Knoxville Art League," *Knoxville Journal*, Aug. 22, 1928.

"Melrose, the County Seat of the Late Maj. Thomas O'Connor," *Knoxville News-Sentinel*, Aug. 20, 1922.

Moore, Mrs. John Trotwood. "The Tennessee State Library in the Capitol," *THQ* 12 (1953), 3–22.

Patten, Z. Cartter. "A History of the Mansion on the Tellico River," *THQ* 10 (1951), 366–69.

Rudy, Jeanette C. *Historical Two Rivers: A Pictorial Review of Two Rivers Mansion*. Nashville: Blue and Gray Press, 1973.

"Sale of Relics at the Old Homestead," *Nashville Daily American*, May 30, 1888. [Belmont; Belle Monte]

Egyptian Revival

Bunting, Robert F. *Manual of the Presbyterian Church, Nashville, Tennessee, with a Brief History from its Organization, November, 1814 to November 1868*. Nashville: Southern Methodist Publishing House, 1868.

Hoobler, James A. "Karnack on the Cumberland," *THQ* 35 (1976), 251–62.

Wills, Jesse E. "An Echo from Egypt. A History of the Building Occupied by the First Presbyterian Church, Nashville, Tennessee," *THQ* 11 (1952), 63–77.

———. *The Towers See One Hundred Years. The Story of the First Presbyterian Church Building, Nashville, Tennessee*. Nashville: The author, Apr. 12, 1951.

The Architecture of Southern Nationalism

"Belle Meade: A Maine Editor's Visit to the Great Stock Farm," *Nashville Daily American,* June 7, 1884.

Caldwell, Mary French. *Andrew Jackson's Hermitage.* Nashville: Ladies' Hermitage Association, 1933.

Dorris, Mary Currey. *The Hermitage, Home of General Andrew Jackson . . . .* Nashville: Ladies' Hermitage Assoc., 1913; rpt. 1959.

Fort, Chloe Frierson. "A New Life for Rattle and Snap," *Nashville Tennessean Magazine,* Apr. 25, 1954.

Gower, Herschel. "Belle Meade: Queen of Tennessee Plantations," *THQ* 22 (1963), 203–19; *LTH,* 25–44.

Horn, Stanley F. "The Hermitage, Home of Andrew Jackson," *Antiques* 100 (Sept. 1971), 413–17.

———. *The Hermitage, Home of Old Hickory.* Richmond: Garrett & Massie, 1938; rev. ed. New York: Greenberg, 1950; rpt. Nashville: Ladies' Hermitage Assoc., 1960.

———. "The Hermitage, Home of Andrew Jackson," *LTH,* 5–21.

Ladies' Hermitage Association. *The Hermitage: Home of Andrew Jackson, A History and Guide.* Nashville: Ladies' Hermitage Assoc., 1967.

"Rattle and Snap." A Sketch unsigned, undated, postmarked Nashville, Aug. 24, 1931. TSLA.

Appomattox to the Centennial

Beasley, Ellen. "The End of the Rainbow," *Historic Preservation* 24, No. 1 (Jan.-Mar. 1972), 19–23.

Bruce, A.C. "Design for a School House," *American Builder* 8–9 (Dec. 1873), 275.

Brumbaugh, Thomas B. "The Architecture of Nashville's Union Station," *THQ* 27 (1968), 3–12.

Cummings, Frank, and Katherine L. Trewitt. *History of St. Luke's Episcopal Church, Cleveland, Tennessee, 1867–1967.* Cleveland: St. Luke's Episcopal Church, 1967.

Davis, Louise Littleton. "The Parthenon and the Tennessee Centennial," *THQ* 26 (1967), 335–53.

Henderson, Jerry. "Nashville's Ryman Auditorium," *THQ* 27 (1968), 305–28.

History, Building and Site, and Services of Dedication at Nashville, Tennessee, January 1, 1876. New York: Trustees of Fisk Univ., 1876.

History of the Grand Ole Opry House. Nashville: WSM Broadcasting Co., n.d.

History of Second Presbyterian Church, Memphis, Tennessee. Memphis: Adams Printing and Stationary Co., n.d.

Holly, Henry Hudson. "St Luke's Memorial Hall, University of the South, Tennessee," *American Architect and Building News* 3 (May 11, 1878), 165.

Hughes, Eleanor D. "The Fontaine House of the James Lee Memorial," *THQ* 27 (1968), 107–17.

McGaw, Robert A. *The Vanderbilt Campus: A Pictorial History,* Jan. 1979.

Reynolds, Ann Vines. "Nashville's Custom House," *THQ* 37 (1978), 263–77.

Reynolds, Richard S. "History of Glen Leven." MS in possession of Glen Leven Presbyterian Church, Nashville.

Smith, William C. "John M. Lea Store Building, Nashville, Tennessee," *American Architect and Building News* 35 (Mar. 26, 1892), 206, pl. 848.

———. *The New State Prison of Tennessee. A Paper Read Before the Engineering Association of the South, at Nashville, Tennessee, December 13, 1894.* Nashville: Brandon Printing, 1895?

DESCRIPTIONS OF TOWNS AND PLACES

References to later anthologies in which original descriptions are reprinted in part or entirely appear in parentheses after the entry for the original work.

Alexander, James Edward. *Transatlantic Sketches, Comprising Visits to the Most Interesting Scenes in North and South America, and the West Indies.* Philadelphia: Key and Biddle; London: R. Bentley, 1833.

Asbury, Francis. *The Journal of the Rev. Francis Asbury, Bishop of the Methodist Episcopal Church, from August 7, 1771, to December 7, 1815 . . . .* 3 vols. New York: N. Bang and T. Mason, 1821; ed. Elmer E. Clark, J. Manning Potts, and Jacob S. Payton. Nashville: Abingdon Press; London: Epworth Press, 1958. [*ETT,* 287–313; *NST,* 193–95; *THQ* 15 (1956), 253–68].

Baily, Francis. *Journal of a Tour in Unsettled Parts of North America in 1796 & 1797,* ed. Augustus de Morgan. London: Baily Bros., 1856; rpt. abridg. ed. Jack D. Holmes, Carbondale: Southern Illinois Univ. Press, 1969. (*ETT,* 383–430.)

Baird, Robert. *View of the Valley of the Mississippi, or the Emigrant's and Traveller's Guide to the West . . . .* Philadelphia: H.S. Tanner, 1832; 2d ed., 1834.

Bedford, John R., ed. "A Tour in 1807 Down the Cumberland, Ohio and Mississippi Rivers from Nashville to New Orleans," *THM* 5 (1919), 40–68.

Buckingham, James Silk. *The Slave States of America.* 2 vol. London and Paris: Fisher, Son and Co., 1842; rpt. New York: Negro Univ. Press, 1968.

Cartwright, Peter. *Autobiography,* ed. W.P. Strickland. Cincinnati: Cranston and Curtis; New York: Hunt and Eaton, 1850; rpt. 1856; rpt. Freeport, N.Y.: Books for Libraries Press, 1972. (*NST,* 196–97.)

"The City of Nashville—Its History, Population, Resources, Manufactures, &c.," *Commercial Review of the South and West* 1 (1846), 502–8.

Conner, Juliana. MS Diary. Alexander Brevard Papers, 1751–1911. North Carolina Department of Cultural Resources, Division of Archives and History. (Williams, *Historic Madison,* 479–88.)

Cundiff, Ruby Ethyl. *Nashville, Past and Present, Portrayed in Books: A Bibliography.* Nashville Branch, American Assoc. of University Women, 1936.

De Schweinitz, Frederick C. *Report of the Journey of the Brethren Abraham Steiner and Frederick C. De Schweinitz to the Cherokees and the Cumberland Settlements.* MS Diary. Moravian Archives, Bethlehem, Pa. (*ETT,* 443–521.)

Dillon, Thomas, to James McHenry, May 1796. *Virginia Magazine of History and Biography* 12 (1904–5), 259–64. (*ETT*, 355–60.)

Dow, Lorenzo. *Perambulations of Cosmopolite; or Travels and Labors of Lorenzo Dow . . . .* Rochester, N.Y.: Orrin Scofield, 1842. This work appeared in various versions and editions from 1804. (*NST*, 186–87.)

Edson, Andrew S. "How Nineteenth Century Travelers Viewed Memphis Before the Civil War," *WTHSP* 24 (1970), 30–40.

Featherstonhaugh, George William. *Excursion Through the Slave States, From Washington on the Potomac to the Frontier of Mexico, With Sketches of Popular Manners and Geological Notices.* 2 vols. London: J. Murray, 1844; New York: Harper, 1844; rpt. Negro Univ. Press, 1968.

Federal Writers' Project, Works Progress Administration for the State of Tennessee. *Tennessee: A Guide to the State.* New York: Viking, 1939; rpt. Hastings House, 1945, 1949.

Foster, Augustus John. *Jeffersonian America: Notes on the United States of America Collected in the Years 1805–6–7 and 11–12 by Sir Augustus John Foster, Bart,* ed. Richard Beale Davis. San Marino, Calif.: Huntington Library, 1954.

Gilmore, James Roberts [Edmund Kirke]. *Down in Tennessee and Back by Way of Richmond.* New York: Carleton, 1864; rpt. Westport, Conn.: Negro Univ. Press, 1970; rpt. Freeport, N.Y.: Books for Libraries Press, 1971.

Ingraham, Joseph Holt. "Dots and Lines . . . or, Sketches of Scenes and Incidents in the West," *Ladies' Companion* 11 (1839), 38–41, 69–71, 123–24, 196, 243–44.

———. "Sketches in the West," *Ladies' Companion* 13 (1840), 67–68, 139–40, 202–3, 215–16; 14 (1841), 91–92, 127–28, 185–86, 281–82.

———. *The Sunny South.* New York: G.G. Evans, 1860; rpt. Negro Univ. Press, 1968.

[Ingraham, Joseph Holt]. "A Letter from Nashville," *Port Folio* 1 (1847–48), 276–79.

"Memphis," *Memphis American Eagle,* Nov. 18, 1842.

"Memphis, A New Town on the Mississippi," *Portfolio* 9 (1820), 489–94.

"Memphis As Seen By a Visitor," *Daily Memphis Enquirer,* Apr. 3, 1849.

Michaux, François André. *Travels to the Westward of the Alleghany Mountains in the States of Ohio, Kentucky, and Tennessee, and Back to Charleston by the Upper Carolines . . . .* London: B. Crosby and J.F. Hughes, 1805. (*ETT*, 327–31; *NST*, 183–86; Thwaites, III, 105–306.) Another translation: *Travels to the Westward of the Alleghany Mountains, in the States of Ohio, Kentucky, and Tennessee, and Return to Charleston, through the Upper Carolinas . . ,* trans. B. Lambert. London: J. Mawman, 1805.

Morris, Eastin. *The Tennessee Gazetteer.* Nashville: W.H. Hunt, 1834; rpt. ed. Robert M. McBride and Owen Meredith, Nashville: Gazetteer Press, 1971.

Morse, Jedidiah. *The American Gazetteer.* Boston: Thomas S. Hall and Joseph Andrews, 1797; rpt. New York: Arno Press and *New York Times,* 1971.

Nashville Daily American, May 12, 1887.

"Nashville and her Manufactures," *Tennessee Farmer and Mechanic* 1 (1856), 170, 221–22, 281–82, 407–8.

"Nashville and her Manufactures, New Series," *Tennessee State Farmer and Mechanic* 2 (1857), 21–22, 69–70, 119, 169–70.

Olmsted, Frederick Law. *A Journey in the Back Country.* 2 vols. New York: Mason Brothers, 1860; rpt. Schocken Books, 1970.

"Our City," *Memphis American Eagle,* Dec. 23, 30, 1842; May 19, 1843.

"Our City," *The Parlor Visitor* 2 (July 1854), 63.

"Our City-Rents," *Memphis American Eagle,* Dec. 30, 1843.

Parton, James. *Life of Andrew Jackson.* 3 vols. New York: Mason Bros., 1860; rpt. Johnson Reprint Corp., 1967.

Rogers, George. *Memoranda of the Experiences, Labors, and Travels of a Universalist Preacher.* Cincinnati: J.A. Gurley, 1845. [Williams, *Historic Madison,* 479–88.]

Ross, Frederick A. *Autobiography.* Typescript in McC.

Royall, Anne Newport. *Letters from Alabama on Various Subjects . . . .* Washington, D.C.: The author, 1830; rpt. University: Univ. of Alabama Press, 1969. (*NST*, 201–2).

Ruffner, Henry. "Notes of a Tour from Virginia to Tennessee in the Months of July and August, 1838," *Southern Literary Messenger* 5 (1839), 44–48, 137–41, 206–10, 269–73. (Schwaab, 341–63.)

Schwaab, Eugene L., ed. *Travels in the Old South.* 2 vols. Lexington: Univ. Press of Kentucky, 1973.

Sharp, J.M. *Recollections and Hearsays of Athens: Fifty Years and Beyond.* Athens, Tenn.: The author, 1933.

"A Short Topographical Sketch of the Fourth Chickasaw Bluff," *Fort-Pickering American Eagle,* Feb. 28, 1842.

Smith, J. Gray. *A Brief Historical, Statistical, and Descriptive Review of East Tennessee, United States of America . . . .* London: J. Leath, 1842; rpt. Spartanburg, S.C.: Reprint Co., 1974.

Strothers, David H. [Porte Crayon]. "A Winter in the South," *Harper's New Monthly Magazine* 15 (1857), 433–51, 594–606, 721–40; 16 (1858), 167–83, 721–36; 17 (1859), 289–305; 18 (1860), 1–17.

[Tannehill, Wilkins]. "Nashville and Its Prospects," *Port Folio* 1 (1847–48), 17–18.

———. "Nashville As It Is," *Nashville Orthopolitan,* Oct. 17, 1845.

———. "Nashville As It Was," *Nashville Orthopolitan,* Oct. 16, 1845.

———. "Nashville—Retrospective, Present, Prospective," *Port Folio* 1 (1847–48), 177–78.

———. "The Town We Live In." *Port Folio,* 1 (1847–48), 340–41, 379–81; 2 (1848–49), 19–20, 51–52, 81–82, 153–55, 241–42, 337, 379; 3 (1849–50), 81–82, 145–46, 177–78, 305–6, 369–70.

Thomas, Jane Henry. *Old Days in Nashville, Tenn.: Reminiscences By Miss Jane H. Thomas.* Nashville: Publishing House of the Methodist Episcopal Church, South, 1897; rpt., Charles Elder, 1969.

Thwaites, Reuben Gold. *Early Western Travels, 1748–1846.* 32 vols. Cleveland: A.H. Clark, 1904–7; rpt. New York: AMS Press, 1966.

Walsh, Frances. *The Annals of St. Cecilia Convent, 1860–1888.* Nashville: Dominican Sisters, 1969.

Williams, Emma Inman. *Historic Madison: The Story of Jackson and Madison County Tennessee From the Prehistoric Moundbuilders to 1917.* Jackson, Tenn.: Madison County Historical Society, 1946.

[Williams, L.P.]. "Nashville As It Is," *Nashville City and Business Directory, 1860–61.* Nashville: L.P. Williams, 1860, pp. 25–113.

Williams, Samuel Cole. *Early Travels in the Tennessee Country, 1540–1800.* Johnson City, Tenn.: Watauga Press, 1928; rpt. Nashville: Blue and Gray Press, 1972.

———. "Nashville As Seen By Travelers, 1801–1821," *THM,* ser. 2, no. 1 (1930–31), 182–206.

PICTURE BOOKS

The souvenir albums of the late nineteenth century and the nostalgic picture books of the twentieth are valuable sources:

Art Album of the Tennessee Centennial and International Exposition, Held in Nashville, May 1 to October 31, 1897. Photographs by W.G. and A.J. Thuss. Nashville: Marshall and Bruce, 1898.

Art Work of Chattanooga. Chicago: W.H. Parish, 1895.

Art Work of Chattanooga. 9 pts. Chicago: Gravure Illustration Co., 1917.

Art Work of Chattanooga, Tennessee. Chicago: Gravure Illustration Co., 1906.

Art Work of Hamilton County. Chicago: W.H. Parish, 1895.

Art Work of Knoxville. 12 pts. Chicago: W.H. Parish, 1895.

Art Work of the City of Memphis. 12 pts. Chicago: W.H. Parish, 1895.

Art Work of Memphis, Tennessee. 9 pts. Chicago: Gravure Illustration Co., 1900.

Art Work of Memphis, Tennessee. 9 pts. Chicago: Gravure Illustration Co., 1912.

Art Work of Nashville. Chicago: W. H. Parish, 1894.

Art Work of Nashville, Tennessee. 9 pts. Chicago: Gravure Illustration Co., 1901.

Centennial Album of Nashville, Tennessee. Nashville, 1896.

City of Nashville Illustrated. Nashville, 1890.

Crawford, Charles W. *Yesterday's Memphis.* Seemann's Historic Cities Series No. 25. Miami: E.A. Seemann, 1976.

Egerton, John, et al. *Nashville: The Faces of Two Centuries, 1780–1980.* Nashville: Plus Media, Inc., 1979.

Glimpses of Nashville, Tennessee. Compliments of J.S. Reeves and Co. Nashville: E.W. Softly, n.d.

History of Maury County, Tennessee in Pictures, vol. 1. Columbia, Tenn.: Columbia Historical Society, 1966.

Huddleston, Ed. "Big Wheels and Little Wagons." Published in installments, *Nashville Banner,* Oct. 5-Dec. 7, 1959.

Jones, Ira P. *The City of Nashville Illustrated.* Nashville: The author, 1890.

Knoxville: Fifty Landmarks. Knoxville: Junior League of Knoxville, 1976.

Knoxville, Tennessee Centennial Souvenir. Issued by *Knoxville Daily Tribune,* May, 1897.

Lubschez, Ben J. *Eight Photographs of Nashville, Journal of the American Institute of Architects* 7 (1919), 251–58.

Memphis Appeal, "Souvenir Edition, December, 1890, 50th Anniversary, 1840–1890, and Celebrating the Erection of the Appeal Building."

Memphis Evening Scimitar. "Art Supplement to the Greater Memphis Edition . . . April, 1899."

Picturesque Chattanooga, Tennessee, with Historical and Descriptive Sketches. Neenah, Wis.: Art Publishing Co., 1890.

Plunkitt, Kitty. *Memphis: A Pictorial History.* Norfolk, Va.: Donning Co., 1976.

Smith, Reid. *Majestic Middle Tennessee.* Prattville, Ala.: Paddle Wheel Publications, 1975.

Wittemann, A. *Memphis Illustrated in Photo-Gravure from Recent Negatives.* New York: Albertype Co., 1892.

———. *Nashville, Tenn. in Photo-Gravure from Recent Negatives.* New York: Albertype Co., 1892.

Zibart, Carl F. *Yesterday's Nashville.* Seemann's Historic Cities Series No. 16. Miami: E.A. Seemann, 1976.

EMBELLISHED AND PANORAMIC MAPS

Chattanooga, 1871, by A. Ruger. St. Louis, Mo.: A Ruger [1871].

Chattanooga, 1886, by H. Wellge. Milwaukee: Norris, Wellge and Co. [1886]. [This map was published under the title *Chattanooga, County Seat of Hamilton County, Tennessee, 1886* as a supplement to the *Chattanooga Daily Times,* March 23, 1887.]

City of Nashville and Edgefield, Davidson County, Tennessee. Lithography by P.S. Duvall and Son's Lithographic Establishment. Philadelphia: Haydon and Booth, 1860.

Clarksville, 1870. N.p.: Stoner and Ruger [1870].

Harriman, 1892, by George E. Norris. Brockton, Mass.: George E. Norris [1892?].

Jackson, 1870, by A. Ruger.

Knoxville, 1871.

Knoxville, Tenn., County Seat of Knox County, 1886. Milwaukee: Norris, Wellge, 1886.

Map of the City of Memphis and Its Environs Including Fort Pickering. Memphis: Tod and Crider, 1850.

A Map of the City of Nashville, with Public Buildings &c. Engraved by Dolittle and Munson. Embellishments by Samuel B. Munson. Cincinnati: A.J. Ayres, 1831.

Memphis, Tenn., 1870: Bird's Eye View of the City of Memphis.

Memphis, 1887. Milwaukee: Henry Wellge and Co. [1887?].

Nashville, Tenn. Milwaukee: H. Wellge, 1888.

COMMERCIAL REVIEWS

After 1865 commercial associations and book manufacturers often published illustrated reviews whose purpose was to describe a city or region and its businesses. These commercial reviews often contain a good deal of information about architecture, including local architects, as well as important lithographs, engravings, and photographs. The important commercial reviews published by or about Tennessee cities before 1897 include:

Commercial and Statistical Review of the City of Memphis, Tenn., Showing Her Manufactures, Mercantile and general Business Interests, Together With Historical Sketches of the Growth and Progress of the "Bluff City;" also Sketches of the Principal Business Houses and Manufacturing Concerns. N.p.: Reilly and Thomas, 1883.

Cornman, John. *Nashville: An Illustrated Review of Its Progress and Importance*. Nashville: Enterprise Publishing Co., n.d.

Greater Knoxville Illustrated. Nashville: American Illustrating Co. [1910?].

Halley, R. A. *The City of Nashville; Advantages Possessed by Tennessee's Capital as a Home and as a Place of Business*. Nashville: Foster and Webb, 1903.

History and Illustrations of Knoxville, Tennessee. Post "C" (Tenn. Division), Travelers' Protective Assoc. of America, 1896.

Hopkins, G.M., comp. *Nashville Atlas*. Philadelphia, 1889.

"Industrial Number Descriptive of and Illustrating Knoxville of Today," *American Journal of Commerce* 17, no. 28 (Dec. 1903).

Memphis: An Illustrated Review of Its Progress and Importance. Memphis: Enterprise Publishing, 1886.

Morrison, Andrew. *Knoxville, Tennessee*. The Englehardt Series: American Cities, vol. 25. St. Louis: George W. Englehardt, 1925.

———. *Memphis, Tenn., the Bluff City, Mistress of the Valley of the "Lower River."* St. Louis and Memphis: George W. Englehardt Publishers, 1892.

———. *The City of Nashville*. The Englehardt Series: American Cities, vol. 24. St. Louis: George W. Englehardt, 1891.

Nashville, Tennessee: The Rock City of the Great and Growing South. American Journal of Commerce. New York: *American Journal of Commerce*, n.d.

Pen and Sunlight Sketches of Chattanooga. N.p.: American Illustrating Co., n.d.

Pen and Sunlight Sketches of Nashville. N.p.: American Illustrating Co., 1911.

Reilly, J.S. *Knoxville, Past, Present and Future, embracing historical sketches of its growth and progress from its establishment to the present time, together with outline of Tennessee History. Also a review of its Manufacturing, Mercantile and general business advantages, together with Statistics of the magnitude of operations in the different times and inducements offered to all Capitalists. To which is added Sketches of the Principal Business Houses and Manufacturing Concerns of the Metropolis of East Tennessee*. N.p., 1884.

Robert, Charles E. *Nashville and Her Trade for 1870*. Nashville: Roberts and Purvis, 1870.

HOUSE CARPENTERS AND ARCHITECTS

The most complete indexes to biographical information about American architects are the *Avery Obituary Index of Architects and Engineers* (Boston: G.K. Hall, 1963) and Henry F. Withey and Elsie Rathburn Withey, *Biographical Dictionary of American Architects* (Los Angeles: Hennessey and Ingalls, 1956; rpt. 1970). The most important sources for nineteenth-century Tennessee architects are, besides censuses and contracts, the Manufacturers' Census of Tennessee, 1820, a microfilm copy of which is in TSLA; and Joseph L. Herndon, "Architects in Tennessee until 1930: A Dictionary." M.S. thesis, Graduate School of Planning, Columbia Univ., 1975. See also:

Beasley, Ellen. "Tennessee Cabinetmakers and Chairmakers Through 1840," *Antiques* 100 (July-Dec. 1971), 612–21.

Ravenel, Beatrice St. Julien. *Architects of Charleston*. Charleston: Carolina Art Assoc., 1945; 2d ed., 1964.

Wodehouse, Lawrence. *American Architects from the Civil War to the First World War: A Guide to Information Sources. The Art and Architecture Information Guide Series, vol. 3*. Detroit: Gale Research, 1976.

———. *American Architects from the First World War to the Present: A Guide to Information Sources. The Art and Architecture Information Guide Series, vol. 4*. Detroit: Gale Research, 1977.

Original biographical sources are rare, the exceptions being Thomas Hope's letters (McC); Drury P. Armstrong's Diary (McC): Nathan Vaught's manuscript autobiography, "Youth and Old Age" (TSLA), written in 1882; a few of Heiman's letters (TSLA), and Harry Lee Swint, ed., "With the First Wisconsin Cavalry, 1862–1865; The Letters of Peter J. Williamson," *THQ* 2 (1943), 333–45, 432–48.

Of the architects who worked in Tennessee before 1897, William Strickland has been the subject of greatest scholarly interest. See:

Elliot, Elizabeth Porterfield. "Legacy of Architectural Beauty Left to City by Strickland," *Nashville Tennessean*, May 29, 1927.

Gilchrist, Agnes Addison. "Latrobe vs. Strickland," *JSAH* 2 (July 1942), 26–29.

———. "William Strickland," *Pennsylvania Magazine of History and Biography* 67 (1943), 272–79.

———. *William Strickland: Architect and Engineer, 1788–1854*. Philadelphia: Univ. of Pennsylvania Press, 1950; 2d ed. New York: Da Capo Press, 1969.

Gilliams, E. Leslie, "A Pioneer American Architect," *Architectural Record* 23 (1908), 123–25.

McNabb, William Ross. "Another Look at William Strickland." M.A. thesis, Vanderbilt Univ., 1971.

Mahoney, Nell Savage. "William Strickland and the Building of Tennessee's Capitol, 1845– 1854," *THQ* 4 (1945), 99– 153.

———. "William Strickland's Introduction to Nashville," *THQ* 9 (1950), 46– 63.

Newcomb, Rexford. "Early American Architects: William Strickland," *The Architect* 10 (July 1928), 453– 58.

On Adolphus Heiman and his work see:

Frank, John G. "Adolphus Heiman: Architect and Soldier," *THQ* 5 (1946), 35– 57.

"The Gallant Dead," *Nashville Republican Banner,* Nov. 17, 1869.

Morrow, Sara Sprott. "Adolphus Heiman's Legacy to Nashville," *THQ* 33 (1974), 3– 21.

Parrent, U. Clinton, Jr. "Adolphus Heiman and the Building Methods of Two Centuries," *THQ* 12 (1953), 204– 12.

Patrick, James. "The Architecture of Adolphus Heiman," *THQ* 38 (1979), 167– 87, 277– 95.

Other studies and sketches on architects whose works were built in Tennessee before 1897 include:

"Alexander Campbell Bruce," *National Cyclopaedia of American Biography,* III, 361.

"Charles Coolidge Haight," *Architectural Record* 41 (April 1917), 367– 69.

Coolidge, Harold Norman, Jr. "Samuel Sloan (1815– 1884), Architect." Ph.D. diss., Univ. of Pennsylvania, 1973.

Herndon, Joseph L. "Clegg and Crutchfield—Early Builders of East Tennessee." Typescript in McC.

Howell, William W. "Hugh Cathcart Thompson: Native Tennessee Architect." B. Arch. thesis, Univ. of Tennessee, 1975. Copy in Nashville Room, Nashville Public Library.

Hughes, Ellen. "Two Master Architects of Early Memphis: Edward Culliat Jones, 1822– 1902, and Mathias Harvey Baldwin, 1827– 1891." Typescript in Memphis Room, Memphis Public Library.

"Reuben Harrison Hunt," *National Cyclopaedia of American Biography* XXVIII, 178.

Schuyler, Montgomery. "Great American Architects Series—No. 6: The Works of Charles Coolidge Haight," *Architectural Record,* Suppl. to June 1899 issue, 1– 83.

Scully, Arthur, Jr. *James Dakin, Architect: His Career in New York and the South.* Baton Rouge: Louisiana State Univ. Press, 1973.

Tate, Susan Douglas. "Thomas Hope of Tennessee, c. 1757– 1820." M.S. thesis, Univ. of Tennessee, 1972.

Tomlan, Michael A. "George F. Barber." Typescript in McC.

———. "George Franklin Barber (1854– 1915), Carpenter, Architect, and Publisher," *JSAH* 35 (1976), 261– 62.

———. "Joseph F. Baumann (1844– 1920): Architect of the First Knoxville." B. Arch. thesis, Univ. of Tennessee, 1973.

Upjohn, Everhard M. *Richard Ujohn: Architect and Churchman.* New York: Columbia Univ. Press, 1939.

Walter, Thomas U., Joseph M. Wilson, and Frederick Graff. "Obituary—John C. Trautwine," *Journal of the Franklin Institute* 116 (Nov. 1883), 392– 96.

Weathersby, Robert W. II. "J.H. Ingraham and Tennessee: A Record of Social and Literary Contributions," *THQ* 34 (1975), 264– 72.

Wood, Mrs. Halsey. *Memoires of William Halsey Wood.* Philadelphia: The author [1938?].

ARCHITECTURAL THEORY AND AESTHETICS

The local architectural aesthetic of the early nineteenth century was derived from the common sense school of Edinburgh and Glasgow, from Francis Hutcheson, Henry Home, Thomas Reid, and John Witherspoon. The single treatise written locally and containing an architectural aesthetic was by Samuel Doak:

"Lectures on Human Nature. Adapted to the Use of Students at Colleges, Academies or in other Schools or in Private. To Which is Added an Essay on Life, by Rev. John W. Doak, D.D. & M.D.," ed. John W. Doak. Jonesboro, Tenn.: F. Gifford & Co., 1845.

Local appreciation of the architectural theory of the Greek Revival was partly the result of the tendency of southerners to see themselves as the heirs of classical culture. During the 1840s the *Guardian* (published at the Columbia Female Institute), the *Naturalist* (published in Nashville), and other Tennessee periodicals echoed the defense of classicism which was encouraged regionally by *De Bow's,* the *Southern Literary Messenger*, and the *Southern Quarterly Review*. The following titles are characteristic:

"The Athens of the West," *Guardian* 2 (1842), 129.

Eichbaum, J. "What Editions of the Classics Should Be Used in Our Schools and Colleges?" *Naturalist* 1 (1846), 85– 87.

"Essays on the Fine Arts," *Guardian* 2 (1842), 46– 47, 56– 57, 72– 73.

Moore, Henry. "The Study of the Classics," *Guardian* 1 (1841), 106– 8, 125– 27, 139– 40, 173– 74.

Smith, J. Fowler. "Education Among the Ancient Greeks," *Naturalist* 1 (1846), 84, 161– 71, 179– 80.

Grecian architecture and its intrinsic aesthetic had been ably defended by George Tucker of the University of Virginia as early as 1814 in an essay "On Architecture" in *Essays on Various Subjects of Taste, Morals, and National Policy* (Georgetown, D.C.: J. Milligan, 1822). This classical aesthetic was very much alive in Nashville in the 1840s. Professor Nathaniel Cross of the University of Nashville presupposed it in *An Address Delivered Before the Alumni Society of the University of Nashville. Oct. 7, 1846* (Nashville: Burton and Billings, 1846). Strickland wrote an essay on Grecian theory, "The Three Orders of Architecture— Wisdom, Strength, and Beauty," which Tannehill published in *Port Folio* I (1847–48), 321–23. Other essays on Grecian or classical design written locally include:

Strickland, William. "Fine Arts," *Nashville Daily Orthopolitan*, Sept. 16, 1846.
———. "Sketches of Roman Architecture," *Nashville Daily Orthopolitan*, 11 articles, May 22-June 24, 1846.
[Tannehill, Wilkins]. "The Greek and Roman Order of Architecture—Their distinctive Characters," *Port Folio* 3 (1849–50), 325–26.
———. "Orders of Architecture," *Port Folio* 2 (1848–49), 194–95, 239.

In the 1840s the romantic horticultural and agricultural theories of Andrew J. Downing became popular in Tennessee, at least with the periodical press. Among the articles inspired by Downing were:

Foster, Charles [C.F.]. "Rural Architecture," *Southern Lady's Companion* 1 (1847–48), 78.
"Hints to Beginners in Ornamental Planting," *Tennessee State Farmer and Mechanic* 1 (1856), 65–68.
"The Importance of the Beautiful," *South-Western Monthly* 1 (1852), 47.
Ingraham, J.H. [Visitor]. "The Nashville Horticultural Society and Garden," *Naturalist*, ser. 2, no. 1 (1850), 85–86.
——— [I.]. "Rural Taste," *Naturalist* 1 (1850), 185–88.
"The Late A.J. Downing," *South-Western Monthly* 2 (1852), 142–44.
"A National Architecture," *Tennessee State Farmer and Mechanic* 2 (1857), 409–10.
"The Orchard," excerpted from *Fruits and Fruit Trees of North America* by A.J. Downing, *Naturalist* 1 (1846), 447–52.
"Ornamental Cultivation," *Tennessee Farmer* 3 (1838), 348.
"Ornamental Gardening," *Tennessee State Farmer and Mechanic* 1 (1856), 249–51.
Phillips, Wendell. "Lost Arts," *Guardian* 8 (1848), 71–75.
"Rural Architecture," *Naturalist* 1 (1850), 117–19.
"Village and Farm Cottages," *Tennessee State Farmer and Mechanic* 1 (1856), 318.

The first work on ecclesiastical Gothic published in the United States was John H. Hopkins, *Essay on Gothic Architecture, with Various Plans and Drawings for Churches, Designed Chiefly for the Use of the Clergy* (Burlington, Vt.: Smith and Harrington, 1836). Hopkins' work, which linked Gothic architecture and the practical concerns of the clergy, antedated the writings of Pugin and Ruskin. These gave rise to the English ecclesiological movement, through which the thesis that Gothic was distinctively Christian was popularized. The definitive study is by James F. White:

The Cambridge Movement: The Ecclesiologists and the Cambridge Revival. New York: Cambridge Univ. Press, 1962.

Almost as soon as the theories of Pugin's disciples Benjamin Webb and John Mason Neale were established in England and publicized through the *Ecclesiologist*, the influence of the movement was felt in the United States, even in the Southwest. The *New York Ecclesiologist*, published in imitation of the English original, was inaugurated in 1848 and continued until 1853. On the American movement see:

Brown, Benton. "Quest for the Temple: A Study of the New York Ecclesiological Society 1848–1855, and its effect upon the architectural setting of worship in the Episcopal Church in the United States of America 1840–1860." S.T.M. thesis, General Theological Seminary, 1968.
The Constitution of the New-York Ecclesiological Society, Adopted at the Primary Meeting, Held on Friday, March 3d, 1848. New York: The Committee, 1851.
The Laws of the New York Ecclesiological Society, together with a Statement of the Object and Intended Operation of the Society, adopted at the Primary Meeting, Held on Friday, March 3d, 1848. New York: The Committee, 1848.
Patrick, James. "Ecclesiological Gothic in the Antebellum South," *Winterthur Portfolio* 15, no. 2 (Summer 1980), 99–118.
Transactions of the New-York Ecclesiological Society, 1855. New York: David Dena, 1857.
Puseyite Developments or Notices of the New York Ecclesiologists by a Layman, Dedicated to their Patron, the Right Rev. Bishop Ives of North Carolina. New York: Bedford, 1850.

On symbolism, the architectural theory of the New York society, see the writings of Frank Wills (listed below) and:

Hopkins, John H., Jr., "Symbolism in Church Architecture," *New-York Ecclesiologist* 2 (1849–50), 77–81.
Ives, Levi Sillman. *The Address at the Laying of the Corner Stone, St. Mary's Church, Burlington, New Jersey.* Burlington: E. Morris, 1847.

The *Transactions* for 1855 named three architects members of the New York Ecclesiological Society, Frank Wills, Richard Upjohn, and J.W. Priest. Two built churches in Tennessee, and both wrote on Gothic church architecture:

Upjohn, Richard. *Rural Architecture: Designs, Working Drawings and Specifications for a Wooden Church, and Other Rural Structures.* New York: Putman, 1852. rpt. Da Capo, 1975.
Frank Wills. *Ancient English Ecclesiastical Architecture and Its Principles, Applied to the Wants of the Church at the Present Day.* New York: Stamford and Swords, 1850.
———. "Form and Arrangement of Churches," *New-York Ecclesiologist* 1 (1848–49), 53–54; 103–6.
———. Letter to the editor, Feb. 20, 1850, *New-York Ecclesiologist* 2 (1849–50), 94–95.
———. "Reality in Church Architecture, Substance of a Paper read at the quarterly meeting of the New-York Ecclesiological Society, April, 1848," *New-York Ecclesiologist* 1 (1848–49), 8–12.

On symbolism and ecclesiolgy in Tennessee see:

"The Consecration; St. John's Chapel, Maury County," *Guardian* 2 (1842), 153.

Page, David C. [Rector of Calvary Church, Memphis]. "St. John's Church, Maury County, Tennessee," *Guardian* 13 (1848), 200.

"St. John's Church, Maury County, Tennessee," *Guardian* 2 (1842), 143.

Tomes, Charles. *Address Delivered at the Laying of the Corner Stone of the Church of the Holy Trinity by the Rector of Christ Church, Nashville, May 29, 1852.* Nashville: South-Western Monthly Office, 1852.

The controversy surrounding the consecration of St. Andrew's, Monroe County, occasioned an extensive literature in the church press:

"Abuse of Episcopal Authority," *Churchman* 27, no. 46 (Jan. 7, 1858), 364.

"Bishop Otey," *Episcopal Recorder* 35, no. 49 (March 6, 1858), 194.

"Bishop Otey's Letters," *Banner of the Cross* 19, no. 8 (Feb. 25, 1858), 60.

A Broad High Churchman, "The 'Church Ornament' case in Tennessee," *Churchman* 27, no. 51 (Feb. 11, 1858), 403.

Filius Ecclesiae, "The Riverside Case," *Churchman* 28, no. 9 (Apr. 22, 1858), 66–67.

————"Government by Law," *Episcopal Recorder* 35, no. 47 (Feb. 28, 1858), 186.

"Is He a Churchman? Then He's Fond of Power," *Churchman* 27, no. 44 (Dec. 24, 1857), 346.

"Is He a Churchman? Then He's Fond of Power"—No. 2, *Churchman* 27, no. 51 (Feb. 11, 1858), 403.

Otey, James Hervey. "The Riverside Case," *Episcopal Recorder* 35, no. 52 (March 27, 1858), 205.

Otey, James Hervey, to the editors, Feb. 2, 1858, *Episcopal Recorder* 35, no. 47 (Feb. 20, 1858), 185.

Otey, James Hervey, to the editors of the *Churchman,* Jan. 22, 1858, in *Banner of the Cross* 19, no. 6 (Feb. 11, 1858), 41.

"The Riverside Case," *Churchman* 28, no. 7 (Apr. 8, 1858), 52–53.

"The Riverside (Tenn.) Case," *Churchman* 28, no. 12 (May 13, 1858), 90. [J.W.J. Niles to the editors of the *Epsicopal Recorder,* April 8, 1858; Margarett W. Niles to the editor of the *Episcopal Recorder,* April 10, 1858.]

"St. Andrew's, Riverside, Tennessee," *Churchman* 27, no. 50 (Feb. 4, 1858), 400. [James Hervey Otey to the editor, Jan. 22, 1858.]

"Stringent Episcopacy," *Epsicopal Recorder* 35, no. 44 (Jan. 30, 1858), 174.

"The Tennessee Case," *Episcopal Recorder* 35, no. 49 (March 6, 1858), 194.

"The Tennessee Controversy," *Churchman* 28, no. 6 (Apr. 1, 1858), 44.

"The Tennessee Episcopacy," *Churchman* 28, no. 12 (May 13, 1858), 96.

Partly as a result of the Gothic Revival and ecclesiology and of the changing character of regional religion, the local press began in the forties to urge and justify the building of costly churches. See:

"Clean Meeting Houses," *Banner of Peace and Cumberland Presbyterian Advocate,* Nov. 7, 1844.

Jones, William P. "Beauty and Glory of the House of God," *Parlor Visitor* 3 (1855), 64.

"Log Churches," *Guardian* 3 (1843), 58.

Stacey, A.G. "Piety and Beauty," *Home Circle* 1 (1855), 364–66.

"Taste and Religion," *Home Circle* 1 (1855), 35–37.

Functionalist theory was current in Tennessee by 1883, when W.C. Smith read his paper "Architecture," published in the *Nashville Daily American* on June 11, before the Nashville Art Association. The paper, which called for honest architectural expression of new building techniques, anticipated Joseph Warren Yost's better known essay "The Influence of Steel Construction and of Plate Glass Upon the Development of Modern Style," which was read in Nashville on Oct. 21, 1896, published in the *Proceedings of the Thirtieth Annual Convention of the American Institute of Architects,* 1896, pp. 52–58, and reprinted in part in Lewis Mumford, ed., *Roots of Contemporary American Architecture* (New York: Reinhold, 1952), 152–58, and entirely by the American Institute of Architects (Washington, D.C., 1962).

ARCHITECTURAL BOOKS

During the late eighteenth and early nineteenth centuries, architects and house carpenters were influenced by two types of architectural books: handbooks published privately or by carpenters' companies to describe standard practice and establish prices, and the elegant treatises of English architects, written partly to enhance their authors' reputations, partly to advocate new theories and styles. Of the latter none antedating 1840 has thus far been discovered in Tennessee, though it is difficult to believe that none circulated in the state. Of the former the most influential was *The Rules of Work of the Carpenters' Company of the City and County of Philadelphia* (1786), recently reprinted with an introduction by Charles E. Peterson (New York: Bell, 1971). No copy of the Philadelphia book has been found in Tennessee. The only other eighteenth-century carpenter's handbook known is Thomas Hope's, now in possession of McC:

Pain, William. *The Builder's Golden Rule, or the Youth's Sure*

Guide: Containing the Greatest Variety of Ornamental and Useful Designs in Architecture and Carpentry . . . . To Which is Added an Estimate of Prices for Material and Labor. London: H.D. Steel, 1782.

Other books available in the South before 1897 are cataloged in:

Park, Helen. "A List of Architectural Books Available in America Before the Revolution," *JSAH* 20 (Oct. 1961), 115–30.

Nichols, Frederick Doveton. "The Early Architecture of Virginia: Original Sources and Books," *American Association of Architectural Bibliographers' Papers* 1 (1965), 81–125.

Hitchcock, Henry Russell. *American Architectural Books.* Minneapolis: Univ. of Minnesota Press, 1962.

Roos, Frank J., Jr. *Bibliography of Early American Architecture.* Urbana: Univ. of Illinois Press, 1968.

The most important author of architectural books in Tennessee before 1897 was George F. Barber. His first collection, containing only eighteen designs, was *Modern Artistic Cottages, or the Cottage Souvenir, Designed to Meet the Wants of Mechanics and Home Builders* (DeKalb, Ill.: Tyrell and Fay, 1888), and was published with more than one cover design. After moving to Knoxville, Barber published *The Cottage Souvenir No. 2* (Knoxville: S.B. Newman, 1891), 120 designs, and in the following year a revised and enlarged edition was published. *New Model Dwellings and How Best to Build Them* (Knoxville: S.B. Newman, 1894) and *Artistic Homes; How to Plan and Build Them* (Knoxville: S.B. Newman, 1895) followed. Barber continued to publish his books of designs until 1907.

George Barber was also editor of the only significant architectural periodical inaugurated before the centennial, *American Homes – A Monthly Journal Devoted to Designing, Building, and Beautifying the Home*, published at Knoxville from 1895–1904. In 1891 a single issue of *The Southern Builder and Decorator* was published at Nashville by F.W. Kreider. Tennessee architects occasionally published books popularizing their own work. See:

Carpenter, J. Edwin R. *Artistic Homes for City and Suburb.* Nashville: Birdsall and McNish, 1892.

Selections from the Executed Work and Sketches by Thompson and Zwicker, Architects, Nashville. Louisville: Southern Publishing and Advertising Co., 1896.

Antebellum architects sometimes published engineering surveys and reports. See:

Morrison, D. *Proceedings of the Board of Mayor and Aldermen of the City of Memphis, Tennessee, on the subject of a Western Armory, and Naval Depot and Dockyard at Memphis: Together with the Report of Col. D. Morrison, Civil Engineer; the Report of the Committee Appointed by the Board, etc.* Memphis: Appeal Office, 1842.

Trautwine, John C. *Some Remarks on the Internal Improvement of the South.* Philadelphia: The author, 1839.

Strickland was nearly as famous for his engineering surveys and reports as for his architecture, but none of these touched on Tennessee.

COMPANIES AND MECHANICS' ASSOCIATIONS

The Carpenters' Company of the City and County of Philadelphia left its mark on the Southwest through immigration and the publication of its *Rules of Work* (see above). The Philadelphia Company was descended from the London Carpenters' Company, on which see Edward Basil Jupp, *An Historical Account of the Worshipful Company of Carpenters* (London: W. Pickering, 1848; rpt. Pickering and Chatto, 1887).

The European tradition fostered not only American guild companies such as the Philadelphia Carpenters' Company and the Bricklayers' Company of the City and County of Philadelphia (see George L. Wren, *Bulletin of the Association for Preservation Technology* 3 [1971], 73–75), but the mechanics' associations from which trade unions grew and tradesmens' benevolent associations such as the Ancient and Honorable Mechanical Company of Baltimore. The only documentary evidence of the company formed by Knoxville carpenters in 1801 is the copy of the agreement Thomas Hope inscribed in his *Builder's Golden Rule*, and the Nashville Mechanical Society formed about 1801 is known only from contemporary newspaper accounts. By the time the Mechanics' Institute and Library Association of the State of Tennessee was formed in 1844, the movement had gained the interest of the local press.

On mechanics' associations see:

"Agricultural and Mechanical Associations," *Naturalist*, ser. 2, no. 1 (1850), 317–19.

Constitution of the Mechanics' Institute and Library Association of Tennessee. Instituted at Nashville, May, 1841. Incorporated January, 1844. Nashville: J.F. Morgan, 1854.

"Mechanics," *Naturalist* 1 (1850), 211–12.

Mechanics' Institute of Tennessee. *Report of the First Annual Exhibition.* Nashville: John F. Morgan, 1855.

———. *Report of the Second Annual Exhibition.* Nashville: Smith, Morgan and Co., 1856.

———. *Report of the Third Annual Exhibition.* Nashville: Bang, Walker and Co., 1857.

TECHNIQUES AND MATERIALS

The techniques of the antebellum house carpenter are poorly documented and little studied. The following writings are helpful:

Field, Walker, Jr. "A Re-examination into the Invention of the Balloon Frame," *JSAH* 2 (Oct. 1942), 3–29.

Nelson, Lee H. "Eighteenth-Century Framing Devices," paper presented at the National Park Service Historic Structures Training Conference, Philadelphia, 1961.

Rempel, John I. "Notes on the Evolution of Timber Framing, 1650–1836," *Bulletin of the Association for Preservation Technology* I, no. 3 (Dec. 1969), 15–18.

Shurtleff, Harold R. *The Log Cabin Myth: A Study of the Early Dwellings of the English Colonists in North America.* Cambridge, Mass.: Harvard Univ. Press, 1939.

Eighteenth- and nineteenth-century American brickmaking has also been little studied, though Joseph Arnold Foster's six part *Contributions to a Study of Brickmaking in America* (Claremont, Calif.: The author, 1968–71) does much to remedy this neglect. The following sources also provide background for the study of brickmaking in Tennessee:

Claiborne, Herbert A. *Comments on Virginia Brickwork Before 1800.* Boston: Walpole Society, 1957.

Loth, Calder, "Notes on the Evolution of Virginia Brickwork from the Seventeenth to the Late Nineteenth Century," *Bulletin of the Association for Preservation Technology* 6, no. 2 (1974), 82.

Harrington, J.C., "Seventeenth Century Brickmaking and Tilemaking at Jamestown, Virginia," *Virginia Magazine of History and Biography* 58 (1950), 16–39.

Glass was imported to Tennessee from Pennsylvania, New Jersey, and Virginia throughout the nineteenth century. See:

Hull, Maude Polland, *Early Glass-Making in Virginia.* Richmond: Jones Printing, 1933.

McKearin, George S. and Helen. *American Glass.* New York: Crown, 1941.

Moore, N. Hudson. *Old Glass—European and American.* New York: Tudor, 1946.

Quynn, Dorothy MacKay. "Johann Friedrich Amelung at New Bremen," *Maryland Historical Magazine* 43 (1948), 155–79.

Shadel, Jane S. "Robert Hewes, Glass Manufacturer," *Journal of Glass Studies* 12 (1970), 140–48.

The antecedents of Tennessee iron manufacturing were the Pennsylvania and Virginia industries. See:

Bining, Arthur Cecil. *Pennsylvania Iron Manufacture in the Eighteenth Century.* Harrisburg: Pennsylvania Historical Commission, 1939.

———. *Pennsylvania's Iron and Steel Industry.* Gettysburg: Pennsylvania Historical Assoc., 1954.

———. "The Iron Plantations of Early Pennsylvania," *Pennsylvania Magazine of History and Biography,* 57 (1933), 117–31.

Bruce, Kathleen. *Virginia Iron Manufacture in the Slave Era.* New York: Century, 1931.

Swank, James M. *History of the Manufacture of Iron in All Ages.* Philadelphia: The author, 1884.

On the manufacture of iron in Tennessee before 1865 see:

Fink, Paul M. "The Bumpass Cove Mines and Embreeville," *ETHSP* 16 (1944), 48–64.

"The First Heat," *Naturalist* I (1850), 160.

"Furnaces and Forges," *THM* 9 (1925), 190–92.

Hunt, Raymond F., Jr. "The Pactolus Ironworks," *THQ* 25 (1966), 176–96.

Pactolus Journals, Feb. 1811–June 1815; Jan. 1821–Nov. 1824; Oct. 1825–Apr. 1828. Southern Historical Collection, Univ. of North Carolina.

Phelps, Dawson A., and John T. Willett. "Iron Works on the Natchez Trace," *THQ* 12 (1953), 309–22.

Williams, Samuel C. "Early Ironworks in Tennessee Country," *THQ* 6 (1947), 39–46.

On eighteenth-century finish hardware see:

Streeter, Donald. "Early American Wrought Iron Hardware: English Iron Rim Locks, Late 18th and Early 19th Century Forms," *Bulletin of the Association for Preservation Technology* 6, no. 1 (1974), 40–67.

Index

(References to illustrations are in **bold type**)

Carondelet, Baron Francisco Luis Héctor de, 77
Carpenter, J. Edwin R. (1867–June 11, 1932), 184
Carpenters' companies, 18–19; II, n.11
Carpenters' Company of the City and County of Philadelphia, 18, 32
Carpenters' Hall, Philadelphia, 18–32
Carrick, Samuel, 51, 120
Carroll, William, 85, 86, 121
Carter, Alfred Moore, house, Elizabethton, 21, **85**, 89, 95
Carter, Elizabeth McLin, V, n.62
Carter, Fountain Branch, house, Franklin, 95
Carter, John, 58, 60, 61, 64, 69, 89, 214; house, Elizabethton, 13, 16, 17, 21, **23**, **50A**, **58**, 61, 65–66, 69
Carter, John (Lancaster Co., Va.), 37
Carter, Landon, V, n.62
Carter, Robert (Councilor), 37
Carter Co. *See* Elizabethton; Watauga
Carter's Grove, James City Co., Va., 13
Carthage, Smith Co., 121. *See also* Smith County Courthouse
Caruthers, Robert L., 123; house (Bobo-Ligon Funeral Home), Lebanon, 123, **131**, 170
Castalian Springs, Sumner Co. *See* Bearden house; Cragfont; Wynne Inn
Castalian Springs Inn. *See* Wynne Inn
Cate, Elijah, house, Niota, 95, **96**
Cathedral of Our Lady of the Seven Dolors (St. Mary's Catholic Church), Nashville, 137–38, 146, **155**
Cathedral of St. John and St. Finebar, Charleston, 145
Centennial. *See* Nashville Centennial Exposition; Tennessee Centennial Exposition; Philadelphia Centennial
Central Baptist Church, Memphis, 189, **213**
Central Block, Chattanooga, **226**
Chambers, Maxwell, 71
Chapel of the Cross, Mansdale, Madison Co., Miss., 112, 115
Charleston, S.C., 16, 18, 31, 32, 56, 57, 119, 183. *See also* Bank of the United States; Brewton house; Cathedral of St. John and St. Finebar; Charleston Hotel; Drayton Hall; Izard House; Manigault house; Orphan House; St. Michael's Church
Charleston Carpenters' Society, 18
Charleston Hotel, 140
Charleville, Jean du, 58
Charlotte, Dickson Co., 35, 95, 99. *See also* Dickson County Courthouse; McRaie house
Chase, William H., 146
Chattanooga, Hamilton Co. *See* Adams Block; Carnegie Library; Chattanooga Times Building; First Methodist Church; Glass Building; Hamilton County Courthouse; Lookout Mountain Inn; Richardson Building; Second Presbyterian Church
Chattanooga Times Building (Dome Building), Chattanooga, 200, 206, **238**
Cheairs, Nathaniel, house (Houston Hall Farm, Rippavilla), Spring Hill, 177, 181, **193**
Cheairs Place. *See* Cheairs, Nathaniel, house
Cheatham, Adelicia Hayes Franklin Acklen, 151, 152
Cheatham, William A., 151
Cheekwood, Nashville, 14
Chenault, David, house (Greenfield), Gallatin, 95

Chester Inn (Bell Tavern, Union Hotel, Planter's House), Jonesboro, 60
Chickasaw Bluffs, 56
Childress, John, house. *See* Rokeby
Childrey, Stephen (early 19th c.), 22
Chimneys, 69
Chisholm, John, house. *See* House on Front Street
Choragic Monument of Lysicrates, 5, 118, 131, 132
Choragic Monument of Thrasyllus, 153
Chote, Monroe Co., 57
Christ Episcopal Church (Zion Church), Brownsville, 107, 111, **121**
Christ Episcopal Church, Nashville (1831), 1, 5, 7, 9, 40, 109, 112, 113, 143, 159; (1894), 189
Christ Episcopal Church, Rugby, 210
Christian Church, Nashville (1852), 137, **154**. *See also* Vine Street Christian Church
Chucky, Greene Co. *See* Earnest, Felix, house; Earnest, Henry, house
Church Hill, Hawkins Co., 58, 65
Church of the Advent (First Church of Christ, Scientist), Nashville (1866), 112, 115, **125**, 145
Church of the Assumption, Philadelphia, 145
Church of the Holy Trinity, Nashville, 113, 115, **124**, 145, 180
Church of the Nativity, Huntsville, Ala., 112
Church of St. Mary, Memphis. *See* St. Mary's Episcopal Church
Church Street Methodist Church, Knoxville (1879), 189, **212**
Cicero, 120, 140
Cincinnati, O., 29, 140, 183
City and Country Builder's and Workman's Treasury of Designs, 37
City Architecture, 157
City Hall, Charleston. *See* Bank of the United States
City Hotel, Memphis, 5
City Hotel, Nashville, **5**, 101, 102
City Hotel Block, Nashville, 187, 197, **207**
City Offices, Nashville. *See* Market House and City Offices
Claiborne Co. *See* Speedwell
Clark (Clerk), John, 54
Clarksville, Montgomery Co. *See* Lewis house; Masonic College of Tennessee; Smith house; Stewart house; Tip Top
Cleague, Samuel (c. 1781–c. 1850), 31, 95, 99, 131; house, Athens, 89, 92
Cleveland, Bradley Co. *See* St. Luke's Episcopal Church
Cleveland Hall, Donelson, 131
Clifton Place, Columbia, 89, 171
Clinton, Anderson Co., 213
Clouston Hall, Franklin, 21, 26, 83, 95
Clover Bottom, Donelson (c. 1798), 42, 45; (1859), 165, 182, **185**
Clyce, William H. (c. 1815–post-1868), 29, 31, 33, 129, 131, 183, 187
Coalmont, Grundy Co., 211
Cobb, William, 17; house, *see* Rocky Mount
Cochran, Gifford A., 166, 170

Architecture in Tennessee was composed on
the Variable Input Phototypesetter in ten-point
Garamond with one-point spacing between the lines.
Garamond type was also used as display. The book
was designed by Jim Billingsley and Judy Ruehmann,
set into type by Williams, Chattanooga, Tennessee,
printed offset by Thomson-Shore, Inc., Dexter,
Michigan, and bound by John H. Dekker & Sons,
Grand Rapids, Michigan. The book is printed on
S.D. Warren's Lustro Offset Enamel Dull, an
acid-free sheet designed for an effective life of
at least three hundred years.

THE UNIVERSITY OF TENNESSEE PRESS
KNOXVILLE